Circle Gardening

Number Fifty-Six

W. L. Moody Jr. Natural History Series

Texas A&M University Press
College Station

Circle Gardening

Growing Vegetables outside the Box

Kenneth E. Spaeth Jr.

First edition

This paper meets the requirements of ANSI/NISO Z39.48-1992 (Permanence of Paper).
Binding materials have been chosen for durability.
Manufactured in China through FCI Print Group

Library of Congress Cataloging-in-Publication Data

Names: Spaeth, Kenneth E., Jr., author.
Title: Circle gardening: growing vegetables outside the box / Kenneth E. Spaeth Jr.
Description: First edition. | College Station: Texas A&M University Press, [2017] | Includes bibliographical references and index.
Identifiers: LCCN 2017007157 | ISBN 9781623495565 (book/flexbound (with flaps): alk. paper)
Subjects: LCSH: Vegetable gardening. | Circle gardening.
Classification: LCC SB320.9 .S63 2017 | DDC 635—dc23 LC record available at
https://lccn.loc.gov/2017007157

Contents

Preface

The circle gardening methods described in this book provide the most simplified approach I know of to growing vegetables. Throughout the various chapters, I include photos from my garden: I know the method works. You can establish circle plots in a small to large garden anytime during the year and be ready for spring-summer-fall-winter plantings, depending on your particular climate. The important thing is to get started. Whether you are new to vegetable growing or have years of experience, the method of planting in circles has been used for millennia (chapter 7). You do not have to understand all the details related to gardening at first; some of us like to jump right in, while others may want to study things through. This book follows a logical sequence of steps and contains material that will increase your knowledge of soils and plants.

- Decide on your gardening goals and objectives (chapter 1). Think about what you want to accomplish and grow. Will you use organic methods exclusively, or a combination of organic and conventional methods (chapter 2)?
- Plant vegetables in circle plots to mimic the clumped distribution of plants in nature (chapter 3). Diversity is important in your garden (chapter 3).
- Locate your garden in the best location you can (chapter 5).
- When you have time, develop a detailed plan (chapter 8). Find gardeners in your area and establish friendships and gain local knowledge.

- Enhance and improve your soil (chapters 4 and 9).
- Start small and work up to more ambitious goals. Develop a planting plan (chapters 7 and 8).
- Know your local climate, its positive aspects and the limitations it imposes, and identify plant hardiness and growing zones (chapter 6 and appendix C).
- Obtain soil amendments/fertilizers (chapter 9, appendixes B and D), seeds of adapted cultivars and varieties (chapter 5), and basic gardening tools, water hoses, and so forth (chapter 9).
- Establish your garden plot (chapter 7), apply soil amendments (chapter 9 and appendixes B and D), and protective measures for pets, wildlife, and so forth (chapter 10). Some simple fencing ideas are given throughout the book.
- Plant seeds and transplants correctly (chapter 9 and individual Vegetable Guides).
- Maintain adequate moisture; water when necessary (chapter 9).
- Be vigilant, evaluate growth and vigor of your plants, control weeds, apply fertilizers as necessary, and inspect garden daily for pests. Before you undertake any remedial actions to control a problem, identify the cause of the problem (chapter 10 and individual Vegetable Guides).
- Harvest vegetables at their peak and enjoy your harvest.

Acknowledgments

One morning as I awoke, I was fretting over finding a publisher and/or agent who would show interest in my book. I felt that my idea of "circle gardening" could help many people be successful in growing vegetables, and I was anxious to make some progress. Then a thought or message came from nowhere: "It only takes one person to make it happen." That individual was Shannon Davies (director of Texas A&M University Press), whom I later met at an exhibit booth at a science conference. Thank you, Shannon, for letting me pitch the book idea to you and for your insight in promoting it.

Above all I want to thank my wife, Angela, for her support and patience, especially in taking care of the farm chores when I was in the middle of an idea and writing. Her wise reminder "Kommt Zeit Kommt Rat" (in the course of time and deliberation, problems will find solutions) kept the book moving along.

I also wish to thank Peggy Young, Dr. Mark Nearing, and Clark Harshbarger for their encouragement and review of the book. Also, thanks to Stacy Eisenstark (acquisitions editor for the natural environment and agriculture) for final organization and layout, and to Laurel Anderton (copyeditor) for final editing and proofs—you're both amazing.

Finally, I want to mention my mother, who encouraged me and bought supplies so I could start my first vegetable garden at 12 years of age.

Circle Gardening

GARDENING ESSENTIALS

FIGURE 1. Assortment of circle plots in home vegetable garden. *Far right*, cover crop for future tomato plants. Photo by author.

1

Circle Gardening

A Simple, Natural Vegetable Gardening Method

In this book, I present a simple planting and management method that can produce results with a minimum of resources. I discuss the advantages and practicality of planting in circle arrangements. There is also an ecological basis for clumping plants in a circle plot (chapter 3). This book is a step-by-step guide for the beginner but also contains more advanced plans that you can use as your confidence and experience grow. Likewise, experienced gardeners (Master Gardeners, etc.) will find science-based information on a variety of subjects.

Vegetable gardening is actually an intervention where you interact with, modify, alter, and manage the environment to grow plants that are not naturally adapted to or found in a particular location in nature. Most of the vegetables we grow are improved cultivars and varieties that no longer resemble their ancestors. In the "Selected Vegetable Guides" section of this book, information is given about the origin and development of some of our vegetable crops. It is estimated that about 400,000 plant species inhabit our planet; of these, over 20,000 species are edible plants, and fewer than 20 provide 90% of our food. Growing your own vegetables can provide many benefits as well as supplement and enrich your diet.

In time, gardeners learn how their particular climate, location, and soils interact to produce a unique gardening result. Learning the basics of gardening can help you get started, but the real fun is the individual journey that a gardener takes. Unexpected results and discoveries all depend to a certain extent on your intuition and the decisions you make along the way. A gardener soon realizes that gardening is a "delicate dance" with nature that often requires unplanned decisions and periodic changes in management (improvisation), some of which may not have been in the original garden plan.

The objectives of this book are simple:

1. Inspire you to start or reestablish a vegetable garden
2. Help you achieve gardening success
3. Help you grow a garden with a minimum amount of time, expense, and resources
4. Help you become more self-sufficient
5. Create excitement and joy in life from simple pleasures
6. Provide technical information
7. Anticipate technical information that you will eventually need

As gardeners, we all have our successes and failures, and after years of experience and observation, we develop certain ideas and notions. Some gardeners may be dedicated to particular cultural methods; my advice is to keep an open mind, try new ideas, and try breaking away from some old established notions and rules. Agriculture, including vegetable gardening, is a science and an art. You may disagree with some aspects of the book and the science presented—science constantly disagrees with itself. Nevertheless, the objective of science is to understand the nature of the world through testing and observation. Max Planck (1858–1947), originator of modern quantum theories, stated: "Science cannot solve the ultimate mystery of nature. And that is because, in the last analysis, we ourselves are part of nature and therefore part of the mystery that we are trying to solve." Nevertheless, we press on with science and our personal efforts to perceive nature's patterns—especially those of us who farm and garden. I have observed over time that some gardening approaches work well for some individuals, but not for others. Inherent talent also plays a part in gardening, but you can succeed if you have the proper attitude, follow a prescribed workable method, and keep trying. There are so many variables in nature that can affect your gardening efforts, and sometimes, unexpected serendipities occur that defy explanation.

Overview of This Book

I have seen many successes and failures in growing crops and garden vegetables. Many people would like to start a vegetable garden but often make excuses: lack of time, resources, or space; past failures; and inability to perform the hard work. As gardeners, we all share these problems; therefore, I have developed and evolved some simple techniques to help solve them. Circle arrangements as well as square, rectangular, and other abstract designs in gardening have been around for a long time. Throughout the years, I have gravitated toward the circle arrangement out of necessity. As a scientist, I later realized that growing plants in clusters mimics natural plant distribution in the wild (more on this subject in chapter 3). Our ancestors have been planting in clusters and circle arrangements for millennia (see "Three Sisters" planting, chapter 7). Why circles? The geometric form of the circle has been known since the beginning of time, in celestial bodies and in many organisms in nature (flowers, stems, mushrooms, seeds, berries, fruit, sand dollars, pearls, snails, and cross-sectional design sections of worms, snakes, blood vessels, bubbles). In the mechanized world, the circle is also a dominant geometric shape (wheels, ball bearings, gears, pipes, gun barrels, cannons, wire). The circle is a perfect geometric shape; it has the largest area for a given perimeter. Nobel physicist Richard Feynman stated: "Why is nature so symmetrical? No one has any idea why."

Often, our garden resources are limited: topsoil (depth and quality), space, organic materials, tools, time, strength to do the work, and water (its lack or expense). These limitations have influenced, motivated, and inspired me to experiment. Like most challenges in life, adversity can strengthen and cause us to explore other avenues. We must remind ourselves that there are many methods and ways of doing things, especially growing vegetables in the home garden.

My concept does not require a substantial outlay of money, resources, or energy. Most vegetable gardening books inundate the beginner with materials and methods. Upon reading my first gardening books, I was overwhelmed with all the required materials. I thought, where would I obtain manure and compost? I did not have a truck, rototiller, or tractor; lumber, masonry, or tools; the money to build raised beds; hot and cold frames; or organic materials to start a compost pile. The large, well-stocked building and garden centers we have now did not exist then. I experienced all the constraints that beginning gardeners face.

This book starts with a motivational theme; my intention is to help gardeners overcome trepidation about starting a vegetable garden. Science Notes on particular subjects are included in text boxes throughout the book chapters. Personal Notes also supplement the text with observations and excerpts from my experience.

Motivation

Self-reliance has many benefits; it is essential to our physical, temporal, and spiritual well-being. Planting a garden, even if small, can help you have a greater feeling of self-reliance. Gardening has physical, psychological, social, temporal, and spiritual benefits. Regular physical activity in the garden can help you gain strength and health. When working in the garden, all your senses are stimulated—sight, smell, hearing, and, ultimately, taste. Picture a beautiful day with the sun shining, the birds singing, and the smell of the earth while you have happy and peaceful thoughts, watch your vegetables and flowers grow, and anticipate enjoying the taste of what is to come. Experience this truly positive endeavor on a daily basis.

I include a quote from Jo-Anne van den Berg-Ohms at John Scheepers Kitchen Garden Seeds that touched and inspired me: "The spirit and care with which gardeners sow seeds, tend gardens and celebrate seasonal bounty is invaluable, and must never be underestimated. It's extraordinary, how just one life crafted around the garden and the kitchen can impact so many. It's contagious goodness borne of one's passion for gardening, cooking, and the magic of seeds. It enhances every aspect of life: the cadence of our days, our physical health and well-being, our connection to the seasons, how well we eat, sleep and feel, and the joy that we feel and share for the world that we help create."

If you are a beginning gardener, I encourage you to start your first gardening project and begin a new adventure in your life—be bold! As Johann Wolfgang von Goethe (1749–1832) said: "Whatever you can do or dream you can, begin it. Boldness has genius, power and magic in it!" For those whose gardens are a memory, begin again; for those actively engaged, challenge yourself to try new things and increase your knowledge.

There are many benefits to gardening and growing your own food:

- Communing with nature and watching the miracle of food growing in your own garden
- Reflecting on spiritual issues
- Having fun and experiencing more joy
- Increasing your knowledge of nature and the environment
- Improving your family's health
- Teaching children and family members valuable skills
- Augmenting the family budget and saving on groceries

- Getting physical exercise and improving psychological health
- Socializing with other family members or friends who enjoy the work and experience
- Renewing your cooking skills and enjoying better-tasting food
- Reducing your environmental impact and food waste
- Beautifying the landscape and aesthetics of your home
- Eliminating concerns about food safety
- Developing the scientist in you—experimenting
- Practicing self-sufficiency

Growing Your Own Food: Trends and Statistics

Throughout the world, the statistics regarding hungry and undernourished people are staggering: almost 850 million people in developing countries. The Food and Agriculture Organization (FAO) of the United Nations states that food is cheaper and diets are better than they were 40 years ago, but malnutrition and food insecurity threaten millions. As the world's population expands from 6.7 billion to the projected 9.2 billion by 2050, the world's dwindling natural resources and the unequal distribution and availability of food will continue to be major political and social challenges to governments. Livestock and crop production currently occupy about 38.6% (19.4 million square miles) of the earth's land area. In order to produce enough food for the 2050 population, about double the crop production of today will be needed. As developing countries begin to prosper, there is an increased demand for meat, eggs, and dairy products. As these preferences and demands expand, more corn and soybeans are needed for animal feed. Agricultural scientists have proposed several strategies to feed the world in the future: (1) curtail the conversion of tropical rain forests and other marginal lands to farmlands; (2) increase production and grow more food on existing farms; (3) increase efficiency of vital resources such as water, fertilizers, and pesticides; (4) shift diet preferences and rely less on using crops to feed large livestock animals; and (5) conserve the food we have and reduce waste. In the United States, about 73% of the total crop calories are used for animal feed and fuel production, and 27% for human consumption. The percentages vary throughout the world; however, India devotes more of its crop calories (89%) to human consumption than any other highly populated country.

Wherever there is a little plot of land, some food can be produced with a minimum of resources. That is what this book is all about:

Some favorite selected motivational garden quotes that may "touch a nerve"

Nothing is more the child of art than a garden. —Sir Walter Scott

Gardening is the purest of human pleasures. —Francis Bacon

The man who has planted a garden feels that he has done something for the good of the world. —Vita Sackville-West, poet and novelist, 1892–1962

Earth laughs in flower. —Ralph Waldo Emerson

Flowers always make people better, happier, and more helpful: they are sunshine, food and medicine to the soul. —Luther Burbank, botanist, 1849–1926

I have never had so many good ideas day after day as when I worked in the garden. —John Erskine, educator and author, 1879–1951

Gardening is something you learn by doing—and by making mistakes; like cooking, gardening is a constant process of experimentation, repeating the successes and throwing out the failures. —Carol Stocker, American gardening columnist

Who has learned to garden who did not at the same time learn to be patient? —H. L. V. Fletcher, 1949

The best place to seek God is in a garden. You can dig for him there. —George Bernard Shaw, 1856–1950, in *The Adventures of the Black Girl in Her Search for God*, 1932

A garden is a grand teacher. It teaches patience and careful watchfulness; it teaches industry and thrift; above all it teaches entire trust. —Gertrude Jekyll, 1843–1932

There is no spot of ground, however arid, bare or ugly, that cannot be tamed into such a state as may give an impression of beauty and delight. —Gertrude Jekyll

I perhaps owe having become a painter to flowers. —Claude Monet

No occupation is so delightful to me as the culture of the earth, and no culture comparable to that of the garden. —Thomas Jefferson

Though an old man, I am but a young gardener. —Thomas Jefferson

One of the most delightful things about a garden is the anticipation it provides. —W. E. Johns, 1893–1968, creator of "Biggles" and *The Passing Show*, 1937

To forget how to dig the earth and tend the soil is to forget ourselves. —Mahatma Gandhi

---

Courtesy of Down Garden Services, 2012. Gardening quotes: On gardening in general, Down Garden Services, Down, Northern Ireland, http://www.downgardenservices.org.uk/quotes.htm.

plant a few circle plots, and if you follow the instructions in this book, you will be amazed at how much food you can grow in a 4- to 5-foot-diameter circle. A tremendous amount of land lies vacant throughout the United States, not including cropland, pastureland, or rangeland. Most of these vacant lands are in grass cover and include roadways, vacant lots, and overgrown weedy areas, as well as extensive lawns. There is no need to fear and fall prey to scare tactics regarding future food shortages in the United States. As I mention throughout this book, small fertile garden areas can produce an amazing amount of produce. If Americans need to grow more of their own food, the resources exist, but some changes in the culture relative to maintaining lawns and ignoring odd vacant areas will be needed. In highly populated countries with limited arable land resources, you can see small productive vegetable garden plots tucked here and there; people are already using their odd land areas more efficiently to produce local food for individual families and communities. Small vegetable gardens are commonly referred to as allotment, community, kitchen, and *potager* (poh-tah-ZHAY) gardens. Allotment and community gardens are often individual noncommercial gardens for growing food plants. *Potager*, the French word for "kitchen or vegetable garden," pertains to gardens in which an assortment of vegetables, herbs, fruits, and flowers are grown. Potager gardens are esthetic works of art that make use of symmetry, balance, and proportion.

According to the US Department of Agriculture (USDA), the United States imports about 32% of its fruits and nuts, and 13% of its vegetables. In many communities, farmers' markets are popular and increasing, but the statistics show that locally grown food accounts for a very small percentage of vegetables sold nationally. The National Gardening Association conducted research on the impact of home and community gardening in America in 2015 and found that 90 million (about 75% of US households) spent $36.1 billion on their lawns and gardens in 2015, with an average of $401 per household. According to the National Gardening survey, spending was highest among baby boomers, college graduates, and married households (age group 18–34) with annual incomes over $75,000. The most popular gardening activities were food and flower gardening (36% and 34% of households, respectively).

In an earlier report in 2009, the National Gardening Association found that homeowners grew vegetables because of better taste, money savings, food quality, food safety, economic reasons, and recession. Favorite vegetables (percentage of gardens that included specific vegetables) were tomatoes (86%), cucumbers (47%), sweet peppers (46%), beans (39%), carrots (34%), summer squash (32%), onions (32%), hot peppers (31%), lettuce (28%), peas (24%), and sweet corn (23%).

Suggestions and Ideas for Areas Where Resources Are Limited

If resources are limited (land, physical strength, motivation, money, time, knowledge, etc.), and you wish to be involved in growing some of your own produce, there are many different avenues to achieve your goal. Gardening can be a challenge, and we all have limitations, be it limited land area for a garden; fragile erodible soils; inadequate rainfall or irrigation; limited resources for purchasing seeds and fertilizer; unavailability of seeds, tools, and fertilizer; physical handicaps; lack of knowledge, equipment, time, and manual help in taking care of a garden; and personal health and disability issues. Many people like the community-supported gardening idea (fig. 2); however, this concept can be scaled down to include a few relatives, friends, neighbors, or a combination of all the above.

In summary, circle gardening can bring you the following advantages and benefits:

- Grow produce using less space, money, resources, and time.
- Maximize new technology to your advantage, such as drip irrigation and organic farming and gardening methods.
- Garden with friends, relatives, or neighbors; share resources.
- Get involved with a community garden effort.
- Obtain free information about growing vegetables at extension offices and on the Internet.
- Trade resources, one talent for another.
- Join a local garden club.
- Enroll in Master Gardener Program.
- Grow plants from seeds and avoid the expense of buying transplants. The cost of buying transplants has increased significantly, and the trend is away from economy packs (6 to 12 plants in a tray) to single 4-inch or larger plants. If you wish to grow a larger number of plants—for example, 12 tomato or pepper plants—the cost can be prohibitive, and your profit or savings margin will be substantially less.
- Grow heirloom varieties and cultivars and save your own seeds. The cost of buying hybrid seeds each year can be high.

- Trade seeds with fellow gardeners.
- Find local farmers and livestock producers who will let you haul away manure for free. Explain your situation and you will find the agricultural community to be very generous.
- Share labor and gardening expenses with friends and neighbors.
- Encourage family members to participate and allocate garden responsibilities.
- Participate in church and community projects.
- If you live in an apartment or condominium, you can generally grow a little food in pots and planters.
- Create a neat, attractive, and productive garden.
- Join and get involved with 4-H Youth Development Projects.
- Start a small vegetable garden, master the basics, and then expand your efforts year by year.
- Learn to can and freeze your produce.
- Trade excess produce for other food items.
- Rely on personal inspiration and spiritual guidance.
- Teach others by example.
- Prioritize what is important in your life.

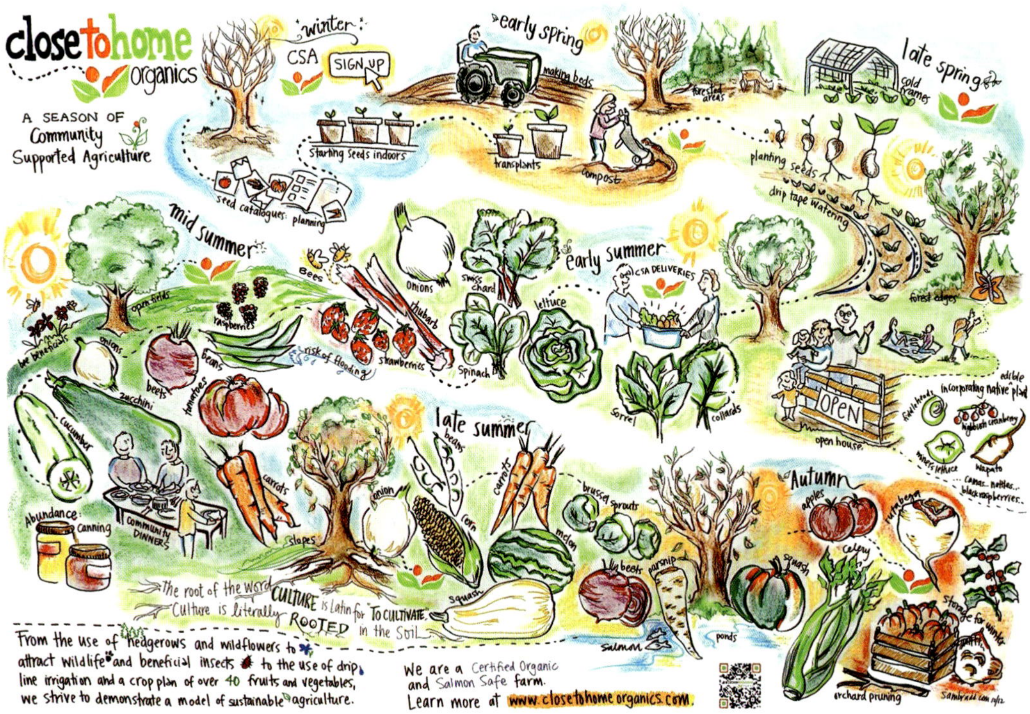

FIGURE 2. A season of community-supported agriculture. Drawing courtesy of Sam Bradd, 2013, http://www.sambradd.com/.

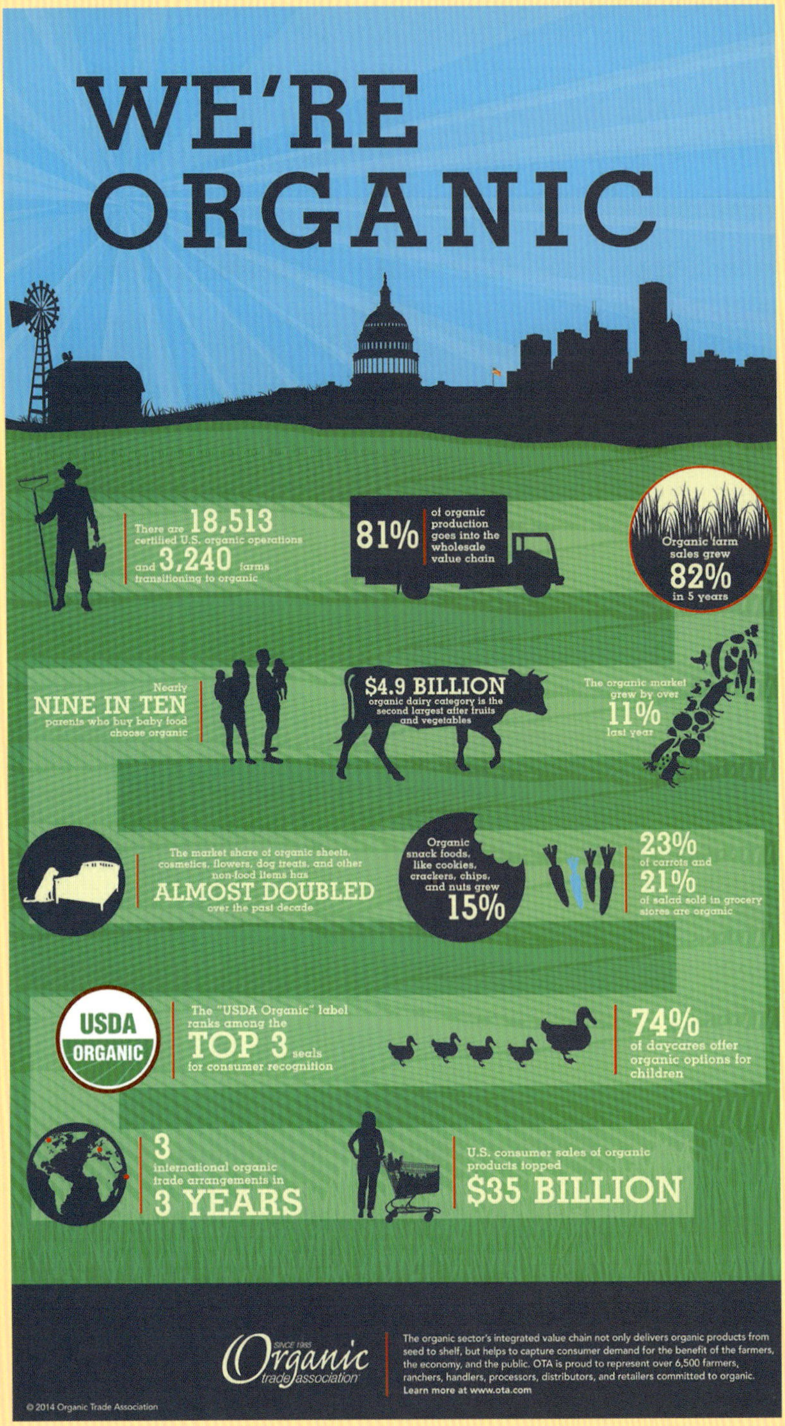

FIGURE 3. Organic food statistics. USDA Agricultural Marketing Service, 2012, National Organic Program, http://1.usa.gov/organic-certification.

2

Garden Pathways

The Organic and Conventional Debate

If you are currently growing or planning to grow your own vegetables, you undoubtedly have underlying motivations. Taste, food safety, self-sufficiency, enjoyment of a hobby, mental and physical health, nutrition, and the desire to produce food without chemicals have various levels of meaning to all of us. As a gardener, you need to make a decision as to how you wish to grow your own food. Do you want to adhere to a strict regimen of organic methods, where additions of organic soil-building components such as compost, animal manure, and organic fertilizers are used? The US Department of Agriculture has strict guidelines about "certified organic" (see the section titled "Certified Organic: What Does It Mean?"). Alternatively, are you willing to use some chemical fertilizers when pests or diseases threaten your crop? Every farmer and gardener has to decide on what strategies to use (natural, chemical, or combinations thereof). As you will learn in the chapters to come, growing vegetables organically is not an automatic key to success. There are many variables involved in the equation to successfully grow vegetables. However, there is a high correlation between healthy soils and healthy plants. The benefits associated with healthy, fertile soil include the following:

- optimal soil organic matter,
- optimal soil structure,
- more stable pH and more nutrients available to plants,
- optimal soil aggregate stability,

- adequate supply of macronutrients,
- adequate supply of micronutrients,
- active populations of microorganisms and mycorrhizae,
- active soil fauna (earthworms),
- optimal soil water-holding capacity,
- optimal infiltration capacity, and
- balanced populations of beneficial microorganisms versus pathogens

Success in organic gardening requires diligence in improving your soil health through a combination of actions such as building organic matter, rotating crops, and using a variety of soil amendments (manure, compost) over time. Improving and enriching soils with organic amendments takes time (see chapters 4 and 9). Although healthy soil and organic practices provide a degree of insurance in your gardening success, they do not ensure immunity to plant diseases and pests, or the effects of climate (drought or excessive wet cycles, erratic temperatures, cold snaps, and extreme heat). To some extent, the farmer and gardener can modify the effects of climate, but there are limits. The probability of a successful vegetable garden is vastly improved if you practice and use organic principles, especially if you have decided to use some conventional farming practices as well.

There are trade-offs, advantages, and disadvantages to using organic, conventional, and integrated farming methods, and you, the gardener, need to make your own decisions and choices. I am certainly an advocate of organic farming methods, but I also recognize the potential benefits that modern science offers. We each have to find our happy medium, what we feel comfortable with, and what formula works for us.

Three Agricultural Methodologies: Conventional, Integrated, and Organic

Sir Arthur Keith (1866–1955) stated: "The discovery of Agriculture was the first big step toward a civilized life." Agriculture has played a key role in the development of human civilization. Until the Industrial Revolution in the eighteenth and nineteenth centuries, the vast majority of the human population labored in centuries-old sustainable agriculture. Humans started cultivating edible plants in the Neolithic age (7,000–10,000 years ago). By 3000 BC, land preparation, irrigation, and pruning were practiced in Egypt. When did agriculture start to transition from largely organic means to more conventional methods? One of the most notable discoveries was the Haber-Bosch method (1909) for synthesizing ammonium nitrate, one of the key ingredients in chemical synthetic fertilizer. During the last fifty years, the use of inorganic chemical fertilizer (ICF; 10 million tons per year in 1960) has significantly increased and is projected to reach 200.5 million tons in 2018. Inorganic chemical fertilizer started out as an amendment to soil along with recycled nutrients such as crop residues and animal manure. During the era of the "green revolution" (World War II to the present), there has been a trend toward more reliance on ICF and pesticides throughout the world.

Pesticides are not new to agriculture; before 20 BCE, humans used pesticides to protect their crops. Sulfur, arsenic, mercury, and lead were applied to crops to kill pests. In the nineteenth century, natural pesticides such as pyrethrum (derived from chrysanthemums) and rotenone (produced from the roots of tropical plants) were discovered. The pesticide dichlorodiphenyltrichloroethane (DDT) was synthesized in 1874 and was first used as an insecticide in 1939 to control malaria and typhus among civilians and troops during World War II. After the war, DDT was made available for use as an agricultural insecticide, and soon its production and use became widespread. In the 1940s, manufacturers began to produce large amounts of synthetic pesticides. Pesticide use in the United States has increased 50-fold since 1950, standing at 516 million tons in 2008.

"Conventional agriculture," also called "modern agriculture" or "industrial farming," is a system that incorporates current technological and scientific information, which can include single crops grown in one or more seasons; crop rotations and cover crops; synthetic and organic fertilizers and pesticides; external energy and labor efficiency; dependence on high-yield hybrid cultivars and genetically modified plants; and often dependence on capital investments and agribusiness and marketing strategies. Conventional farming systems are highly varied around the United States, throughout the world, and from farm to farm. We cannot ignore the fact that conventional agriculture has steadily raised productivity; consumers in the United States and Canada have enjoyed abundant and relatively inexpensive food for well over a century. The US Department of Agriculture and World Bank have estimated that 70%–90% of the increase in food production today is the result of modern technologies in conventional agriculture, not of increasing land under cultivation. When you consider the challenges of growing food for the world, consider that insects and plant diseases are constantly adapting and pose considerable challenges. Over 400 species of insects and mites and more than 70 fungal pathogens have adapted and have developed resistance to pesticides. In addition, there is continual public concern over the use of pesticides and their effect on the environment and our health. Therefore, science must keep in step with these challenges.

Integrated Pest Management (IPM) is a logical step between conventional and organic methods and advances a set of strategies that growers can use to reduce pesticide use by matching inputs to a specific need. The IPM strategy focuses on using alternative control methods, reducing input costs, preserving resources, improving soil health, and protecting human and environmental health. In many instances, IPM and conventional agriculture are constantly melding. This discussion about conventional and organic agriculture is not about pinning one method against the other. Let's be clear that the debate between organic and conventional agriculture in the United States is not about whether food is grown in a "good" or "bad" way. For example, many organic growers use conventional farming techniques, and some conventional growers use organic methods. The topic is complicated; in many situations the two methodologies are more intertwined than you might expect.

"Organic farming" generally emphasizes natural agronomic production practices and principles, green or environmentally friendly inputs, and organic soil amendments and pesticides. According to the USDA National Organic Standards Board (NOSB), organic agriculture is defined as "an ecological production management system that promotes and enhances biodiversity, biological cycles, and soil biological activity. It is based on minimal use of off-farm inputs and on management practices that restore, maintain, or enhance ecological harmony." The primary goal of organic agriculture is to "optimize the health and productivity of interdependent communities of soil life, plants, animals, and people." Also, organic food handlers, processors, and retailers must adhere to organic standards that maintain the integrity of organic agricultural products. Organic farming systems rely on crop rotations, crop residues, animal manures, legumes, cover crops and green manures, and organic and biological pest control to enhance and maintain soil productivity, supply plant nutrients, and control insects, weeds, and other pests. In order to convert agricultural fields from conventional to organic, no prohibited substances can be used for a period of 3 years before the harvest of an organic crop.

There are many heated debates about the pros and cons of the three farming methods mentioned previously. Organic agricultural systems and production have developed a reputation of being environmentally friendly and sustainable. There are many advantages to organic farming such as maintenance of soil fertility and health, avoidance of synthetic chemicals and fertilizers, less pollution potential (but not always), cover crops and rotation, a more positive "green footprint," and animal-welfare concerns; however, no system is perfect from an environmental point of view. Agriculture and farming interactions with the environment are extremely complex, and there are misconceptions, myths, and confusion concerning conventional and organic farming methods. There are always trade-offs with any agricultural methodology. For example, many conventional farmers use no-till or reduced tillage practices. Seeds are planted with special seed drills into the previous crop's stubble. Herbicides are often used to control existing weeds so tillage is not necessary. In contrast, organic farming may have to rely more on tillage practices to control weeds, which can lead to soil erosion when the soil is bare. Tillage may also disturb nesting birds, worms, and invertebrates as well as use more fossil fuels, thereby increasing pollution from nitrogen oxides; it is also associated with oxidation and loss of organic matter. Organic matter is often applied to both organic and conventional fields, but tillage speeds up the loss of organic matter in the soil. Given this argument, which method is more environmentally friendly? There lies the quandary.

All three agricultural methods—conventional, IPM, and organic—use pesticides and an assortment of chemical products. Organic methods use natural products, with no synthetic fertilizers, sewage sludge, or genetically engineered plants. It is important to remember that although organic pesticides are natural, this does not imply that they are always less toxic than synthetic pesticides. The USDA publishes the National List of Allowed and Prohibited Substances for organic crop and livestock production and identifies synthetic substances that may be used and nonsynthetic (natural) substances that may not be used. The list also identifies nonorganic substances that may be used in or on processed organic products.

Organic and Conventional Farming: Effects on Soil Health

Healthy soil has many roles: it is linked to clean air and water; productive crops, forests, and grazing lands; and the overall aesthetics of our landscapes. Healthy soils also sustain plant and animal life, including the soil fauna or soil food web (collective terms for all the organisms living within the soil such as earthworms, nematodes, protozoa, fungi, bacteria, blue-green algae, and various arthropods). The mineral structure of the soil and the soil fauna can filter, buffer, break down, and detoxify organic and inorganic materials. Carbon, nitrogen, phosphorus, and many other nutrients go through a cycling process in the soil. Finally, soil health is directly related to how well the soil acts as a medium for plant growth. Both organic and conventional farming systems depend on healthy soil; without it, production is not sustainable.

There are inherent soil characteristics that we cannot easily change, such as its physical structure, topographical features (e.g., slope), color, texture, soil horizons (diagnostic soil layers), and mineralogy. However, we can manipulate and enhance soil pH, fertility, nutrient concentrations (nitrogen, phosphorus, potassium, and micronutrients [the rarer elements]), organic carbon, soil aggregate stability, and soil microflora. For example, clayey soils may be enhanced with organic materials to improve soil surface workability, nutrients, and aggregate stability, which are associated with increased water infiltration. Additions of organic matter over time (years) will improve fertility such that plants will be able to utilize soil nutrients at a more constant, sustainable level. Likewise, to a certain extent, sandy-textured soils may also be improved with additions of organic matter. However, be aware that significant short-term improvement of soils with high sand or clay content is limited because of the inherent physical properties of the soil.

What are the potential benefits of using organic nutrient sources for growing plants?

Agriculture is trending back to more natural organic nutrient sources such as manure, compost, and cover crops. Integrated approaches utilize available organic and chemical fertilizers. Organic methods tend to be more appealing to home gardeners since they are more able to manage the addition of organic materials in their garden settings. However, in large-scale production agriculture, agricultural scientists and producers point out that in order to produce abundant food, both organic and synthetic fertilizers have specific and important roles. Research shows the following:

- Organic nutrient sources are beneficial to soil physical, chemical, and biological properties. Maintaining or increasing organic matter in the soil improves soil aggregate stability (the soil particles are less likely to disintegrate upon wetting), resulting in better water infiltration, improved drainage, and soil tilth; lower bulk density; higher porosity and infiltration capacity; and improved drainage.

- Soil microbe diversity and biomass, organic matter, and nitrogen mineralization potential are often greater in organically enriched soils compared to conventionally managed fields where synthetic fertilizers are extensively used on a regular basis.
- As with any nutrient source, organic or synthetic, careful management is necessary to avoid potential environmental impacts (pollution).
- Assessment of crop yields (organic vs. conventional) can be difficult because of variability in nature (climatic conditions) and in the organic materials themselves. Organic materials are composed of complex compounds that have varying degrees of available nutrients and release rates. There can be potential problems associated with nutrient leaching from long-term applications of manure. Excess accumulation of nitrogen and phosphorus can occur. Organic phosphorus can be leached and transported by water runoff to streams, rivers, and lakes, causing pollution and degraded water quality. Too much of a good thing can have negative results.
- Soils have a carbon equilibrium level that is controlled by climate, vegetation, and the physical properties of the soil itself. Do not assume that raising the organic carbon content of your soil is a continuous linear, upward progression or that increases in soil organic carbon levels will remain constant over time.
- Where macronutrients and/or micronutrients are limited, specific organic and synthetic fertilizers can help compensate.
- Chemical fertilizers used alone are not a long-term solution where soil quality and health are limited.

Our Food Philosophy

A generation of young people during the late 1960s and early 1970s became aware of the dangers of foods produced with pesticides. During that time, the organic and health food movement was stimulated by people such as Adelle Davis, natural food advocate and author of *Let's Have Healthy Children*; Nobel prize winner Linus Pauling (proponent of megadoses of vitamin C); Rachel Carson, author of *Silent*

Spring; and Robert Rodale, author of organic gardening and farming publications. In my first gardening book, *The Basic Book of Organic Gardening*, edited by Robert Rodale, he said this about organic gardening: "The first step in becoming an organic gardener is to think about the step you are taking. Consider that you are embarking on a new adventure—a voyage of discovery into the world of nature's wonders . . . your organic garden will be a demonstration of the cleanliness and spirituality of nature's design for life on this planet." During the 1960s and 1970s, much of the literature on the value of organic foods came from nonscientific sources—magazine articles, newspapers, and logic. Today, there are published peer-reviewed scientific studies comparing pesticide residue levels and nutrition of organic versus conventionally grown foods.

There is a need to synthesize and interpret the claims and risks attributed to organically and conventionally grown produce. Organically raised produce does not use synthetic fertilizers and pesticides, but organic growers do have access to nonsynthetic (natural) substances, which have varying toxicities. However, there are other health risks associated with the plants we eat besides chemical residues (see table 1). Microbial and pathogenic organisms, mycotoxins, natural plant toxins, other human contaminants, and undesirable eating habits (unbalanced diets) pose greater threats to our health than pesticide residues. There is no scientific evidence to suggest that organic foods may be more susceptible to microbial contamination than conventionally grown produce.

Science points out that organic crops under stress from climate, insects, and weeds can stimulate the production of beneficial secondary plant metabolites (polyphenolic antioxidants) and naturally occurring poisonous toxins (natural pesticides). Plants produce toxins that are natural defense mechanisms against pests and predators. D. H. Janzen stated this about plants: "The world is not green. It is colored lectin, tannin, cyanide, caffeine, aflatoxin, and canavanine. And there is a lot of cellulose thrown in to make the mix even more inedible."

Most of us depend on others to produce our food, manage our water supply, and produce our fiber—there is no way we can control every aspect of the food and water that we depend on. Every time you visit the market, you make decisions about the products you buy. Many of us rely on name brands that we trust. If we desire to reduce our risk of various diseases, or combat a current illness, food purity and nutrition are probably a top priority. Whether your choice is toward vegetarianism, veganism, a macrobiotic diet, or a balance of all food items, there is the question of organic versus conventionally grown foods. Most health-conscious people want to avoid exposure to pesticides and residues on their food, especially pregnant women, parents of young children, and people battling disease.

Our food philosophy often changes with the onset of health problems. What seemed appropriate before may no longer be valid. How do we unravel the truth for ourselves? This is the challenge. If we are observant and rely on common sense, scientific advice, and spiritual inspiration, I believe we can maneuver our way to the truth for ourselves. We must be mindful, however, that our particular philosophy and diet regime may not fit the needs of others.

In today's markets, organically grown foods are more prevalent and available, but some organic foods are difficult to find or may be too expensive and beyond our budget. Since the early 1990s, the organic food industry has experienced a geometric increase in organic food sales, and the Organic Trade Association reports that organic food sales have reached $35 billion annually (fig. 3). Organic food items are the fastest-growing commodity in America's grocery stores. About 82% of US families are now buying organic foods, clothing, body and hygiene care, dietary supplements, pet food, and other products. Also, about 56% of US consumers say they prefer organic foods, but such foods often come with a 10%–60% price premium. Studies show that the main reasons consumers purchase organic foods are to (1) enjoy freshness, health, and nutrition; (2) avoid the use of pesticides; (3) enhance food safety; (4) avoid genetically engineered or modified foods; (5) increase environmental soundness and quality; (6) promote animal welfare (free-range animals); (7) eat wholesome food that is reminiscent of the past; and (8) support the local economy. As we make our choices at the market, we may contemplate the following questions: What exactly is an organically grown vegetable, and am I really buying a "healthier" product? How are organic products different from nonorganic? Why are organically grown produce and food items usually more expensive? Can I trust organic produce grown outside the United States? How can I maximize my food choices to prevent or help cure disease? What is the truth behind organic, and what are our options? Before you know it, you are in a quandary. Making these choices for ourselves and our family can be difficult and stressful because we may never really feel secure about the food we buy. Let us explore these issues and try to make some sense out of them.

Certified Organic: What Does It Mean?

In 1990, Congress enacted the Organic Foods Production Act (OFPA) as part of the 1990 Farm Bill. The OFPA mandated that the USDA develop more uniform national standards for organically produced agricultural products. As a result, the National Organic Program (NOP) was created and is administered by the USDA Agricultural Marketing Service, which develops, implements, and administers national production, handling, and labeling standards for organic products. Producers who meet the NOP standards may label their products "USDA Certified Organic."

According to the Agricultural Marketing Service, "Organic is a labeling term that indicates that the food or other agricultural product has been produced through approved methods that integrate cultural, biological, and mechanical practices that foster cycling of resources, promote ecological balance, and conserve biodiversity. Synthetic fertilizers, sewage sludge, irradiation, and genetic engineering may not be used." A product is considered organic in the United States when it (1) has been certified organic, and (2) contains 95% or more organic ingredients.

The Agricultural Marketing Service currently defines two categories of organic: (1) "'100% Organic,' which has 100% organic ingredients (excluding water and salt)," and (2) "'Organic,' which has at least 95% organic ingredients. The other 5% of the product cannot include genetically modified foods (GMOs), but can include non-organic items, if organic of that item isn't commercially available." Organic farming operations with yearly sales of $5,000 or less are exempt from certain certification requirements.

What about the remaining 5% of ingredients? The USDA has proposed 38 minor ingredients (food colorings, fish oils, hops, chipotle chilies, bay leaves, rice starch, whey protein concentrate, and natural sausage casings, to name a few) that are not organic in origin for this approved list. The consumer who buys and pays more for organic would undoubtedly prefer that all the ingredients on an "organic" label be organic. On foods such as fruits and vegetables, look for a small sticker version of the USDA organic label or check the signage in your grocery store produce section for this seal. Producers of products that contain at least 70% organic ingredients may label them "made with organic ingredients" but may not use the organic seal.

FIGURE 4. An organic product must bear the USDA organic seal.

What is the difference between "organic" and "natural"? Do they mean the same thing?

On some food product labels you may see the words "natural," "all natural," "free range," and "hormone and antibiotic free." Do not confuse these terms with "organic," because they do not meet the criteria and organic standards set forth by the USDA.

What are the USDA rules concerning imported produce? All food certified and sold as organic in the United States must be produced and handled in accordance with US standards. Organic food products from foreign countries must be certified by a USDA-accredited certifier. The dynamics of international trade are complex, as are the intricacies of organic certification. The USDA has accredited certifying agents in many foreign countries to help verify that NOP requirements are being met. Yes, there are instances of fraud and misuse of the organic label on both US and imported produce. However, most of the news reports on this issue state that there is little evidence that fraud is widespread, and the USDA is continually investing more resources into preventing fraud.

Risks Associated with Pesticide Use

Many of us have questions about pesticide residues on our food. Various environmental and organic groups have ranked commonly purchased fruits and vegetables as to their potential pesticide residues (the "Dirty Dozen" being the most likely to have such residues). The lineup varies somewhat from publication to publication, but it generally starts with apples, strawberries, grapes, celery, peaches, spinach, sweet bell peppers, nectarines, cucumbers, cherry tomatoes, potatoes, hot peppers, kale, collard greens, zucchini, lettuce, and blueberries. If you wish to purchase organic fruits and vegetables, these lists may help you prioritize your purchases.

There are four main ways pesticides can enter the food chain: (1) post-harvest residues, (2) farm pesticides, (3) pesticides on imported food, and (4) pesticides that persist in the environment even though they are now off the market. Surveys show that the main reason consumers purchase organic foods is to avoid pesticides. This is a valid concern, but few consumers realize that there are more-potent food safety hazards such as pathogenic microbial agents, mycotoxins (toxic chemical products produced by fungi/molds), phycotoxins (toxins produced by algae in shellfish and other marine animals), phytotoxins (toxins produced by plants), unbalanced diet, food additives, and others (table 1).

TABLE 1. Ranking of food hazards related to human health

Potential food hazards		
Rank	**Acute** (conditions could be severe and sudden in onset)	**Chronic** (long developing)
1	Microbial agents	Mycotoxins
2	Phycotoxins	Human contaminants
3	Some phytotoxins	Some phytotoxins
4	Mycotoxins	Unbalanced diet
5	Human contaminants	Phycotoxins
6	Food additives	Microbial agents
7	Pesticide residues	Food additives
8		Pesticide residues

Source: Magkos, Arvaniti, and Zampelas (2006).

Note: Food hazards are rated from most to least potent on two scales based on acute and chronic effects, regardless of whether the food is grown organically or conventionally.

A systematic review of several recent studies of nutrient and contaminant levels in foods shows that although pesticide residues can be higher for conventionally grown produce, the vast majority of residues are well within tolerable limits as set by the Environmental Protection Agency. At present, although there are periodic outbreaks of *E. coli* and *Salmonella*, there is no conclusive scientific evidence to instill distrust in current agricultural and industrial food production.

Organic and Conventional Farming: Nutritional Comparisons

What can science presently tell us about nutritive content and taste differences between organic and conventionally grown vegetables? Many consumers have the perception and belief that organic foods are more nutritious than conventional foods. Many studies have attempted to quantify differences in crop and soil attributes resulting from conventional and organic production methods. However, science has not produced any concrete definitive answers regarding nutritional differences between organic and conventionally grown produce. You may wonder why science cannot clear up the controversy. The reason is there are too many variables that can confound experiments. Homogeneity of soil physical and chemical structure and properties, fertility, soil microorganisms, and climate are difficult to control in field experiments. Experienced farmers and gardeners know that fluctuations among these factors affect the final productivity and quality of the crop. Climatic fluctuations such as sudden hot or cold spells or dry and wet cycles can affect the quality of the crop and, ultimately, taste. Add the availability of nitrogen, phosphorus, potassium, and micronutrients; organic matter content; mycorrhizal fungi populations, and potential pests and disease organisms to the equation. Now try to deduce which factors influence the overall quality of the crop. Can the difference be fully explained by organic versus conventional growing practices? Therein lies the problem.

One of the high-ranking reasons consumers buy organic is taste. A comparison of organic and conventionally grown produce from the grocery shelf is simply not possible because of all the factors that can affect quality. The vegetables we buy at the store can be any number of different varieties and cultivars; they have been grown under different climatic, soil, and fertility conditions; and they have been managed, harvested, and handled differently from field to store. Taste is subjective. From my experience, the taste and texture of homegrown produce is associated more with varieties and cultivars, and with harvesting vegetables at their peak. For example,

SCIENCE NOTE • Taste Comparisons between Organic and Nonorganic Vegetables

Although consumers have the perception that organically grown produce tastes better, sensory evaluations have been inconsistent. Consumers were not able to detect differences in taste between organic and conventionally grown tomatoes, cucumbers, and onions. Other taste test comparisons have shown little difference between lettuce and green beans; conventionally grown carrots were chosen over organic; organic broccoli was preferred; and organic potatoes were more bitter. Glycoalkaloids were 100 times greater in organically grown potatoes. The two main glycoalkaloids in potatoes are a-solanine and a-chaconine. Potatoes produce chlorophyll, which causes greening, and solanine at the same time. High levels of chlorophyll (which is not harmful) often accompany high solanine content in potatoes, which can be toxic if consumed (3 to 6 milligrams per kilogram of body weight can cause death). Do not eat green potatoes!

many tomato lovers prefer the taste of heirloom varieties. There is a basis to this preference, no doubt, but subjectivity does enter in. In homegrown-tomato taste tests I have participated in, the winning characteristics were inherent qualities such as sweetness or flavor, not whether the fruit was grown organically or conventionally.

How does one decide on the issues surrounding organic versus conventionally grown foods? While there are reports indicating that organic and conventional fruits and vegetables may differ in a variety of sensory qualities such as taste, smell, and texture, the findings are inconsistent. Unraveling all the facts about the foods we eat is a monumental task. As stated in the beginning of this chapter, most health-conscious people buy organic to avoid exposure to pesticides and residues on their food. However, science points out that pesticide residues are not the only risks to our health; improper diet has far more implications and poses far more risks to our health than eating conventionally grown foods (with or without pesticides and/or chemical fertilizers). In an article titled "Are Organic Veggies Better for You? Maybe, or Maybe Not, Either Way, It's a Useless Debate," James McWilliams states: "Let's first focus on what we eat before we start fighting over the details of how, exactly, it's grown." I offer the following advice: moderation in all things, and reliance on spiritual inspiration, your body's response to food items, common sense, and scientific and medical advice. In the home garden, by all means practice organic principles as best you can. My belief is that homegrown produce is a positive step toward a healthy life for ourselves and our families.

FIGURE 5. Ecology of the garden with interacting factors. Figure by author.

3

Garden Ecology

As a gardener, you will be applying and practicing scientific concepts used by ecologists, agronomists, soil scientists, botanists, climatologists, and horticulturists. When you stop to think about it, the vegetable gardener has to balance many factors, only some of which can be controlled (fig. 5). For example, building soil health, choosing the best time to plant specific vegetables, selecting the varieties and cultivars that are best for a given climate, considering and caring for plants with different botanical and growth characteristics, and diagnosing and treating diseases and pests are but a few variables the vegetable gardener needs to address on a yearly basis. Often, our best-laid gardening plans may need to be changed or modified because of the many unexpected situations that can arise. Natural plant communities and their corresponding ecosystems are complex culminations of an infinite number of interrelationships that have been in force for millennia. Climate, soils and soil flora, plant composition, and animal and human impacts are constantly changing, morphing our environment in unpredictable ways. With so many shifting variables in a given environment, we should never expect a consistently uniform, predictable outcome. In agriculture, we must always be on guard and willing to improvise at any time. When unpredictable situations occur, such as drought, flooding, cold or hot temperatures, insect infestations, plant diseases, or market changes, success in agriculture often depends on when and how we intervene. As gardeners, we need to be able to accept a certain amount of failure during any given year. For example, tomatoes may have done well this year, but corn did not. As explained in later chapters, your location, soils, and climate will be conducive to growing certain vegetables successfully, while other vegetables may always be a challenge. Rare is the situation in which all vegetable crops perform splendidly at any given location. If you are new to gardening, find out what vegetables do well in your locale and start with those. Over time, you will find your knowledge increasing and may realize that you are using scientific methods to help understand and solve problems.

As gardeners, we often interject our personal and cultural beliefs, which may be derived from our own or others' observations, to develop a specific gardening theory or conclusion. In time, others may make particular observations and arrive at the same conclusion, and soon the belief becomes entrenched in gardening folklore. For example, when hot and sweet peppers are planted close together, the sweet pepper fruits develop unpredictable hot and spicy flavors. Perhaps the gardener remembers that this phenomenon does not always occur. Subsequently, he or she makes a common conclusion: do not plant hot and sweet peppers together; the hotness is transferred to the sweet peppers, and you may likely have all hot-tasting peppers. This is an example of inductive reasoning, where we make observations that may or may not result in a consistent pattern; nevertheless, we formulate a conclusion. The hint in this example is that this pattern does not always occur, but a conclusion is made just the same. Be aware of the hazard of inductive reasoning: our observations and generalizations may not be correct. In the case of hot and sweet peppers, science has shown through experimentation that this phenomenon is a myth. Pepper plants have perfect flowers that self-pollinate; therefore, the hot gene is not transferred during the growing year. However, peppers will occasionally cross-pollinate, and because the hot gene in peppers is dominant, the seeds from plants that have cross-pollinated during the previous growing season might produce fruit with unpredictable flavors. This is the risk of saving pepper seeds from hot and sweet plants grown close together. If a gardener does not save seeds and replant them, a mistake can still be made by a seed grower—to avoid cross-pollination between hot and sweet peppers, they must be separated by at least 500 feet.

Vegetable gardeners who have been gardening for a number of years usually conduct experiments, but they may not realize it. For example, do you compare varieties and cultivars for productivity, taste, or disease resistance; practice companion planting; evaluate and compare various soil amendments; or test foliar applications of fertilizer and the effects of plant pruning? If you are an experimenter, I encourage you to keep notes about your results.

The Garden Ecosystem

When you consider all the factors in figure 5, both biotic (living) and abiotic (nonliving chemical and physical factors in the environment), the probabilities of different outcomes from season to season and year to year are numerous and unpredictable. In a healthy soil, insects, earthworms, and myriad microorganisms such as algae, fungi, and bacteria interact (some compatibly, others competitively) with each other while at the same time reacting to light, temperature, precipitation, soil moisture, nutrients, and plant roots in the soil. Many home gardens may have surprisingly high biodiversity. Jennifer Owen, in *The Ecology of a Garden: The First Fifteen Years*, documented yearly fluctuations of 1,757 animal species and 422 plant species in her garden in Leicestershire, England, between 1972 and 1986.

In a well-balanced, healthy ecosystem, the garden can function in relative harmony. I say "relative harmony" because in the natural environment there is never true equilibrium. There is always a "tug-of-war" going on in nature. You may perceive a beautiful garden, a pristine stream, an old-growth forest, a high-elevation alpine zone with wildflowers, or a prairie, but be assured that these ecosystems have experienced many disturbances (ecologists call them perturbations) during their development over time. During some years and groups of years, there may be relative equilibrium; however, there are also periodic droughts, extreme cold and hot temperatures, insect plagues, wildfire, floods, and animal impacts. To be realistic, the best we can hope for is to establish "relative" equilibrium and harmony in our garden.

As gardeners, we have the ability to manipulate the environment to a point, but there are many factors we cannot control. We can manipulate the timing of planting seeds and growing or hardening plants for transplant; override drought to a certain extent by irrigating and by preserving moisture with mulches; deal with unexpected frost by covering plants with tarps; use garden solar fabrics on unusually hot, intensely sunny days that can burn tender leaves; manage insect infestations to a certain extent by organic (beneficial insects and other biological control organisms) and inorganic means; improve soil fertility with soil amendments; and use plant varieties and hybrid vigor to our advantage.

Some people may be under the impression that using a strict regimen of organic principles in the garden environment means that all is well. Unfortunately, as long as we live in our terrestrial world,

SCIENCE NOTE • Ecology in the Garden

Perhaps you never realized this, but a gardener is actually a practicing plant ecologist. Plant ecologists study the interactions between plants and their environment. The environment includes many aspects such as climate, landscape features and topography, geology, soils, organisms in the soil, and animals—especially herbivores. Include past and present disturbances (natural and human) throughout time, and you soon realize how complex the environment is.

What does ecology have to do with your garden? In new and established gardens, it is helpful if you step back and evaluate the history of the garden. By doing this, you can understand your soil resource and what the garden might be capable of. Questions that should be considered are the following: What type of soil do I have? Is it sandy, silty, clayey, or a combination of these textures? Has the topsoil been eroded or scraped away by construction? What was the original vegetation—forest, grassland, or other plant community—at my location? When the garden was established, what was the prior state of the vegetation? What is the quality of the soil, and are the soil flora and microorganisms active? What is the climate throughout all 12 months, including timing and amount of precipitation, and temperature fluctuations (especially diurnal fluctuations, or fluctuations between night and day) during the growing period?

The more you learn about the ecology of your garden location, the more successful your gardening experience will be!

nature will impose its will. The goal in agriculture, organic or otherwise, is to grow crops and raise animals while actively managing pests and diseases by cultural strategies. The advantages are great where soil organic matter and fertility are in balance: plants are healthy, soil water-holding capacity is increased, and soil flora and fauna are active. Even when all these factors are optimal, equilibrium in the garden can be disrupted by forces beyond our control. The first line of defense against perturbations (pests and natural disturbances) is to use preventive strategies to buffer the garden and create resilience.

Why I Plant Vegetables in Circle Plots: Mimicking Nature's Patterns

I used to plant my vegetables in rows, but circumstances and limiting resources in my Texas garden stimulated the scientist in me: I thought, there must be a more efficient way to plant and grow vegetables! In my case, my soil is very limiting (in the depth of its topsoil and its alkalinity); irrigation is necessary in my climate because of erratic rainfall (and my only water source is a well); my profession requires me to travel several times a month, and I have to depend on family members to take care of the garden; and the act of bending down is hard on my back and knees. I started planting groups of vegetables in smaller plots and eventually settled on the circle arrangement for a number of reasons. I explain the benefits of circle plots in detail in chapter 7. I find that circles are efficient and convenient for a variety of reasons such as ease of building soil health, planting, weeding, watering, harvesting, and fencing for protection (fig. 5). The physical requirements of bending and crouching are also greatly reduced.

Circle gardening mimics natural plant distribution. I had done research and published a paper on plant spatial patterns in a scientific journal, but I did not realize at that time the connection between the clumped plant pattern commonly exhibited in nature and planting vegetables in circles in my vegetable garden (see Science Note on the next page). When I started writing this book and listing the positive attributes of circle plots, I contemplated the ecological aspects of natural plant distribution for many plants; then I realized why my garden was doing so well. Clumped planting arrangements have been used for thousands of years by indigenous people in both arid and humid environments throughout North and South America. In the "Three Sisters" arrangement, corn, squash, beans, and other plants that attracted pollinators were planted together because they were recognized as having compatible and mutualistic attributes (more on this in chapter 6).

Plant Diversity in the Garden

Plant diversity is important in the garden because greater variety aboveground is associated with greater diversity of living organisms in the soil. Microorganisms, including mycorrhizae, other fungal species, bacteria, algae, and other living organisms (from insects to

SCIENCE NOTE • Ecological Basis for Planting in Circle Arrangements

Terrestrial plant communities, whether forests, grasslands, or deserts, exhibit various distribution patterns. The three main distribution patterns in nature are clumped, random, and uniform. Animal species and populations demonstrate inherent distribution patterns: fish swim in schools; bison, mountain goats, and antelope live in herds; and cougars, tigers, and polar bears are solitary animals. The next time you visit a natural, relatively undisturbed forest or grassland, try to observe the habit of certain plants. For example, you may see a patch of evening primrose, Indian paintbrush, coreopsis, Texas bluebells, blackberries, live oak, or aspen trees. Regularity in plant communities seems to be uncommon. Likewise, departure from randomness and a predilection toward clumping is common among many plants in the wild.

If you see plants growing in a clumped arrangement, try to visualize the environmental and biological reasons behind this spatial arrangement. A clumped arrangement is nonrandom, which may imply some environmental or biological preference, or perhaps some other environmental restraint. It may also suggest habitat heterogeneity—a particular habitat may be more favorable for a given plant species, for example in soil type, soil depth, soil texture, microrelief, aspect (north, south, east, or west), available water, fractured bedrock, available light, microclimate, and so on. A clumped arrangement may also be favorable for plant reproduction—new plants are initiated via runners, rhizomes, or stolons, or seeds are dispersed close to the parent plants. In contrast, a random pattern of vegetation may denote environmental homogeneity and/or nonselective plant requirements. Uniform plant distribution may be related to competition for nutrients, light, or some other interaction between individuals.

Several different factors or combinations of factors may be responsible for plant spatial patterns: (1) environment (wind, water, soil, light, aspect, elevation, and the amount, timing, and form of precipitation); (2) reproductive mode (seed dispersal, clonal clumps due to runners or rhizomes; (3) territorial behavior in animals; and (4) competitive effects. Some plants exhibit allelopathy (a competitive effect from a chemical toxin that inhibits other plants). The following are some examples of plants and the allelotoxins they contain:

- Black walnut (*Juglans nigra*), juglone
- Tree of life (*Ailanthus altissima*), ailanthone

- Spotted knapweed (*Centaurea maculosa*), cnicin
- Sorghum (*Sorghum* spp.), sorgoleone
- Rye (*Secale cereale*), hydroxamic acids
- Wild mustards (*Brassica* spp.), thiocyanates
- Tobacco (*Nicotiana rustica*), nicotene
- Rice (*Oryza sativa*), momilactones
- Pea (*Pisum sativum*), pisatin

Extracts from the leaves and stems of eggplant have been shown to express autotoxicity, which inhibits germination of tomato, pepper, cucumber, and eggplant itself. In summary, many plants have allelopathic toxins in stems, leaves, flowers, roots, or fruits, which may inhibit shoot or root growth and/or limit nutrient uptake. The allelopathic effect may facilitate a clumped distribution pattern.

earthworms), thrive when aboveground plants are robust. Diverse plant species (including flowering plants that attract pollinators) and various varieties and cultivars of vegetable plants promote garden health. Chances are there is greater balance between nonpathogenic versus pathogenic microorganisms in gardens containing a diversity of plants than there is in monocultures of corn or other singularly grown crops. Throughout the centuries, agricultural skills and methods have been developed and confirmed through the success and higher productivity of crops. Early traditional farmers realized the importance of plant diversity in their plots and fields, which resulted in (1) more stable food production, (2) less crop failure, and (3) reduced insect and disease incidence. Throughout the world today, traditional agroecosystems using high plant diversity as a management tool provide about 15%–20% of the global food supply. For example, the Huastec Indians in Mexico incorporate various planting strategies such as planted and fallow crop fields, highly diverse home gardens (80–125 species), and forest plots. The accumulated plant diversity totals about 300 plant species. In West Java, Indonesia, the *pekarangan* (home garden) and *kebun-talun* (shifting cultivation) cropping systems commonly contain about 100 or more species (plants for building materials are 42%, fruit trees 18%, vegetables 14%, and the remainder are medicinals, ornamentals, spices, and other cash crops). Farmers in the Andes traditionally plant about 50 potato varieties. Home gardens can contribute to the conservation of biodiversity, and more diverse gardens are associated with more resilience to diseases and pests. An added advantage to increasing diversity in the garden is the attraction of pollinating insects.

In natural plant communities, plant diversity is not static from year to year. Yes, specific cadres of dominant and subdominant plants are largely maintained over time. Plant species wax and wane to a certain extent because of varying climate. During wet years, certain plants may appear and then may not be seen again for some time. Many plant species seem to be able to lie dormant, as latent roots and/or seeds, during stressful periods. When external disturbances such as grazing, burning, flooding, and drought occur, plant diversity and plant community composition change. This change is a major theme of study among plant ecologists. By increasing and changing plant diversity in our vegetable gardens, we can mimic nature. Nature seems to thrive because of randomness in climate, the favorable result being a disruption to diseases and pests. Variety seems to be a key to health in the garden: plant different vegetables from year to year or rotate where you plant them, use different cultivars and varieties, increase diversity by planting flowers that attract pollinators, and use different cover crops during dormant periods to build soil health.

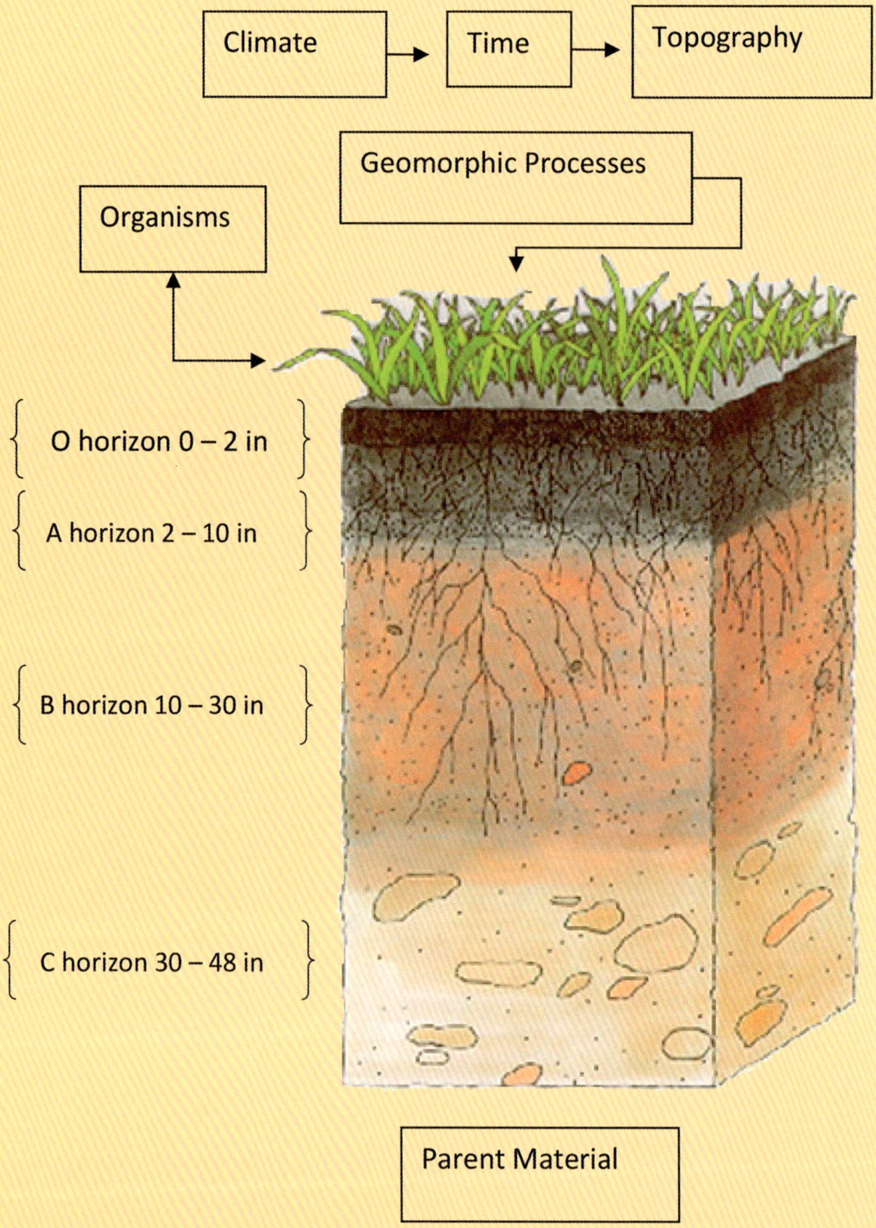

FIGURE 6. Soil profile showing layers (soil horizons) and soil-forming factors. Courtesy of USDA NRCS, 2013, http://www.nrcs.usda.gov/wps/portal/nrcs/detail/soils/survey/office/ssr7/profile/?cid=nrcs142p2_047970.

4

Soil

A Living Entity

Soil is the basis for nearly all land use, from agriculture to mining to construction. For the home gardener, soils and soil health are everything. I am intentionally including this chapter on soil as a living entity before the chapter on establishing a garden because the subject deserves special attention, and the knowledge you gain here will assist you in building your circle plots. What you grow depends on the soil. Of course climate and the care and management of your garden are other major factors in gardening, but soils are the foundation. If you want to succeed at growing vegetables, you need to learn and know about your soils. You can avoid some of the technical aspects of soils for only so long. Understanding that soil is a living entity will open new windows of awareness and broaden your gardening experience. As you learn about soil texture, organic matter, pH, and compost, begin investigating these dynamics in your own garden. When you mix your finished compost into your soil, notice the pleasant earthy smell—this is a good sign. Look at the crumbly nature of the compost, the brown hues of the decomposed materials, and think about how this organic matter is going to improve your soil. There is no single pathway to improving soil health, but adding organic matter and compost is a good start. Be solicitous about bagged compost for sale in garden and building centers, as I find that this material is now largely woody in nature—not really compost. Experiment with various organic soil amendments. If you are not averse to using synthetic fertilizers, experiment with combinations of both. How do soil microbes react to additions of organic matter? How do soil microbes synthesize fertilizers? These answers are included in this book. As your soil knowledge grows, you will see nature in a different light, and you will be able to diagnose the status of soils in many different settings. In time, as you examine the vigor and color of plants, you will immediately begin to formulate the status of soil health—in your garden, lawn, public flower beds, crop fields, or pastures. Have the soils been eroded? Has the topsoil been scraped off, or is it compacted and lacking in nutrients? What are the diagnostic signs of healthy soil? Remember, healthy soils and productive lands are not limitless. Soil erosion has plagued many civilizations throughout history, including the United States, and it is still a problem throughout the world. Agricultural statistics say that 99.7% of our food calories come from the land (less than 0.3% come from the oceans and other aquatic ecosystems). Throughout the world, soil loss is depleting about 25 million acres of cropland per year, which amounts to approximately 75 billion tons of soil loss from agricultural systems per year. Soil erosion occurs about 10 to 40 times faster than the rate at which it can rebuild.

What is soil? Soil is a product of the environment and is a dynamic matrix of minerals, gases, liquids, organic materials, and living organisms that serves as a medium to support plant growth essential to life on Earth. The length of time required for soil development is measured in millennia. The worldwide average for soil development is 1 centimeter in 178 years, or 1 inch in 452 years. To help put this into perspective, 1 centimeter of soil spread over 1 acre is approximately 58.1 tons; 1 inch of soil spread over 1 acre is about 147.5 tons. The rate of soil development varies depending on the soil formation factors listed in figure 6.

How do soils form and develop? Soils evolve or develop from interactions with climate, a host of living organisms, the primary geological material (also referred to as parent material), and the topography of the land or terrain (fig. 6). The slope of the land, its north, south, east, or west aspects, the slope shape, and the elevation are related to topography. Hans Jenny (soil scientist, 1899–1992) described the soil-forming process with the following equation:

> soil formation = function of climate, potential biota–plants and animals, relief, soil parent material, and time

Soil scientists identify and describe soils in layers. These layers are called horizons and are usually indicated by symbols, for example, O, A, E, B, C, and R (fig. 6). In circle gardening, we will be manipulating the O and A horizons by adding additional mulches, manure, compost, and other soil amendments. For practical purposes, let's simplify the concept of soil horizons so that the information can be useful to the home gardener. An O horizon is the uppermost surface layer of the soil and is composed of organic matter, which can be undecomposed or partially decomposed litter such as hay, leaves and needles, moss, and lichens. In some instances, the O horizon may be very thin or nonexistent for a number of reasons. This layer may be raked away during normal lawn and ground maintenance, it may be eroded, or it may be in the process of decomposition, depending on local climatic conditions. As you progress from the O to the C horizon, organic matter typically decreases.

Next is the A horizon, which is the uppermost mineral horizon. In nontechnical terms, this layer is your topsoil layer and can contain decomposed organic material. Professional soil scientists use soil color as a discernible characteristic to identify and classify soils. They use a Munsell Color Chart, which contains color chips much like those you find at a paint store, to determine hue (yellowness to redness), value (lightness or darkness), and chroma (color intensity or brightness). Following the A horizon, an E horizon could exist (not shown in fig. 6). The E horizon is a zone where silicate clay, iron, and aluminum oxides or a combination of these may have leached downward, making this horizon characteristically lighter in color than the A horizon above or the B horizon below. The B horizon, often referred to as subsoil, typically forms below the A horizon and contains less organic matter. The C horizon is unconsolidated material (broken-up rock). Plant roots usually do not easily penetrate this layer, except through cracks and fissures. Very little organic material is found in the C horizon. The R layer (not shown in fig. 6) is hard bedrock with very little evidence of weathering. Granite, basalt, quartzite, limestone, and sandstone are examples.

Getting to Know Your Soil

As gardeners, we may often wonder, what kind of soil do I have, and what can I grow in it? Many agricultural and gardening publications recommend sending soil samples to a lab. I recommend that you start with a basic evaluation using the Soil Health/Quality Indicator Scorecard in appendix A and then send the soil for analysis. You can use this scorecard to evaluate soil quality and health of both new and existing gardens. The scorecard is a subjective evaluation, but it can provide a relative baseline of conditions using the number of indicators in each column. The indicator columns are undesirable and/or unhealthy, and desirable and/or healthy, with the middle column intermediate between these two. Not all the indicators represent an unhealthy situation; for example, texture, color, and infiltration capacity may depend on the inherent characteristics of your soil—the norm for your soil type. Many of the indicators can be improved and managed, for instance, pH, organic matter, biological activity, infiltration, compaction, water-holding capacity, and overall soil health.

Should you obtain a soil test? This information is always useful, but be aware that the report will be somewhat technical. Most soil test labs provide basic information on soil pH, some macronutrients (phosphorus, potassium, calcium, magnesium, sodium, sulfur), salinity (soluble salts) and cation exchange capacity (CEC). CEC is the ability of negatively charged soil particles (clay and organic matter) to attract and retain positively charged ions called cations (calcium, Ca^{++}; magnesium, Mg^{++}; potassium, K^{+}; sodium, Na^{+}; ammonium, $NH4^{+}$; aluminum, Al^{+++}; and hydrogen, H^{+}), and many other micronutrients. Clay and organic matter in the soil have net negative charges and will attract these positively charged cations, just as the poles of a magnet attract their opposite charge. Sands are typically low in colloids and therefore low in cations, whereas silt loams and clay loams have a higher CEC, and humus has a very high CEC. In a soil lab report, CEC is reported in metric units (milliequivalents per 100 grams of soil [meq/100 g] or cmol/kg; 1 meq/100 g = 1 cmol/kg) that home gardeners most likely will not understand. As a guideline, CEC in sandy-textured soils is below 9 cmol/kg, in loamy soils 9 to 20 cmol/kg, and in clayey soils above 20 cmol/kg. The percentage of soil clay, clay type, and organic matter content influence CEC: as soil clay and/or organic matter content increase, CEC increases. CEC is a useful indicator of soil fertility, as it indicates the ability of the soil to supply three important plant nutrients: calcium, magnesium, and potassium.

Soil analysis data is worth the testing expense. Some labs may include nitrates and organic matter. Tests for micronutrients, organic matter, soil texture, and detailed salinity often require additional fees for each test (check online soil lab services through your state agricultural extension, university, and private labs). Routine soil tests will usually not provide information about soil name, some physical characteristics, the relation to other adjacent soils and the landscape, general potential productivity of adapted crops, or information about how the soil is suited for a building site or for growing crops. Other sources also provide this type of information (see below). Investigate and determine your soil type via the USDA Natural Resources Conservation Service (NRCS) Web Soil Survey (WSS) on your computer (http://websoilsurvey.nrcs.usda.gov/app/HomePage.htm; click on "Start WSS"). You can access the largest natural resource information system in the world, which contains soil maps and data about your soils (soil type and name, texture, organic matter, pH, etc.). This data is based on undisturbed soils. If your soil has undergone disturbance from construction, erosion, or long-term cropping, the data may no longer be representative. If these factors have altered your soil over time, reductions in topsoil depth, organic matter, and fertility have most likely occurred. More than 95% of the private land in the United States is mapped and identified. Generally, the WSS does not include public land owned and managed by the US Forest Service, Bureau of Land Management, or other federal agencies (though there are some exceptions in which public lands are mapped through cooperative agreements).

In addition, there is an application (app) for iPhone and Android users in which global positioning system (GPS) technology locates your position on the landscape and links with NRCS soil survey data. An app called "Soil Web: An Online Soil Survey Browser" provides summaries of soil type based on the current location of a smartphone in the field. This app was developed by the California Soil Resource Lab at the University of California–Davis and the University of California Division of Agriculture and Natural Resources in collaboration with the NRCS (http://casoilresource.lawr.ucdavis.edu/soilweb/).

The WSS and Soil Web app will identify the soil map unit and soil components within the map unit for your property location, specifically the spot where you are standing. A soil map unit is a collection of soil areas or nonsoil (miscellaneous) areas delineated in a soil survey. Map units are assigned a name that uniquely identifies the area in a particular soil survey area, and these differ in minor or major ways from other units in the survey area. Map units consist of one or more components, and usually there are several component names in a soil map unit. For example, one soil component may occupy 70% of a map unit, while other, more minor components make up the remaining 30%. By reading the soil component descriptions, you can narrow down the appropriate soil component that is represented in your garden or field.

PERSONAL NOTE • Has Your Soil Been Disturbed?

You may or may not have firsthand knowledge about the history of your homesite or your existing or planned garden site. Be aware that your soil most likely has been altered or disturbed during the construction of your home. During construction, your topsoil may have been eroded, scraped away, or buried under subsoil materials. During the landscaping process in home building, contractors and landscapers often apply a relatively thin layer of topsoil. This is also problematic for gardeners, as it creates an unnatural boundary layer between the topsoil and the hard, compacted subsoil. This subsoil layer will impede development of plant roots and can also affect percolation of soil water. This is also a common problem when raised beds are constructed and new soil is placed over the existing soil (see discussion on the next page).

Mixing clayey soils over sand, or sandy soils over clay, can have significant effects on water movement in your soil. Abrupt changes in soil texture or subsurface compaction layers have varying effects on water movement in soils. Soil scientists classify these texture layers and other dense layers as claypans, fragipans (dense, compacted layers other than claypans), sand, and gravel layers. In clayey soils over sand, water must move from fine to coarse pores, resulting in water accumulation at the clay/sand interface. Eventually, gravity or hydrostatic pressure will force the water into the sand layer (fig. 7). Reverse the situation, with sandy over clayey soil, and water will accumulate and may form a perched water table, resulting in extremely slow or nonexistent water flow, depending on conditions (fig. 7).

If you are building a home, discuss stockpiling your topsoil with your contractor. It is advisable to cover the topsoil pile with a breathable material to prevent it from eroding, drying out, and growing weeds. Another option is to plant a quick-growing crop such as wheat or oats.

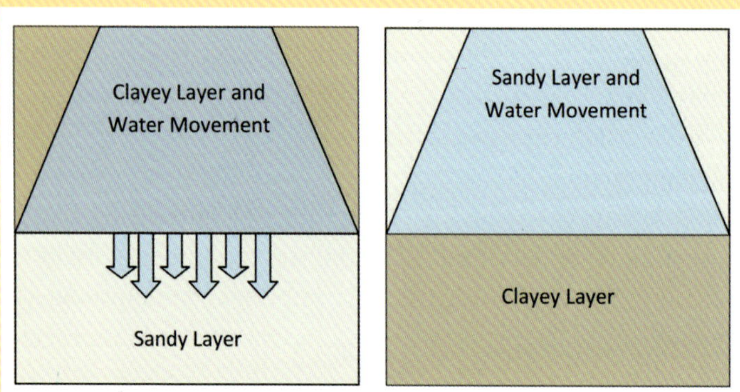

FIGURE 7. Soil texture changes can affect water movement in soil. Redrawn and adapted from Whiting et al. (2011).

Common problem encountered with raised garden beds: One of the most common problems gardeners encounter in raised bed gardening occurs when they place topsoil over compacted soil or soil of a different nature. In constructing raised beds, you must incorporate new material with the existing soil to a depth of at least 8 to 12 inches (some references quote 24 inches). If you place topsoil over compacted soil or soil of a different nature (sand, clay) in a raised bed, it is likely that your plant roots will stop at the interface between the added soil and the existing soil. Vegetable plants can develop extensive root systems, yet in most garden environments (see chapter 5), a large percentage of the fibrous roots occupy the top 9 to 12 inches of soil. In summary, there are two potential problems with placing one soil on top of another without thorough mixing or removal of the poor soil substrate: both water movement and root development may be impaired. If you find that your raised beds are not working well, the only alternative is to mix your new soil into the existing soil, at least to 12 inches.

Irregular soil texture layers: If you water and fertilize your plants regularly, yet your plants seem to wilt and die, you may have a perched water table, in which the roots are submersed in standing water where they eventually rot and die. This is common where a thin layer of topsoil has been placed over impervious or compacted soil layers. Check by digging a hole a few feet deep to look for abrupt changes in artificial soil layers. The primary reason why so many gardeners set up raised beds is to provide a stratum of deeper soil in which roots can grow. However, many gardeners find that their raised beds do not meet their expectations. Do not pile or place new soil materials over compacted layers when setting up raised beds. There are several alternative choices:

1. If extreme soil texture layers exist, such as clayey soil over sand, sand over clay, an impervious dense layer, or gravel, excavate existing soil beyond the average depth of the vegetable root zone and backfill with a homogeneous soil.

2. Topsoil may be shallow, but there are no impervious layers below, and natural soil layers seem undisturbed. Dig in and mix topsoil with high additions of organic matter (decomposed manure and compost) to a depth beyond the average depth of the vegetable root zone. Check Web Soil Surveys for a profile description of your soil.

Soil Physical Properties

Soil properties are important to the vegetable gardener because vegetable crops grow better in certain types of soils and conditions. Soil physical properties determine the general character and behavior of a soil. These properties include texture, structure, density, strength, permeability, porosity, color, stability (aggregate stability—how well the soil aggregates hold together), mass or bulk density, and thermal properties related to temperature dynamics. Soil texture and structure are two important physical properties that either help or hinder your gardening experience. Infiltration of water into the soil and moisture-holding capacity are partially dependent on soil physical properties such as texture, structure, particle or aggregate stability, and degree of compactness (bulk density).

Aggregate stability in soil is an important concept to recognize, as it is related to organic matter content. Aggregate stability refers to how well soil aggregates hold together. Soil aggregates are particles that are bound together into larger particles as a result of biological activity in the soil. Soil microorganisms secrete compounds, fungi form hyphae (threadlike structures), and earthworms secrete mucus (coelomic fluid that enables them to move more easily in the soil and lines their burrow paths to keep them from collapsing), all of which stabilize and aggregate soil particles, like organic glues. Generally, soil aggregates less than a quarter of a millimeter are held together by older, more stable organic compounds, whereas aggregates larger than a quarter of a millimeter form from more recent biological activity and organic material. Larger aggregates are more fragile and less stable but are good indicators of soil health. Tillage practices, aboveground impact by livestock, and foot traffic can degrade aggregate stability.

Infiltration is also affected by chemical properties in soils and by organic matter content. Whatever type of soil you have, your goal is to enhance the soil with organic matter so that infiltration, tillage, workability, structure, and fertility are improved. As you work the soil by digging, hoeing, and cultivating, you will soon appreciate how soil physical properties affect your work in the garden.

Soil Texture or Particle Size

The most obvious soil physical property is texture or particle size, and it is important for gardeners to know the texture of their soils. This important property is directly related to how well certain crops will grow. Soil is classified into textural classes that are determined by the contribution of sand, silt, and clay (fig. 8). In general, fine-textured soils have more clay, whereas coarse-textured soils contain more sand. Technically, sand particles are between 0.05 and 2 millimeters in size and are visible to the naked eye. Silt particles are smaller, ranging from 0.002 to 0.05 millimeters and are not visible to the naked eye. Clay particles are the smallest, less than 0.002 millimeters. Clay particles have a large surface area and a tremendous capacity to absorb and store water. Very fine clay particles act as colloids and if added to water stay in suspension—they do not settle out. The ratio of sand, silt, and clay will determine the workability (tilth) of your soil, the speed of water infiltration, the amount of water that can be stored in your soil, the stability of the soil aggregates (small, stable, BB-sized particles that hold together when wetted), and many other physical properties. Soil texture also influences what types of soil organisms may inhabit your soil and how plant nutrients and fertilizers function in your garden.

As gardeners can attest, vegetables can be successfully grown in a wide spectrum of soil textures; however, most vegetable crops have certain textural preferences. Personally, I have had more success with potatoes in my Idaho sandy loam garden than I had in my Kansas clayey soils. Growing potatoes in clayey soils was hard work, my yields were lower, and I had more small potatoes than large, but they were good nevertheless—size is not everything. I offer a note of encouragement: do not be deterred from growing certain vegetables because your soils may not be optimal in terms of texture. Go ahead and plant. You can always improve tilth by adding organic matter, but be aware that soil texture cannot be altered by merely adding sand (do not do this) or organic matter (see Science Note, next page).

The WSS will give you information about the percentages of sand, silt, and clay on your property. Keep in mind that the soil information from the WSS is a coarse representation because the mapping scale depends on the complexity of the soil patterns on your landscape and the expected intensity of land use. In other words, the scale of soil mapping can vary from place to place, and small, unique areas are usually not delineated.

Checking Soil Texture

Percentages of sand, silt, and clay can be obtained from laboratory tests, a county soil survey published by the NRCS, or WSS. To use the soil texture triangle, you need the percentages of sand, silt, and clay. You can perform your own soil texture test by feel. Check your soil by

SCIENCE NOTE • Altering Soil Texture

The gardener can alter texture in planting pots and in raised beds by adding topsoil. However, changing soil texture on a larger scale in the garden is usually not practical, as large amounts of other soil with preferred textural qualities would need to be imported and mixed into the existing soil. It is important to note that increasing and building up organic matter by adding compost, peat moss, or manure does not change texture. Organic soil amendments certainly improve soil health, but soil texture refers to the relative abundance of mineral particles composed of sand, silt, and clay.

What about adding sand to your garden plots to ameliorate clayey soils? Adding sand to a heavy-textured soil can create problems. In sandy soil, coarse grains have large pores (air) between the particles. Sand grains of different sizes do not create or enlarge pore space when they are added to and embedded in a fine-textured clayey soil—they create a situation similar to concrete. If you want to try to modify soil texture in planting beds or circle plots, add a soil of a different texture (preferably a good topsoil mix), not sand. Improving the organic content of the soil can also work wonders in clayey soils, making them more friable (a term pertaining to soils that are more workable and crumble more easily).

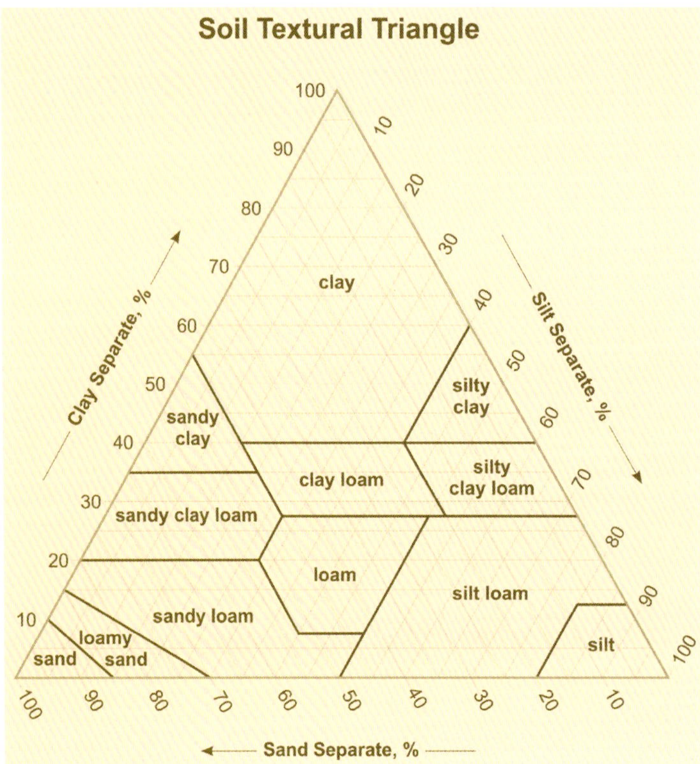

FIGURE 8. Diagram showing the ranges of texture as expressed by percentages of sand, silt, and clay. There are 12 textural classes in the USDA Soil Texture Triangle. USDA NRCS, 2015, http://www.nrcs.usda.gov/wps/portal/nrcs/detail/soils/survey/?cid=nrcs142p2_054167.

taking a walnut-sized amount in your hand. When you moisten the ball, what does it feel like?

- Sandy, gritty
- Smooth and powdery, not sticky
- Sticky and clayey

Compare your texture analysis with the description of your soil in the NRCS soil survey. If you believe the results of your texture test differ from the mapped soil description, take some soil to your local NRCS office.

Improving Soil Health

In the home garden, improving soil health involves a combination of efforts. Adding organic matter (animal manure and compost), planting green cover (manure) crops over winter, limiting the extent and types of certain cultivation practices, and using mulches are all associated with improving soil health. Other soil amendments, principally fertilizers, can be used to correct and/or provide the necessary nutrients for your plants. The Soil Health/Quality Indicator Scorecard in appendix A explains how you can evaluate your existing soil conditions.

SCIENCE NOTE • Using the Soil Texture Triangle (fig. 8)

Example 1. A soil test identified 15% clay, 60% sand, and 25% silt. First start with clay and draw a horizontal line at 15% (the line should be parallel to the base of the triangle, labeled sand. Next locate the sand percentage (60%) and draw a diagonal line upward parallel to the silt axis. You could also locate the silt percentage (25%) and draw a diagonal line parallel to the clay axis, but all that is needed are 2 of the 3 soil components. In this example, 15% clay, 60% sand, and 25% silt intersect in the box called sandy loam. The textural triangle allows you to see other, closely related textural classes.

Example 2. Clay 70%, sand 25%, silt 5%. The textural class would be clay.

Example 3. What is a loam soil? A loam contains 10%–25% clay, 22%–55% sand, and 30%–50% silt.

Loss of soil through erosion, loss of soil organic matter (SOM), and loss of soil nitrogen (N) are the consequences of tilling the soil and incorporating surface plant residues and litter deeper into the soil. The soil surface is usually a more active zone for microorganisms and contains more organic matter and nutrients. As this layer is mixed with subsurface soil through tillage, the soil will usually appear lighter in color—tillage dilutes organic matter and nutrients. Most deeper subsoil layers are less fertile and contain less humus and organic matter. This is true in large farm fields as well as in your home garden. In some of the best agricultural lands throughout the Great Plains in the United States, it has been estimated that 35%–50% of the SOM and N were lost during the first 50 years after tillage began. Soil scientists estimate that for each 1% decrease in SOM via tillage and erosion, about 1,000 lb. organic N/acre and an inch of potential water storage capacity are lost. Soil loss and SOM turnover occur rapidly at the onset of tillage but eventually reach equilibrium if soil erosion is controlled by conservation practices and management. Even though some cultivation and incorporation of organic matter into circle plots is necessary, the addition of SOM compensates for what is lost via decomposition.

SOM is formed as a direct result of soil microbial activity. The potential productivity of a soil is related to SOM concentrations in disturbed and undisturbed soils. SOM content varies considerably in natural ecosystems. Soils in desert regions are typically low in SOM (less than 1%); prairie soils of the Midwest have 4 to 8% SOM; histosols, formed from organic deposits in wetland areas (marshes, bogs, ponds, and swamps) can have 20 to 30% SOM (fig. 9), and peat soils up to 80%. Climate is a major factor in SOM development and accumulation over time. Average SOM content in temperate climates can range from 0.4 to 10%; in humid regions the average range is 3 to 4%, and in semiarid climates, 1 to 3%. SOM is associated with 95% of soil N, 40% of soil phosphorus, and 90% of soil sulfur. About 90% of the terrestrial carbon mass on Earth is sequestered in forests and agricultural lands.

Tillage or cultivation of soils has a profound impact on the accumulation and amount of SOM. First, physical disturbance, mixing, and exposing the soil to the air increases SOM oxidation and eventually depletes it. Exposed soil is also susceptible to wind and water erosion, which can further deplete topsoil, SOM, and plant nutrients. Proper conservation management systems can maintain sustainable levels of soil loss. Second, as surface plant residues and SOM are incorporated and distributed deeper into the soil profile, microbial activity, rate of decomposition, and availability of nutrients are slowed down considerably. This is the reason soil conservationists promote reduced and/or no-till cropping systems—less soil disturbance leads to a greater amount of SOM accumulation over time.

A

B

FIGURE 9. *A*, Excavated soil profile showing organic matter content. Histosols contain the highest organic matter content of all soils. *B*, A mollisol formed under grassland (prairie) vegetation. This dark, deep, very productive soil has a friable surface and is high in native fertility and organic matter. Photos courtesy of USDA NRCS, Washington, DC.

Importance of Soil Organic Matter

SOM is an integration of biological and mineral components and includes plant and animal residues in various stages of decomposition that may vary considerably in different soils. SOM has many roles such as providing a substrate for soil flora and microbes, supplying a nutrient reservoir, enhancing moisture storage, and acting as a soil conditioner. Soil organic carbon is specific to the amount of carbon in SOM. See the organic matter fact sheet in appendix B.

Organic matter has a profound effect on soil physical and chemical properties and processes and, ultimately, plant growth. The interrelationships among all these factors create a complex, dynamic web with the environment. For example, SOM influences and enhances soil structure, granulation, aggregate stability, and porosity, which are related to hydrologic factors such as infiltration capacity. Increasing organic matter results in increased water infiltration, water-holding capacity, and subsequent available water for plant growth; deep percolation into the soil profile, which can recharge groundwater and eventually aquifers; and subsurface lateral flow to streams and springs. The ramifications of organic carbon in soils are immense—entire books have been written on the subject.

The primary source of organic matter is plant tissues; animal waste products are secondary. On a weight basis, plant tissue contains between 60 and 90% water (depending on the plant species). The remaining dry matter (averaging about 25%) comprises mostly carbon, oxygen, and hydrogen. The organic dry matter fraction of dead plants consists of carbohydrates (sugars, starches, and cellulose, 15%–60%; lignin, 5%–30%; hemicelluloses, 10%–30%); proteins, 2%–15%; fats and waxes, 2%; and other compounds such as polyphenols (tannins and other acids), 2%. When plants die, these compounds are decomposed into simpler compounds by microbes. Collectively, these organic materials are called humus, which tends to have a low decomposition rate and is subdivided into humic and nonhumic substances. Humic components are natural substances and are the most abundant form of organic matter (60 to 80%) in terrestrial and aquatic environments.

Four basic categories or pools of organic matter are differentiated based on the availability and turnover times of potential nutrients. They are the living (soil food web or soil flora), the active or recently dead (identifiable material), the slow decomposing, and the stable humus. The living component constitutes the potential release of the organic carbon and nitrogen that have traditionally been unaccounted for, that is, tied up in protein, amino acids, nucleic compounds, and other organic compounds.

The active SOM pool comprises recent plant residues in the early decomposition phase. Active SOM turnover may take months to years, and nutrients mineralized by microorganisms are important to plant growth. Nitrogen fixed from rhizobia associated with legume roots is part of the active SOM pool. Nutrients from animal manure also become part of the active SOM pool. Organic matter in the active SOM pool enhances infiltration capacity and ease of soil tillage. The slow-decomposing SOM pool is a source of more long-term mineralized nitrogen and phosphorus contributed from the active and stable SOM pools. Nutrient turnover takes years to decades. Additions of organic materials to the soil eventually end up in the slow SOM pool. Roots from crops, cover crops, and legumes decompose more slowly than aboveground leaf tissue and over time become part of the slow SOM pool. The stable humus SOM pool contains organic materials that are hundreds to thousands of years old. The SOM pool is also referred to as the passive organic matter pool or humus that is part of the clay/humus complex (humins and humic acids). Nutrient removal by plants has little effect on the stable SOM pool. The stable SOM pool contains 60 to 90% of the total organic matter in the soil.

SOM tends to increase with clay content. The interaction of clay particles and organic matter slows the decomposition process. Soil organic content tends to be higher at the base of slopes and hills where conditions are moister and vegetation production is greater compared to middle and upper slopes. North-facing hillsides and slopes usually have higher SOM content than south slopes. Well-aerated soils with

TABLE 2. The four basic groupings or pools of soil organic matter and relative turnover times of potential nutrients

Components of SOM	Pools of carbon
Living	(Living) intact plant and animal tissues and microorganisms
Active, fresh organic residue	(Active and slow) can contain recognizable plant residues
Slow-decomposing SOM	Active and slow
Stable-humus SOM	(Stable) some humic substances in soil solutions may supply some micronutrients for stimulating plant growth

Source: Author, from many sources

high porosity tend to have lower organic matter because of their high rate of decomposition. High soil moisture is necessary in order to prevent desiccation and death of soil microbes. Saturated conditions brought about by poor drainage or flooding have a negative effect on oxygen soil content and decomposition (soil-denitrifying bacteria die in anaerobic conditions), and soil pores are blocked. Decomposition of SOM occurs at temperatures between 77 and 104°F. At temperatures below 77°F, the rate of decay gradually decreases, and it virtually stops at the freezing point.

Living Organisms in the Soil

Aeration and the supply of free oxygen, moisture, temperature, nutrients, the composition of organic residues, and living flora are all interrelated during the decomposition process. The soil flora includes vertebrates (mice, moles, gophers, etc.), earthworms, mollusks (slugs and snails), mosses, lichens, blue-green algae, arthropods, nematodes, rotifers, ciliates, amoebae, protozoa, fungi (yeasts, molds, rusts, mushrooms), bacteria, and viruses (fig. 10). Soil microbes play crucial and specific roles in terrestrial ecosystems such as participating in biogeochemical processes, regulating productivity, contributing to nitrogen and carbon cycles, acquiring nutrients for plants, and forming soil. Unknown to many people, soil microbes comprise the vast unseen majority of genetic biodiversity on Earth. Recently, scientists have updated their estimates from around 8.7 million microbes to about 1 trillion species, 99.9% of which are undiscovered. One gram of soil can contain as many as 10^{10} to 10^{11} bacteria, 6,000–50,000 bacterial species, and up to 650 feet of fungal hyphae.

What happens to organic matter as it is being decomposed by soil microorganisms? Some misconceptions may exist about this topic, including the idea of continual accumulation and buildup of organic matter in soils. There is a limit to how much SOM can accumulate and remain at a constant level in soils that are not histosols—it is not an endless increasing progression (unless the site is a peat bog). On average, most of the carbon added to soil from organic matter during the year returns to the atmosphere as carbon dioxide. Most of the carbon is oxidized, while only about 25%–33% remains in the soil as live biomass (organisms, ~ 5%), humic substances (~ 20%), and nonhumic fractions (~ 5%). That is why organic matter buildup in soils is a slow process. Organic residues on the soil surface decompose much more slowly than SOM incorporated into the soil because they are not in direct contact with soil microorganisms.

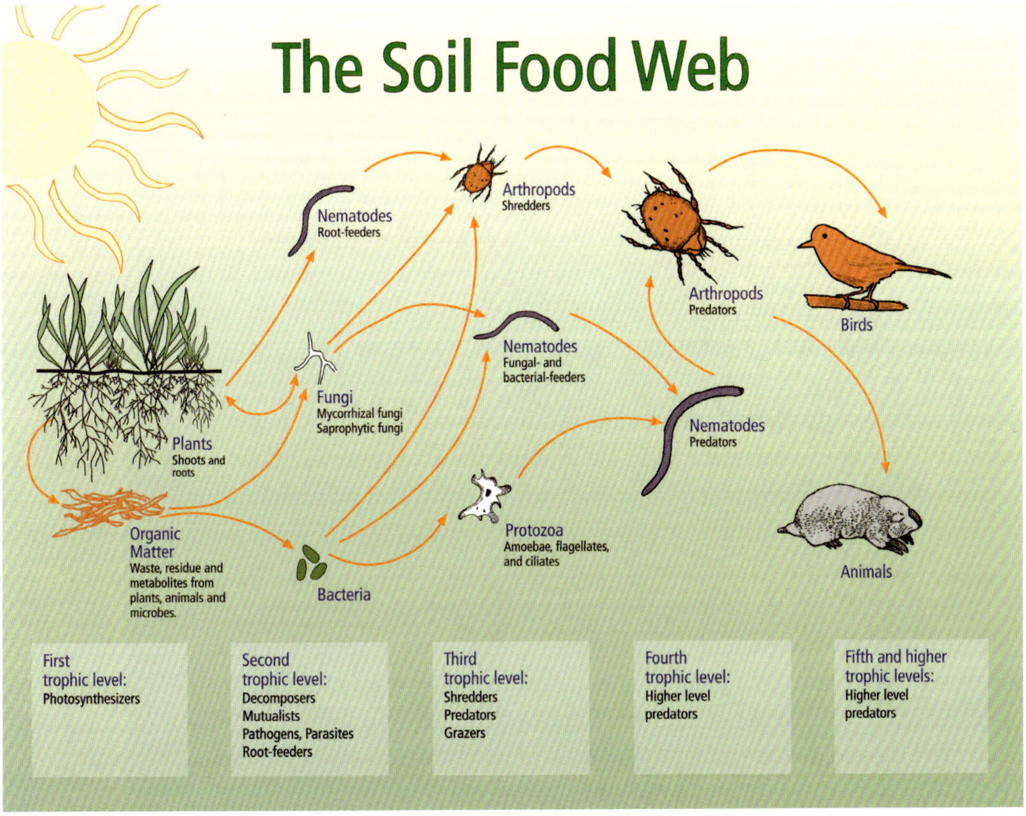

FIGURE 10. Various organisms in the soil food web. Courtesy of USDA NRCS, Soil Biology Primer, www.nrcs.usda.gov/wps/portal/nrcs/detail/national/soils/?cid=nrcs142p2_053860.

Does organic matter continue to increase at a constant level over time? As soil develops, the decay of plant material (surface litter and roots) gradually starts to build organic matter. In the absence of high natural erosion rates, SOM accumulates over long periods at a progressive rate until a constant level is reached—in equilibrium with climate, soil properties, the plant community, and decomposition processes. Once SOM has reached equilibrium, some years will have a positive buildup of organic matter, and other years a negative loss; however, the long-term average is constant or zero.

What Are Mycorrhizal Fungi and Why Are They Important?

Mycorrhizae (from the Greek *mycos*, meaning "fungus," and *rhiza*, meaning "root") are symbiotic filamentous (feathery) fungi that form symbiotic relationships with plant roots in forests, pastureland, rangeland, and cropping systems. The association between plants and mycorrhizae was observed by Albert B. Frank in 1885, and today scientists have found mycorrhizae in almost all terrestrial ecosystems. Research on mycorrhizae continues with high-tech molecular tools that are increasing our knowledge of the biology, biodiversity, and evolution of these fungi.

Mycorrhizal studies are a major theme in soil ecology and agricultural journals. Both conventional and organic farmers recognize the benefits of maintaining healthy soils and the positive effects of arbuscular mycorrhizae (AM) on crops. Intensive soil disturbance practices such as tillage, monocropping, seasonal fallow periods, and inorganic fertilizers have been shown to reduce benefits provided by AM. Circle gardening can have a positive effect on the ecology of AM because of reduced tillage as well as the addition of organic matter and less dependence on fertilizers high in nitrogen and phosphorus.

Mycorrhizal fungi (MF) can penetrate and live inside the cortex of plant roots, occupy root surfaces, or surround epidermal root cells. MF provide the link between plant roots and the soil; the fungal hyphae also grow outward from the plant roots into the surrounding soil where they seek and supply plant nutrients. MF obtain carbohydrates (glucose and sucrose) from plants—between 10 and 50% of plant photosynthates, depending on fungal type (AM or ectomycorrhizae, EM)—and in return provide increased soil nutrient absorption to the plant. The relationship between plants and mycorrhizae has been observed in fossil records dating back 460 million years. Mycorrhizal associations with plants are the norm in the plant kingdom; about 50,000 fungal species (about 0.5%–10% of the total number of probable fungal species on Earth) and 250,000 plant species participate in such associations. There are four main mycorrhizal groups: about 74% of all plant species are associated with AM, about 9% with orchid mycorrhizae, about 2% with EM, and about 1% with ericoid mycorrhizae. There are plants in the Brassicaceae, Crassulaceae, Orobanchaceae, and Proteaceae families that are nonmycorrhizal. In the home garden, such plants include cabbage, broccoli, cauliflower, and brussels sprouts, all in the Brassicaceae family.

Mycorrhizae provide significant but varying amounts of nitrates and phosphates to plants, especially where soils lack abundant nutrients. For example, AM can provide up to 80% of plant phosphorus and up to 20% of plant nitrogen, whereas EM can provide up to 80% of both nitrogen and phosphorus. MF also improve the availability of immobile nutrients such as copper and zinc. Studies show that most plant roots are colonized by multiple MF, which are not host specific. An interconnected underground fungal network of AM exists in plant communities containing shrubs, grasses, and herbaceous forbs. In temperate forests, the fungal network comprises largely EM.

Fungal hyphae provide three advantages in addition to the symbiotic relationship of nutrient uptake in plant root hairs: (1) the hyphae are numerous and have more area and volume than root hairs; (2) they are attracted to nutrients; and (3) they are smaller than root hairs and can extend into and around soil aggregate spaces and pores. To put AM in perspective, estimates show that 1 teaspoon of soil can contain the equivalent of up to 8 miles of mycorrhizal hyphae. The benefits of AM are summarized below:

- Increased absorption of nutrients and water.
- Improved phosphorus uptake.
- Protection of host plant from damping-off fungal and root rot diseases.
- Impeded uptake of heavy metals in the soil (zinc, cadmium, and manganese).
- Enhanced production of plant hormones that affect cell division, stem elongation, seed germination, and other physiological functions.
- Improved soil aggregate stability, which is a diagnostic feature that soil-plant specialists use to identify soil health. Stable soil aggregates and air spaces in the soil are enhanced by MF, which produce a gelatinous compound (glomalin) that binds soil particles and improves infiltration capacity. Compaction by foot traffic, livestock, vehicles, and cultivation causes the breakdown of soil aggregates.

MF can also exhibit neutral or negative effects on plants. Research has shown that AM can suppress seedling growth during the first few weeks after germination because of donated carbon allocation from the seedling to developing fungi, which can result in decreased seedling survival. However, in many ecosystems, the long-term positive gains increase as the plant matures. Studies show that increasing the availability of nitrogen (nitrogen fertilization) can unbalance the mutualistic relationship between fungi and plants, and parasitism can occur. Insufficient light can also affect a plant's ability to allocate photosynthates to MF, which in turn decreases fungal benefits to plants. In vegetable gardens with excess shade, not only is photosynthesis reduced because of insufficient sunlight, but the decreased activity of AM may also affect plant thriftiness. Perhaps science will shed more light on this in the future.

Many disturbance activities can diminish mycorrhizal populations in your soil: tillage, chemical fertilization, crop monocultures, erosion by wind and water, topsoil removal, construction and site preparation, fumigation, pesticides, and invasion of alien and nonnative plants. Bare ground consisting of compacted soils and patchy, nonvigorous vegetation is probably a sign of inactive or virtually eliminated MF populations, along with soil loss, chemical factors in the soil, and nutrient deficiencies.

Some mycorrhizae are specific in their ability to enhance drought tolerance, pathogens, and nutrient uptake. Plants associated with MF are usually more competitive and able to tolerate stress caused by climate and the environment. Commercial AM cultures are available; however, in large-scale farming operations and large garden areas, the application of AM cultures is not always economically feasible. Introductions of MF are usually not needed unless your soil has been severely disturbed and the topsoil removed. The problem with AM applications to crop fields is that AM colonization and subsequent plant responses are unpredictable since a diverse mix is needed (AM from the Glomeraceae, Gigasporaceae, Scutellosporaceae, and Acaulosporaceae families).

Managing Mycorrhizae

Mycorrhizal populations in your garden soil can be managed with the following techniques:

- Grow a wide variety of plants in the garden: flowers, vegetables, legumes, and nonleguminous plants.
- Avoid growing the same crops in the same location year after year. Monocultures are associated with decreased AM colonization and depleted populations.
- Keep soil tillage to a minimum.
- Avoid heavy applications of fertilizer with phosphorus.
- Inoculate soil with decomposed mulches and soil from undisturbed plant communities in your area.
- Purchase and use commercial mycorrhizal preparations according to directions. Nursery and landscape professionals use these products, and commercial production of MF for agricultural use has been ongoing for over a decade. Commercial mycorrhizal preparations are relatively expensive, but another advantage of growing in circle arrangements is that you will need only a small fraction of material to inoculate depleted soils.

- Use cover crops to protect soils during winter months and to build up soil health. Forage oats by themselves or in mixtures with other plants (winter wheat, clover, vetch, turnip, and radish) have been found to maximize AM potentials.

TABLE 3. Minimum and maximum pH ranges for commonly grown vegetables in the home garden

Vegetable	Minimum pH	Maximum pH
Potatoes	4.8	5.5
Sweet potatoes	5	5.9
Eggplants	5.5	6.5
Peppers	5.5	6.5
Cucumbers	5.5	6.8
Lima beans	5.5	6.8
Tomatoes	5.5	6.8
Bush and pole beans	5.5	7
Parsnips	5.5	7
Pumpkins	5.5	7.5
Sweet corn	5.5	7.5
Cabbage	5.8	7
Carrots	5.8	7
Turnips and rutabagas	6	6.5
Onions	6	6.7
Broccoli	6	7
Cauliflower	6	7
Chives	6	7
Lettuce	6	7
Peas	6	7
Radishes	6	7
Spinach	6	7
Beets	6	7.5
Summer and winter squash	6	7.5
Asparagus	6	8

Note: This list ranks vegetable crops in order of their preference for acidic, neutral, and alkaline soil pH.

Importance of Soil pH

The most important attribute that affects chemical and biological processes in the soil and plant growth is the acid-alkaline status of the soil. This is quantified by measuring soil pH, or the concentration of hydrogen ions in solution. In nature, certain plants have adapted to or prefer specific ranges of soil pH; conifer forests in humid regions are adapted to acidic soils, whereas some arid and semiarid regions tend toward alkaline or saline (salty) soils. Alkaline soils often have a calcium (calcium carbonate, limestone) or gypsic (gypsum-rich) component, and in areas of low rainfall, these materials do not leach beyond the root zone.

Vegetable plants can tolerate a range of pH; however, we must strive to maintain pH ranges that are preferable. Table 3 shows optimal pH ranges for common vegetables.

The chemistry of pH is a complex concept that we are intimately associated with on a daily basis (table 4). When you put lemons in your drinking water or lemon juice on fish, eat an apple, apply vinegar on your salad, or drink coffee or beer, you are experiencing acidity. Likewise, if you use antacid tablets, you are experiencing alkalinity (table 4). Neutrality, or a pH of 7, is in the middle range between acidic and alkaline—examples are distilled water (pH = 7.0) and human blood (pH = 7.4). What makes foods, chemicals, and soils acid or alkaline (on a scale of 0 to 14) is simply the concentration of hydrogen (H^+) and hydroxide (OH^-) ions. Totally deionized water has a pH of 7, and an equal concentration of H^+ and OH^- ions ($H_2O \leftrightarrow H^+ + OH^-$). Both H^+ and OH^- ions are present in solutions. A solution is acidic if the H^+ ions exceed the OH^- ions, whereas OH^- ions dominate basic solutions. Increasing pH means the H^+ ions are decreasing. The pH scale is logarithmic, not linear. A solution with pH = 1 (battery acid) has ten times (not twice) the H^+ than lemon juice (pH = 2). Conversely, bleach (pH = 12) is ten times more alkaline than ammonia (pH = 11). Lye (pH = 13) is one hundred times more alkaline than ammonia (pH = 11). Chapter 9 discusses ways to manage soil pH in the garden.

TABLE 4. Average pH of various chemicals and products in our daily lives

hydrochloric acid	**0**
battery acid	**1**
lemon juice	**2**
vinegar	**2.2**
apples	**3**
coffee, wine, beer	**4**
tomatoes	**4.5**
rain water	**5.5**
milk	**6.8**
distilled water	**7**
human blood	**7.4**
seawater	**8**
baking soda	**8.3**
antacid tablet	**9**
milk of magnesia	**10**
ammonia	**11**
bleach	**12**
lye	**13**

5

Plant Attributes and Basic Botany

Considering and Choosing Adapted Plant Varieties and Cultivars

As you browse through seed catalogs, my favorite pastime, there are many varieties and cultivars to choose from. As a beginning vegetable gardener, and before I started my agricultural training and career, I selected varieties and cultivars based on the descriptions and pictures in the seed catalogs. How did that work out? Actually, I had some great gardens and never really thought about locally recommended varieties. I had a lot of success, not because of my gardening skills but because of the soil and climate at my location. Lyon County, Kansas, tucked into the Flint Hills, has some amazingly fertile soils (mollisols), and the climate is not extreme in terms of summer temperature fluctuations. Rainfall is dependable, most of the time. However, when I moved out West and later to the South, I had to start paying attention to varieties and cultivars. My southern Idaho garden was prolific; I felt as if I were in "vegetable paradise." Finally, I achieved success with potatoes in Star, Idaho, that I never achieved in Kansas (potatoes love the sandy loams and climate of southern Idaho). In Idaho, my vegetable garden was in a bottom area where cool air drained during the evenings. In this setting, my broccoli plants produced all summer, an example of a unique microenvironment. In northern Idaho (Moscow), I had to pay close attention to the growing season and cooler temperatures. In my garden in Laramie, Wyoming (elevation nearly 7,200 feet), tomatoes were difficult to mature, but it was possible if I started plants early in a cold frame. Cool-season vegetables grew very well with very little interference from insect pests. However, the scenario changed when I moved to east-central Texas: I now have to pay attention to varieties and cultivars that are adapted to hot temperatures and humidity. In my Texas garden, spring does not last long, and hot temperatures and humidity rise quickly in late spring and summer. I have to pay attention to specific tomato, onion, some pepper, and corn cultivars. However, there are advantages to my Texas garden that I did not experience in more northern states: I can grow spinach, lettuce, Swiss chard, and the cole crops late into the winter season with protection, and I can plant several repeat crops of squash in the summer.

Do not be awed by seed catalog descriptions such as "most productive," "enormous size," "extra sweet," "early bearing," and "big profits." Although such claims may be accurate, do not choose varieties and cultivars based on these criteria.

Vegetable Varieties and Cultivars

Seed catalogs include names for all the vegetable plants (for example, 'Big Boy,' 'Better Boy,' 'Celebrity,' 'Early Girl,' 'Brandywine,' and 'Beefsteak,' all registered trademarks). What is the difference between a cultivar and a variety? Often these terms are used interchangeably, but technically, they are different. A variety is or was found growing in the wild; a cultivar is a plant grown from selective breeding in cultivation. Good cultivars are propagated and bred to maintain particular characteristics from generation to generation. For example, most of the plants in our vegetable gardens are cultivars. Some heirlooms are cultivars because they were chosen and perpetuated by selecting the best plants over time. Typically, you will not find 'Big Boy' tomatoes growing wild in nature. The cultivar name is written in plain text (not italicized) within single quotation marks and appears after the scientific name (for the tomato, genus = *Solanum*, species = *lycopersicum*) of the source species. For example, *Solanum lycopersicum* 'Big Boy' is a proprietary tomato cultivar of W. Atlee Burpee and Company. In 1942, Dr. Oved Shifriss (1915–2004) was director of research and a plant breeder for W. Atlee Burpee. He developed hybrids of cucumber, eggplant, cantaloupe, watermelon, and the famous 'Big Boy' tomato, which appeared in 1949. The 'Big Boy' cultivar is still popular, but its exact parentage is a trade secret. Many gardeners look forward to and enjoy experimenting with many of the varieties and cultivars available from seed companies, seed saver exchanges, and fellow gardeners.

How do you determine the best varieties and cultivars (V&C)? One way is to check V&C lists provided by state and county extension services, local Master Gardeners, local plant nurseries, and gardening neighbors. It is also wise to check plant hardiness zone adaptability to your climate, and to compare data for V&C with respect to days to maturity, and maturity characteristics. The following is a list of considerations regarding adapted V&C:

1. Adaptation to extremes in temperature, cold versus hot.
2. Tolerance of heat and humidity.
3. Optimal recommended soil texture.
4. Adaptation to salinity, if that is a problem in your soils.
5. Disease resistance—consider specific problematic diseases and insects in your area.
6. Pollination—open-pollinated (heirlooms) or hybrid.
7. Growth habit, vine versus compact vine versus bush; determinate or indeterminate tomatoes, pole versus bush beans, and so on.
8. Taste preferences, acidity, sweetness, and so on.
9. Nutritional value—many new cultivars are bred for high nutritional value.
10. Aesthetic preferences: color, shape, and appearance.

Part of the fun of gardening is experimentation. Try heirlooms and hybrids, and if you want to go the full measure, try breeding some of your own cultivars. I offer some practical information that may help you decide which cultivars will work for you. For example, in many locations throughout the United States, spring temperatures may not last as long as you need. Cool-season crops such as the brassicas (broccoli and cauliflower) may tend to bolt or flower before the head matures. Here is where shorter-season cultivars may make a big difference. The same idea applies to other spring crops such as lettuce and spinach. Choose cultivars that do not bolt quickly and become bitter.

It is very tempting to offer suggestions on various cultivars, but it is impractical to discuss specific cultivars in this book because (1) too much climatic variability exists throughout the United States and Canada, (2) opinions about certain cultivars are often based on subjectivity and bias (taste, for instance), and (3) cultivars sometimes come and go quickly. For example, some of my favorite cultivars are no longer available in seed catalogs. My recommendation for beginning gardeners is to choose the most disease-resistant cultivars (hybrids if necessary) and give yourself the best chance for success. No one likes to see their tomatoes and cucumbers succumb to wilt and other diseases.

If you want to buy transplants (tomatoes, peppers, eggplant, cauliflower, cabbage), check out your more local plant nurseries and ask questions about what cultivars are best for your locale. The best option is to grow your own plants from seeds, as you will have much more control over selecting and obtaining adapted varieties. Try to find a seed company located in your part of the country, whether northern, western, eastern, or southern based. In seed catalog descriptions, look for information that is pertinent to maturity, adaptations to hot temperatures, ability to mature in colder climates, and so forth—do your research! One final thought: very few climates and gardening environments are conducive to success for every vegetable. There may be some vegetables that simply elude you and will not perform up to your expectations. Think about regions of the country where specific vegetables and fruits are grown—they grow there for a reason.

Days to Maturity

"Days to maturity" (DTM) in seed catalogs and on seed packets can be misleading. Information about the number of frost-free days a cultivar needs can help in cultivar selection, especially for warm-season crops. With hardy cool-season crops, you have more flexibility regarding frost-free days, because these crops can tolerate light frosts. DTM can mean several things depending on the type of vegetable. Most seed catalogs state the DTM from transplant and from sowing.

Some gardeners calculate DTM when the true leaves of the seedling appear, which usually adds another week. As days become shorter toward fall, adding 2 weeks will compensate for late summer/fall crops. Information on DTM is meant to serve as a guide; the times are approximate because there are many factors that can influence maturity of a crop. Weather is the main factor, as cold weather can slow growth, and too much or too little rain can affect the DTM. More precise DTM data can be obtained only by keeping detailed records in your own garden for a couple of years.

Open-Pollinated and Hybrid Plants

Do you want to use open-pollinated varieties (heirlooms) and keep seeds, use hybrid varieties, or both? There are advantages to both: seeds from open-pollinated varieties are usually less expensive than those of hybrids and in many situations perform well, but hybrid varieties have the potential to be more vigorous and robust and may have built-in disease resistance. Open-pollinated cultivars have many desirable attributes such as flavor and seed-saving ability, and some heirlooms may have certain disease resistance to pests in environments similar to where they were originally selected and grown.

In the gardening world, an "heirloom" can be a variety or cultivar that has been passed down through generations of family and friends because of special characteristics. It can be an old, rare, or antique variety. In my mind, "heirloom" denotes a plant propagated vegetatively through cuttings or grown from open-pollinated seeds, a "purebred variety." These seeds can be saved and will grow true to the original open-pollinated variety. Heirloom cultivars have a history and often an unknown provenance, which leads the gardener to wonder where and how they developed. Often heirloom seeds are passed down by family or friends and may have some unique stories and history of their own. From an ecological perspective, heirloom vegetable varieties constitute the genetic pool of biodiversity. Maintaining plant biodiversity in the crop gene pool is important to agriculture because it allows for development of new cultivars that can adapt to changing environmental conditions and threats from diseases and pests. The Food and Agriculture Organization has estimated that in the last 100 years, about 75% of crop species diversity has been lost. In response, various organizations (about 1,750 seed banks) have been collecting plant varieties to protect and foster genetic diversity in food crops. Many old heirloom varieties have been lost; however, there are many dedicated seed-saving organizations, including Seed Savers Exchange, Native Seeds/SEARCH, International Board for Plant Genetic Resources, and Southern Seed Legacy Project, all in the United States; Seed Savers Network in Australia; Seeds of Diversity in Canada; Irish Seed Savers Association in Ireland; and the Heritage Seed Library in the United Kingdom. Professional plant breeders and conservation biologists acknowledge the need for biodiversity in agriculture. Maintaining biodiversity and preserving heirloom varieties depends largely on the contributions and involvement of amateur gardeners.

A resurgence of heirloom varieties and cultivars is in vogue, and seed catalogs now offer many choices. In contrast, hybrid plants are produced by crossing two different open-pollinated cultivars (often by hand), and the resulting F1 hybrid will produce the desired effect for that seed. Producing hybrid cultivars is often laborious—a pure line sometimes involves several generations of crosses to achieve the desired features—and this procedure can take many years. Planted seeds from F1 hybrids will not result in the parent hybrid, as the same crossing process has to be repeated to re-create the desired F1 hybrid. Seed catalogs now advertise heirloom tomato varieties grafted onto hybrid rootstock.

What are the advantages and disadvantages of open-pollinated varieties (including heirlooms) and hybrids? Productivity, vigor, uniformity, faster growth, and disease resistance are major advantages of hybrid plants. Commercial crop production relies on these traits, and productivity can be up to 25% higher with hybrid cultivars. The disadvantages of hybrids are that they are more costly and can require more exacting cultural requirements and care. Seeds saved from F1 hybrids will probably not resemble the parent plant, and second-generation (F2) hybrid seeds are usually associated with lower-yielding plants. Can hybrid seeds be saved and planted? If so, what will be the result? Home vegetable gardeners can try dehybridizing the hybrids, saving the seeds from assumed hybrids and growing the next generation of F2 plants. However, remember that selling and marketing seeds from patented hybrids is illegal. If F2 plants closely resemble the original hybrid variety, then the plant may actually be a pure-breeding variety. Do not be deterred: plant seeds from your hybrid variety. You may be surprised at the results—the missing F2 characteristic may be only color, size, shape, length of maturity, or some unseen disease resistance.

Hybrids are advantageous for plants (corn and brassicas) that exhibit inbreeding depression (a loss of plant vigor associated with inbreeding). There is only a small advantage for developing hybrids for vegetable crops that are normal inbreeders or outbreeders. Hybrid corn cultivars display more uniformity in size and shape, an advantage for commercial producers who harvest corn with combines. Superior performance and productivity of hybrid varieties is magnified in commercial crop settings with the use of prescribed fertilizer rates and pesticides, and optimal weather conditions.

Open-pollinated plant varieties that have evolved in a particular locale and climate can outperform hybrids when field and weather conditions may not be optimal. Judy Barrett's book *What*

Makes Heirloom Plants So Great states that one of "the biggest advantages of heirloom plants is their strong will to live." Heirloom and old open-pollinated varieties have stood the test of time, especially where they originated. Through natural selection, heirlooms have developed genetic resiliency. During the drought and high summer temperatures in Texas in 2012, my only tomato variety that produced was an heirloom called 'Porter.' Interestingly, V. O. Porter, a gardener and seed enthusiast from Stephenville, Texas, developed the 'Porter' tomato around 1914 to withstand the heat and humidity of Texas.

Genetically Modified Plants

Is a plant hybrid a genetically modified organism (GMO)? No, these should not be confused with each other. Genetically modified plants are developed using techniques of biochemical and genetic engineering. Genetic engineering typically involves either synthesizing a gene to perform a certain function, or extracting a desired gene from another organism. In either case, the desired gene is linked with various other genes and DNA. Genetic engineering involves biochemical processes that are performed in a laboratory, whereas breeding plant hybrids is performed in the field or greenhouse and does not manipulate DNA, create artificial genes, or transfer genes from another organism. Many vegetable seed companies state in their catalogs that they do not knowingly buy or sell GMO seeds or plants.

As of this writing, about 94% of all soybeans and 89% of corn planted on US farms are GMOs. Also, genetically modified wheat has been developed but has not been approved for commercial planting. Other main GMO crops in the United States are cotton, sugar beets, and rapeseed. Genetically engineered corn, canola, and soybeans are typically used as ingredients in prepared foods—for example, cornstarch in soups and sauces, corn syrup as a sweetener, and canola oil in mayonnaise, salad dressings, breads, cereals, and snack foods. If you are interested in the GMO and food safety debate, many books and articles are now available on the subject. To be sure, this debate is highly emotionally charged.

Seed Facts

In circle gardening, you will be planting seeds or transplants into circle beds. Before you begin planting, I would like to review a few facts about seeds. A seed is a ripened ovule that varies in size, shape, texture, and color. For example, on average there are approximately

5–8 corn seeds/gram; 635–750 carrot seeds/gram, 900 lettuce seeds/gram, 317 tomato seeds/gram, and 5–8 zucchini seeds/gram. The main parts of a seed are the seed coat, which can be thin, thick, papery, or hard, and the embryo. The embryo is actually a miniature plant with one or two (seldom more) attached leaves called the cotyledons. Food stored in the seed includes carbohydrates, proteins, and fats in varying proportions depending on the plant species. For example, legume seeds (beans, peas) have a higher protein content and are one of the best sources of vegetable protein.

Most plant seeds undergo a rest cycle before they germinate and develop into seedlings. A germinated seedling depends on the stored food in the seed. Rest periods for seeds vary according to the species. Once a seed is dispersed from a plant, one of three scenarios occurs: (1) the seed may not be dormant and can germinate at any time, (2) the seed can be nondormant but quiescent (germination is inhibited because of an environmental condition), or (3) the seed can be dormant. Many different environmental triggers affect seed germination. Some plants use climatic cues such as temperature, moisture, drought, light, or a combination of these at particular times of the year.

Manipulation and specialized plant breeding can reduce or eliminate seed dormancy; however, many vegetable and flower species still maintain some form of seed dormancy. For example, cucumber and spinach seeds have mucilaginous layers that inhibit gas exchange and are active during ripening and after seed drop. These active layers perpetuate primary dormancy, mainly because the semipermeable layer restricts aeration and leaching of inhibitors. During dry storage at room temperature, cucumber seeds lose dormancy after 5–30 days. Lettuce seed requires red light to germinate, but this requirement is lost when temperatures drop below 73°F. Lettuce seeds are induced into thermodormancy at temperatures above 77°F. Most vegetable seeds are ready to plant from the packet.

The home vegetable gardener should not be overconcerned with seed dormancy. The most important factors for seed germination are heat and moisture (different levels for specific vegetables). In general, temperatures should be constant to optimize germination. Proper moisture is essential, as water triggers a series of chemical reactions in the seed that soften and weaken the seed coat. Oxygen also influences germination, and as new growth begins, oxygen interacts with the seed's stored food to make energy. Squash, pumpkin, and cucumber are particularly sensitive to low oxygen levels in the soil.

Garden Botany: Plant Structure (Morphology)

Morphology is the size, shape, and structure of an organism. Many vegetable cultivars now offer a number of different morphological characteristics. Carrots come in all sizes, colors, and shapes; squash is available as a vine, semivine, or bush type; cucumber plants can have vining or compact bush habits; peas can be bush types or vines; and tomatoes can be determinate or indeterminate.

Stems

Stems are the plant organs that support leaves and reproductive features. They are composed of nodes (the solid part) and internodes (the part between two nodes) and may have a jointed appearance. Internodes are easy to see on grasses and horsetails (*Equisetum* spp.). Within the stem is a vascular system (the plant's circulatory system) that transports water, carbohydrates, minerals, and other substances. Water and nutrients flow upward from the roots in the xylem tissue (from the Greek *xylon*, meaning "wood"). Carbohydrates produced by photosynthesis in chloroplasts in the plant cells of leaves and stems move downward in the phloem (from the Greek *phloos*, meaning "bark"). Monocots and dicots have different xylem and phloem tissues. The xylem and phloem in dicots is arranged in concentric rings with the phloem surrounding the xylem. In woody dicots, xylem is the principal or only woody tissue. In monocots, the xylem and phloem occur together in vascular bundles. In dicots, there is a cambium layer consisting of actively dividing cells between the xylem and phloem. The cambium layer produces xylem internally and phloem externally. In woody stems, bark is produced external to the cambium. There is live bark, which is made of both living and dead cells and conducts food and solutes, and dead bark, which is composed of dead cells and protects the plant.

There are several types of specialized structures (thorns, spines, prickles, stolons, rhizomes, and corms) on various plants. Thorns are modified stems, as on mesquite (*Prosopis glandulosa*), hawthorn (*Crataegus* spp.), and honey locust (*Gleditsia triacanthos*). Spines are modified leaves, stipules, or extensions of leaf veins (as in cacti). Prickles are extensions of the plant cortex and epidermis and are analogous to hairs, which can be woody and coarse, as in roses (*Rosa* spp.). Some varieties and cultivars of squash, cucumber, and pumpkin can have harsh prickles on the stems and leaves.

Plants with climbing stems are called vines or lianas and tend to grow up trees, rocks, and walls because they are usually not strong enough to support themselves. Some vines have tendrils, which can be modified stems or leaves or parts of leaves (e.g., grapes, poison ivy, cucumbers, and melons).

Leaves, stems, and roots can all play a role in vegetative reproduction, but stems are often more active reproductive organs. A stolon is a stem that creeps above and along the ground and sports adventitious roots, which eventually form new erect stems and plants. Strawberries have long, leafless stolons that are often called “runners.” A creeping underground stem is a rhizome; roots generally originate at the nodes or may be scattered along the whole length of a rhizome. In the vegetable garden, a thickened rhizome, or tuber, is the edible organ of the Irish potato (*Solanum tuberosum*). The sweet potato (*Ipomoea batatas*) is a modified lateral tuberous root. Another modified stem is the corm, which is more common in monocots. Corms are short, rigid, erect underground stems (as in crocus, gladiolus, and Chinese water chestnuts) where carbohydrates are stored. They can be covered by layers of leaf bases, which make them less conspicuous. A bulb is different from a corm and has thickened leaves or bulb scales that surround the short, erect stem. Onions are short bulb scales and are differentiated from the foliage leaves.

Leaves

Leaf morphology is adapted to perform various important functions such as photosynthesis, respiration, and transpiration. The leaf, including its size and shape, is probably the most obvious part that gardeners notice. There are several diagnostic leaf features: (1) arrangement on the plant, (2) duration—deciduous or evergreen, (3) simple or compound form, (4) characteristic venation, (5) shape of leaves and leaflets; and (6) stipules. Leaf anatomy includes the blade and petiole (leaf stem), an axillary bud at the junction of the stem and petiole, stipules (a pair of basal appendages), and stomata (leaf cells specialized for gas exchange).

In flowering plants, leaf shape is diverse and ranges from a simple one-leaf blade to a compound leaf in which each blade is subdivided into two or more leaflets. Leaf arrangements vary among plant species and cultivars and are classified as alternate, opposite, or whorled. The tomato plant typically has compound leaves, although some appear simple, with an alternate arrangement, but some leaves may appear opposite because of serration on the leaf margins. Carrot leaves are compound, each leaf consisting of several finely divided leaflets, and are alternate with the upper leaves becoming nearly opposite. Cucumber leaves are simple, alternate, palmately veined, and often lobed. Onions display simple, narrow leaves in a basal rosette or circular arrangement. Bean leaves are compound and alternate, with many small leaflets, sometimes with tendrils and stipules at the base of each leaf. Lettuce leaves are simple and form a rosette in which all leaves are similar in height.

Roots

Roots are amazing! For example, alfalfa roots have been found in a mineshaft at 128 feet, although typically the majority of alfalfa roots are found at 5 to 6 feet, depending on dryland or irrigated conditions. Mature apple tree roots can penetrate to a depth of at least 30 feet and extend laterally between 25- and 30-foot rows; a 100-year-old pine was estimated to have 310 miles of roots with 5 million root tips. In the vegetable garden, a mature tomato plant has a fibrous root system with many lateral roots. Tomato roots can penetrate 50 inches and have a 5-foot-diameter spread. Carrot roots can extend to 30 inches, with a 2.3-foot spread. Onions, which are typically shallow rooted, can also develop 20–200 white fibrous roots to depths of 18–32 inches, with a lateral spread of 12–18 inches from the center of the plant. Table 5 gives the average primary depth of vegetable, cover crop, and fruit plant roots (80% of root mass) with which available water is usually extracted (exceptions and maximum greater depths exist).

Roots are the underground organ of plants; in contrast to stems, which grow against gravity, roots grow in the direction of gravitational force. Plant roots have several basic functions: they anchor the plant in the soil, absorb and conduct water and nutrients, and serve as food (carbohydrate) storage organs. There are many different types of root morphologies. Most of our garden vegetables have five basic root structures:

- Taproot—the primary downward-growing root with small hairlike roots called secondary or lateral roots (carrot).
- Fibrous roots—many small, delicate roots that form a netlike mass (grasses, corn, beans).
- Fleshy roots—a combination of a taproot and fibrous roots (tomatoes, peppers, squash).
- Adventitious roots—roots produced by a plant organ other than the root itself (stem brace or prop roots on corn, the whitish bumps on a tomato stem).
- Tuberous roots—modified lateral roots, enlarged to function as a storage organ (sweet potato). Tuberous roots can be produced at

the end, in the middle, or over the entire root. Tuberous roots store carbohydrates for the plant from year to year.

Other underground plant organs that you may be familiar with include bulbs, corms, and tubers. Potatoes are stem tubers, developing from rhizomes that enlarge into a storage organ, whereas sweet potatoes are tuberous roots. The enlarged area of the root tuber may occur at the end or middle of the root or may involve the entire root.

Corn and sorghum exhibit a special root type called prop or brace roots, which provide additional structural support to the plant. These are adventitious roots that develop from the vertical stem and grow downward toward and into the soil. Prop roots are more common in

TABLE 5. Average primary rooting depth (80% of root mass) of vegetable, fruit, and cover crop plants where available water can be extracted in well-drained, deep soils

Crop	Depth (feet)	Crop	Depth (feet)
Alfalfa*	5–6	Grasses*	2–5
Asparagus	5	Lettuce	1–2
Beans, dry	2–3	Melons	2–3
Beans, green	2–3	Mustards*	2
Beets, table	2–3	Onions	1–2
Berries, blue	4–5	Parsnips	2–3
Berries, cane	4–5	Peas*	2–3
Broccoli	2	Peppers	1–2
Brussels sprouts	2	Potatoes, Irish	2–3
Cabbage	2	Potatoes, sweet	2–3
Cantaloupes	3	Pumpkins	3–4
Carrots	2–3	Radishes*	1
Cauliflower	2	Spinach	1–2
Clover*	2–3	Squash	3–4
Corn, sweet	2–3	Strawberries	1–2
Cucumber	1–2	Sunflowers*	4–5
Eggplant	2	Swiss chard	1–2
Fruit and nut trees	4–5	Tomatoes	3–4
Garlic	1–2	Turnips*	2–3
Grains*	3–4	Watermelon	3–4
Grapes	5	Wheat*	4

*Plants can be used for cover crops and/or green manure.

monocots and in many subtropical trees such as red mangrove (*Rhizophora mangle*) and banyan (*Ficus benghalensis*).

Plant Development: Flowers, Fruits, and Pollination

Our cultivated vegetable garden plants develop the flowers and fruits that the gardener strives for (fig. 11). Flowers and fruits may appear one time, continuously, or seasonally. In each of the Vegetable Guides, botanical information is given for leaves, stems, fruits, seeds, and roots.

Vegetable plants have either perfect (bisexual) or imperfect (unisexual) flowers. Perfect flowers contain both sexual parts—stamens and pistils—in each flower (fig. 12). Imperfect flowers are missing at least one sexual part. Plants bearing only perfect flowers are called hermaphrodites or hermaphroditic plants. The majority of our vegetable crops have perfect flowers, including tomatoes, peppers, eggplants, peas, and beans. Plants with imperfect flowers are classified as either monoecious or dioecious. Monoecious is Greek, from *mono*, "one," and *oikos*, "household." Monoecious plants have both male (staminate) and female (pistillate) flowers on the same plant. Examples are corn, squash, melons, pumpkins, and strawberries. Dioecious (two-household) plants have imperfect flowers, and the male and female flowers are borne on separate plants (spinach, asparagus).

The cucumber has some interesting flowering dynamics. The cucumber is typically monoecious; however, plant breeders have created new varieties that have only female flowers, while others have a greater proportion of female to male flowers. There are usually 10–20 male flowers for every female flower. The female blossom of the cucumber is attached to the end of an immature fruit, whereas the male flower is attached to a straight stem. Cucumber breeders in the 1960s began developing gynoecious cucumbers in which female or pistillate flowers were produced at every node. Seed packages of gynoecious hybrid cucumbers are now blended with about 15% monoecious hybrid seeds for pollination. Greenhouse cucumber varieties have been developed (seedless, nonbitter) in which fruit set occurs without pollination (parthenocarpic, meaning "virgin fruit").

For many of our vegetable crops (table 6), pollination is essential. In the plant world, about 80% of plant species rely on animals, mostly insects, to pollinate flowers. The remaining 20% rely on wind—grasses rely largely on wind pollination. The most significant pollinating insects are bees, flies, butterflies, and moths. Bees are the

Figure 11

FIGURE 11. Edible plant parts of popular garden vegetables. Figure by author.

dominant pollinator of crop plants in temperate climates, flies take on more importance as pollinators in higher elevations and higher latitudes, and beetles are important pollinators in tropical and equatorial areas (tropical rain forests). Bees tend to demonstrate constancy by visiting flowers of the same species, often returning to the same flowers. Butterflies and moths are also important pollinators but demonstrate less constancy and visit flowers of many different plants—they seem to be attracted to flowers where nectar is readily available. As pollinators, butterflies and moths are generally not as effective as bees; nevertheless, they are beneficial for transferring pollen among plants. Other animals involved in pollination are bats (which pollinate trees in the tropics and saguaro cacti in the deserts of the United States and Mexico); hummingbirds in the Americas; sunbirds in Africa; sugar gliders in Australia; and lemurs in Madagascar. You can attract pollinating bees and butterflies to your garden with an assortment of flowering plants.

In our home gardens, vegetables demonstrate either inbreeding or outbreeding. Inbreeding vegetables are self-pollinated, while outbreeding plants require another plant of the same variety for pollination. Inbreeding plants are prone to varying degrees of inbreeding depression. Inbreeding depression results from small, isolated populations of plants in which germination and plant yields diminish over time. If you wish to save seeds, consult *Breed Your Own Vegetable Varieties* by Carol Deppe and *Seed to Seed* by Suzanne Ashworth.

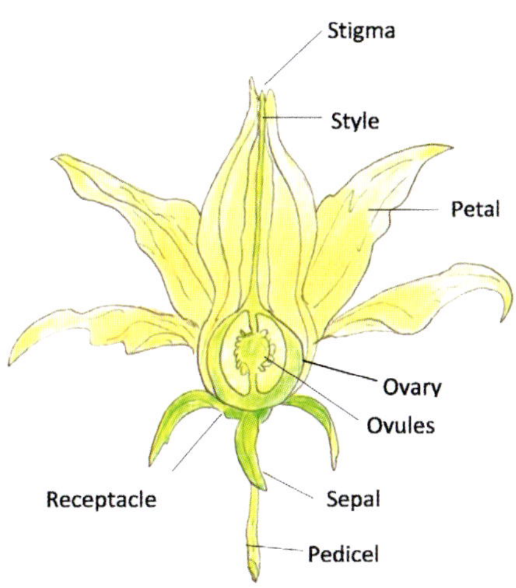

FIGURE 12. Details of the tomato flower. Figure by author.

TABLE 6. Summary of pollinators, predominant breeding systems, and flower types of common garden vegetables

Vegetable	Pollination	Predominant breeding system	Flower type	Notes
Beans (snap)	Self-pollinating	Inbreeding	Perfect	Protogynous, cleistogamous*
Beets	Wind	Outbreeding	Perfect	
Broccoli	Honeybees, solitary bees, flies	Outbreeding	Perfect	
Cabbage	Bumblebees, solitary bees, flies	Outbreeding	Perfect	
Carrots	Flies, solitary bees, honeybees, flies	Outbreeding	Perfect	
Cauliflower	Bumblebees, solitary bees, flies	Outbreeding	Perfect	Self-pollinate more readily than other brassicas
Corn	Wind	Outbreeding	Monoecious	Displays severe inbreeding depression
Cucumbers	Honeybees, squash bees, bumblebees, leafcutter bees, solitary bees	Outbreeding	Monoecious, some new cultivars have only or almost all female flowers	Does not cross with muskmelons, watermelons, squash, or pumpkins
Eggplants	Bumblebees, solitary bees	Inbreeding	Perfect	Protogynous
Lettuce	Flies, other insects	Inbreeding	Perfect	Partly cleistogamous
Peas	Self-pollinating, assorted insects	Inbreeding	Perfect	Cleistogamous
Peppers	Honeybees, stingless bees (*Melipona* spp.), bumblebees, solitary bees, hoverflies	Inbreeding	Perfect	Protogynous
Radishes	Bees, assorted insects	Outbreeding	Perfect	
Spinach	Wind	Outbreeding	Dioecious	
Squash, pumpkins, zucchini	Honeybees, squash bees, bumblebees, solitary bees	Outbreeding	Monoecious	
Tomatoes	Bumblebees, solitary bees, thrips	Inbreeding	Perfect	Protogynous

*Protogynous: a hermaphroditic (perfect) flower in which the female reproductive organs come to maturity before the male; cleistogamous: a self-pollinating flower.

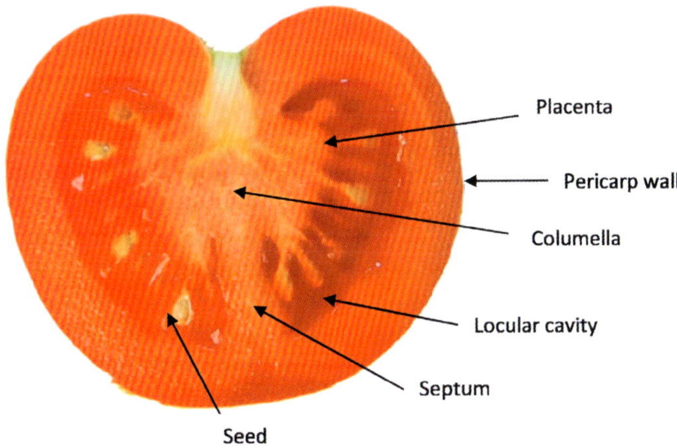

FIGURE 13. Anatomy of the tomato. Figure by author.

Fruits of Your Labor

Fruits are the ripened ovaries of a flower and contain other structures that develop with maturity. After fertilization takes place and the embryo develops, the surrounding ovule becomes the fruit (fig. 13). The development of plant fruits occurs after successful pollination and fertilization. The botanical purpose of the fruit is the protection and dissemination of the seeds. Some plants can develop fruit without pollination and fertilization (parthenocarpic). Examples of parthenocarpic fruits are greenhouse cucumbers, seedless grapes, navel oranges, and pineapples. As we grow our vegetables, other palatable plant parts are produced, including edible roots, tubers, stems, leaves, seeds, and flower clusters. There are two broad categories of fruit: fleshy and dry. Fleshy fruits develop succulent tissues, as in peaches, plums, and cherries, whereas in dry fruits the entire pericarp (the fruit wall of the ripened ovary) becomes dry at maturity (as in cereal grains, nuts, and dry legumes). Fruits are further categorized into simple, aggregate, or multiple fruits.

Botanically, there are many types of fruits. Peaches, plums, cherries, apples, apricots, strawberries, blueberries, and bananas may come to mind when we think of fruits, but do botanists technically consider them fruits? What is the fruit of the tomato plant? Let's go pick berries. Botanically, the tomato fruit is a true berry, a fleshy fruit in which the entire ovary wall ripens into a soft pericarp where the seeds are embedded. Examples of berries include the tomato, pepper, grape, banana, orange, blueberry, and gooseberry. The pepo is a berry with a hard rind (as in the persimmon, pomegranate, pumpkin, watermelon, and cucumber). Strawberries and raspberries develop from multiple ovaries and are considered aggregate fruits, not true berries. The seeds in strawberries are achenes, as are those of buckwheat, dandelion, and sunflower. A caryopsis is a grain (as in corn and cereal grains). The mulberry, fig, and pineapple are multiple fruits; apples, pears, and quinces are pomes; peaches, cherries, plums, olives, and walnuts are drupes; and beans and peas are legumes.

FIGURE 14. First severe freeze. Photos by author.

6

Climate Considerations

Depending on where you live, vegetable gardening is usually a spring and summer activity, but in some southern climates plants can grow virtually all year. With careful planning, you can extend your vegetable production. What type of climate do you live in? What can you grow in your climate? Most of North America is considered temperate, with the exception of Hawaii (Hawaii is in the tropics but has a varied climate because of elevation and orographic influences) and Puerto Rico (which is tropical). Some areas in the southern portions of the United States are thought of as subtropical and tropical. Knowledge of your local climate and the microclimate in and around your garden location is of primary importance to your success as a gardener.

There are five basic climate factors: (1) temperature, (2) precipitation, (3) relative humidity, (4) light, and (5) wind. You will likely see some of the best and worst your climate has to offer in a 10-year period. As a gardener, you will be the first to recognize a dry spell—your nongardening neighbors may not notice the trend for some time. Likewise, a frost or impending frost is at the top of the gardener's "watch list" in the spring and fall. Many cooperative extension offices, local garden centers, and fellow experienced gardeners can provide you with a wealth of knowledge if you are new to an area. Gardening calendars may be available through local extension and Master Gardener groups that provide information about gardening activities month by month. You can manipulate some climate factors on a small scale. For example, irrigate when dry; cover sensitive plants with row covers, tarps, blankets, or sheets during a frost; and use solar row covers to protect crops from high-intensity light and heat. There are also more chill- and frost-tolerant cultivars available for certain vegetable crops. However, large-scale farms do not have the luxury of manipulating the climate in the ways the home gardener can. These farms have to plan carefully, plant according to frost-free dates, and hope for the best (as far as rainfall and its timing). Irrigation at the farm scale requires careful planning and equipment.

Temperature

Temperature plays an enormous role in gardening and dictates when and what vegetables can be grown in your area. Minimum winter temperatures are a big factor that affects plant survival. Because vegetable crops are grown as annuals, minimum winter temperatures are not as critical. However, anyone who grows ornamental shrubs and flowers, fruit trees, berries, and grapes needs to be keenly aware of minimum and maximum winter temperatures. Also, do not underestimate the effect of maximum temperatures and humidity during the summer. Many vegetable crops will not flower and pollinate during high day and night temperatures in the summer (see specifics in individual crop descriptions). Most locations throughout the United States have pros and cons associated with how vegetable crops respond to the climate. Cool-season crops may be grown throughout the season at higher elevations or in more northern climates, but the season may be too cool and short for long-season tomatoes. Various tomato cultivars are bred specifically for certain climates.

There are three basic climate aspects to consider: (1) macroclimate, (2) mesoclimate, and (3) microclimate. Macroclimate broadly defines the climate of a region (tens to hundreds of miles), and weather data is available from climate stations (identified by city). Minimum and maximum monthly temperatures and average monthly precipitation, relative humidity, and wind speed are available for cities in most counties throughout the United States. The next smaller scale, mesoclimate (tens of yards to miles) is influenced largely by elevation and topography. The smallest scale is microclimate (tens of yards to inches). Microclimate can be affected by natural or artificial barriers and structures such as trees, shrubs, soil depressions, windbreaks, boulders, buildings, fences, and roadways. There is a degree of overlap between mesoclimates and microclimates. A low spot in the garden could be a frost pocket that freezes when slightly elevated surrounding areas do not; that low spot may also accumulate runoff, and the soil may be poorly drained. Trees and shrubs shading the garden can create microclimates, and some areas of the garden may not receive full sun all day.

Temperature and Vegetable Plant Physiology

In plants, algae, and certain types of bacteria, photosynthesis results in the release of molecular oxygen and the removal of carbon dioxide from the atmosphere. During photosynthesis, glucose and other complex carbohydrates are produced and can be used when plant cells need energy (fig. 15). The process of photosynthesis transforms the sun's energy, which is stored as glucose for later use. Glucose (a simple sugar) comprises three elements: carbon, hydrogen, and oxygen—the three basic elements of all organic compounds. Plants use glucose in several ways:

1. Part of the glucose supply is used to form fiber, or cellulose.

2. Glucose can be converted into starch that can be converted back to glucose when the plant needs it. For example, in potatoes, glucose becomes a complex carbohydrate, or starch. Starch is also found in wheat, rice, and all whole grains. Plants use glucose for food storage in seeds.

3. Glucose can be broken down during the process of plant respiration, thus releasing energy stored in the glucose molecule. Where photosynthesis is the process of chlorophyll transforming light energy into chemical energy that is stored in plant cells as glucose, respiration utilizes food in cells, releasing chemical energy and heat for plant growth and other life processes. More simply, respiration is the process by which the plant uses carbon in the form of sugar fixed during photosynthesis to grow. Photosynthesis occurs in the light, but respiration does not require light and occurs continually in every plant cell.

Plants have specific physiological adaptations to various elevation, temperature, and moisture regimes. Plants exhibit three basic photosynthetic pathways: cool season (C_3), warm season (C_4), and the pathway used by succulents and cacti (CAM). All these pathways depend on environmental factors such as light intensity, temperature, and the availability of carbon dioxide, water, and certain minerals. A shortage of any one of these can limit photosynthetic rate and efficiency. C_3 photosynthesis was known before the discovery

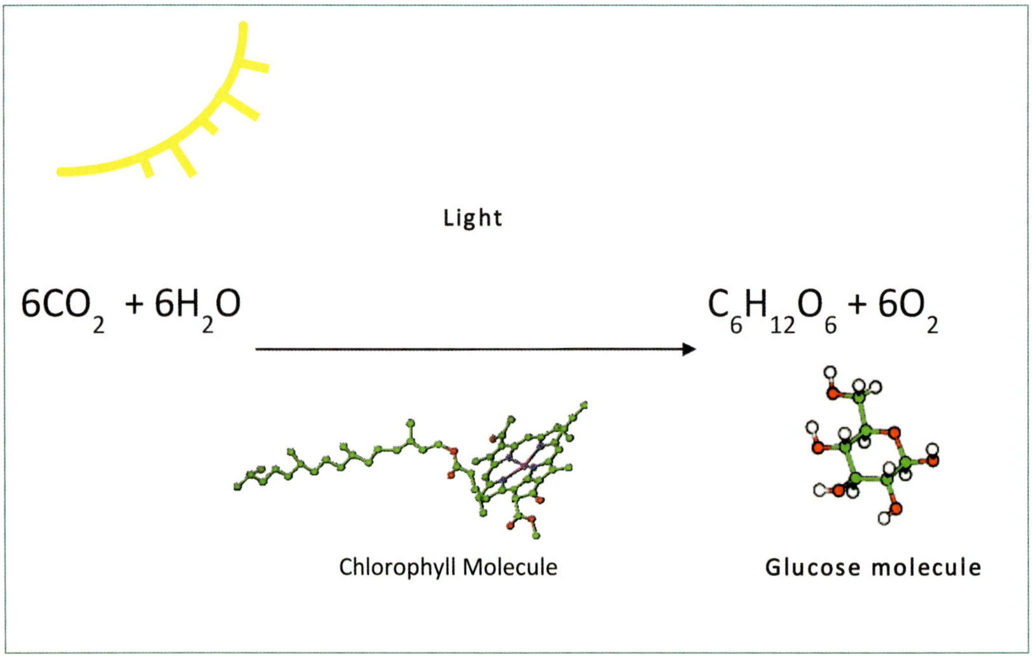

FIGURE 15. Photosynthesis, the process of carbon metabolism in plants, occurs in plant chloroplasts. Radiant energy, water, chemical energy, and carbon dioxide drive the synthesis of organic compounds (glucose) and release oxygen to the atmosphere. Spaeth (2001).

of C_4 photosynthesis in the mid-1960s—science considers C_4 a relatively recent evolutionary phenomenon (developing over the past 30 million years). Plants with C_4 photosynthesis are significantly less numerous than C_3 plants (7,500 C_4 species; nearly 250,000 C_3 species). Of the three photosynthetic pathways, C_4 photosynthesis is the most efficient for plant growth.

Each photosynthetic process has unique biochemistry and is linked to how well plants grow during cooler conditions in spring or hotter conditions in summer. Optimal temperatures for photosynthesis in cool-season plants (C_3) range from 68 to 86°F, while optimal temperatures for warm-season plants (C_4) are between 86 and 104°F. Keep in mind that these are just averages; some crop species may be able to function outside these ranges, but they may be stressed. The C_3 class contains the largest group of vegetable plants cultivated by gardeners: lettuce, spinach, beets, carrots, radishes, tomatoes, potatoes, peppers, cucumbers, broccoli, and cabbage; corn is a C_4 plant. Environmental conditions can cause variation in the photosynthetic process. Plants with C_4 photosynthesis usually have the highest photosynthetic rates, and CAM plants the lowest.

Garden Vernacular Related to Temperature Preference of Vegetable Plants

In the gardening world, a particular vernacular is used to refer to the temperature preferences and adaptability of plants that is not based on photosynthetic biochemical pathways. Gardeners classify vegetables as cool season (spring and fall plants), warm season (summer plants), hardy, semihardy, tender, and very tender (table 7).

Table 7 shows germination temperatures, time to germination, and optimal growing temperatures during the season. As a general guide, plant the hardy cool-season vegetables such as spinach, Swiss chard, onions, leeks, shallots, peas, radishes, cabbage, kale, turnips,

TABLE 7. Temperature requirements and average days needed for seed germination

Vegetable (temperature sensitivity)	Soil temperature requirements for seed germination				Optimal growing temp. (°F) during the season
	Minimum temp. (°F)	Optimal range (°F)	Optimal temp. (°F)	Avg. number of days to germination	
Lettuce (SH)*	35	40–80	75	2–7	60–65
Spinach (H)	35	45–75	70	6–21	60–65
Onions, leeks (H)	35	50–95	75	6–16	55–75
Beets (SH)	40	50–85	85	4–10	60–65
Broccoli (H)	40	45–85	80	3–10	60–75
Cabbage (H)	40	40–95	85	4–5	60–75
Cauliflower (SH)	40	45–85	80	3–10	60–65
Carrots (SH)	40	45–85	80	6–21	60–65
Peas (H)	40	40–75	75	8–25	60–65
Radishes (H)	40	45–80	80	3–5	60–65
Swiss chard (H)	40	50–85	85	7–14	60–70
Corn (T)	50	60–95	95	4–7	60–75
Tomatoes (T)	50	60–85	85	5–14	70–85
Beans (T)	60	60–85	80	5–10	60–75
Cucumbers (VT)	60	60–95	95	3–7	65–75
Muskmelons (VT)	60	65–95	90	5–10	65–75
Sweet peppers (VT)	60	60–95	85	8–25	70–75
Hot peppers (VT)	60	60–95	85	8–25	70–85
Squash (VT)	60	70–95	95	4–9	65–75

Note: All vegetables listed use the C_3 photosynthetic pathway, except corn, which uses C_4.

*Temperature sensitivity: H = hardy; SH = semihardy; T = tender; VT = very tender.

collard greens, and other hardy salad greens in early spring. These vegetables can tolerate frosts down to 25°F–28°F; some plants such as the very hardy spinach, kale, and collard greens can tolerate freezing temperatures down to the low 20s. When planting cool-season and hardy vegetables, I always err on the side of planting early. In fall gardens, spinach, cabbage, and collards taste sweeter after a frost. The semihardy vegetables should be planted when the danger of hard freezes is past, but they can usually tolerate light frosts (29°F–32°F). The tender and very tender plants should be planted after the last spring frosts (warmer weather, 65°F–90°F). County and state extension offices and Master Gardening groups usually publish a planting calendar, and state extension services usually publish a guide listing planting dates for all vegetables.

Humidity

A discussion of humidity is included because humidity has a direct effect on plants. Two concepts related to humidity often cause confusion. "Absolute humidity" or just "humidity" is the actual amount of water vapor in an air sample, measured in grams per cubic meter of gas. "Relative humidity" (RH), the term we are probably most familiar with, is the ratio of the actual amount of water vapor present compared to the maximum amount of water the air could hold at the present temperature (the ambient temperature) and is measured as a percentage. Hot days can feel hotter because of high humidity; in contrast, low humidity is associated with dry throat, eyes, and nose, and you may generate static upon touching certain objects. Horticulturists specify certain humidity requirements for various species of houseplants; however, in the vegetable garden we have little control over the effects of humidity on our plants. Our only control is not to water plants from above and wet the foliage; water from below and not during evening hours.

Humidity has a direct influence on transpiration in plants. When a plant is turgid and water balance is sufficient (saturated), water vapor is transpired to the atmosphere. The process of water loss in the plant is called transpiration. Most of the water absorbed by the plant is transpired or lost via stomata as water vapor. More than 90% of the water that a plant takes up is transpired and lost to the atmosphere. If we perspired this much, we would have to drink 20 gallons or more of water per day. Water is the basis of metabolic processes in plants and is used in photosynthesis and the synthesis of hormones, chlorophyll, and other plant pigments. The exchange of gases in pho-

TABLE 8. NOAA's National Weather Service Heat Index

Temperature (°F)

Relative Humidity (%)	80	82	84	86	88	90	92	94	96	98	100	102	104	106	108	110
40	80	81	83	85	88	91	94	97	101	105	109	114	119	124	130	136
45	80	82	84	87	89	93	96	100	104	109	114	119	124	130	137	
50	81	83	85	88	91	95	99	103	108	113	118	124	131	137		
55	81	84	86	89	93	97	101	106	112	117	124	130	137			
60	82	84	88	91	95	100	105	110	116	123	129	137				
65	82	85	89	93	98	103	108	114	121	128	136					
70	83	86	90	95	100	105	112	119	126	134						
75	84	88	92	97	103	109	116	124	132							
80	84	89	94	100	106	113	121	129								
85	85	90	96	102	110	117	126	135								
90	86	91	98	105	113	122	131									
95	86	93	100	108	117	127										
100	87	95	103	112	121	132										

Likelihood of Heat Disorders with Prolonged Exposure or Strenuous Activity

Caution · Extreme Caution · Danger · Extreme Danger

Source: National Weather Service Heat Index, National Oceanic and Atmospheric Administration (NOAA), 2016, http://www.nws.noaa.gov/os/heat/index.shtml.

tosynthesis requires moist cell surfaces. When the amount of water absorption by roots falls below the amount being transpired, leaves may wilt and stomata close. Stomata remain closed at night when plants are restoring water balance.

Higher humidity (RH) is associated with slower transpiration rates and less water loss from the plant. Weather forecasters use a complex heat index (HI) equation to indicate how hot it actually feels when RH and air temperature are both considered. As RH increases, the HI temperature increases (table 8). For example, if the temperature is 90°F and the RH is 50%, the HI temperature is 95°F. Increase the RH to 75%, and the HI temperature increases to 109°F.

Using Climate Tools in Gardening

There are a number of sources of information about your particular climate:

- Plant hardiness zones and maps (appendix C).
- Freeze-free period (also known as frost-free period) maps and tables (appendix C).
- Long-term average monthly precipitation and temperature data.

Plant Hardiness Zones

Plant hardiness zones are useful in establishing whether particular plants will flourish and grow (appendix C). Climate growing-zone maps are useful tools to help gardeners grow and propagate successful gardens. Hardiness zones give gardeners a general overview of macroclimate temperature extremes for their particular location so that they can select adapted and tolerant plants for landscaping and garden use. Remember that climate zones are guidelines to determine the hardiness and survivability of various plants and trees in a specific geographic area. Plants have temperature thresholds, and these are especially important when selecting ornamentals, certain vegetable varieties, cultivars, and fruit trees. Often, the tags and labels on purchased plants at a nursery will provide information about the temperature regime to which the plant is adapted. Many seed catalogs also provide hardiness zone information about plants and particular cultivars. When in doubt, ask the nursery staff, seed company specialist, or extension specialist about adaptability to your particular zone. The hardiness zones generally refer to winter temperature adaptability. Equally important, especially in hotter climates, you need to know the upper limits of summer temperatures. Certain vegetable and fruit tree varieties may not be well adapted to grow in hot and humid temperature zones.

The USDA Agricultural Research Service (ARS) Plant Hardiness Zone Map (PHZM) is the standard in the United States. The new PHZM now allows you to zoom in to regional and state levels via Geographic Information System (GIS) technology and find your zone by inputting your zip code. The PHZM climate database utilizes 30 years (1976–2005) of data and includes sophisticated algorithms to account for geographic and topographic characteristics such as elevation and proximity to bodies of water. The American Horticultural Society publishes a Plant Heat Zone Map, and the Arbor Day Foundation in Nebraska City, Nebraska, has also developed a similar hardiness zone map. Comparable maps are available for Canada, Europe, Australia, Africa, Asia, and throughout the world.

The climate zones in the USDA PHZM map are divided into 10°F zones, which are based on the average annual extreme minimum winter temperature. The USDA warns that the lowest temperature is an average, not the lowest temperature that may ever occur. For example, if you garden in Zone 5a, you can expect average annual extremes to drop as low as -15 to -20°F. However, during rare climatic events, temperatures may drop lower than the average ranges.

Freeze-Free or Frost-Free Dates

Gardeners need to be familiar with the freeze-free period (also known as frost-free period and frost-free date). The National Oceanic and Atmospheric Administration (NOAA) publishes maps showing the number of days that are available for crop production between the last spring frost and the first fall frost (appendix C). The freeze-free period is an important consideration because different vegetable crops need various lengths of time to mature and bear fruit. For example, the freeze-free period for Dallas, Texas, is about 240 days; for Boston, Massachusetts, about 150–160 days; for Sacramento, California, about 300 days; for Laramie, Wyoming, about 90 days; and for Portland, Oregon, about 170 days. If a seed catalog specifies that a cultivar takes 110 days to mature and bear fruit, and the freeze-free period in your area is 90 days, there may not be enough time for the plant to mature.

Frost risk levels are useful in agriculture. For example, for Dallas, Texas, there is a 90% chance that the freeze-free period will be longer than 240 days, or a 10% chance that it will be shorter (appendix C). Some areas are too detailed to distinguish zones on the map; as an alternative there are various websites that provide frost-free period data by zip code.

NOAA defines three freezing regimes: light freezes, 29°F–32°F; moderate freezes, 25°F–28°F; and severe freezes, 24°F or less. NOAA has two maps that show spring freeze occurrence (10% probability of 32°F or less on a later date; appendix C), and fall freeze occurrence (10% probability of 32°F or less on an earlier date; appendix C).

In addition to maps (appendix C), NOAA publishes spring and fall freeze/frost probability data in a table format for states and cities throughout the United States. This data gives 10 to 90% probabilities of spring and fall frost occurrence. Freeze/frost tables are available for most major cities and states throughout the United States. As an example, tables 9 and 10 show freeze/frost probabilities for certain dates and for the number of freeze-free days at three temperature thresholds for my location in Weatherford, Texas. Table 9 shows that for Weatherford, in Parker County, Texas, there is only a 10% chance that the first moderate freeze (28°F) in the fall will occur near October 29 (or a 90% chance that one will occur after that date), and there is a 90% chance that a moderate freeze will occur near December 3. Likewise, there is a 10% chance of a late spring light freeze (32°F) near April 16 or shortly thereafter, but a 90% chance of a freeze near March 12. Table 10 shows that there is a 90% chance that the frost-free (36°F) period from spring to fall will exceed 190 days (or a 10% chance that it will be equal to or less than 190 days). There is a 10% chance that the freeze-free period (36°F) will extend to about 229 days.

TABLE 9. Probability of freeze/frost occurrence for Weatherford, Parker County, Texas

	Probability of occurrence								
Temperature	10%	20%	30%	40%	50%	60%	70%	80%	90%
Spring 32°	Apr 16	Apr 10	Apr 6	Apr 2	Mar 29	Mar 26	Mar 22	Mar 18	Mar 12
Spring 28°	Apr 6	Mar 30	Mar 25	Mar 21	Mar 17	Mar 13	Mar 8	Mar 3	Feb 24
Spring 24°	Mar 25	Mar 15	Mar 9	Mar 3	Feb 26	Feb 21	Feb 15	Feb 8	Jan 30
Fall 32°	Oct 22	Oct 28	Oct 31	Nov 3	Nov 7	Nov 10	Nov 13	Nov 17	Nov 23
Fall 28°	Oct 29	Nov 3	Nov 7	Nov 11	Nov 14	Nov 18	Nov 21	Nov 26	Dec 3
Fall 24°	Nov 5	Nov 12	Nov 18	Nov 22	Nov 26	Dec 1	Dec 6	Dec 11	Dec 18

Source: Adapted from W. J. Koss, J. R. Owenby, P. M. Steurer, and D. S. Ezell, *Freeze/Frost Data* (Asheville, NC: National Climatic Data Center, National Oceanic and Atmospheric Administration, January 1988), http://www.crh.noaa.gov/Image/oun/climate/freeze/freezefrost.pdf.

TABLE 10. Probability of freeze-free days at three temperature thresholds for Weatherford, Parker County, Texas

Temperature threshold (°F)	Freeze-free period (days)		
	Probability		
	10%	50%	90%
36	229	209	190
32	244	226	208
28	275	249	224

Source: Adapted from W. J. Koss, J. R. Owenby, P. M. Steurer, and D. S. Ezell, *Freeze/Frost Data* (Asheville, NC: National Climatic Data Center, National Oceanic and Atmospheric Administration, January 1988), http://www.crh.noaa.gov/Image/oun/climate/freeze/freezefrost.pdf.

Note: Percentages indicate the probability of a longer-than-specified freeze-free period (days).

FIGURE 16. Improving soil health with manure, compost, and mulch. Soil amendments can be concentrated in the circle plot arrangements to improve soil health. Photo by author.

7

Establishing the Garden

The Circle Concept—Advantages

By using the circle planting method, you can grow a considerable amount of produce in a small space (fig. 16). Circle plots can squeeze into spaces from very small to large. Commercial and professional growers and "truck vegetable" farmers often utilize the traditional row system because they need to use machinery for cultivating, planting, and harvesting their crops. A well-planned and well-managed garden with vegetables planted in rows is aesthetically very pleasing. However, for the home gardener, I believe planting in small circle plots is a more efficient method.

Use circle plots for the following purposes:

- Eliminate the cost of buying border materials, including wood or masonry. If you have existing raised beds, please continue using them; however, try the planting and cultural techniques described throughout this book.
- Reduce the time and work needed to plant and maintain your garden.
- Concentrate your water, fertilizer, compost, and manure resources within the circles. Fewer resources are needed because you are not spreading them over the entire garden area. Note that in time, fertility will gradually disperse to the empty spaces in the garden as mulch decomposes—organic materials are inevitably dispersed throughout the garden.

- Replant quickly and easily; repeated planting or sowing of seeds once your circle beds are established can be accomplished quickly with minimum effort. No major soil cultivation is needed.
- Save your back, with less bending and moving up and down planted rows, or maneuvering around larger raised-bed arrangements.
- Weed quickly and easily. Once you have enhanced the soil with organic matter and it begins to become more friable and less compacted, weeding with a small spade or your fingers around tender seedlings is usually all that is needed. No expensive tools are necessary.
- Establish and build compost piles in situ (on-site). Why create compost in one location only to move it to other locations? Too much work!
- Easily protect beds against pets and small wildlife by using wire fencing, which is easy to arrange in a circle. Wooden stakes maintain the shape.
- Mimic the distribution of wild plants and maximize production and yield.
- Once your plots are established, use them year after year.

Circle Plots Explained

The premise of circle gardening is based on limiting and reducing the work, expense, and effort needed to build borders out of wood or masonry or excavate existing soil and replace it with expensive soil mixes. A circle 3 to 5 feet in diameter is formed into a convex mound with a built-up rim (fig. 17). Mulch is used around the circle perimeter to eliminate weeds and erosion of the plot perimeter (figs. 16 and 17). The mulch border (I use spoiled hay and straw) also helps maintain the circle border or lip that prevents water from running off during irrigation. Compost piles can be constructed and maintained on the circle plot, so you do not have to bother with moving the heavy material from another location. The circle plots are built slightly convex in order to improve drainage. Seedlings and growing plants always seem to perform better in an elevated soil profile compared to a flat, compacted seedbed. Circle beds are easy to protect against pets and small wildlife. I use green vinyl wire mesh, which can be obtained in rolls at building and hardware stores. I cut the wire rolls to a height of about 2½ feet (chapter 9). I do not use cages around all my vegetables, just the ones the rabbits seem to like. Adjust the height of your protective circle fence to meet your specific needs. Soil amendments and fertilizers can be added to the circle plot prior to, during, and after the growing season. Once your circle plots are established, you can use them year after year. No major cultivation or soil preparation is needed; just replenish soil nutrients, do some light cultivation, and plant.

The expense of circle gardening is significantly reduced because you are not applying soil amendments (compost, manure, fertilizer)

A

B

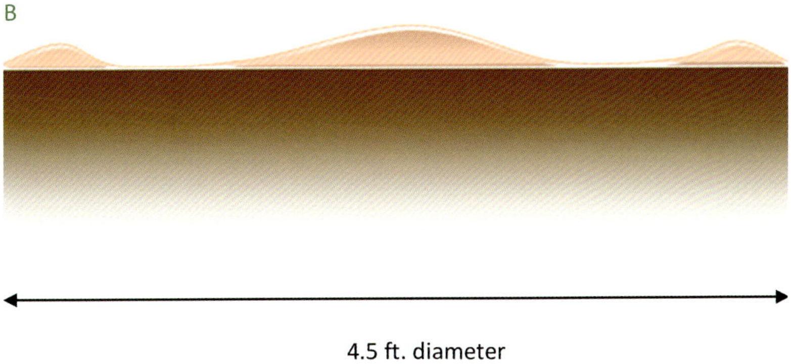

FIGURE 17. *A*, Circle plot 4½ feet in diameter with a slightly convex (mounded) center, a raised soil border, and mulch on the periphery for weed control. The mulch also provides a clean area on which to kneel beside the plot for seeding, weeding, and harvesting. *B*, Side view of circle plot. Figures by author.

and water over the entire garden area. Periodic additions of mulch around the circle plots will improve soil health over time as the materials decompose. Various formulations of compost, decomposed animal manure, and topsoil are available in 40–50-pound bags at nursery, building supply, and hardware centers. The amount of soil amendments needed and the cost of applying them to circle plots are a fraction of the amount and cost for the entire garden area (fig. 18). Some gardeners are concerned about extraneous salts, herbicides, and antibiotics in commercially bagged animal manure. If this is a concern, do some research on the supplier and the product. I have not seen any harmful effects to my soil or plants from the commercially bagged compost and manure that are available in my area. Talk to professional nursery staff; they are knowledgeable about the products they sell. I have also noticed that some commercially sold compost preparations in 40- to 50-pound bags contain a high percentage of woody material. Avoid these and try to find compost that is not just ground-up woody material.

Efficiency of Small, Concentrated Circle Garden Plots

The circle planting method uses less compost, fertilizer, and water because these resources are concentrated in the planting area instead of over the entire garden. For example, if you wanted to apply 1 inch of compost on an area 10 by 10 feet, it would require 0.31 cubic yard (about 403 pounds). Applying 1 inch of compost on 4 circle plots in the same size area would require half the amount (50.4 square feet, 0.16 cubic yard, or 208 pounds) (fig. 18). For those starting new gardens, this is a more efficient use of resources. You may wonder, what about the fertility status of the interspaces? It is important to mulch around your circle plots to enable you to work around the garden, even during wet conditions. The mulch also provides weed control around the plots. With additions of mulch over time, and as the mulch decomposes, soil health and fertility are improved.

What is the efficiency of packing plants with circular architecture into square, rectangular, or circle plots? Interestingly, many mathematical treatises study this phenomenon—the subject is quite technical and mathematically robust. Circle packing is a geometric study of the arrangement of circles (of equal or unequal diameters) in a given geometric shape with no overlap, but with all circles touching. In the garden, our growing plants do overlap and form a network, often with many layers of foliar cover. Mathematically, planting plants with circular architecture—cabbage, for example—in square

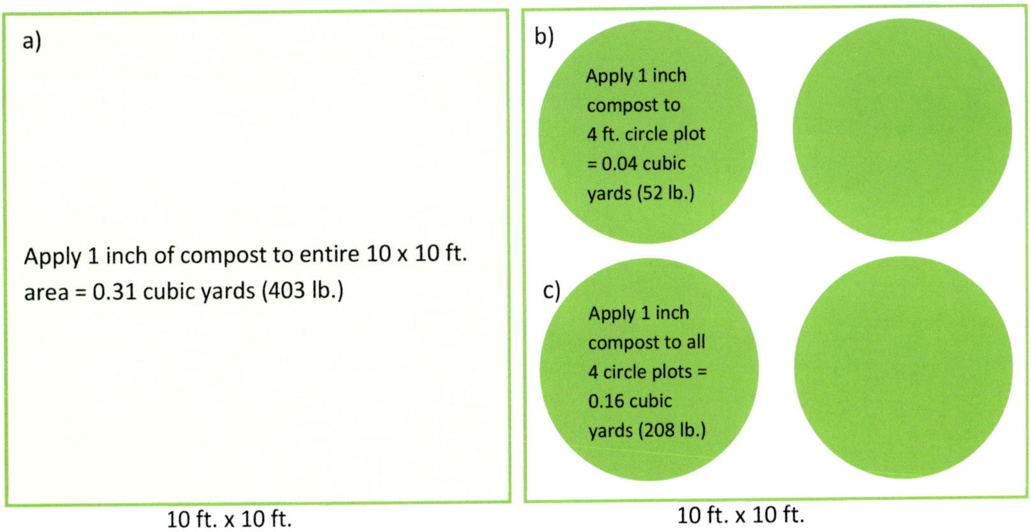

FIGURE 18. Comparison of compost applied at 1-inch depth to a 10-foot-square plot versus four 4-foot-diameter circle plots. Note: a cubic yard of compost weighs between 1,000 and 1,600 lb.; average = 1,300 lb.

plots is slightly more efficient than planting them in a circular plot (fig. 19); however, as the example on the next page shows, the gain in efficiency is only one plant. Certain websites will calculate how many circles of a given diameter will fit into a larger circle, rectangle, or square. In the scale drawing (fig. 19), the packing density of 1-foot-diameter plants into a rectangle of 20 square feet is 18 plants, and in the circle it is 17 plants. In reality, the argument for spacing and density of plants is not really significant for the home garden. As I have mentioned, I find the circle planting arrangement easier to plant and care for than crawling along a row.

Garden Location

Adequate topsoil on a well-drained site that receives full sunlight would fulfill the most important criteria in selecting a garden location (fig. 20). Distance from trees and shrubs is also important: locate your garden at least 10 feet from tree and shrub borders and drip lines in order to prevent shading and keep roots from competing for water and nutrients. If you have walnut or pecan trees, plant your garden 50–60 feet away, as these trees produce a substance called juglone, which is toxic to other plants. The International Society of Arboriculture provides some good rules of thumb about how far tree roots can spread: "(1) Tree root systems extend out 2–3 times the

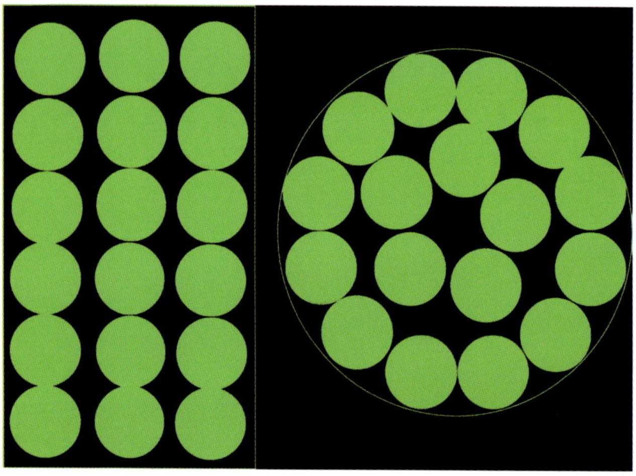

FIGURE 19. Packing circular plants (1-foot diameter) into a rectangle (3.33 feet wide x 6 feet long = 20 square feet) and a circle (5-foot diameter = 20 square feet). Diagram to scale: rectangle = 18 plants; circle = 17 plants.

FIGURE 20. Criteria associated with a good garden location. Photo by author.

dripline; (2) most roots are in the top foot of soil; (3) roots extend out about 1.5 times the height of the tree; and (4) more than 60 percent of the absorbing root system is beyond the dripline."

Some vegetables can tolerate some shade, but I need to emphasize that they will not produce as well as those grown in full sun (table 11). In my experience, vegetable plants grown in partial shade never reach their full potential, and the result is disappointing. When a

TABLE 11. Basic light requirements for the vegetable garden

Full sunlight		
Beans	Melons	Potatoes
Broccoli	Okra	Pumpkins
Cauliflower	Onions	Squash
Cucumbers	Peas	Tomatoes
Eggplants	Peppers	Watermelons
Partially shade tolerant		
Beets	Collard	Parsley
Brussels sprouts	Kale	Radishes
Cabbage	Lettuce	Spinach
Carrots	Mustard	Turnips

recommendation says full sun, it means "full sun." My best advice is to find a sunny location for your vegetable garden.

If your garden site is not optimal, you can make improvements. Many city and suburban homeowners may have little choice about where to place a garden plot because of space. However, there are still some situations that you should try to avoid. Gardening against the foundation of a home, whether on the north, south, east, or west side, is generally not suitable. I have seen some successful vegetable gardens placed against the foundations of homes, but the summer climate was moderate. On the south side of a home foundation, the site may be too hot, as solar energy from the sun is reflected off the house. Likewise, do not plant vegetables on the north side of the house because of excessive shade. East and west locations receive partial sun, but west exposures in many areas can also get very hot during late afternoon. Another concern related to planting food crops near house foundations is polluted soil. Lead and arsenic and other heavy metals tend to be highest in the drip zone around a house. Vegetables can take up heavy metals from the soil. In addition, treatments for termites may have used organochlorine pesticides such as chlordane. Chlordane was used in the United States from 1948 to 1988, after which it was banned. Chlordane adheres to soil particles, has low solubility, and does not percolate easily with groundwater. It maintains a long residual effect in soil, as it does not readily break down—it may persist for 25–35 years.

Often the back end of a yard, perhaps with a fence behind the plot, is a good location, as it is not in the direct path of children or pets. If you have a pet that digs, you will need to fence off the garden location. If your land or lot is on a steep slope, you will have to take some precautions to control runoff and erosion with a terracing scheme. If you are a country homeowner with one or more acres, you have more choices for your garden location. Whether your garden is in town or in the country, there are both common and unique factors to consider.

Both town and country gardeners may have to protect their gardens from digging pets, but the country homeowner will most likely have to deal with wildlife as well. During all my gardening years, I have contended with deer, armadillos, rabbits, skunks, raccoons, feral hogs, coyotes, gophers, woodchucks, birds, and snakes. In the country, escaped cattle, sheep, and goats occasionally visit the garden. In Texas, my most challenging and destructive animal has been the feral hog. The only solution with feral hogs is trapping them in a hog cage with baited food inside. Fortunately, licensed individuals in my area have the equipment and knowledge to catch hogs. I have solved the deer problem with an electric fence, and knee-high woven wire placed around the circle plots has kept the rabbits, skunks, and armadillos from causing too much damage.

Garden size depends on several factors such as the amount of land available, the amount of produce you wish to grow (family needs), and the time available to take care of the garden. Vegetables all have different spacing requirements, and this ultimately determines what you can successfully grow. For small garden areas, vining plants such as melons, winter squash, pumpkins, and cucumbers may not be practical. However, there are now bush and semibush cultivars for winter squash, cucumbers, pumpkins, and melons that are adaptable to small spaces and even patio pots. Corn and potatoes may also be limited if you have a very small garden; however, nothing is impossible, and corn can be grown against a fence on the north side of the garden and potatoes can be grown in circle plots and in containers.

Where space is limiting, you will need to consider which vegetables are your favorites and which can be practically grown. If you like peppers, it makes more sense to grow them as opposed to potatoes because of the difference in their cost at the market. Specialty yellow, orange, red, and purple peppers are priced at a premium. If you like salad, by all means consider various cultivars of salad greens—again, all the prewashed salad greens at the store are expensive. Onions are easy to grow and can be stored throughout the winter. Most people love tomatoes—how can they be left out? Tomatoes are treated somewhat differently in the circle gardening concept, as only one plant occupies a given circle. Legumes such as beans can be planted around the perimeter (a modified "Three Sisters" arrangement; fig. 21). I rotate my tomatoes around the garden each year to avoid diseases, but lately I have been planting additional tomato plants randomly throughout the garden in odd leftover spaces. The growth form and habit of the brassicas (broccoli, cabbage, cauliflower, and brussels sprouts) lend themselves quite well to the circle plot arrangement. One last bit of advice for new gardeners is to underestimate the size of your garden and build up to more ambitious plans. New gardeners need to "find their stride" to learn how much garden they can handle and take care of. Experienced gardeners learn how to keep in step with planting, weeding, and care of the garden. For example, in large gardens, weeding may be done on a schedule rather than by visual need. Yes, the weeds may be small or inconsequential, but they grow fast and can soon overtake tender plants like carrots, beets, and lettuce.

FIGURE 21. Traditional Native American "Three Sisters" companion planting of corn, beans, and squash. Drawing by author.

Garden Site Indicator Scorecard

In appendix A of this book, you will find the Garden Site Indicator Scorecard. Go through each indicator on the scorecard at the garden location. Each indicator is based on your subjective evaluation and is rated as poor, tolerable, or best. Some indicators, highlighted in red, are critical. If an indicator score occurs in a red box, find another garden location. Likewise, if some of the indicators are rated poor, all is not lost; they may be improved or corrected depending on the extent of the situation.

Preparing the Garden Soil

Unfortunately, preparing the soil is probably one of the steps that inhibits people from establishing a garden and growing vegetables. Breaking up sod can be hard work if you do not have the right tools. Traditionally, a rototiller is often used to break up sod and start a new garden. However, you do not need a rototiller to start creating circle plots. Circle plots can be established with a sharpshooter shovel, pitchfork, and other common garden tools (fig. 22). Mulch can be used to smother out grass sod and weeds around plots. Plastic or canvas tarps can also be placed on the soil surface (with edges weighed down) to kill or weaken grass sod and weeds. Once the unwanted vegetation is dead or subdued by smothering with a tarp, it is easier to cultivate the garden plots. Once the circle plots are established, you will not need to turn over the soil in the entire garden with a cultivating machine each gardening season. Before you plant, mix and incorporate soil amendments directly into the circle beds, using the steps in figure 22.

If you wish to break up sod over a larger garden area, a rototiller and/or a tractor with a cultivating implement is the most practical course of action. If you do not wish to invest in a rototiller, they can be rented. If you do not already own a rototiller and are not familiar with them, be sure to go over each step in the instruction manual and have a knowledgeable person show you how to properly operate the machine and go over safety issues. Rototillers come with front or rear tines, and each has its pros and cons. I currently own a heavy-duty rear-tine machine, but I have also owned front-tine machines, and I like them both. As I have mentioned in previous chapters, once the circle plots or beds are established the first year, do not use a rototiller or machine to cultivate the garden. I use hand tools to incorporate soil amendments and prepare my new seedbed, as shown in figure 22.

Follow these steps:

Step 1. Moisten the circle area (4½ to 5 feet in diameter) a few days before turning over sod and work one circle at a time based on your strength and energy level. Repeat this process several times over a 2-week period, taking care to bury the sod pieces so they break down.

Step 2. Chop up the sod, repeating periodically until the sod is dead and clumps start to disappear.

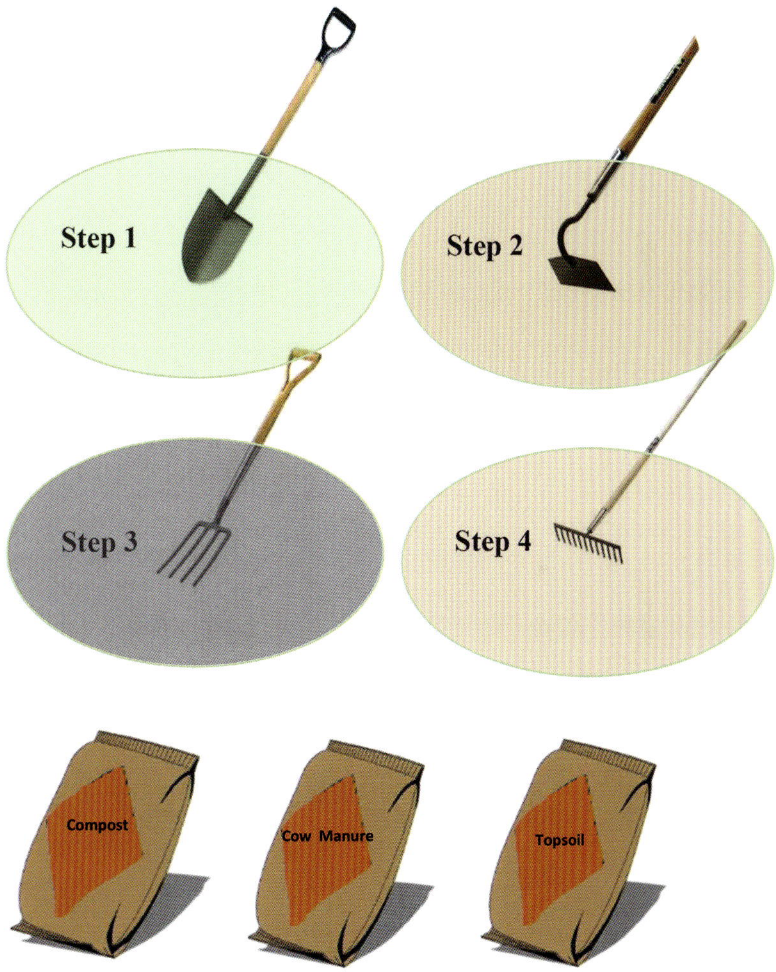

FIGURE 22. For established gardens, mark out several circle plots and proceed to step 3. If starting from scratch, start at step 1 and prepare the soil in 4 steps.

Step 3. After the sod has died and is partially decomposed, apply 20 to 40 pounds each of the three basic soil amendments (compost, decomposed cow manure, and topsoil), depending on the condition and fertility of your soil (fig. 23). You can add other fertilizers such as blood meal, bone meal, and other animal manures (appendix B), depending on the soil nutrient requirements of the plants you wish to grow. You can use small amounts of preplanting synthetic fertilizers, which are not organic, at your own discretion. Check appendix B for amounts. If you are not experienced with different fertilizers, add less and build up fertility gradually. You can always add more nutrients as your plants are growing. I gauge fertilizer and the fertility of my circle plots by how the plants are growing—their vigor and color (see individual Vegetable Guides).

Step 4. Keep the circle plots moist, not wet, and continue to mix the soil and break down clods. Try to achieve a nice friable, crumbly texture. If your soil contains high clay content, you may need to add more topsoil. Do not add sand to your circle plots and soil (see Science Note in chapter 4). Build up a small berm around the outside perimeter of the plot to prevent water runoff during irrigation. Create a slightly convex shape toward the middle (center) of the plot (fig. 17).

One of the strongest advantages to growing vegetables using circle or other raised-bed designs is that once the soil has been worked into a state adequate for planting seeds (the seedbed), you will no longer need either muscle or a machine to work your soil. Your circle beds will become more friable (mellow) over subsequent seasons with the addition of organic amendments. In my circle beds, I have not

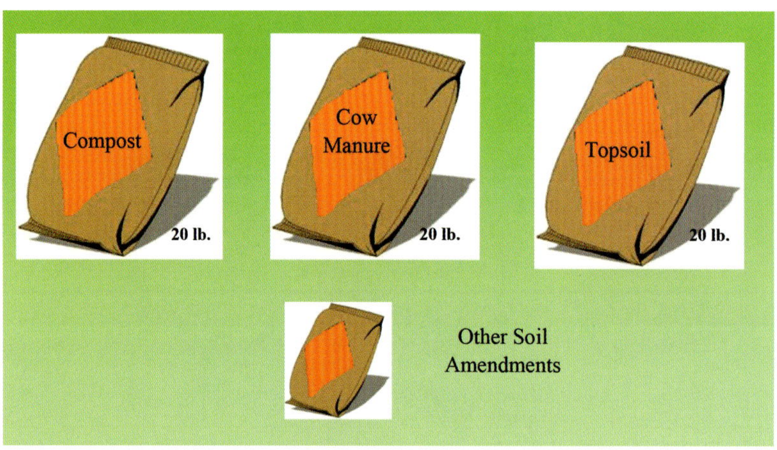

FIGURE 23. Basic soil amendments added to circle plots.

"plowed" or cultivated them with a machine since I established the garden 10 years ago. I use a hay fork or heavy pitchfork to turn and mix organic matter into my soils. My clay loam soil has become mellow and friable and is now easily worked. It now takes about 10 minutes to turn over the decomposed compost and prepare the circle bed for planting.

Over time, as you continually add compost and manure to your garden circles, you will create a nutrient pool that your plants will use gradually throughout subsequent years. Adding compost and manure to your garden on a regular basis, especially during the first few years, can modify your soil surface and create a friendlier and healthier environment for seeds and growing plants. With the creation of an organically rich soil surface environment, preparation of the seedbed will be easier compared to the intensive deep tillage methods used in row crop systems. Preparation of the furrow for seed placement, and especially covering the seeds with a friable, organically rich soil, will ensure that your seeds have every advantage for germination and seedling emergence. Heavy, clayey soils tend to form hard crusts after they have been cultivated and wetted. Small, fragile vegetable seedlings such as lettuce, spinach, and carrots have difficulty emerging in such soil, and your stand of plants may turn out spotty or irregular.

The addition of compost, decomposed manure, and topsoil will quickly pay for itself with fresh, healthy vegetables. There is no strict rule about what soil amendments are needed; it depends on your soil type, the condition and health of the soil, and what products are available locally. If you are starting a brand-new vegetable garden, you are going to be in a testing phase during the first year. This includes the following:

- Decide on your garden philosophy (totally organic versus a combination of organic and synthetic) (chapter 2).
- Be honest about what resources are available to you. Can you supply all plant nutrient needs with organic products? Consider the availability and cost of the products you wish to use.
- Evaluate your soil quality and health (use the Garden Site Indicator and Soil Health/Quality Indicator Scorecards in appendix A).
- Evaluate existing fertility.
- Determine what soil amendments may be needed now and in the future (appendixes B and D).
- Start with plants that are easy to grow and relatively trouble-free (chapter 8).

- Apply fertilizer in small amounts throughout the growing season (chapter 9, appendixes B and D).
- Aim to improve and sustain soil fertility over time.
- Assess whether your plants are healthy and disease resistant (chapter 10).
- Finally, evaluate the production and quality of your harvest.

Almost every vegetable garden is going to need fertilizer, especially nitrogen, phosphorus, and potassium. A starter rate, a low or partial rate of the total fertilizer requirement, is usually recommended. Many experts recommend several gradual additions of fertilizer throughout the growing season.

Continually evaluate how well your plants are growing with the starter. Monitor and assess the vigor and color of your seedlings. If they appear to be spindly, grow slowly, demonstrate an overall lack of vigor, and are not a healthy green, you will need to consider another small fertilizer application. You may be wondering, what is a healthy green color for specific vegetables? This is subjective, but as a rule, there should be no yellow hues to the plant. Examine the leaf color and texture of vegetables at a grocery store or roadside market. Look at images or photos of healthy vegetable plants in books or on your computer. This can give you some idea of what your vegetable plants should look like when they are actively growing and healthy (fig. 24).

FIGURE 24. Healthy green color of zucchini, cucumbers, and Swiss chard.

A

FIGURE 25. *A*, Italian parsley; *B*, Swiss chard; *C*, okra; *D*, assorted circle plots of onions and lettuce. Photos by author.

B

Garden Design and Layout

This chapter provides garden plans and schemes, and step-by-step guides for the beginning and experienced gardener. Diagrams and instructions are given that anticipate common questions and events. The schemes start out with easy-to-grow vegetables and proceed to gardens with more variety (less commonly purchased vegetables, flowers, and some berry bushes).

C

D

Garden Design and Layout: Plans and Schemes—Beginner to Experienced

Planning what to grow in a garden really comes down to one important point: What do you like to eat? More-experienced gardeners like to experiment and try vegetables that they have not grown or tasted before. I like okra but never tried growing it until a few years ago. Okra plants are especially adapted to the circle arrangement and are highly adapted to southern climates. The plants were stunning, especially the flowers (fig. 25C), and they produced a good crop without any insect problems. One year, my local feed and farm store gave me kohlrabi seeds instead of cabbage, and I thought that aliens had altered the plants until I found out about kohlrabi—they are interesting plants. I admit I have never grown parsnips, nor am I familiar with them as a culinary item. They have a long growing season, about 100 days, so I plan to experiment with them. I have a penchant for trying vegetables that are out of the ordinary, such as Hubbard squash, pattypan summer squash, kohlrabi, rutabagas, colored carrots, specialty colored peppers, orange cauliflower, Swiss chard, and odd orange and blue pumpkins (Jarrahdale).

Just Starting Out?

For beginning vegetable gardeners, I propose that you consider some of the easier vegetables. However, as soon as I say a vegetable crop is easy or hard to grow, someone will disagree. In the gardening world, some vegetables give some people fits, and for others they cause no trouble. Whether growing a specific vegetable is "easy," "moderate," or "problematic" remains somewhat subjective. Notice I use the word "problematic" instead of "difficult." "Problematic" leaves the door open, because sometimes these vegetables may be easy, depending on your environmental conditions. Many factors can influence certain vegetables or cause them to be problematic. Certain climates (seasonal temperatures), rainfall distribution and amount, soil type, fertility, insect pests common to your area, and finally your skill level affect the outcomes. In table 12, I have ranked various vegetables from easy to difficult, based on my experience. Success with certain vegetables varies by individual, and this is where the "art" of gardening takes precedence—if you wish, ignore the list and try growing whatever you want.

Certain things come to mind to recommend for beginning vegetable gardeners. I find that vegetables with larger seeds are easier for the beginner (summer and winter squash, corn, beans; table 12). Right away, an exception emerges, because although lettuce seeds are small, lettuce is easy to grow. However, the small seeds can be difficult to measure out and place evenly with your fingers—usually several seeds fall in one spot. Seed companies now sell pelleted lettuce seeds, which makes the chore of planting them easy. With regular, nonpelleted seeds, it is very easy to overseed and use up your seed packet before you finish planting your beds. A second consideration for beginners is to start with vegetables that produce aboveground fruit. I recommend working with your soil, enhancing it with organic matter, and getting to know its strengths and limitations. Belowground vegetables like carrots, beets, and potatoes can be grown later, after you improve the soil.

TABLE 12. Average number of seeds per ounce and seeds per gram for common garden vegetables, sorted from largest to smallest, and ease of growing these vegetables

Vegetable	Avg. no. Seeds/oz.	Avg. no. Seeds/g
Beans	90	3
Peas	110	4
Corn	155	5
Zucchini	180	6
Watermelons	600	21
Cucumbers	1,000	35
Melons	1,200	42
Swiss chard	1,400	49
Spinach	2,000	71
Beets	2,200	78
Radishes	2,500	88
Peppers	4,500	159
Broccoli	7,000	247
Cabbage	7,500	265
Cauliflower	8,000	282
Tomatoes	9,000	317
Turnips	9,000	317
Carrots	18,000	635
Parsley	18,000	635
Lettuce	25,000	882

Easy*	Moderate	Problematic
Peas	Bulb onions	Melons
Turnips	Peppers	Cauliflower
Green onions	Okra	Brussels sprouts
Collards	Broccoli	Lima beans
Beans	Tomatoes	Cucumbers
Summer squash	Beets	Carrots
Swiss chard	Spinach	
Lettuce	Potatoes	
Radishes	Sweet potatoes	

Note: Easy, moderate, and problematic ratings are based on author's experience.

Two-plot arrangements

Let's examine a few garden plans for the beginner. Use a circle 3 to 5 feet in diameter. Summer squash can include zucchini, yellow zucchini, yellow straight neck or crookneck, round, or pattypan types. There are compact cultivars of zucchini available. In a two-plot arrangement, the vegetables in table 13 will work well. Many surveys have tried to ascertain which vegetables are easy to grow and which are hard to grow. The main complaints related to difficult vegetables are weed problems and diseases, the high level of management required, and pests. As I looked through the literature on this subject, I was surprised to see some vegetables that I think are easy rated as moderate to difficult, as well as plants that I think require a lot of attention and management rated as easy. For example, I see beets and carrots on the "easy" lists of many publications. If you have a nice, deep, sandy loam, maybe, but I hold these two vegetables in reserve for intermediate to experienced growers. I think cabbage is easy to grow, and it usually falls into the moderate category. If you can control the cabbage worm, cabbage is an easy vegetable. There is so much subjectivity, but the vegetables listed in table 13 are good ones to start with.

In any circle plot, you can plant the entire circle with one vegetable, several related compatible vegetables, or several cultivars of the same vegetable (e.g., leaf lettuce, romaine, and butterhead lettuce; or red, white, and yellow onions). *An important note: if you mix various cultivars of the same species, crossing may occur; therefore, seeds harvested for future crops may not produce the desired results (see individual Vegetable Guides for information about crossing).*

TABLE 13. Vegetable choices for beginners in a 2-plot circle layout

Plot 1 choices	Plot 2 choices
Leaf lettuce varieties	Peppers*
Romaine or butterhead varieties	Summer squash, bush habit*
Spinach	Onion plants or sets
Swiss chard	Shell, snap, or snow peas*
Radishes	Garlic*
Bush beans*	Others (turnips, okra)

*Use mulch to conserve water and prevent soil-borne diseases.

Variations within a circle plot: Example 1

One variation would be to divide up the circle plot and plant different cultivars of the same vegetable. For example, plant 3 lettuce varieties or 4 separate vegetables (radishes, lettuce, spinach, and Swiss chard).

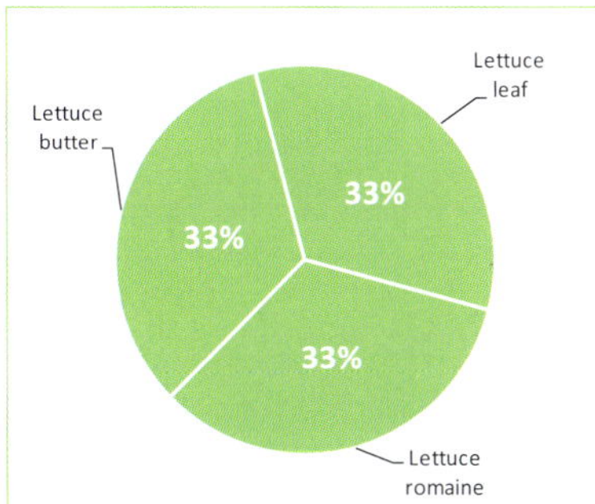

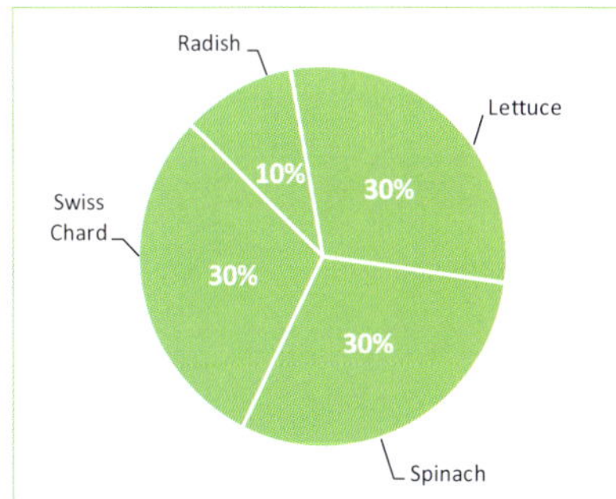

Variations within a circle plot: Example 2

Various members of the onion family can be planted, or various cultivars of peppers. Cross-pollination from insects can occur in peppers; therefore, saving and planting seeds may not produce desired results.

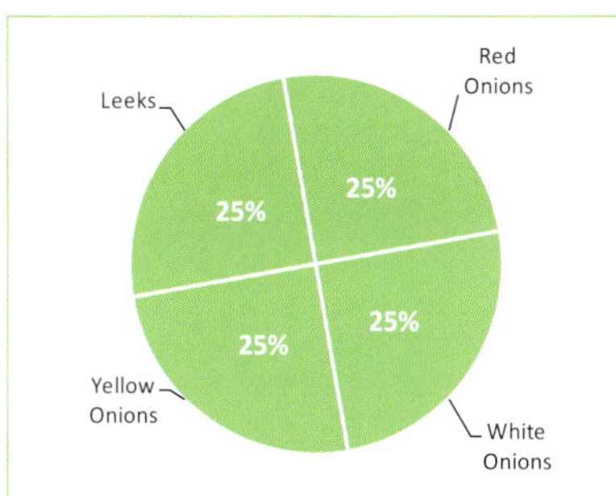

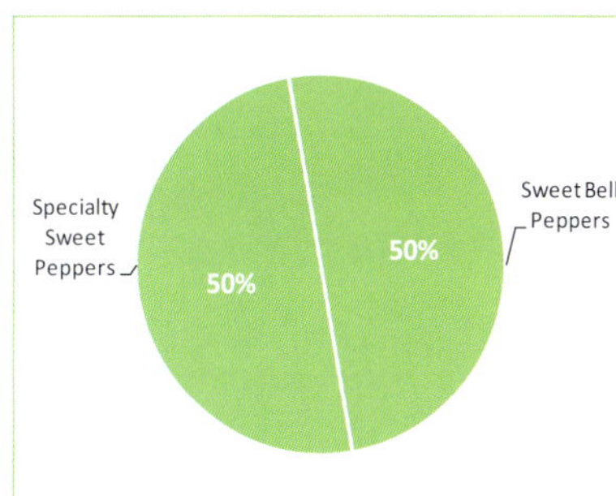

Variations within a circle plot: Example 3

Try different bean cultivars, or different squash cultivars. Cross-pollination in beans and squash (but not among beans and squash) can occur; therefore, saving and planting seeds may not produce desired results.

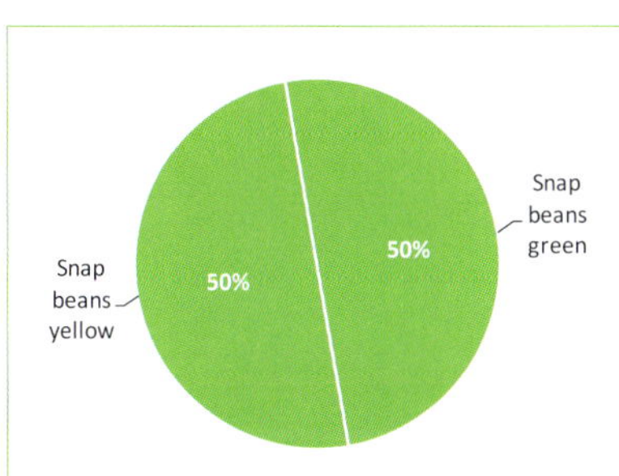

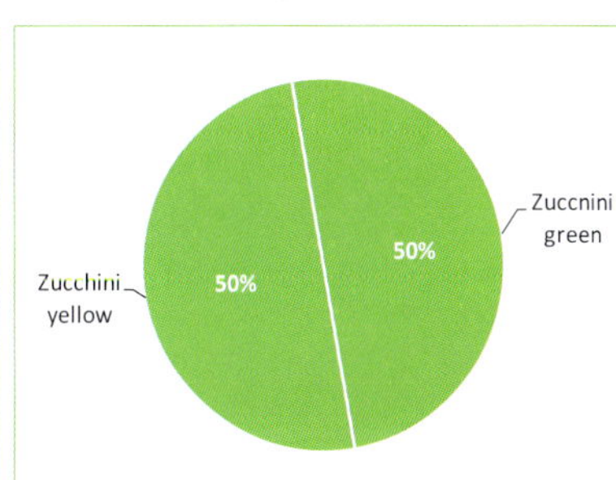

Intermediate Level

The next set of vegetables for intermediate-level vegetable gardeners to grow consists of beets, carrots, parsley or other herbs, parsnips, cabbage, broccoli, tomatoes, and corn. One or several cultivars can be planted. If you do not wish to start your own seedlings and transplants for peppers and the brassicas, you can purchase plants. If you need to conserve space in the garden, use bush squash cultivars. If space is not an issue, plant squash cultivars with a vining habit on outside plots.

In a 4-plot circle garden, any of the plants listed for the 2-plot arrangement can be used. A 4-plot arrangement could include a variety of choices. Use mulch to conserve water and prevent soil-borne diseases.

In a 6-plot circle garden, any of the arrangements listed below or in the examples on the next page could be used. A tomato plant (3 feet in diameter) could also be planted, or a circle of corn with the "Three Sisters" arrangement (corn, squash, beans). At the intermediate level, you can expand beyond 6 plots—experiment. Use mulch to conserve water and prevent soil-borne diseases.

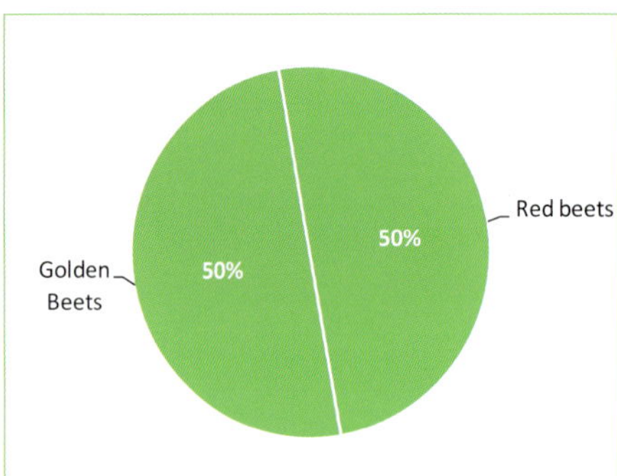

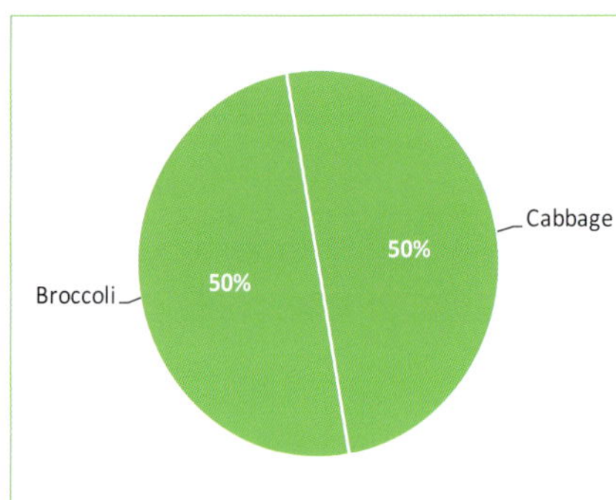

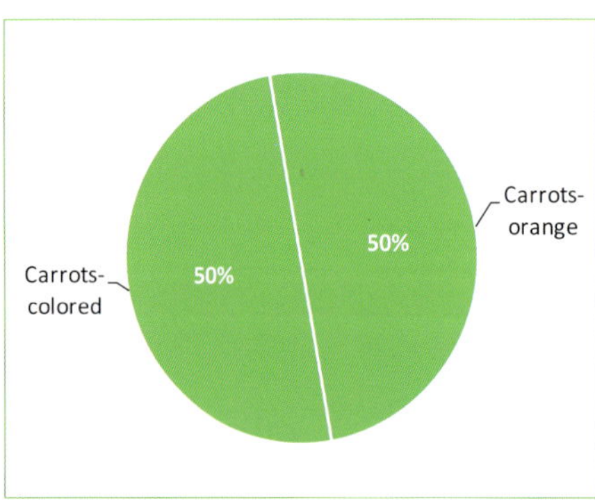

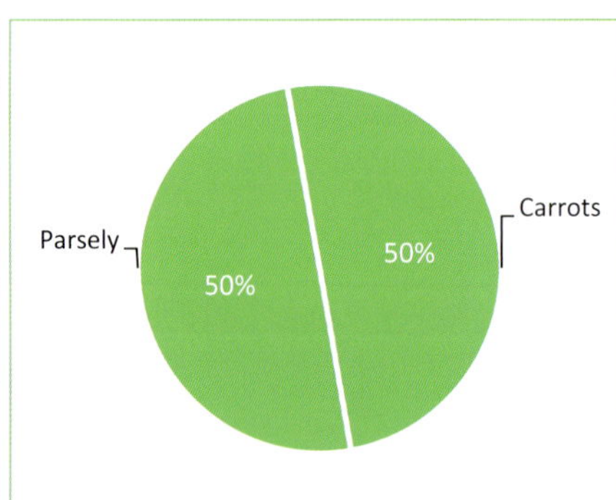

TABLE 14. Three examples of vegetable choices for a 4-plot circle garden

Example 1

Plot 1 choices	Plot 2 choices	Plot 3 choices	Plot 4 choices
⅓ leaf lettuce varieties, ⅓ spinach, ⅓ romaine or butterhead varieties	peppers*	summer squash, bush habit*	all broccoli or all cabbage, or ½ broccoli and ½ cabbage*

Example 2

Plot 1 choices	Plot 2 choices	Plot 3 choices	Plot 4 choices
⅓ lettuce leaf varieties, ⅓ spinach, ⅓ romaine or butterhead varieties	½ sweet bell peppers, ½ specialty sweet peppers*	summer squash, bush habit*	¼ red onions, ¼ white onions, ¼ yellow onions, ¼ leeks

Example 3

Plot 1 choices	Plot 2 choices	Plot 3 choices	Plot 4 choices
golden beets and red beets	broccoli and cabbage	orange carrots, vari-colored carrots, or 2 different varieties	parsley and carrots

*Use mulch to conserve water and prevent soil-borne diseases.

TABLE 15. Two examples of vegetable choices for a 6-plot circle garden

Example 1

Plot 1 choices	Plot 2 choices	Plot 3 choices	Plot 4 choices	Plot 5 choices	Plot 6 choices
⅓ leaf lettuce varieties, ⅓ spinach, ⅓ romaine or butterhead varieties. Can add some radishes.	½ sweet bell peppers, ½ specialty sweet peppers*	summer squash, bush habit*	¼ red onions, ¼ white onions, ¼ yellow onions, ¼ leeks	all broccoli or all cabbage, or ½ broccoli and ½ cabbage*	bush beans*

Example 2

Plot 1 choices	Plot 2 choices	Plot 3 choices	Plot 4 choices	Plot 5 choices	Plot 6 choices
⅓ leaf lettuce varieties, ⅓ spinach, ⅓ romaine or butterhead varieties. Can add some radishes.	½ sweet bell peppers, ½ specialty sweet peppers*	summer squash, bush habit*	corn* (try "Three Sisters" approach but without squash)	carrots or beets, assorted cultivars	1 tomato plant with cage or trellis*

*Use mulch to conserve water and prevent soil-borne diseases.

Advanced Vegetables

As we have discussed, there is some merit to using published information about easy- and hard-to-grow vegetables. Talent and a love for a specific vegetable can make a big difference. It is always possible that what is easy for one person is difficult for another, and vice versa. Climate and soil type really do play an important role in what vegetables are easy to grow in any particular location. Cucumbers, muskmelons, watermelons, winter squash, cauliflower, and eggplant are generally considered moderate to difficult for various reasons. For example, cucumbers are plagued by a number of diseases, need consistent moisture, seem to wilt easily, and develop bitter fruit when hot weather arrives. In Texas, I now grow cucumbers on a tent trellis cut from metal hog panels to prevent many diseases that plague this vegetable. Mulch seems to alleviate diseases related to soil splash. Muskmelons and watermelons require a lot of attention, and water balance is essential. Wildlife also enjoys melons. Often I put dry straw or hay under the fruits. Winter squash has a long growing season. Cauliflower requires diligence when the heads start forming and maturing, insects seem to arrive on schedule, and the bright sun causes discoloration of the heads. Gardeners will often tie some of the leaves over the heads to prevent sunscald and discoloration. See individual Vegetable Guides.

More-Complex Garden Designs

One common attribute of experienced gardeners is that they tend to venture into the unknown and enjoy a certain amount of challenge and experimentation. Generally you will see companion planting, herbs, flowers, berries, fruit trees, and, for the experienced, espalier fruit trees (fig. 26). The French grow an assortment of vegetables, herbs, fruits, and flowers in potager (poh-tah-ZHAY) gardens.

Mandala garden designs with keyhole paths offer unlimited opportunities to express your artistic and creative ideas in gardening designs. Search the Internet for intriguing designs. Visiting a botanical garden is a great pastime and can be inspiring. Be sure to bring a notebook and camera. Experienced gardeners and Master Gardeners may wish to expand their horizons. I have drawn out a plan using circle plots, fruit trees (dwarf and espalier designs), flowers, and berries. Creating diversity is the key to advanced designs.

You may have a desire to take or teach a Master Gardening class, attend a gardening show or series of gardening lectures, participate

Figure 26

FIGURE 26. Advanced potager vegetable garden design. Figure by author.

in and teach at community gardens, take a horticultural class at a university, visit and tour seed company facilities, paint or draw your garden, write poetry about it, join a local gardening club, or spend a year writing about your gardening techniques and philosophies (circle gardening, of all things!).

Experiment with such things as the following:

- Pushing the envelope on spring and fall planting dates.
- Trying different cultivars.
- Saving seeds.

- Breeding your own hybrids.
- Branching out to fruits and berries.
- Landscaping your garden with vegetables, flowers, fruits, and berries (potager garden).
- Building a root cellar.
- Buying or building a greenhouse.
- Experimenting with cold frames.
- Growing plants in a mobile greenhouse.
- Using floating row covers.
- Using low plastic tunnels (French chenilles) or tent cloches (movable covers, from the French for "bell").
- Learning about and using plant propagation.
- Learning about drip irrigation and equipment.
- Setting up a drip irrigation system in your garden.
- Writing articles for a gardening club, Master Gardener program, or garden publication.
- Teaching others.

FIGURE 27. Newly seeded circle plot with Swiss chard. Seeds are placed in concentric circles resembling a target. Plants should be thinned as they grow. Photo by author.

9

Planting and Soil Management

Planting Seeds

There are various techniques for planting seeds:

- In the circle gardening method, plant seeds in small trenches in concentric circles (like a target) and cover with a mixture of topsoil and fine compost.
- Very small seeds (lettuce, carrots, parsley, spinach, beets, Swiss chard) can be broadcast over the surface, raked gently, and sprinkled with a mixture of topsoil and fine compost. If your stand of seedlings is thick, you can thin them later. If a spotty stand emerges, just use your fingers to create a shallow trench and seed by hand.

I recommend seeding by hand in concentric circles (figs. 27 and 28), but do experiment with broadcasting lettuce, spinach, beets, carrots, and parsley. To achieve the concentric circles in figures 27 and 28, I scribe them with the handle of my hoe. Mark the center and start at a radius of 5 inches, then move out 10 inches, then another 10 inches. The total radius of the circle will be 25 inches; therefore, the diameter of the circle plot is 50 inches. Usually the depth of the scribed trenches is about 1 inch. You can adjust the depth of the trench with your fingers as you plant seeds. I kneel beside the circle plot and usually move twice to each side of the plot. Depending on the vegetable, adjust the depth of planting and distance between seeds as per spacing recommendations. I usually plant all my seeds one concentric circle at a time, and then when all the circle rings are completed I cover the seeds with soil to the recommended depth. Planting seeds by hand takes practice, and the small seeds can be challenging if you drop several in one spot. If this occurs, use your finger to spread them. Do not worry about being exact, as you can always thin the plants later.

One of the best new innovations in garden seeds is pelleted seeds. Pelleted seeds are now available from seed catalogs for many vegetables (lettuce, carrots, beets, onions, Swiss chard, basil, fennel, tomatoes, and some flowers). The seeds are coated with an inert material to increase their size, so they can be held in the fingers. The advantages of pelleted seeds are that (1) they are easier to plant and space; (2) heavy thinning is reduced; (3) you can see the seeds as you plant them, as they are usually white or colored; and (4) some pelleted seeds are primed during the pelleting process, which facilitates quicker germination and increases oxygen availability and penetration. The negative side of pelleting some vegetable seeds, such as lettuce, is that storage time is reduced. Lettuce seeds are notoriously short-lived anyway, so I do not see much of a problem.

After you plant seeds, keep the seedbed uniformly moist, but not overwet or saturated. The circle plot method uses a slightly mounded, convex shape; the center is elevated 5–6 inches and tapers down toward the edges to improve drainage. Some seedlings are delicate when they first germinate, and if the soil dries out for a short period without your notice, the seedlings can die. In Texas, if it is sunny and windy and temperatures start edging above 70°F, the soil surface can dry out quickly and newly germinated spinach, lettuce, beets, and carrot seedlings can wilt and die quickly. I gently water every day because I learned my lesson the hard way. One day you notice a nice stand emerging, and then you have 2–3 days of warm, windy, dry weather, and without irrigation, the fragile seedlings are gone. When it does not rain, a daily light watering with a delicate spray will prevent premature loss of your stand. For optimal germination, keep the seedbed moist. It is critical to be alert when young, fragile seedlings are germinating—look at your seedlings every day!

After the seedlings have developed a few leaves, you can start mulching with a fine compost. You can continue applications of compost for mulching as the plants develop and mature. I like to use the fines that fall to the bottom of my hay feeder that the goats ignore. For example, repeated additions of a soil/compost mix around leek stalks are a necessity. I depend on mulch to give the plants added sup-

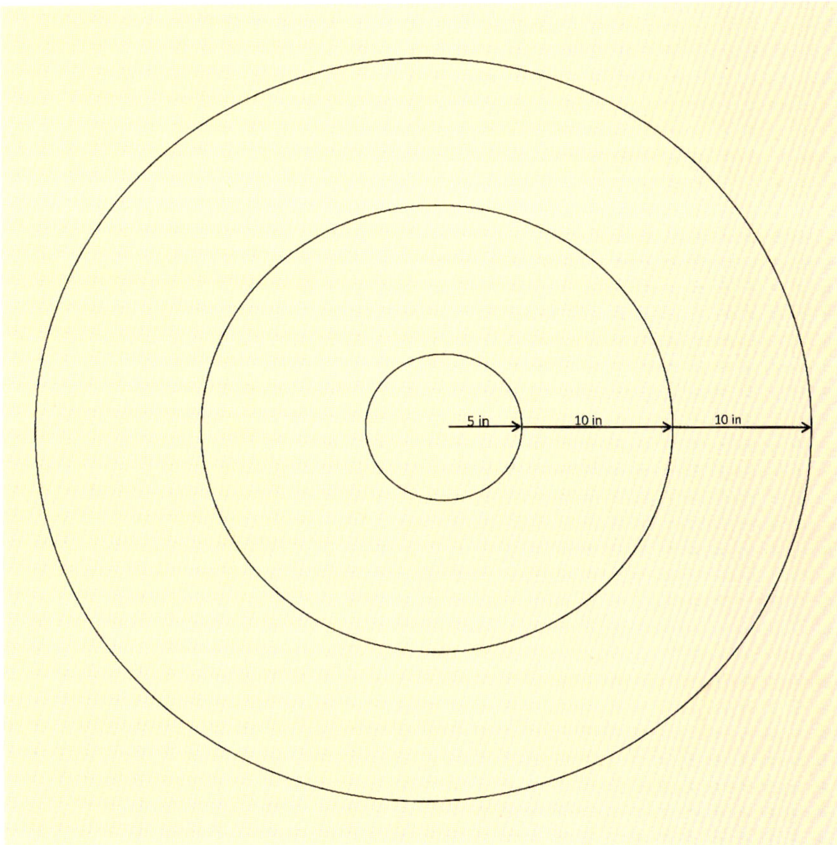

FIGURE 28. Scheme for lettuce in a 50-inch-diameter circle (≈ 14 square feet). Table 16 shows plant density (number of plants per ring) at spacings of 3, 6, and 12 inches. Spacing depends on the cultivar, type of lettuce (iceberg; butterhead, Bibb, or Boston; cos or romaine; leaf), and growing objectives, such as mature plants or baby greens. Figure by author.

TABLE 16. Number of plants in circle plot rings at various spacings

Distance from center of circle (inches)	Circumference of ring (inches)	Number of plants at various spacings		
		3 inches	6 inches	12 inches
5	31	10	5	3
15	94	31	16	8
25	157	52	26	13
Total plants		93	47	24

port and to protect the leaves and fruits from soil contact, reducing the chances of soil-borne fruit and leaf diseases. For example, in my pepper circles, I continually add mulches of spoiled and discarded hay from the barn. The mulch decomposes throughout the growing season as I water the plants. This creates a nice friable soil surface that optimizes infiltration capacity. Whether you seed by hand into a furrow or broadcast your seeds, you can always thin out plants or interseed in the gaps. Planting, weeding, and harvesting can be accomplished by sitting or kneeling next to the circle. The gardener needs to move only twice to each side, or three times for a larger circle plot, to accomplish the tasks of planting, thinning, and weeding.

Transplants

Transplanting established plants from pots is an efficient way to plant certain vegetables. If you buy transplants at a nursery, you will find that they are not always of equal quality from place to place. For example, if you walk up to a rack of transplants at a store and see wilted, spindly, yellowish, or pale green plants (in either shade or sun), go elsewhere. Do not take it for granted that your local vendor is selling cultivars that are best adapted to your area—do your homework and have a list of the best cultivar names. If you are cost conscious or want to plant adapted cultivars, starting your own transplants from seeds is the best idea. If you want to start your own transplants, you have several options of where to start them: (1) indoors with grow lights, (2) outside in a cold frame, (3) in a portable or permanent greenhouse, or (4) outside in full sunlight. There are many options for indoor lighting systems; check reputable seed companies, as they usually have a large selection. Many seed companies now offer many options of portable cold frames and minigreenhouses.

Starting Transplants

In the individual Vegetable Guides, I have included detailed specific information about starting and caring for transplants. Some vegetables do best when planted as a transplant, others by direct seeding. The brassicas (cabbage, cauliflower, broccoli, brussels sprouts, collards, and kale), peppers, tomatoes, and eggplants do best as transplants. Cucumbers, squash, melons, beans, peas, corn, spinach, lettuce, Swiss chard, beets, and carrots should be seeded directly into the garden. I have seen these plants in pots for sale at nurseries, but I do not recommend that you buy and plant transplants for this group of vegetables. One reason is the expense, and another is that many of these transplants are often spindly and weak and have a difficult time "hardening off." I have found that squash and cucumber plants may not do well as transplants, as they are extremely sensitive to any root disturbance. What is "hardening off" in the vegetable world? It is simply the process of plants adjusting to the natural environment: outside temperatures, full sun, natural precipitation patterns, and wind.

The biggest challenges to growing your own transpants are (1) starting from seeds, (2) providing the optimal environment, and (3) hardening off the plants. There are many different methods for starting seeds, as I mentioned above. It is a matter of preference. I have tried planting seeds and growing transplants indoors with various lighting systems, outside in a cold frame or in portable plastic minigreenhouses, and outside in full sunlight. Your climate will partially dictate which methods work better than others. In early spring, I have had consistent results with planting seeds such as the brassicas (cabbage, cauliflower, and broccoli) outside in full sun in 4-inch, half-gallon, and 1-gallon pots. Sometimes when freezing temperatures are imminent, I cover the pots with clear plastic. In my southern climate, I let nature determine when they germinate. The only time I move plants is when a frost threatens; then I move them into a shed or garage until the frost passes. For frost-sensitive plants such as tomatoes, peppers, and eggplants, I place the pots in a portable plastic cold frame. Many different styles are available in seed catalogs, or you can improvise and build one.

I like the gallon pot because there is more than enough soil to sustain even moisture, the plants can grow larger, and when you move the plants out to the garden there is less transplant shock. If you use 2- or 4-inch pots, the soil can dry out quickly and seedlings can become desiccated, wilt, and possibly die if you are not tending to them every day. The gallon pots give you more room for error—a day or two of warmer weather will not dry the gallon pot of soil to the point where the plant suffers. Some nurseries give away these pots, and I save them from plants that I have bought at the nursery for the flower beds.

Starting your own vegetable transplants from seeds requires a good fertile potting medium. I usually buy an organic potting medium for starting flowers and vegetables. Sometimes I mix the potting medium with some of my own compost (I used this method for the plants in fig. 29). You can also include a small amount of slow-release fertilizer if the potting mix does not contain added nitrogen, phos-

FIGURE 29. *A*, Tomato; *B*, *C*, pepper; *D*, broccoli. These transplants were seeded outdoors in 4-inch, 1-gallon, and 2-gallon pots and allowed to adjust to natural weather conditions. Photos by author.

A

B

C

D

phorus, and potassium. I have found by experience that potting mixes with slow-release fertilizer do not have enough nutrients for certain plants like tomatoes, peppers, eggplants, broccoli, cabbage, and cauliflower. As these plants grow, I use a small amount of diluted liquid organic fertilizer. There is no hard-and-fast rule. I use the color and stature of the plants as a guide. If my tomatoes appear to be on the light green side and somewhat spindly, I increase the frequency of the liquid fertilizer. Many starter fertilizer formulations are low in nitrogen, phosphorus, and potassium and contain micronutrients (e.g., 3-0-4, 6-4-4, 4-2-6, 4-5-3, etc.). You must be careful not to overdose your plants—go slow with fertilizers even if they are organic. If your plants seem thin stemmed and fall over easily, they are probably lacking in one or more essential nutrients and/or are not receiving enough light. Your plants should appear strong and sturdy as they grow (fig. 29).

Hardening off your transplants requires some improvisation. The goal is to gradually acclimate your plants to the rigors of your climate and to full sun so they can be moved to the garden with a minimum of shock. If done correctly, growing strong plants in larger

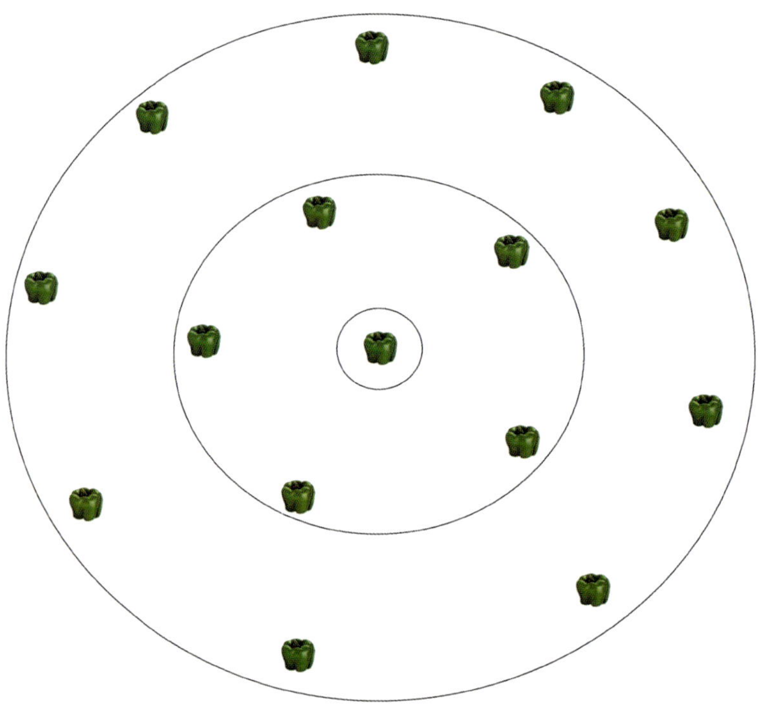

FIGURE 30. Diagram of circle plot (5-foot diameter) for pepper transplants. Spacing between plants in rings is approximately 18 inches. Figure by author.

TABLE 17. Number of plants in circle plot rings at different spacings

Distance from center of circle (inches)	Circumference of ring (inches)	Number of plants at different spacings	
		14 inches	18 inches
14	88	6	5
28	176	12	10
Total plants		18	15

pots, hardening off the plants so they can tolerate full sunlight, and minimizing disturbance to the roots when planting out in the garden will result in almost no transplant shock. The hardening-off process requires gradual movement from a less harsh environment to partial sun, then full sun. Sometimes I use portable plastic greenhouses, and when I remove the plants from that protected environment, I locate them on the north side of the house or in another shady spot for 2–3 days. Then I move them to a location with more light for 2–3 days (usually full sun). I then wait for cloudy skies; this is a good time to move them out to the open garden. If the weather changes and there is full sun, you can always cover the plants with the pot or a fabric covering. If the transplant has been hardened off properly, it should be able to withstand partial to full sunshine. The whole process of hardening off is a slow, systematic procedure. Gradual changes are the rule for hardening off transplants!

Several days before setting out the hardened plant, decrease watering but do not let the plant completely dry out. When I am ready to move transplants to the garden, I wait for an overcast day. Planting transplants is simple with the circle gardening method. Check spacing data for the vegetable, plant around the outside of the circle, and then move inward accordingly (fig. 30). For example, in figure 30, I decided on 18-inch spacing for pepper plants. Refer back to chapter 3 on the ecology of planting in a clumped arrangement.

Dig a hole larger and deeper than the pot and root ball and place some compost and organic fertilizer in the hole. Then cover the fertilizer with about 2–3 inches of soil. Remove the plant gently from the pot, try not to disturb the roots, and try to keep the entire soil-root mass intact. If you used a good potting medium, the roots should be well developed and should hold the soil intact. Place the plant in the hole so the level of the soil in the pot is slightly below the soil level in the garden. I leave a slight depression around the plant so the soil forms a moat to prevent runoff during watering. I always mulch around my transplants to prevent soil splash onto the leaves, for both disease prevention and water conservation (fig. 31).

Companion Planting

Creating plant diversity and applying companion planting concepts in your garden have many advantages: aesthetics, attracting pollinators, birds, and beneficial insects, and repelling and deterring pests. Although commercial farming operations are somewhat limited in creating plant diversity in crop fields, home vegetable gardeners can avoid monocultures, which create an environment where your plants are more susceptible to pests, as in larger patches of corn, squash, pumpkins, and watermelons. Even if your soil is healthy and organically rich, the dynamics of planting in monocultures can supersede your efforts. In the garden ecology chapter, I mentioned that we can strive to create a well-balanced garden ecosystem and hope for relative harmony in the garden, but there is never true equilibrium. There is always that tug-of-war that involves soil organisms—pathogenic and nonpathogenic soil bacteria, fungi, and nematodes—as well as climatic fluctuations that affect plant physiology and development, and plant competition between the same (intraspecific) and different (interspecific) species for water, light, and nutrients. Even in your garden ecosystem, the environmental complexity is beyond comprehension. As gardeners, we strive for relative equilibrium and employ all the tools at our disposal such as improving soil health, fertilizing, irrigating, using adapted cultivars, planting heirlooms and hybrids, and doing companion planting. Many gardeners use companion planting as a means to exploit allelopathic and phytotoxic traits. Allelopathy is a form of chemical competition in which plants release allelochemicals by leaching root exudates or volatile compounds from leaves, stems, fruits, or litter residues in order to inhibit growth of the same or other plant species. Vegetable plants such as eggplant, tomato, cucumber, muskmelon, and watermelon as well as rice, sorghum, and sugarcane have allelopathic properties.

Is there a scientific basis for companion planting? There are numerous popular publications and books on this subject; however, scientific reviews find that most of the literature is tied to a few references with limited scientific support. Figure 31 is a compilation of the most common plant associations found in the popular literature. Be aware that science has not been able to substantiate common linkages and mechanisms associated with companion planting. Many science publications mention that compatibility of vegetable plants is based on anecdotal information (gardener observations). However, many popular publications recommend that this should not be a deterrent to experimentation in the home garden. In the book *Carrots Love Tomatoes*, Louise Riotte states: "All the suggestions given in this book for companion planting are only a beginning . . . your own experiments will lead you into many exciting pathways and discoveries."

Although companion planting is a popular practice and idea among gardeners, I stress that there are other "housekeeping" chores that should be practiced first: improving soil health, using compost, rotating vegetable species, mulching plants, growing cover crops during winter, selecting adapted cultivars and varieties (both heirlooms and hybrids—both may have unique disease-resistant properties in your garden), and increasing diversity with mixtures of flowers and other vegetable crops. You can grow plants such as marigolds, nasturtiums, mint, rosemary, basil, alliums, lavender, lemongrass, and geraniums in pots and move them around the garden. As I delve into the literature on companion planting and the insect-repellent properties of some of the plants listed above, I unfortunately find little supporting scientific documentation.

Is competition greater or less in resource-rich versus resource-poor environments? In the home garden, the latter would most likely resemble a soil with low organic matter and macronutrients (nitrogen, phosphorus, and potassium). One hypothesis predicts that competition is less influential in resource-poor compared to resource-rich environments, while an alternative hypothesis predicts that competition will be similar in resource-poor and resource-rich environments. During the early growth of plants, their germination, emergence, and initial root and shoot development may be especially sensitive to competition; small seedlings may show more sensitivity to competition than mature plants. However, other research shows that competition may be relatively uncommon after germination but may become more critical as plants mature.

Plant competition theories in the scientific literature are not clear or consistent. Personally, I do not think a consistent plant competition model will emerge, because plant communities around the world are unique and are always adapting to new stresses and perturbations. Perhaps intraspecific and interspecific competition, competitive exclusion, and coexistence mechanisms shift as plants and the community as a whole adapt to stressors. As we contemplate the dynamics and complexity of competition, can we ever be sure whether companion planting among vegetable species—each originating from different regions of the globe, belonging to different plant families (fig. 32), and growing close together—actually enhances the growth of each species?

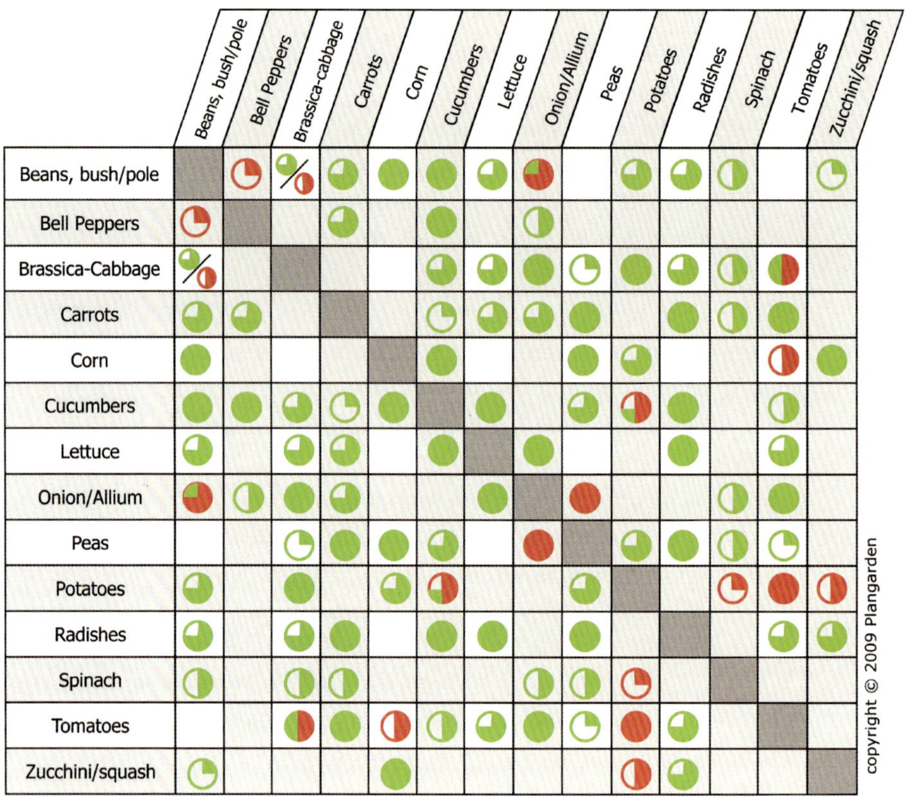

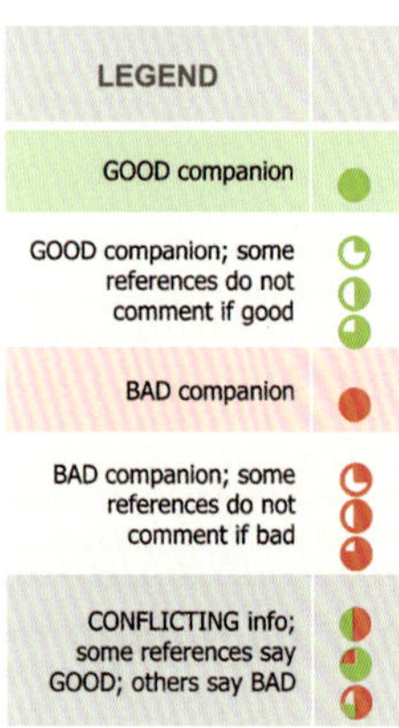

FIGURE 31. Synopsis of companion planting schemes. Plangarden.com, https://plangarden.wordpress.com/tag/companion-planting/.

SCIENCE NOTE • Theories of Plant Competition and Implications for Companion Planting

This science note is included as a further discussion of companion planting. Scientists have produced a number of conceptual models that try to explain plant competition dynamics in plant communities; however, none of them are clear and concise. In nature, organisms grow, reproduce, and die and must compete for life-sustaining resources. No organism lives in isolation, and plants compete for water, light, nutrients, and space. Plant competition is a primary ecological process and denotes a sense of negativism, plants directly or indirectly impacting one another. The main concepts that dominate and pervade the literature are intraspecific competition, interspecific competition, competitive exclusion, coexistence, and symmetrical or asymmetrical competition. Intraspecific competition implies that more closely related species are less likely to coexist; the idea is that individuals of the same species share similar resource requirements. Interspecific competition in natural plant communities focuses on competition between different species. Competitive exclusion considers that two species, evenly distributed and with limited resources, cannot coexist for extended periods. Competitive exclusion may be avoided if the species either develop or have different requirements (e.g., niche differentiation—deeper versus shallower roots, plants requiring high-intensity versus filtered light, larger versus smaller leaves—or differentiation in adapting to varying moisture levels in the soil, or in the ability of a plant to maintain internal water balance). Coexistence is necessary if two or more species are to survive; natural selection in the plant community coincides with maintaining balance for the same contested resources. Niche segregation can be symmetrical or asymmetrical and usually refers to how plant species evolve away from each other and adapt to unique niches or locations in their communities.

Importance of Maintaining Moisture Levels in Circle Plots

Begin watering as soon as you have finished planting seeds or setting out transplants. Keeping a consistent moisture level is important during this time. Avoid periods of wetness followed by days of dryness in your seedbeds. Keep the soil moist, but not saturated, until the seeds germinate. Uneven moisture will affect germination, and

FIGURE 32. Centers of origin of common crop plants. Courtesy of USDA, 2007, General Accounting Office, Washington, DC.

a poor stand of plants can result. Maintaining adequate moisture for transplants can be enhanced by mulch (fig. 33). After transplants have taken root and hardened off in their new environment, they are more resilient to drier soil conditions.

Maintaining consistent moisture is the key to a successful result in the vegetable garden. When seedlings and transplants are well established and growing, try to soak the soil to a depth of 12–18 inches. Some garden guides recommend an inch of water per week, but there are so many variables that can negate this recommendation: with sandy-textured soil, temperatures over 90°F, and dry, windy, hot conditions, an inch of water per week will not be sufficient. You can always dig down into the soil and check the moisture condition. In Texas, when temperatures rise to over 95°F, I have to water about every day, even with a mulch cover around the plants. During very hot conditions, it is difficult to maintain adequate moisture.

During some summers in Texas, I have had to abandon watering plants that require a lot of water, such as potatoes and corn. My water supply comes from a well, and there are limitations. A simple irrigation system can be set up with half-inch polypipe tubing, quarter-inch microtubing, a T barb or 4-way barb, and a connector to half-inch polypipe for a garden hose attachment (fig. 34). I place the microtubing in the circle plot (open ended) in various configurations. One T barb will host two microtubes; use 2 T barbs with 4

FIGURE 33. Kale, about 3 weeks after transplant. Mulch helps prevent diseases and conserves water. Photo by author.

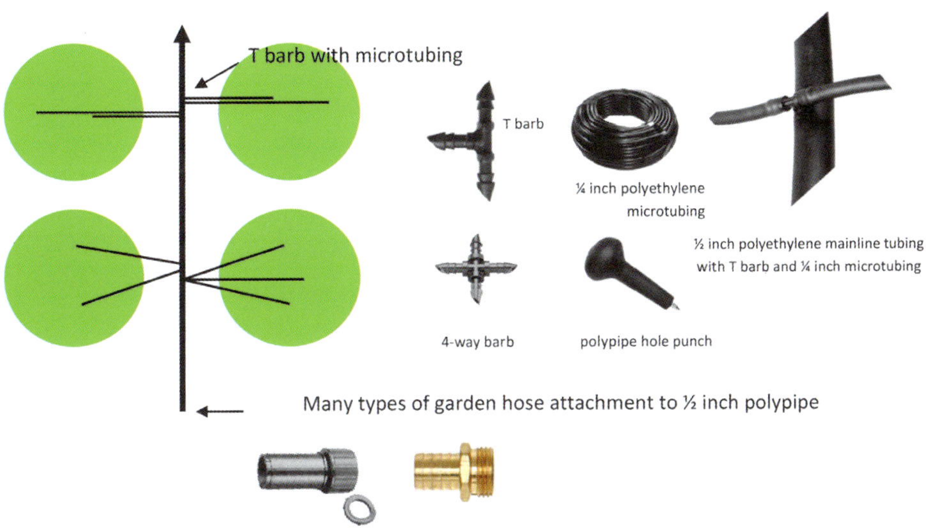

FIGURE 34. Simple drip irrigation scheme with basic needed parts. Figure by author.

microtubes if you want to water circle plots in a shorter time. Timers can be set up on your water spigot or hydrant.

Remember the following important points about irrigating and watering plants:

- Water in the early morning.
- Do not use overhead sprinklers.
- Water in and around the plants; avoid wetting the leaves.
- Use drip irrigation.
- Avoid flooding and excessive runoff.

Maintaining Essential Soil Nutrients

Throughout the year, the vegetable gardener can maintain and enhance soil nutrients by making and using compost, applying fertilizers, and growing cover crops, especially legumes. Seventeen basic essential soil elements are needed for plant growth; they are categorized as macronutrients and micronutrients, or trace elements. Nine of the elements are macronutrients, and they are used in higher quantities than micronutrients. Carbon, hydrogen, oxygen, nitrogen, phosphorus, potassium, calcium, magnesium, and sulfur are macronutrients. More than 90% of plant tissue is made of carbon, hydrogen, and oxygen. Nitrogen, phosphorus, and potassium make up about 1.5% of plant dry weight and are required by plants in relatively high amounts. Three secondary macronutrients—calcium, magnesium, and sulfur—are also important to plants. They are required in lesser amounts than nitrogen, phosphorus, and potassium, but in greater amounts than the micronutrients.

Eight micronutrients that vegetable species use in minute and different amounts (parts per million, or ppm) include iron (Fe), boron (B), manganese (Mn), copper (Cu), zinc (Zn), molybdenum (Mo), nickel (Ni), and chlorine (Cl). A few more elements related to plant growth have now been identified, including cobalt (Co), vanadium (V), sodium (Na), and silicon (Si), although not all plants utilize them. The elements iron, manganese, copper, zinc, boron, nickel, chlorine, cobalt, and molybdenum are necessary but are required in very low amounts. Iron and magnesium are the most abundant micronutrients in the Earth's crust. The remaining six trace elements occur in minute amounts (less than 70 ppm for zinc; the rarest is molybdenum, at 1.5 ppm). The micronutrients are an odd assortment of elements: boron is a light (low molecular weight) nonmetal; iron, manganese, copper, nickel, and cobalt are all metals in the first transition group on the periodic chart of elements (metallic elements); molybdenum is a heavy metal in the second transition group; and chlorine is a toxic greenish-yellow halide gas. With respect to micronutrients, too much or too little can have undesirable effects on plants. For home gardeners, supplemental additions of fish emulsion or meal can provide trace elements that may be lacking in the soil.

Soil tests for the two main macronutrients, phosphorus and potassium, can determine current levels and recommendations if needed. Sometimes nitrogen may be included in lab tests, but the results are usually of limited use because nitrogen levels in soil change with temperature, moisture, activity of microorganisms, and breakdown of organic matter. In the home vegetable garden, especially new garden sites, soil tests can provide a useful baseline for the main macronutrients, pH, and organic matter. Generally, tests for micronutrients are not recommended because of their variable concentrations in the soil, testing limitations, and complex interactions. However, soil labs can provide tests for calcium and magnesium, as well as extractable (available) zinc, manganese, and copper. Sulfur, boron, and iron tests may also be available. Leaf tissue samples, taken around the base of the plants, can provide information about possible micronutrient deficiencies. Soil testing laboratories often offer plant tissue analyses. Before adding any micronutrients to your soil, check with your local extension service for advice about possible micronutrient deficiencies in your particular area. My recommendation is to first evaluate the health and vigor of your plants. Try to rule out disease (especially viral) and verify that soil pH, nitrogen, phosphorus, and potassium are adequate and in balance. Then, if supplements from soil amendments do not remedy problems like yellowish leaves (chlorosis), olive or pale green coloration, bluish tints, yellow streaking in the leaves, or stunted and nonvigorous plants, you may need to consult with local experts about micronutrient deficiencies and send samples for analysis. Foliar-applied micronutrients can be absorbed through plant leaves, but they provide a temporary fix, whereas micronutrient applications to the soil provide a more continuous and lasting solution.

Nitrogen

Our atmosphere contains 78% gaseous nitrogen (N_2), a virtually endless reservoir. Nitrogen is a colorless, odorless, tasteless, and mostly inert gas. An inert gas does not undergo chemical change easily. Most nitrogen in terrestrial environments is found in the soil surface, but the amount still ranges from only 0.2 to 0.5% (the average in cultivated soils is 0.15%). In plant communities, the main limiting factors for plant growth are water, nitrogen, other nutrients, and light. The reason gaseous nitrogen is inert and not directly available to plants is the strong triple bond between nitrogen atoms (N≡N). The two main processes that are able to break the triple bond in nature are lightning and soil microbes. Nitrates (NO_{3-}) are formed during lightning strikes and are transported to Earth with precipitation. Biological nitrogen fixation by microbes (a few species of bacteria and blue-green algae) converts atmospheric N_2 to usable forms. Plant roots take up the microbial products as dissolved nitrate and ammonium ions (NH_{4+}). Some plants prefer one or the other of these ions, but most plants grow well with a balanced mixture of the two. Plants can also use soluble proteins and amino acids of low molecular weight. When mineralized nitrogen and soluble organic nitrogen sources are equally available in the soil, plants utilize a smaller fraction of the soluble organic nitrogen. During uptake of NH_{4+}, plants release hydrogen ions (H_+) to maintain electrical neutrality, which lowers the pH around the roots, while NO_{3-} has the tendency to raise it.

Many plants in the legume family (peas, beans, alfalfa, clover, vetch) develop a symbiosis (mutually beneficial association) with *Rhizobium* and *Bradyrhizobium* bacteria that penetrate root hairs, which causes the formation of root nodules where biological nitrogen fixation takes place. Many legumes require specific species of bacteria—for example, *Rhizobium leguminosarum* biovar *trifolii* inoculates clovers; *Rhizobium leguminosarum* biovar *phaseoli* inoculates string, snap, kidney, and wax beans; *Rhizobium leguminosarum* biovar *viciae* inoculates garden peas, field peas, fava beans, and lentils; and *Sinorhizobium meliloti* inoculates alfalfa and sweet clover. Usually the natural *Rhizobium* population in soils is low; therefore, it is beneficial to inoculate garden legumes with the proper commercially prepared inoculant (available in seed catalogs). Nonleguminous plants (about 200 species) can also develop nodules and fix nitrogen. Most of these plants inhabit forests and wetlands, but they do not include any common vegetable species that I know of. There are other anomalous organisms in nature that are associated with nitrogen fixation: cyanobacteria, the *Spirillum* and *Azotobacter* bacterial genera, and some anaerobic bacteria of the genus *Clostridium*.

Phosphorus

After nitrogen, phosphorus (P) is the second most important element in terrestrial and aquatic ecosystems. Phosphorus concentrations in soil are typically low and largely unavailable to plants because of several reasons: (1) low concentrations in the minerals that are part of the soil parent material, (2) the extent of weathering and leaching, and (3) the formation of phosphorus-containing compounds, which are not readily soluble. Phosphorus becomes available through the mineralization process of organic compounds and through the addition of fertilizers.

Phosphorus is fundamental to the life processes and other aspects of plants: photosynthesis, nitrogen fixation, flowering, seed production and fruiting, root growth, structural tissues in stems, and crop quality (cereals and vegetables). In plant tissues, phosphorus content ranges between 0.1 and 0.4%. Phosphorus migrates to areas of active growth in the plant, such as new leaves and stem tips. Legumes contain higher amounts of phosphorus than nonleguminous plants. Farmers who grow alfalfa and other legumes need to bring phosphorus up to required levels during preparation of the seedbed before the crop is planted. Since phosphorus is insoluble and very little is dissolved in the soil water matrix (usually less than 1 ppm), it is usually necessary to add it in fertilizer form. It is beneficial to add needed phosphorus in advance of planting time. In many soils, phosphorus availability to plants depends on the solubility of mineral compounds containing it (fluorapatite, apatite). One negative aspect of applying phosphorus to cropland soils is that only about 20% of it is used by plants, and the remainder is bound up in the soil. When phosphorus is applied, plants do not need the phosphorus supplied by mycorrhizal fungi; therefore, the fungal relationship is affected, the partnership declines, and the mycorrhizal fungi die off.

Soil organic matter is the predominant source of phosphorus in humid regions. Phosphorus is pH dependent and is restricted at soil pH of less than 6.2 (see fig. 36). Increasing acidity causes the phosphate ions to change to sulfuric acid. Phosphorus also interacts with iron and aluminum compounds that are particularly stable and unavailable to plants under acidic conditions. Adding organic matter and raising the pH with lime can improve phosphorus availability.

An assortment of organic and synthetic fertilizers contain phosphorus (see the "Fertilizers" section later in this chapter). Table 18 shows the average times needed and the amount of nitrogen released by common organic materials. Generally, organic forms of phosphorus (bone meal, raw rock phosphate) become available slowly and are highly insoluble in water. Most phosphorus in manure, more than 75%, is inorganic. For example, about 85% of the phosphorus in feedlot cow manure is available the first year during application, and in composted manure about 73% is available (table 19). Synthetic fertilizers containing phosphorus can provide it relatively fast. Organic gardeners and farmers must rely on long-term applications of organic matter and organic forms of phosphorus.

Potassium

The element potassium (K) is found in minerals such as mica and feldspar, which are common in soil parent materials throughout the world, and in illite, which originates from marine deposits. Plants are heavy users of potassium; they use up to 5 to 10 times more potassium than phosphorus. Plant requirements for potassium and nitrogen are about equal. Plants also tend to remove more potassium from the soil than is actually needed for their metabolism. Potassium is largely removed from the soil resource when crops are harvested from fields and timber is harvested from forests.

Potassium is involved in many plant processes:

- Activates about 60 different enzymes used in plant growth and photosynthesis.
- Is essential for regulating water balance in plants—the opening and closing of stomata.
- Transports water and nutrients in the plant (xylem and phloem).
- Is used in protein synthesis in plant tissues.
- Activates the production of starch (sugars in plants).
- Affects the physical quality of the plant, its yield, and its disease resistance.

How available is potassium in the soil?

About 90 to 98% of the potassium in soil is largely unavailable. The unavailable forms of potassium are in a mineral structure and are slowly available from secondary minerals. On average, only 1 to 2% of soil potassium is available for plants. In most soils, except those with high sand content, total potassium is not the limiting factor for plant growth; it is the rate of change from unavailable to available forms. Available potassium in a soil solution can be lost via leaching (percolation downward into deeper soil layers) and from runoff during rainfall. The potential loss of potassium by leaching and erosion greatly exceeds the loss of nitrogen and phosphorus. The availability of potassium is affected when pH levels reach moderate to strong acidity. In strongly acidic soils, hydrogen ions and hydroxyl aluminum ions are tightly bound to soil colloids, thus preventing potassium availability on the colloid surfaces.

Organic Matter and Nitrogen Deficit

In organic gardening and farming, it is important to know how fast nitrogen from organic sources becomes available to your plants. Nitrogen from some organic fertilizers (manure and compost) is often not immediately available, and applications can have a minimal effect on crop growth during that year because of the slow release of organically bound nitrogen and dependence on environmental factors such as temperature, soil moisture, soil microorganisms, and the characteristics of the organic matter. Release of nitrogen from organic sources involves the biological process of microbial decomposition. Since biological processes are involved with the breakdown and mineralization of organic residues, nitrogen release from organic materials during the growing season is difficult to predict. Mineralization is the biological process in which soil microorganisms decompose (break down) organic nitrogen from an organic source material (plants, manure, or other organic sources). Mineralization depends on several factors such as inherent soil properties, temperature, soil moisture, and the chemical properties of the organic material. The percentage of nitrogen content, time for mineralization, and amount of nitrogen released are highly variable in decomposed manure and compost. The nutrient content of compost is highly dependent on the inherent materials. Various studies show that feedlot cow and dairy manure can range from 0.5 to 2.0% nitrogen, and availability of nitrogen the first year ranges from 9 to 40% of the total nitrogen content.

Why is the carbon-to-nitrogen ratio important in organic gardening and farming?

Incorporating organic matter with high carbon and low nitrogen content will create problems for plant growth, unless nitrogen is balanced by additions of fertilizer (organic or synthetic). In completing the nitrogen cycle during the decomposition process, soil microbes use nitrogen. If sufficiently high nitrogen is not available in the organic material and fertilizer is not used to balance the system, microbes will use mineralized nitrogen from the soil. The higher the carbon-to-nitrogen ratio, the less nitrogen in the source material and the greater the likelihood of a nitrogen deficit. The end result of a nitrogen deficit is poor plant growth and production.

Table 19 shows the average percentage of nitrogen, phosphorus, and potassium that is released and available from common organic materials. Nitrogen compounds in manure are slowly converted to available nitrate, and release during decomposition is gradual. For example, on average only about 35% of mineralized nitrogen is available from raw feedlot manure during the first year, or year of application. The rate subsequently decreases to 15% the second year, 6% the third year, and 2% the fourth year (table 19). Mineralization of composted cow manure is slower on average than that of raw manure: 20% the first year, 8% the second year, 4% the third year, and 1% the fourth year (table 19). In the application of raw cow manure as a nitrogen source, adjustments must be made to meet target applications because manure is still undergoing decomposition and nitrogen is still undergoing mineralization. As a comparison, for synthetic mineral fertilizers such as ammonium nitrate (33% nitrogen), about 50%–80% (average 60%) of the nitrate is readily available as it dissolves in soil water. On average, phosphorus and potassium from some common organic materials such as compost and manure are more readily available the first year of application (table 19).

TABLE 18. Average time needed and amount of nitrogen released by common organic materials

Organic material	Time needed (weeks)	Avg. % nitrogen in material	Avg. % nitrogen released
Urea*	12	46	91–96
Blood meal	12–26	11–12.6	56–75
Feedlot cow manure (raw)	26	0.5–2.5	30–40
Dairy manure (composted)	10–19	0.5–2.0	5.5–20
Poultry manure (decomposed)	12–26	1.8	37–53
Alfalfa pellets	12	3.6	41–52
Yard trimmings (composted woody and grassy materials)	6–19	1.7	4.75
Pelleted organic fish fertilizer	17–19	9.7	77
Rabbit manure	17–19	3.0	63
Rabbit manure (composted)	6–19	1.8	15–19

Sources: Gale et al. (2006); Brady and Weil (1996).

Note: The percentage of nitrogen in organic materials varies among studies.

*Urea is a naturally occurring organic compound, but it is also chemically synthesized.

TABLE 19. Percentages of available N, P, and K released by microbial mineralization for various organic materials

Organic material	Avg. total % N, dry wt.	Avg. % release N, year 1	Avg. % release N, year 2	Avg. % release N, year 3	Avg. % release N, year 4
Feedlot cow manure	0.5–2.5	35	15	6	2
Composted cow manure	0.5–2	20	8	4	1
Poultry floor litter	4.4	50	15	8	3
Fresh dairy manure	0.5–2.1	25	18	9	4
Swine manure	2.1	82	3	1	—

Organic material	Available P %, year 1
Garden compost	30–51
Beef feedlot manure	80–85
Composted feedlot manure	73
Manures in general	> 70
	Available K %, year 1
Dairy compost	73–90
Higher-N animal manures	> 98

Source: Gale et al. (2006); Brady and Weil (1996).
Note: These rates are averages and are somewhat variable because of climate and the types of feed given to the animals. The percentage of nitrogen in organic materials varies among studies.

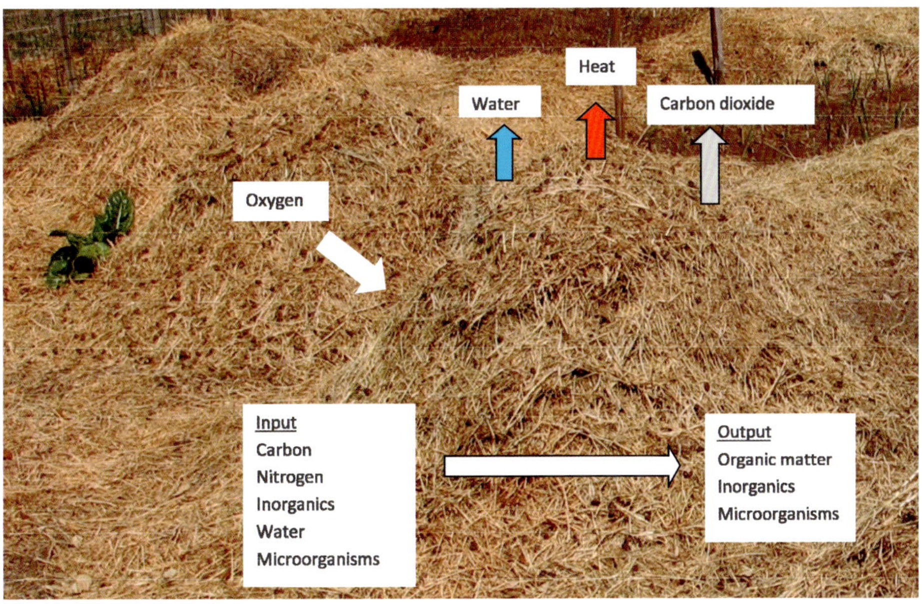

FIGURE 35. Making compost in situ. Set up compost piles in late summer or fall (or anytime) and let nature do its work until spring arrives. Compost can be made at any time of the year when temperatures are above 50°F. Build materials over the entire circle plot (3½ to 5 feet in diameter is sufficient) to a height of about 3 feet. Figure by author.

Compost and Composting

Whether you use organic methods or an integrated approach to farming and gardening, your garden will improve significantly with regular annual additions of compost. Composting yard and barn wastes is a practical and convenient way to deal with these materials. The advantages of using compost include increased water-holding capacity, improved soil structure and friability, enhanced biological properties, and the addition of slow-release plant nutrients. All these factors add up to improved soil health. Depending on the materials you use to make compost, it is usually low in nitrates and ammonium, the two nitrogen compounds that are used by plants. Most garden compost made from litter, and manure from horses, cattle, and hogs, has a total nitrogen content of 0.5 to 0.7% and a moisture content of 50% or more. Composts made with poultry manure can contain up to 1.5% total nitrogen. On a dry weight basis, total nitrogen content of these various composts will be slightly higher (up to 3.5%). Phosphates and potassium are present in compost, but at low levels (usually from 0.5 to 2.0%). Nutrient release from compost is slow but steady over several years (tables 18 and 19). Subsequently, nutrient accumulation becomes additive through constant and repeated applications of compost. Compost, unlike synthetic fertilizers, can provide nearly all the elements required by plants; however, plants that have high nitrogen, phosphorus, and potassium requirements may need a boost, especially in new garden plots. In new garden plots, I recommend that you not depend on compost to supply all your required nitrogen—at least in the short term. Some nitrogen-rich organic materials or inorganic fertilizers will most likely be needed.

Is compost 100% organic matter? Actually, no; although compost is made from organic materials (leaves, hay, kitchen wastes, manure, soil, etc.), there are inorganic minerals and compounds present. Living plants can contain between 2 and 10% inorganic elements and compounds, which when burned remain as ashes. I recommend making compost as easily and cheaply as possible. Compost additives are sold in stores but are not necessary. A healthy soil has all the microbes you need to make compost. Avoid purchasing sterilized topsoil, which has no microbes. Do not make the mistake of using only one ingredient in your compost pile (e.g., leaves, grass clippings, hay). Some essential components that will ensure that your compost pile actually turns into compost include (1) soil; (2) one or more basic bulky organic materials such as leaves, hay, or a mixture of grass clippings (not grass clippings alone) with other bulky materials; (3) a manure source, which can be mixed with organic bedding materials; and (4) another high-nitrogen ingredient.

There are also materials to avoid in your compost:

- Grass clippings on which herbicides and pesticides were used.
- Any parts of black walnut or pecan trees.
- Meat scraps or unwashed eggshells. Eggshells can be contaminated with *Salmonella*, which can survive and multiply for at least 1 year or more in soil.
- Cat litter, which contains fecal material and perfumes.
- Coal ashes, which contain large amounts of sulfur and iron that can injure your plants. Wood ashes can be used sparingly.
- Cat or dog fecal material.
- Dairy products (bury in soil).
- Discarded grease and fats.
- Fish remains (bury in soil).
- Hair, bones, or dead animal remains (these will decompose in specialized commercial compost operations, but such materials are not recommended for the home gardener).
- Lime, gypsum, sulfur, or any chemicals.
- Diseased or insect-riddled plants.
- Rhizomatous weeds that are difficult to kill.
- Leaves of certain trees such as live oak, southern magnolia, and holly, which are too tough and leathery for easy composting.
- Poison oak, poison ivy, or sumac.
- Brush, sticks, or woody material unless shredded.
- Citrus rinds, palm fronds, fruit pits, nutshells, and the cobs, stalks, and husks of corn, all of which break down very slowly.

Making Compost

Simplicity is the goal. There are many different techniques for making compost; for layering, chopping, and shredding the material; and for providing aeration with pipes and gadgets. I make compost in situ—a Latin phrase meaning "in position" (fig. 35). Simply make your compost where you ultimately want it. Why make a compost pile in another location and then move it to where you want to use it later? In the fall after harvest is a good time to start because you can establish your compost piles right on your circle plots or raised garden beds (fig. 35). If you build compost in situ, all you need to do is mix the decomposed material into the soil and prepare the seedbed prior to planting.

Pile up available materials in a homogeneous fashion (mix everything together) into a cone shape over your circle plots. For your compost pile, you will need materials such as leaves, spoiled hay, lawn clippings, a nitrogen source such as alfalfa, blood meal, cottonseed meal, or manure (see organic fertilizers), and finally a dose of soil.

I introduce here the concept of the carbon-to-nitrogen (C/N) ratio of organic materials (explained in more detail in the following pages). All organic material has an inherent level of nitrogen and carbon in its makeup. The proportion of carbon to nitrogen is important to you as a gardener because it is directly related to the availability and release of key nutrients for plant growth, and for subsequent organic matter development and maintenance in your garden. Appendix B includes information on (1) the average carbon and nitrogen content and C/N ratio for commonly available organic materials; (2) average values for major organic materials, timing of release, effect on pH, and notes for commonly used organic fertilizers; and (3) a mathematical method to determine the C/N ratio for making compost. As you contemplate the concept of C/N, an easy rule to remember is that organic materials that decompose slowly have low nitrogen and high carbon levels; organic materials that decompose quickly have a high nitrogen-to-carbon ratio. For example, chicken manure has a low C/N ratio (1 part carbon to 8 parts nitrogen; 1:8), whereas spruce sawdust has a carbon-to-nitrogen ratio of 600:1. No wonder the sawdust from my shop hangs around for two years as a mulch on the garden. I deliberately repeat this concept many times throughout the book because many vegetable gardens suffer from nitrogen deficiency resulting from the addition of organic materials with a high C/N ratio. The literature on making successful compost stresses a C/N ratio of 30:1 because microbes require about 1 atom of nitrogen for every 20–30 atoms of carbon. When you add organic matter to the soil, especially materials with a high C/N ratio (carbon rich), and the moisture and temperature are optimal, the soil microbes harvest nitrogen to break down the carbon-laden material, which can result in a nitrogen deficit—the color and vigor of your vegetable plants will let you know if this is occurring, as they will not be a healthy dark green and will lack vigor.

Here are some basic guidelines for making compost:

1. The C/N ratio can range from 20:1 to 40:1, but 25:1 to 30:1 is ideal. The C/N ratio of organic materials is an important concept in farm-

ing and gardening (appendix B). A ratio is a quantity, amount, or size comparison between two things. Bakers commonly use ratios, and the same concept applies to C/N ratios of organic materials. Carbon is the basic element and building block for living organisms. Carbohydrates contain carbon, which is used for energy, and nitrogen is the basic ingredient in cellular amino acids and proteins. The pH of the materials should be 6.5 to 8.0.

2. The ideal moisture content should be about 40%–65% on a weight basis.

3. Shred materials into smaller particles (⅛ to 2 inches in diameter), mowing leaves so they are free from rocks and stones.

4. Coarser materials should be at the bottom, finer materials on top. As the composting process starts, begin mixing materials.

If you set up your in situ compost piles in late summer or fall, there is plenty of time for nature to do its work and give you a finished product for spring planting. A compost mound 3½ to 5 feet in diameter and 2½ to 3 feet in height is a good size that is easy to manage. If you live in a cold climate, try to gauge when your temperatures finally reach 50°F in spring; your compost piles will begin activating again as the temperatures warm up, but you will probably need at least a month before they are finished. For early spring crops such as salad greens and the brassicas (cabbage family), you may want to hold over some of last summer's compost. If you are in a rush to plant in spring and your compost has not completely decomposed, you can use the rough portions for mulch around the circle.

When should you make compost? You can establish a compost pile anytime you have the materials; however, the actual biological process requires outside ambient temperatures warm enough to start it, at least 50°F. Visualize your compost pile as a mini "biological reactor"; the more nitrogen, the faster and hotter the pile will heat up and produce a finished product. I make compost piles several times a year, often between different crops. After my spring greens fade with the advent of summer, I will build a small compost pile over the old crop. My compost material base is barn litter with manure, soil, and a little alfalfa hay that my animals spill on the ground and discard because of coarser stems. I keep the pile moist and turn it regularly with my hay fork, and if the temperature and moisture are optimal, usually after 2–3 weeks the compost is sufficiently decomposed to incorporate into the soil.

How do you know when your compost is finished?

The time needed to make compost varies from 2 weeks to as long as a year, depending on the materials. Finished compost can be dark to reddish brown and crumbly (it does not need to be powdery), and it should have an earthy odor (no smell of ammonia). The original materials are not recognizable (except woody materials), the pile is cool, and there may be earthworms and other insects at the bottom. If you are not quite sure whether the compost is finished, mix it and keep it moist for another couple of weeks.

Microorganisms and the Composting Process

Initially, the pH of the compost is usually acidic, around 6.0, and as decomposition progresses, further acidification occurs from organic acids (pH of 4.5–5). As temperatures rise and decomposition nears completion, the pH can range between 6 and 8.5, depending upon the composting materials. There are four stages to the composting process: (1) the mesophilic stage, (2) the thermophilic stage, (3) the cooling stage, and (4) the maturing stage. During the thermophilic stage of heating, the common pathogens *Escherichia coli*, *Staphylococcus aureus*, *Bacillus subtilis*, and *Clostridium botulinum* are killed. Aeration or turning is important during this stage to replenish oxygen used by the microorganisms. Pasteurization of harmful organisms occurs during the thermophilic stage when the temperature is 104°F or higher for 5 days, and above 131°F for at least 4 hours. *Salmonella* spp. usually survive for less than 1 hour after the compost pile reaches the upper temperatures of the thermophilic stage. Weed seeds and eggs from parasites (worms, etc.) are reduced during the thermophilic stage, but they are resilient and home composting methods may not eliminate them all. Like most pathogens, they develop resilience to environmental conditions. *E. coli* and *Salmonella* have survived in compost where temperatures reached 129 to 153°F. Higher survivability is associated with drier compost conditions compared to wetter conditions. High moisture content is critical to destroying *E. coli* and *Salmonella* during the thermophilic stage. In short, the removal of microorganisms from compost is complex, and not just the result of heat.

Availability of Plant Nutrients and Soil pH

Gardeners should be aware of two concerns about pH. First, it affects nutrient availability to plants, and second, it affects soil microorganisms. A soil pH range of 5.5–7.0 is a general guideline for most vegetable plants, but it is not optimal for some plants (see table 3 in chapter 4). The ideal pH in the vegetable garden is around 6.5; modification is often needed when pH is below 5.5 or above 7.5. By maintaining proper pH in the vegetable garden, you can avoid nutrient deficiencies dependent on pH.

The Quick Guides for individual vegetables list their recommended optimal pH. Figure 36 shows that strongly acidic soils can negatively affect the availability of calcium, magnesium, potassium, phosphorus, nitrogen, sulfur, and several micronutrients (molybdenum and boron). In contrast, highly acidic soils increase the availability of iron, manganese, zinc, copper, and cobalt, which could extend to toxic levels for plants and microorganisms. A common problem worth mentioning in acidic soils is aluminum (Al) toxicity. Aluminum toxicity is usually not a problem in soils with a pH greater than 5.2. Also, it is not a major concern in organic soils because of low aluminum concentrations. However, at pH levels lower than 5.2, roots can take up this element and a portion can be translocated throughout the plant. If your soils have a pH of less than 5, your plants are not going to grow and produce very well anyway, so aluminum toxicity is a secondary problem—a failed garden is the first symptom. Another element, manganese (originating from the parent soil materials and rocks) can also be toxic in acidic soils (pH 5.6 or lower). Like aluminum, manganese is more soluble in water as pH drops. There are diagnostic plant symptoms associated with aluminum and manganese toxicity. Aluminum toxicity stunts root growth (producing thick, stubby roots) and may turn leaves yellowish (chlorotic). However, many other factors can cause chlorosis as well. Plant symptoms of manganese toxicity are crinkled and cupped leaves with chlorotic spots. If you have highly acidic soils, check with local agricultural experts about reported aluminum and manganese toxicity—a soil test and/or leaf tissue analysis can verify these problems.

Alkaline soils can present special problems related to solubility and availability of plant nutrients. Arid and semiarid soils with subsurface layers rich in calcium carbonate (designated as calcic horizons) can be alkaline. Arid and semiarid regions can also host other problems like saline soils (natural salts with pH < 8.5) and sodic soils (high levels of salt with low soluble salt concentrations and pH > 8.5). If your soils are saline or sodic, you will need some professional advice from local agricultural experts. Specialized irrigation methods, minimal tillage, and organic mulches, which reduce water evaporation from the soil and thus reduce the upward transport of salts to the soil surface, are some ways to deal with this problem. In slightly to moderately alkaline soils, nitrogen, potassium, sulfur, calcium, magnesium, and molybdenum are available for plant growth, while phosphorus, boron, iron, manganese, zinc, copper, and cobalt become limiting (fig. 36). In alkaline soils, the most notable element required for plant growth (phosphorus) starts to become limiting at slight to moderate alkalinity.

Soil pH can have an impact on soil microbes. Fortunately, soil fungi are adapted to a wide range of pH levels. Fungal species tend to be more competitive at lower soil pH, whereas bacteria are better competitors at intermediate to high soil pH. Soil pH can be an effective means of controlling some diseases in the garden. For example, a low pH (equal to or lower than 5.2) can be useful in managing potato scab; soil pH between 6 and 6.6 reduces root and crown rot in wheat; and raising soil pH to 7.0 can control clubroot in the cabbage family.

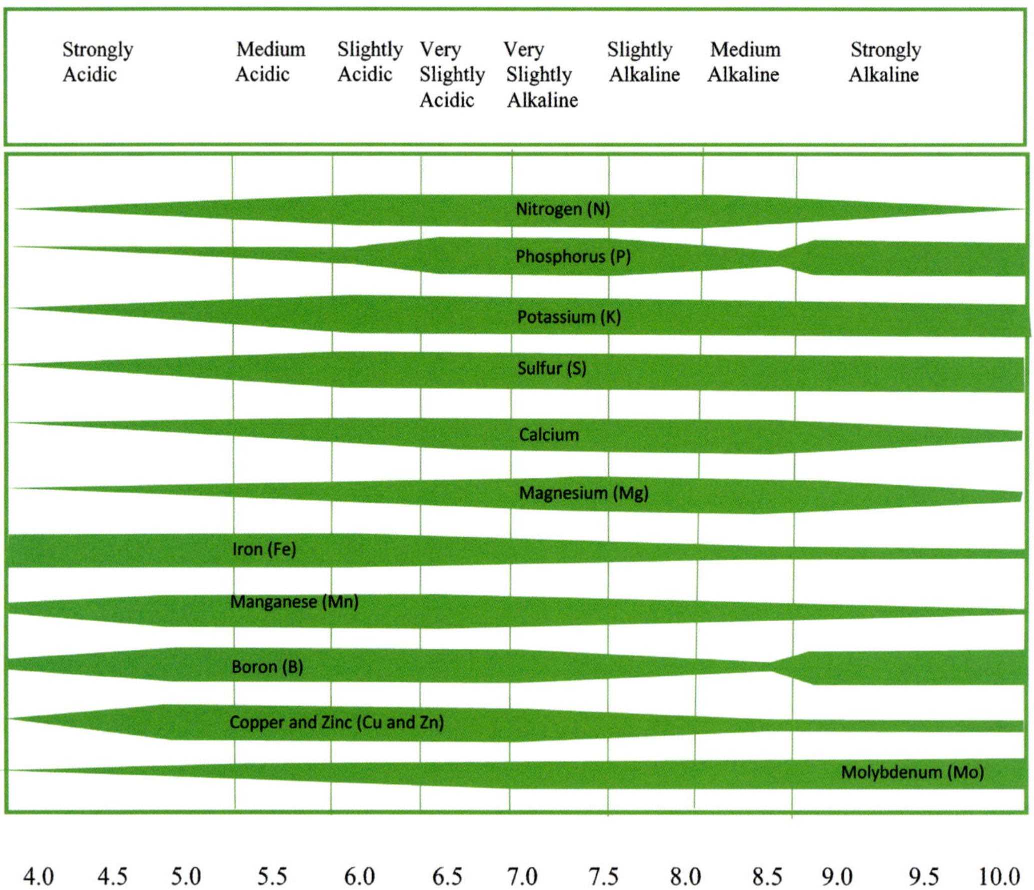

FIGURE 36. Relationship of soil pH and nutrient availability for plants. Figure by author.

Managing Soil pH

Any remedial action for raising or lowering soil pH should be done in conjunction with a soil test recommendation—better yet, use the soil test results and confer with your local agricultural agent. Raising the pH in acidic soils is usually accomplished with agricultural lime, which is natural limestone crushed to a fine powder (do not use hydrated lime, which is highly caustic). Wood ashes can be useful in the garden for certain situations. If available in sufficient quantities, they can be used as an alternative to agricultural lime (average calcium content 20%). Wood ashes are strongly alkaline and should be treated with respect: wear gloves, a dust mask, and eye protection. Do not use ashes from treated lumber or wood with creosote because heavy metals and other pollutants could be present. Wood ashes contain carbonates and oxides and are effective in raising soil pH. Depending on the type of wood that was burned, wood ashes can contain about 1%–2% phosphorus, 4%–10% potassium, and micronutrients such as iron, manganese, boron, copper, and zinc. There may also be trace amounts of heavy metals such as lead, cadmium, nickel, and chromium. They contain no nitrogen. Hardwoods can produce up to three times more ashes than softwoods.

Some wood ashes should be held in reserve for certain insect and disease problems. A small amount sprinkled around the base of a plant can repel maggots, slugs, and snails. Do not let the ashes come in contact with new seedlings or plant roots—moderation is essential; a cupful will do. Wood ashes can help reduce, but not control, the fungus clubroot (*Plasmodiophora brassicae*) in cruciferous vegetables (broccoli, cabbage, cauliflower, brussels sprouts, collards, and kale). Do not apply wood ashes to potatoes because of scab. After wood ashes become wet, they lose their potency (nutrients and insect-repellent properties). If your soils are neutral to alkaline, do not apply wood ashes en masse to your soils; save your ashes for insect and disease control. Increases in soil pH to the alkaline side (> 7.5) are not appreciated by most vegetable plants (fig. 36). If your soils are acidic, (pH < 5.5), wood ashes can be beneficial in raising pH; soil pH of 6.0 to 6.5 can benefit from lesser amounts (not more than 20 pounds of ashes per 100 square feet annually, incorporated to a depth of 6 inches).

I mentioned that organic matter and residues tend to acidify soils. How can organic matter increase and decrease pH? Organic materials such as pine sawdust, peat moss, and coniferous leaves, especially pine needles, are generally low in calcium and nonacidic cations and can lower pH. Manure and leguminous cover crops can increase pH because of higher calcium content (especially poultry manure).

Managing Fertility

Managing and enhancing fertility in the vegetable garden is a constant process. As you build up your soils with manure and compost, in time they should develop into a crumbly, organically rich substrate. Periodic additions of organic matter are necessary because microbes work to break it down, mineralizing nitrogen and other nutrients but also releasing carbon dioxide. The result of this process, the organic carbon cycle, is that organic matter will be lost over time. As a gardener or farmer, you need to decide what types of fertilizer you will use: organic, inorganic, or a combination. Organic gardeners subscribe to totally organic soil amendments. For some gardeners, economics may be an important consideration (see example below). When you purchase organic fertilizers, realize that the cost will be significantly higher than that of synthetic fertilizers. Growers who are or wish to become certified with the USDA National Organic Program (NOP) need to check on substances they use for compliance with the Organic Materials Review Institute.

Fertilizers are soil amendments that guarantee minimum percentages of nutrients such as nitrogen, phosphorus, and potassium (fig. 37). Other elements may be included such as sulfur, boron, copper, iron, and zinc. Organic fertilizers such as seaweed, kelp, and rock-derived nutrients usually list minimum percentages of nutrients. By definition, soil amendments are any materials mixed into the soil matrix, but some soil amendments such as compost do not have legal labels designating nutrient content.

Confusion exists about fertilizer designations (nitrogen, phosphorus, and potassium). Nitrogen content is expressed as N, and P and K occur in the oxide forms P_2O_5 and K_2O (fig. 37). Fertilizer recommendations for P and K are given for the oxide equivalents, not for the pure elemental P and K. A bag of fertilizer with the numbers 10–10–10 contains 10% N, 10% P as phosphorus pentoxide (P_2O_5), and 10% potassium oxide (K_2O), sometimes referred to as potash. One hundred pounds of 10–10–10 would contain 10 pounds of each of the three nutrients. The remaining 70 pounds are a filler material, which provides bulk for easier dispersal. If you purchase a 50-pound bag of 10–10–10, there would be 5 pounds each of N, P_2O_5, and K_2O. How much actual P and K are in P_2O_5 and K_2O, respectively? In P_2O_5, 44% is elemental P, and in K_2O, 83% is elemental K. Many organic fer-

SCIENCE NOTE • Comparing the Price of Nutrients in Fertilizers

Compare the cost per pound of nitrogen for three products:

- The consumer buys a quart of an organic liquid fertilizer (4-4-4) for $30.00 per quart. The actual amount of N in 1 quart of 4-4-4 is 0.10 pound. If the product costs $30.00 per quart, the cost for a pound of N is $300.00 per pound (30 ÷ 0.10 = 300).
- The homeowner buys a 2.75-pound bag of blood meal (12-0-0) for $18.00. In that bag of blood meal there is 0.33 pound of N. The comparative cost of a pound of N is $54.50 (18 ÷ 0.33 = 54.50).
- The homeowner buys a 50-pound bag of ammonium sulfate (21-0-0) for $16.95. In that bag, there are 10.5 pounds of N. The comparative cost of a pound of N is $1.61 (16.95 ÷ 10.5 = 1.61).
- A gardener wants to use manure tea (cow) and purchases 3 manure teabags (0.21 pound per bag) for $12.95. Each manure teabag costs $4.32. Assume the cow manure is 2% N. In the manure teabag there is 0.0042 pound of N (0.21 x 2/100 = 0.0042). The cost per pound of N in one manure teabag is $1,028.00 (4.32 ÷ 0.0042 = $1,028). The per-pound cost of N in the manure teabag is 638.5 times more than the cost from ammonium sulfate (example above).

10-10-10 GUARANTEED ANALYSIS	
TOTAL NITROGEN (N)*	10.0%
1.50% Nitrate Nitrogen	
8.50% Ammoniacal Nitrogen	
AVAILABLE PHOSPHATE (P_2O_5)	10.0%
SOLUBLE POTASH (K_2O)	10.0%
Boron (B)	0.07%
Chlorine not more than	6.00%
Iron (Fe)	0.20%
Magnesium (Mg)	2.00%
Manganese (Mn)	0.25%
Zinc (Zn)	0.25%
Combined Sulfur (S)	10.0%

FIGURE 37. Sample label for a 10-10-10 synthetic fertilizer. Figure by author.

tilizers may contain micronutrients such as sulfur, iron, and zinc, but concentrations may not be listed on the label because levels are either too low or too erratic. Liquid fertilizers also have the same three-number designation, for example, 12-0-12 (N-P-K).

Fertilizers

Organic fertilizers are derived from the remains or by-products of plants and animals. Appendix B lists some commonly used organic nutrient sources. As discussed previously, organic fertilizers rely on microorganisms to break down and mineralize nutrients into usable forms for plants. Microorganisms are active when soil temperatures warm up (> 50°F) and soil moisture is available. Cold and dry conditions will delay and inhibit mineralization. Nutrient release occurs slowly over a long period and may not provide enough nitrogen, phosphorus, and potassium for immediate plant needs. Cottonseed meal, blood meal, bone meal, fish meal, hoof and horn meal, and all animal manures are examples of organic fertilizers. Remember that (1) organic amendments and fertilizers release nutrients slowly over time, so you could experience a nitrogen deficit (see nitrogen discussion); (2) nitrogen in organic materials and products used as fertilizers must be mineralized by soil microorganisms (a temperature- and moisture-dependent process) before the nutrients can become available to plants; (3) the cost of nutrients in organic fertilizers is significantly higher per pound of nutrient than it is in synthetic fertilizers; and (4) with sufficient amounts of organic soil amendments, you will notice that over time your plants will thrive and be supplied with a more constant, steady supply of nutrients.

Animal manure is a common organic fertilizer, and its composition varies depending on the kind of animal, the kind of forage and animal feed, climatic conditions, and management of the manure. Fresh manure typically contains between 30 and 85% water, and the remainder is organic and inorganic solids, other liquids, and gases. In dry manure, about 90% is organic material from digestion of the feed. If animals are fed high amounts of salt and receive medicines such as antibiotics, these materials will occur in the manure. Animal manure contains microorganisms such as bacteria, fungi, actinomycetes, and protozoa. The bacteria classified as enterococci and coliforms are prevalent in manure, and excreted coliform counts can be as high as 18 billion per animal per day.

Animal manures contain different levels of macronutrients and micronutrients; poultry manure contains the highest levels of nitrogen, phosphorus, and potassium (appendix B). Manures applied in low amounts to the garden will not supply adequate nutrients for most vegetables. When applied in high amounts, as over large fields, nitrate leaching and phosphorus runoff can occur, which can lead to excessive plant growth and eutrophication in lakes and other water bodies. It is recommended that composted decomposed manure be used in the home garden. Farming operations often apply fresh manure to fields. Fresh manure will contain slightly higher amounts of nitrogen, but it can also contain viable weed seeds. Guidelines regarding fresh manure and harvest of crops for human consumption vary. Fresh manure can contain various pathogens that can cause food-borne illness to humans (see "Microorganisms and the Composting Process" section). In commercial vegetable operations, 4 months are required after the application of fresh manure before harvest of root crops and leafy vegetables that are in contact with the soil. Some recommendations state 60 days if produce is washed. There are no guarantees that weeds and pathogens are dead in composted manure, whether it is made at home or purchased.

Most synthetic fertilizers available for garden use contain a mixture of nitrogen, phosphorus, and potassium. Other micronutrients may be in the formulation. There are three classes of fertilizer formulations. For example, 10-10-10 is considered a balanced fertilizer; complete fertilizers have nitrogen, phosphorus, and potassium but in unequal amounts (5-10-15); and unbalanced or single-element fertilizers are limited to one nutrient (33-0-0). Commercially prepared organic and inorganic fertilizers include a label with the fertilizer grade.

One important concept to understand with either organic or inorganic fertilizers is that the elements nitrogen, phosphorus, and potassium are not used by plants in pure form. In order for nitrogen to be available to plants, it must combine with oxygen to form nitrate (NO_{3-}) or ammonium (NH_{4+}). Organic forms of nitrogen (proteins and amino acids) must be assimilated by microorganisms, whereas plants can use the nitrate in chemical fertilizer almost immediately.

Application of Fertilizer and Soil Amendments

What is the status of soil nutrients in your garden? Soil tests can take the guesswork out of what levels of nutrients currently exist in your soil, but they do not usually give an indication of nitrogen levels. You can also evaluate the relative fertility status of your garden soil from the plant vigor and productivity of the prior crop (use the Garden Site Indicator Scorecard and Soil Health/Quality Indicator Scorecard to help determine existing conditions). If you are establishing a new garden, evaluate the vigor of current grasses and other plants at the proposed garden site. If you are going to convert a section of lawn into a vegetable garden, examine the vigor, productivity, and color of the turf. Rapid growth and a dark green color are indications of good soil fertility, whereas patchy, slow-growing, yellow turf with a high weed component most likely indicates low fertility.

Home vegetable gardeners typically apply fertilizers by deep soil application, broadcasting, banding alongside seed furrows, or liquid application. In raised beds and circle plots, deep application, broadcasting, and liquid preparations can be used. Working or incorporating manure, composts, or other fertilizer amendments into the soil to a depth of 12 inches is usually sufficient in the home garden. Specific fertilizer recommendations are given in the individual Vegetable Guides. Some vegetable crops may require periodic fertilization (side dressing or liquid applications) at various stages during the plants' growth and development. With experience and trial and error, the home vegetable gardener will be able to determine nutrient and fertilizer needs. When in doubt, always apply small amounts of fertilizer and increase or follow up with additional fertilization in a stepwise progression.

As a vegetable gardener, you will inevitably adopt some form of nutrient management plan. Compost, manure, cover crops, fertilizers, and conservation measures are all part of the gardener's toolbox to improve and maintain soil health. In the vegetable Quick Guides, I provide information on fertilizer application rates for soils with low, medium, and high soil organic matter. Appendix D gives equivalent rates for circle plots 4½ feet and 5 feet in diameter using various soil amendments and fertilizers. Most professional fertilizer recommendations are given in pounds per acre, and many state extension and university publications provide localized fertilizer rates for vegetable crops.

Table 20 shows an example of using a commercial fertilizer rate (average published values from extension bulletins), and calculated equivalent rates using decomposed manure, compost, or a fertilizer blend.

For example, commercial lettuce growers may use 50–120 lb. N/acre depending on soil organic matter and residual fertility, half broadcasted and half used as side dress 3–5 weeks after establishment. Phosphorus rates range from 0 to 150 lb./acre, and potassium from 0 to 200 lb./acre depending on soil test analyses. The equivalent fertilizer rates for a 5-foot-diameter circle plot are shown in table 20 (also see appendix D). With fertilizers, it is often not possible to match

TABLE 20. Fertilizer application to a lettuce circle plot 5 feet in diameter. When nitrogen requirement is met with fertilizer formulation, there can be deficits for P and K.

Soils low in organic matter	Decomposed cow manure N, P_2O_5, K_2O 0.5–0.5–0.5 @ 18% N availability 0.09–0.09–0.09	Compost N, P_2O_5, K_2O 1–1–1 @ 11.5% N availability 0.12–0.12–0.12	Fertilizer blend N, P_2O_5, K_2O 10–10–10
@ recommended rate 100 lb. N/acre	50 lb.	39.2 lb.	0.45 lb. (7.2 oz.)
@ recommended rate 150 lb. P_2O_5/acre	@ 50 lb. deficit = 50 lb./acre	@ 39.2 lb. deficit = 50 lb./acre	@ 0.45 lb. deficit = 50 lb./acre
@ recommended rate 150 lb. K_2O/acre	@ 50 lb. deficit = 50 lb./acre	@ 39.2 lb. deficit = 50 lb./acre	@ 0.45 lb. deficit = 50 lb./acre
Soils high in organic matter			
@ recommended rate 60 lb. N/acre	30 lb.	23.5 lb.	0.27 lb.
@ recommended rate 90 lb. P_2O_5/acre	@ 30 lb. deficit = 30 lb./acre	@ 23.5 lb. deficit = 30 lb./acre	@ 0.27 lb. deficit = 30 lb./acre
@ recommended rate 90 lb. K_2O/acre	@ 30 lb. deficit = 30 lb./acre	@ 23.5 lb. deficit = 30 lb./acre	@ 0.27 lb. deficit = 30 lb./acre

Note: 5-foot diameter = 19.6 $ft.^2$ (see appendix D for more details).

all three plant requirements (nitrogen, phosphorus, and potassium) with one fertilizer blend. Professional farmers can come close with special blended fertilizer mixes. However, in the home garden, we have to approximate. In table 20, for a recommended rate of 100–150–150 (N–P–K), if you applied decomposed cow manure in order to meet the 100-lb. nitrogen requirement, you would have a corresponding 50 lb./acre deficit for phosphorus and potassium. The same scenario plays out with compost and a fertilizer blend of 10–10–10. To more fully meet the phosphorus and potassium recommendation of 150 lb./acre, there are several alternatives. If you apply enough fertilizer to meet the phosphorus and potassium recommendations, you would then have an excess balance for nitrogen (table 21).

TABLE 21. Fertilizer application to a lettuce circle plot 5 feet in diameter, with excess N to attempt to balance P and K

Soils low in organic matter	Decomposed cow manure N, P_2O_5, K_2O 0.5–0.5–0.5 @ 18% N availability 0.09–0.09–0.09	Compost N, P_2O_5, K_2O 1-1-1 @ 11.5% N availability 0.12–0.12–0.12	Fertilizer blend N, P_2O_5, K_2O 10–10–10
@ recommended rate 100 lb. N/acre	@ 75.09 lb. excess = 50 lb./acre	@ 58.7 lb. excess = 50 lb./acre	@ 0.68 lb. (10.8 oz.) excess = 50 lb./acre
@ recommended rate 150 lb. P_2O_5/acre	75.09 lb.	58.7 lb.	0.68 lb.
@ recommended rate 150 lb. K_2O/acre	75.09 lb.	58.7 lb.	0.68 lb.
Soils high in organic matter			
@ recommended rate 60 lb. N/acre	@ 45 lb. excess = 30 lb./acre	@ 35.3 excess = 30 lb./acre	@ 0.41 lb. excess = 30 lb./acre
@ recommended rate 90 lb. P_2O_5/acre	45 lb.	35.3 lb.	0.41 lb.
@ recommended rate 90 lb. K_2O/acre	45 lb.	35.3 lb.	0.41 lb.

Note: 5-foot diameter = 19.6 ft.^{2} (see appendix D for more details).

10

Diseases, Pests, and Weeds

Benefits of Soil Organic Matter and Healthy Soil

When I first started growing vegetables and reading books about vegetable gardening, especially organic gardening methods, organic farming and gardening publications professed that plants grown organically are better able to resist disease and attacks by insect pests. Yes, that made sense: build up your organic matter, soil health, and nutrient levels, and your plants will be healthier. But, I thought, how are organically grown vegetables more able to resist disease and insect pests? When I first started gardening, my impression was that this claim was too good to be true. In the last decade or so, science has been discovering the causal agents associated with healthy soil. For years, gardeners have observed the patterns and results of organic gardening, but it took time for science to catch up and discover the reasons for those results.

In each of the individual Vegetable Guides at the end of the book, I provide a key to aid in diagnosing the most common problems. I refrain from offering detailed control treatments for a couple of reasons: (1) cooperative extension services and university specialists are the experts (and maintain licenses to make recommendations), and it is their role to keep abreast of new treatments in agriculture (organic methods and chemical pesticides); and (2) treatments constantly change with new discoveries and products.

Every gardener is eventually confronted with squash bugs, aphids, Colorado potato beetles, striped cucumber beetles, cutworms, corn earworms, and other insect pests. I do not wish to overplay the subject of diseases and pests, as you may never see or experience some of the diseases I mention in the Vegetable Guides, and your plants may be relatively free of insect problems. It is more likely that insect pests will generally be more of a problem from time to time than plant diseases. Plan ahead and decide what your strategy will be if an insect pest threatens to destroy the plants you are trying to grow for food: Will you try an organic treatment, resort to a chemical insecticide, or forfeit the crop? Whatever your decision, before you use the product, whether organic or synthetic, be sure you read the directions and warnings on the product labels (several times). Find a place to keep your organic and synthetic chemicals under lock and key, away from children and pets—please, no exceptions! I also recommend avoiding many of the "home-brewed" concoctions that appear in some books and on many websites. It is so easy to have an accident and harm yourself, pets, innocent wildlife, or others around you. Cutting up hot peppers in your kitchen while cooking is risky enough: if you forget to wear gloves and wipe your eye or nose, you will not repeat that mistake. Can you imagine blending up a whole batch of hot peppers for a pepper spray, and then having an accident? Do not do it.

Let's be honest—insect problems will arise; they always do at one time or another. But they do not usually come all at once. If you are observant, you can detect egg clusters under the leaves, and any undesirable insect activity. For example, if white butterflies are flying about in your garden, you can expect green cabbage caterpillars. Clusters of small brown dots on squash leaves will develop into squash bugs. Some years, you may have aphids, Colorado potato beetles, striped cucumber beetles, or harlequin bugs, and other years, squash bugs. If you live in an agricultural area where growing crops are thriving, you can expect more insect pests, as their populations are already established. I live in an area with little row crop agriculture, where most of the land is rangeland. Being isolated, I do not see many of the insects that can plague certain vegetables.

Soil Health and Plant Diseases

The soil microcosm is extremely complex. Plants and soil microorganisms have developed symbioses that are beneficial to both. Some mycorrhizae are specific in providing defense against certain plant pathogens. When you are working in the garden, think about the soil, how organic matter provides plant nutrients, and the role of soil microorganisms. Soil organisms, much like people, do not live in isolation; myriad complex biological relationships exist and vary in time and space. In previous chapters I have discussed symbioses between microorganisms and plants in which the relationship is beneficial to both. There are also commensal relationships, in which one organism benefits and the other is not detrimentally affected; parasitism (predation and fungivory), in which one organism benefits and the other does not; and competition, in which both organisms vie for resources, sometimes to the detriment of both. In healthy soils and plant communities, there can be upward of 150 to 200 species of arbuscular mycorrhizae that develop symbioses with more than 95% of plant species (some *Brassica* species are the exception). Most of the gardening literature labels the relationship between mycorrhizae and plant roots as symbiotic-mutualistic for both species. However, science has identified some mycorrhizal relationships as neutral or negative for plants. Arbuscular mycorrhizae can suppress the growth of germinating seedlings because of the photosynthetic carbon allocated to the fungi. Highly fertilized systems of dependent crop plants may be more at risk from mycorrhizal parasitism. Excess and high levels of phosphorus fertilization can decrease mycorrhizal colonization in forest ecosystems. Synthetic nitrogen fertilizers can also change arbuscular mycorrhizal species composition, and fungal species that flourish in fertilized soils may be less beneficial symbionts. Pollution that alters solar radiation levels and thus affects photosynthetic potential can change the delicate mycorrhizal balance. Mycorrhizal populations can be sensitive to ozone-generated plant stress.

Organic gardeners and farmers soon observe that healthy soils are correlated with fewer disease problems. Science has identified the many benefits of healthy mycorrhizae and other soil microorganisms. The challenge now, through experimentation, is to unravel many of the interactions among soil microorganisms, soils, and plants. There is a delicate balance of mycorrhizal populations and species that are mutualistic with plants. Beneficial microorganisms and their association with plant roots produce phytohormones, which can improve and promote plant growth, control insects, detoxify environmental pollutants, and suppress plant pathogens. Management strategies to promote beneficial microorganisms in the garden can include reducing tillage and soil disturbance, using organic soil amendments, rotating vegetable species, and limiting high nitrogen and phosphorus applications. Slow release of organic fertilizers from compost and manure is amenable to mycorrhizal populations. Many soil bacteria (*Pseudomonas* spp., *Bacillus* spp., *Azospirillum*, *Serratia*, *Flavobacte-*

rium, Enterobacter) produce auxins, cytokinins, and gibberellins that stimulate plant growth by increasing root growth. Many fungal and bacterial species in the same respective genera as species that cause problematic diseases, such as *Rhizoctonia*, *Phialophora*, *Trichoderma*, *Pythium*, and *Fusarium* (look at the disease-causing species in the individual Vegetable Guides), are nonpathogenic and reduce the potential damage of their parasitic relatives. Science has accumulated important information that explains why plants growing in healthy soils and balanced ecosystems seem to be more resilient against pests and diseases. Improving soil health by adding organic materials is one of the most important tasks for the home vegetable gardener. The circle gardening technique, in which you concentrate your precious organic resources in the plots where you grow your vegetables, can accelerate the development of healthy soil and the produce you grow.

Identifying Pest and Disease Problems

I recommend getting into the habit of visiting your vegetable garden on a daily basis, which is easier if your garden is near your house. Look at the upper and lower parts of your plants' leaves. Many insects hide there. If you start to see holes where insects have chewed, or your plants are suddenly wilting (from piercing, sucking insects such as squash bugs and aphids), try to find the culprit. If an insect problem arises, the next step is to try to identify the insect. If you do not locate any insect pests, then check the diagnostic keys in the Vegetable Guides for bacterial, fungal, or viral diseases. I have organized some of the common disease vectors for specific vegetables into keys. What part of the plant is showing symptoms—leaves, stems, leaves and stems, roots, fruits, or the entire plant? With practice, you can identify telltale signs of certain insect pests. Is the insect pest a larva or caterpillar? Is it a beetle, aphid, fly, stinkbug (squash bug), leafhopper, or some type of grasshopper? Learn to identify and place the insects in your garden into their respective orders (fig. 38). There are many different kinds of insects; more than 2 million different species have been identified throughout the world, but there may be as many as 30 million insect species yet to be discovered. The number of described insect species in the United States is about 91,000, with 73,000 species that remain undescribed. The majority of described insects in the United States occur in four large insect orders: Coleoptera (beetles, 23,700); Diptera (flies, 19,600), Hymenoptera (ants, bees, and wasps, 17,500), and Lepidoptera (moths and butterflies, 11,500).

Although this information may seem overwhelming, there are similar characteristics for insects in specific orders, which the gardener can recognize over time. General appearance such as shape, size, wings, antennae, legs, color, and other parts can help in placing the insect into its proper order (fig. 38). There are many good field guides to help in identifying insects, with pictorial keys to help identify the orders. If you spend a little time studying illustrations of insects and their scientific orders, you will soon learn to recognize and classify insects into their respective orders. Once you have narrowed down the insect order, do some research on that order with reference to the vegetable hosting the insect. For example, say you have identified a coleopteran (beetle) feeding on your cucumber and squash plants. The beetle is pale yellow with a black head and three black stripes on its back. Once you have arrived at this point, narrowing down the culprit is not too difficult using any of the websites and insect handbooks that describe insect pests by vegetable species (in this case, the striped cucumber beetle, *Acalymma vittatum*).

When growing vegetables, you need to decide what level of damage from pests is tolerable. In my area, I can harvest a good crop of summer squash, but eventually plant growth slows, production drops, and the plants begin to senesce (gradually deteriorate). At this point there is a high probability that squash bugs and stem borers will show up. Instead of overreacting and rushing to treat them, I just thank the plants for their bounty and then pull them up and destroy them. I will replant another squash crop in a week or two and most likely will escape another generation of squash bugs. In time and with experience, gardeners tend to learn how to flow with the ecology of their garden. As I mentioned in the garden ecology chapter, a garden environment is not always in a harmonious state.

Snails and slugs may appear, but they are usually predictable, depending on how shaded and wet your garden is. Some vegetable crops are prone to nematode problems; symptoms are provided in the Vegetable Guides. Sometimes early diagnosis and elimination of a diseased plant may be sufficient. Pull the plant and dispose of it far from the garden—not in the compost pile. The best advice I can give the home gardener is to be constantly vigilant; visit your garden every day, or at least every other day, and practice preventive measures. On the Garden Site Indicator Scorecard, one important point is to try to set up your vegetable garden close to the house and kitchen.

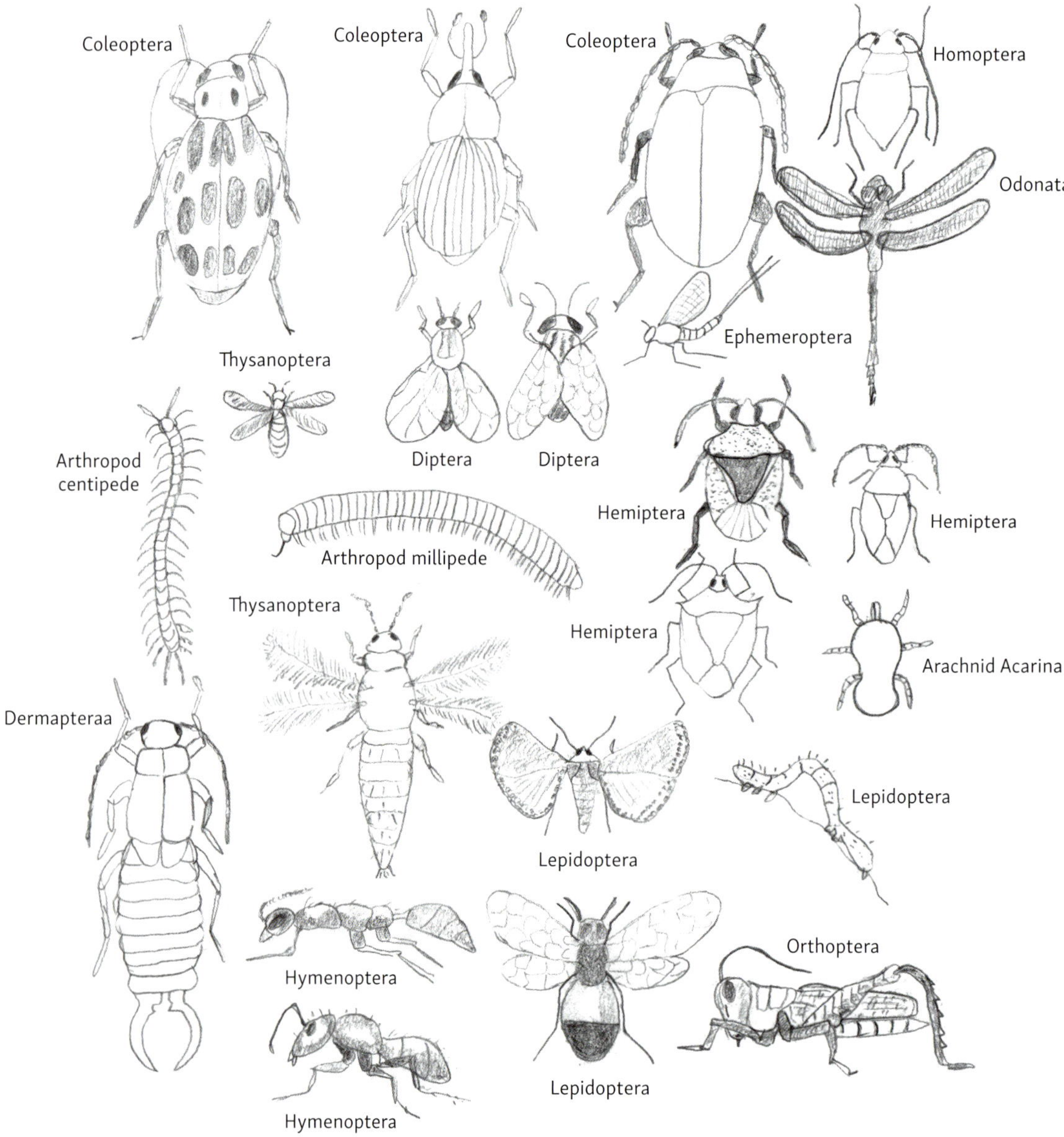

FIGURE 38. Common insect and arthropod orders. Figure by author.

Plant Protection against Pests

What strategies and management practices are available to maintain healthy plants in the garden?

Using adapted cultivars and plants with genetic resistance and preserving soil health and plant diversity in your garden are key concepts in maintaining a healthy garden environment.

Growing resistant or tolerant vegetable cultivars is an important management tool in controlling disease. Plant breeders are constantly working to improve disease resistance while maintaining the flavor, yield, and quality of vegetables. You will find numerous hybrids throughout many seed catalogs. When you see cultivars with disease resistance, remember that the plants are not completely immune to those listed diseases. It is more accurate to view the cultivar as having more tolerance to a particular disease. A resistant cultivar may show less damage from a disease or it may require fewer pesticides, but the plant may still be affected. Again, the vegetable gardener needs to be on constant alert. Disease-resistant plants are still prone to other problems such as drought, low fertility, weed competition, and insects.

As you look through seed catalogs, you will notice that not all plants have been bred to resist all diseases. For example, one tomato cultivar may be resistant to F2 = *Fusarium* wilt race 2, TMV = Tobacco Mosaic Virus, V = *Verticillium* wilt, and N = Nematodes; while another cultivar is resistant to LB = Late Blight, EB = Early Blight, and FCR = *Fusarium* Crown and Root Rot. If a specific disease is causing problems, try to find a resistant cultivar as a means to manage it.

Summary of cultural practices to manage plant diseases

- Rotate vegetable crops in circle plots. The concept is to break the cycle of specific pest species and diseases. For example, do not plant members of the onion, cabbage, nightshade (tomatoes, eggplants, peppers), and squash families in the same plot in consecutive years.
- Use cultivars adapted to your area. Many hybrid cultivars have been bred to resist certain pathogenic plant diseases.
- Use adapted heirloom varieties with natural resilience.
- Increase diversity of plants in the vegetable garden, including herbs and flowers. Plant floral and herb borders in or around the garden to create biological diversity and reduce crop pests.
- For cover crops, use plants with allelopathic properties to suppress soil-borne pests and diseases. For example, planting a cover crop of radishes or grasses such as tall fescue or rye in the fall as a winter cover can reduce the effects of certain weeds and nematodes in and around your circle plots. Certain radish cultivars have been bred specifically for use as a cover crop to improve soil structure, and for their pathogen-resistant qualities (GroundHog, Nitro, Sodbuster, Bio-till, Graza, and Tillage radishes, all registered trade-

marks; also white Daikon radishes, which are a nontrademarked cultivar).

- Improve soil health.
- Build up and maintain soil organic matter.
- Encourage mycorrhizae and other microbes in soil.
- Remove and discard diseased plants.
- Do not place diseased plants in compost piles.
- Eliminate weedy plants that are hosts to vegetable pests.
- Remove plant debris and litter at the end of the growing season.
- Eliminate poor drainage in soil.
- Avoid overhead irrigation.
- Avoid water and soil splash onto leaves.
- Use mulch to maintain moisture and prevent soil splash onto leaves.
- Buy disease-free seeds.
- Use hybrid plants.
- Minimize water stress and maintain adequate moisture levels for plants.
- If a problem is severe, eliminate the crop and destroy it.
- Use pesticides (organic and inorganic).
- Use a more random planting scheme and separate plants throughout the garden.

A

FIGURE 39. *A, B, C,* Small wire mesh fences around circle plots work well to deter small animals. *D,* Five polywires form an electrically charged fence for deer. Photos by author.

B

C

D

Other Animal Pests

Environmental and climatic factors as well as weeds, insects, diseases, and other animals compete with our efforts in the vegetable garden. Many small animals such as rabbits, woodchucks, skunks, armadillos, raccoons, gophers, mice, and birds are members of the ecosystem surrounding your garden. Most of these animals visit the garden when you are not around, or in the evening. They all have their particular habits and idiosyncrasies. Figure 39 shows some of the protective measures I use to thwart certain animals.

I constructed a simple 4½-foot polywire fence powered by an electric fence charger to deter deer. Before I built the fence, deer ate the entire garden in one night. This fencing setup has solved that problem for 10 years. When I first set up the fence, I drilled holes in small hotel-sized perfumed soaps, sprayed pieces of cloth with cheap perfume, and put blood meal in socks and tied them all randomly on my fence and in my fruit tree branches. Now I only occasionally turn on the charger. I recently had an experience with feral hogs. They are the most formidable animal foe that I have experienced; they can bulldoze through your garden in one night.

Polywire is a handy product, which comes in a roll or on a spool that you can wind up. Polywire is a flexible polyethylene rope with stainless-steel fibers that conduct electricity. I have 5 polywires surrounding the garden fastened to wooden posts with plastic brackets. By the gate, each polywire is fastened to an insulated spring handle that is used to unfasten it. New Zealand has pioneered the modern sporadic-pulse electric fence charger, and there are several companies that supply products to the United States and throughout the world. My charger can operate on 4 D batteries, a 12-volt marine battery, or a solar charger, or it can be connected to an electrical outlet.

The electric fence does not deter rabbits, skunks, and armadillos. I use a vinyl-coated wire mesh fence, which comes in rolls 4½ feet high and 50 feet long. I cut it down to about 2½ feet and form a circle fence around plots, held in shape with wooden stakes (fig. 39). I have found this system sufficient to deter these animals. In the case of woodchucks, you may want to bury the fencing a few inches deep. Skunks and armadillos dig around the circle plots looking for beetle grubs but do not damage the plants inside the fence. Raccoons are more devious and are usually attracted to ripening corn. They do not seem interested in leafy vegetables inside the circle plot fence. You can also increase the height of the wire mesh.

The following is an assortment of remedies to thwart larger animals. The trick is to constantly mix up the sequence of remedies so the animals do not become accustomed to any one tactic.

- Electric fencing
- Permanent woven-wire fencing
- Small circular cages or fencing around circle plots
- Human articles such as old shoes
- Scarecrows
- Colorful flagging material, aluminum foil flagging, bright colors
- Bells, wind chimes, pinwheels; anything that creates noise in the wind
- Mesh netting
- Perfumed soaps with holes drilled and hung on stakes around the garden
- Cheap perfume sprayed on cloths that are hung on stakes
- Socks filled with some blood meal and hung on stakes
- Fake snakes and owls
- Portable battery-powered radio
- Commercial animal or varmint repellents
- Human or dog hair in cheesecloth pouches
- Baby powder
- Repellent plants (catnip, garlic, lavender, mint, thyme, rosemary, onion)
- Rabbit-repellent plants—marigold, garlic, onion
- Ferret droppings from pet store
- Gopher traps for gophers
- Trained dogs
- Cats

Weeds

Many gardeners feel that weeds are their biggest enemy in the vegetable garden. When I gardened in rows, yes, I needed to be diligent and hoe out the weeds at least once a week. With the traditional row system, I learned that regularity was the key. If you go out to your garden every few days, take the hoe with you and work for a short time. Hoeing out small weeds is much easier than trying to eliminate grass and herbaceous weeds that have been neglected for 2 or more weeks.

I used to think that the success of my garden was proportional to the amount of work I did. There are tricks to gardening: using mulch for weed control can reduce your garden chores and simplify the weeding dilemma. Basically, weed control is all about staying ahead of the weedy plant species and not letting them become entrenched. Weed species tend to elongate their roots quickly, which usually makes them difficult to pull out or cultivate with a tool.

In the circle gardening system, as I mention throughout the book, weeding will not be your number one problem. Most of my time is now spent keeping up with garden irrigation. As your garden becomes more established, weed seeds *will* progressively diminish in your circle plots. By the third year, you will see that weeds will no longer be a problem. I kneel down beside my circle plots and weed around with my fingers when seedlings become established. This task takes about 10 minutes. I may do this one or two more times as the plants grow. For larger plants such as the cole crops, peppers, onions, and so forth, I mulch inside the circle plot. I also place spoiled hay around my circle plots to keep weeds under control and provide stability to the perimeter of my plots (fig. 39). By using the hay mulch, I never weed between my plots. The mulch also provides a surface where I can walk and maneuver around the garden—even after a rain. An added bonus is that the mulch decomposes and adds organic material to the soil. When the mulch becomes thin, I simply put another layer on. Rodale Press published a book by Ruth Stout in 1973 called *The Ruth Stout No-Work Garden Book: Secrets of the Year-Round Mulch Method*. Ms. Stout adopted a year-round permanent mulch gardening method, which virtually eliminated the tilling and weeding associated with traditional gardening.

One interesting observation I have made over the years but have never read about is the ability of weeds to mimic or camouflage themselves among the plants they are growing with. Figure 40 shows an oat plant that germinated from a previous cover crop growing among garlic plants. Both plants are monocots, but I did not notice the oat plant for some time. I often see this phenomenon: pigweeds, lamb's-quarters, grasses, and other weeds seem to blend into stands of vegetable plants. Look for this weed "camo" characteristic in your own garden.

FIGURE 40. Camouflaged oat plant among garlic plants; see white circle. Photo by author.

SELECTED VEGETABLE GUIDES

History, Culture, and Quick Guides

FIGURE 41. Beans display tremendous diversity. Antique bean packets courtesy of Wikamedia Commons, Français: Variétés de haricots (*Phaseolus vulgaris*) publiées dans *Les plantes potagères* Vilmorin-Andrieux et Cie, 1891. Yellow wax beans, courtesy of BBB seeds, http://www.bbbseed.com/. Romano type beans courtesy of Wikamedia Commons, photo by Rasbak, 2005. Basket of beans, courtesy of The National Garden Bureau Celebrates 2003 as the Year of the Bean.

Beans

(*Phaseolus vulgaris*)

Beans are one of the most important domesticated legumes throughout the world. Green beans are a healthy food; they are low in calories, contain no saturated fat, and are a good source of vitamins (A, C, and K, folate, niacin, pantothenic acid, pyridoxine, riboflavin, thiamine) and minerals (iron, calcium, magnesium, manganese, iron, zinc, and phosphorus). On any given day in the United States, about 14% of the population eats dry beans. In order of productivity, North Dakota, Michigan, Nebraska, Minnesota, Idaho, California, Washington, and Colorado are the top-producing states of dry beans. There is tremendous diversity in beans with respect to shape, size, color, ecological adaptation, taste, and use (fig. 41). Seed Savers Exchange has collected over 4,000 heirloom varieties. Vegetable seed companies offer many varieties of beans to suit the home gardener; the most popular are snap beans, Romano or Italian beans, and lima beans. Snap beans are known by many different names such as string beans, bush beans, green beans, and garden beans. The pods are harvested before the seeds become large and mature. Cooks commonly snap or break the pods into bite-sized pieces; hence the name snap beans. Snap beans are available as bush beans or the taller pole or runner beans.

The stringless bean ('Green Pod,' offered by Burpee Seeds) was bred by Calvin Keeney in New York State in 1898. The next most popular stringless bean, 'Tendergreen,' appeared in 1925. Much later, in 1962, 'Bush Blue Lake' (a combination of the 'Blue Lake' pole bean with a bush type) was introduced. The pole bean 'Kentucky Wonder' was introduced by Ferry-Morse Seed Company in 1877 and is still a popular cultivar. Beans are not hybridized and remain open-pollinated cultivars. Breeders today select for tenderness, stringlessness, and disease resistance.

Both the bush and runner types of beans have round ('Blue Lake' type) and flat ('Kentucky Wonder') pods. Seed catalogs offer many cultivars of bush and pole beans. Scarlet runner beans are also grown for fresh use but require milder temperatures and moist growing conditions. The popular emerging "edamame" are immature soybeans, traditionally used in Chinese, Japanese, Indonesian, and Hawaiian cuisine, and are now available in seed catalogs.

When growing beans, you have a choice of bush beans or pole beans. Bush beans have a shorter life span, produce heavy crops in a relatively short time, take up less space in the garden, and usually do not suffer from diseases because they are short-lived. Bush beans are especially adapted to the circle plot method and can be planted in succession after the first crop has matured and waned. Pole beans require support, poles, trellises, or tepee arrangements. Either pole beans or bush beans are adaptable to the "Three Sisters" arrangement. Pole beans are slower to produce than bush beans, but they bear over a longer period throughout the summer. Taste is a matter of choice.

In the home garden, bush beans with green, yellow, and purple pods are probably the most popular because of their short stature, productivity, quick maturity, and ease of growing without support. Green bush beans are also known as string beans because of the fibrous string that grows along the suture of the pod. Plant breeders have reduced the stringiness of bush and snap beans. The decision to plant bush beans or pole beans depends on the gardener's preference; although pole cultivars generally bear over a longer period and produce a greater yield in the same amount of space. The Romano or Italian beans produce flat pods, which I think are a novelty, and they are fun to grow. Many cooks report that Romano beans have a stronger flavor. Lima beans usually require a longer growing season.

Beans are in the legume family (Fabaceae, formally Leguminosae) and are the second most important plant family that we use for food next to the grass family (Poaceae), to which all our grains crops belong (wheat, oats, barley, corn, rice, rye, millet). The legume family contains about 440 genera and 12,000 species. Legumes are an important source of protein, oil, and forage for livestock. The legume family is widespread over the world but is especially adapted to the temperate regions of both the Northern and Southern Hemispheres.

The genus *Phaseolus*, which includes our beans and limas, consists of more than 150 species.

Science has identified two key locations and gene pools where beans were domesticated: the Andes of Peru and the Lerma Santiago basin of Mexico. Research indicates that beans were domesticated later than maize, but they reached North America at about the same time. The exact date of bean domestication is not precisely known, but beans have been identified in archaeological sites dating back 10,000 years in Argentina and 7,000 years in Mexico. These two gene pools diverged about 11,000 years ago. The Mesoamerican beans are typically smaller (pinto, great northern, small red), while the Andean beans are larger (red and white kidney beans). Other legumes have been traced to Eastern cultures (20,000 years ago); lentils were used by the ancient Egyptians, and faba (fava) beans in their wild form were first collected in Afghanistan and the Himalayan foothills. Fava beans were cultivated by the ancient Greeks but were associated with death because of their dark spots. After years of war in the ninth century, Charlemagne ordered chickpeas to be planted and grown. The common bean found its way to Europe in the sixteenth century.

Native Americans focused on bean varieties that could be grown and dried easily and stored over the winter. These attributes were more of a priority than fresh, tender pods. When Christopher Columbus arrived in the New World, he encountered 5 kinds of domesticated beans: common beans (*Phaseolus vulgaris*), lima beans (*P. lunatus*), tepary beans (*P. acutifolius*), scarlet runner beans (*P. coccineus*), and polyanthus beans (*P. polyanthus*). The tepary bean is a more drought-tolerant legume native to what is now Texas, New Mexico, and Arizona and was a major food staple of southwestern Native Americans. This is the bean that was most likely planted together with corn and squash in the "Three Sisters" arrangement. In 1605 Samuel de Champlain observed the Three Sisters arrangement in the Kennebec region: "With this corn they put in each hill three or four Brazilian beans (*Febues du Bresil*), which are of different colors. When they grow up they interlace with the corn, which reaches to the height of from five to six feet; and they keep the ground very free from weeds." Many other early explorers in the New World documented the bean associated with Native Americans. In 1535 the French explorer Jacques Cartier, known chiefly for exploring the Saint Lawrence River and giving Canada ("kanata") its name, saw fields of maize (corn), beans, and squash in an Iroquoian village (Stadacona), later to become Quebec City. Henry Hudson found beans in cultivation during his exploration of the Hudson River in 1609 (now Rensselaer County, New York). In 1614, Captain John Smith also observed that Native Americans in New England had beans.

Culture and Planting

Beans are easy to plant since they have large seeds. They grow best at temperatures between 70 and 80°F; therefore, it is advisable to plant 7 to 10 days before the last spring frost. When temperatures are below 50°F and above 90°F, bean production and quality are reduced. High night temperatures above 90°F will affect self-pollination, and flowers will drop. Beans are very sensitive to frost, and if it threatens, plots should be covered. Beans will grow in a wide variety of soils, but medium-textured soils are best. Soil pH requirements are toward the acidic side (5.5 to 6.5). During the previous fall, prepare the seedbed in advance with additions of compost and decomposed manure. Prior to planting in spring, add more organic material if necessary and work into the soil to a 12-inch depth.

Since beans are legumes, they require less nitrogen, phosphorus, and potassium than most vegetable crops. Even though legumes develop nodules on the roots where *Rhizobium* bacteria fix nitrogen, it is still advisable to use some nitrogen fertilizer (about 40 lb./acre). Depending on the levels of phosphorus and potassium, these requirements are also considerably lower than for most vegetable crops. For soils low in phosphorus, 80 lb. P_2O_5/acre is sufficient, and for soils high in phosphorus, use 40 lb./acre. For soils low in potassium, use 60 lb./acre, and for soils high in potassium, use 20 lb. K_2O/acre. Use table 32 in appendix D to convert fertilizer rates (lb./acre) to equivalent rates for circle plots.

If you use organic fertilizers such as decomposed manure and compost, be aware that only a fraction of the nitrogen is available the first year (the amount varies, but for manure I use 18% availability as reported in the literature, and for compost about 11.5% N availability) (chapter 9, tables 18 and 19). It is advisable to inoculate the seeds with *Rhizobium* bacteria prior to planting. Packets are available from seed companies, and inoculation helps increase the formation of nodules on the roots. Also, be aware that many species of legume require a specific inoculum.

In organic gardening and farming systems, there is a time lag associated with amendments such as compost and manure. The gardener has to compensate by adding more organic matter to reach target rates. For a new garden, nutrients may be insufficient if you depend on compost and manure alone. Use some of the organic amendments that release nitrogen more quickly, but realize that the downside of this is that high-nitrogen organic products are relatively expensive. After several years of adding organic matter to your garden, the balance of nutrients will reach more desirable levels. The best way to evaluate your soil fertility is by examining the vigor and appearance of the plants. If the plants are growing slowly and appear yellow and spindly, you need to add soil amendments that release nutrients quickly.

In the circle plot arrangement, diameters of 4½ to 6 feet work well. Start planting seeds on the outside rim of the circle, placing seeds 2 to 4 inches apart (fig. 42). Move 14 to 18 inches toward the center of the circle and scribe a seed furrow, much like a ring on a target. In the home garden, plant seeds 1 to 1½ inches deep. Commercial growers vary the depth according to their environmental conditions (½ to 3 inches).

Diseases and Pests

Several excellent references for growing beans are quite detailed and give recommendations for various diseases and other pests. Consult your state or university cooperative extension service for up-to-date information on pest and disease control products. Many bean diseases can be prevented and managed using good rotation practices (use nonlegumes, preferably after corn or grains), removing the previous year's residue, avoiding overhead watering or irrigation (water at ground level), using certified disease-free seed, and using disease-resistant cultivars. Below is a key for common bean diseases and a list of insects and other pests.

Diseases

Leaves and pods

- Dark brown cankers exist along leaf veins and petioles. Pods are infected with small round dark spots with sunken centers. Fungal disease, **Anthracnose** (*Colletotrichum lindemuthianum*). In cool, humid, wet conditions (60 to 80°F), spores are released from lesions during rain or overhead irrigation, and from soil splash onto plant. Fungus overwinters on bean residue and/or seeds. On seeds, fungus is concealed under seed coat; therefore, it is hard to treat with fungicides. Manage disease on seeds by maturing seed crop under warm, dry conditions. Some cultivars have been bred

A

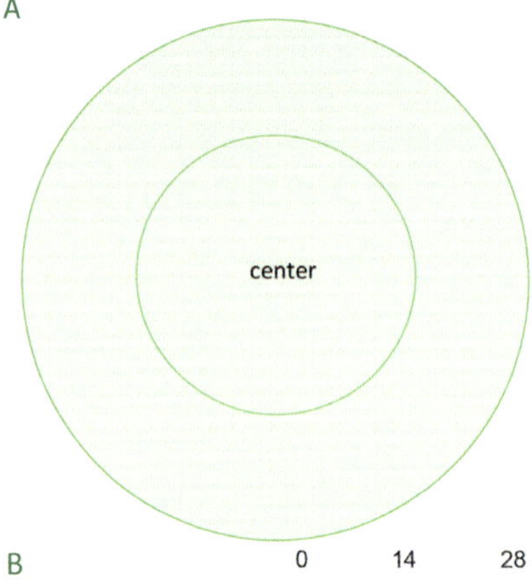

B

FIGURE 42. *A*, Snap beans in a circle plot. *B*, This example uses a circle 4.6 feet (56 inches) in diameter. Plant in concentric rings starting with the outer edge and work toward the center. Table 22 shows the number of plants at 2- and 4-inch spacings.

TABLE 22. Number of plants at 2- and 4-inch spacings in circle plot rings of different size

Radius (inches)	Diameter (inches)	Circumference (inches)	Plants @ 2-inch spacing	Plants @ 4-inch spacing
28	56	176	88	44
14	28	88	44	22
Total plants			132	66

for resistance. Avoid overhead watering and irrigation. Minimum of 3-year crop rotation, especially for bean seed production.

- Infection begins with small, water-soaked spots, more visible on leaf undersides. Spots develop a greenish-yellow border, and eventually a brown spot appears and leaf tissue deteriorates and falls out, creating holes in leaves. Pods can be infected and will have brown water-soaked spots and be distorted or twisted. Early infection can look like halo blight. Bacterial disease, **Bacterial Brown Spot** (*Pseudomonas syringae* pv. *syringae*). Disease is transmitted by infected seeds. Rotate crops every 3 to 5 years (corn and grain crops are good rotation plants).
- Infection begins with small water-soaked spots between leaf veins and on margins of leaves, giving a scalded appearance; can also appear on pods. Spots enlarge and are irregular in shape, 1 inch or more in diameter. Spots turn brown, dry out; lesions along edges of leaves and on pods can turn reddish brown and produce slimy exudates. Seeds appear shriveled or poorly formed, while some are normal. Bacterial disease, **Common Bacterial Blight** (*Xanthomonas campestris* pv. *phaseoli*). Bacteria spread by wind, rain, irrigation, overhead watering, contaminated tools, and machinery. Wet, humid, and warm conditions favor the disease. Overwinters on plant residue and on seeds; seed-borne disease. Use 5-year crop rotations.
- Plants wilt easily during water stress, bacteria block the xylem system in plants. Disease is often confused with common bacterial blight, but more irregular interveinal necrotic lesions with yellow borders form. Disease spreads during hot, dry, and droughty conditions. Bacterial disease, **Bacterial Wilt** (*Curtobacterium flaccumfaciens* pv. *flaccumfaciens*). Seed borne; use 2- to 3-year crop rotations, and resistant cultivars.

Leaves, stems, and pods

- Rotting of stems, pods, flower blossoms, and petioles occurs, with white-cottony growth; plants may wilt. As disease progresses, the white mycelium hardens and darkens. Fungal disease, **White Mold** (*Sclerotinia sclerotiorum*). Soil-borne disease, fungus overwinters in soil as sclerotia (long-lived dark structures that produce spores). Use a 5-year crop rotation. Allow soil to dry between watering and irrigation, avoid wetting plants with sprinklers. Upright cultivars have better airflow and tend to show fewer symptoms.

- Infection occurs in early growth phase on leaves, stems, and/or pods. Yellow or white raised spots appear on upper and lower leaf surfaces. These enlarge and form reddish-brown circular pustules about ⅛ inch in diameter, which contain microscopic summer spores (urediniospores). Pustules can also have yellow halo appearance, and during severe infections leaves can curl, dry up, and fall off the plant. Pod development can be affected and seed size reduced. Fungal disease, **Bean Rust** (*Uromyces appendiculatus*). Fungal spores are released from the pustules, which have a rusty appearance. The spores rub off leaf surfaces, while other blight diseases do not. Near the end of the season, pustules appear as brownish-black overwintering spores (teliospores). Disease is not seed borne and is promoted during wet, cool to moderate daytime temperatures (65 to 85°F) and cool nights. Bean rust can recycle every 10 to 14 days. Use crop rotations of at least 3 years, remove all previous year's bean residue, and do not wet plants or use sprinkler irrigation.
- Disease usually begins as spots with a water-soaked appearance on leaves (1/16 inch in diameter, visible on leaf undersides), stems, and pods. As disease progresses, yellow-green halo caused by a bacterial toxin (about ½ inch in diameter) develops. Pods can appear shriveled and discolored. Bacterial disease, **Halo Blight** (*Pseudomonas syringae* pv. *phaseolicola*). Disease develops during warm, wet weather. Bacteria spread by wind, rain, watering, and feeding insects. Seed-borne disease; rotate crop and use resistant cultivars.
- Infected leaves and pods are greenish-yellow with a dark green mosaic pattern. Plants appear distorted, curled, stunted, nonvigorous, and spindly, especially young plants. Viral disease, **Bean Common Mosaic Virus (BCMV)** and **Bean Common Mosaic Necrosis Virus (BCMNV)**. Virus is spread by aphids and transmitted to seeds. Use certified disease-free seeds and resistant cultivars.

Insect and other pests

- Aphids: Cowpea Aphid (*Aphis craccivora*), Bean Aphid (*Aphis fabae*), Pea Aphid (*Acyrthosiphon pisum*), Green Peach Aphid (*Myzus persicae*);
- Tarnished Plant Bug (Lygus Bugs): (*Lygus hesperus, L. elisus*);
- Leafminers (*Liriomyza sativae, L. trifolii*);
- Grasshoppers (*Schistocerca americana* and others);
- Weevils: Cowpea Weevil (*Callosobruchus maculatus*), Broad Bean Weevil (*Bruchus rufimanus*), Bean Weevil (*Acanthoscelides obtectus*);

- Darkling Beetle (*Blapstinus* spp.);
- Cucumber Beetles: Western Spotted Cucumber Beetle (*Diabrotica undecimpunctata*), Western Striped Cucumber Beetle (*Acalymma trivittatum*);
- Mexican Bean Beetle (*Epilachna varivestis*);
- Empoasca Leafhoppers (*Empoasca fabae, E. solana*);
- Beet Leafhopper (*Circulifer tenellus*);
- Spider Mites: Twospotted Spider Mite (*Tetranychus urticae*), Strawberry Spider Mite (*T. turkestani*), Pacific Spider Mite (*T. pacificus*);
- Armyworms: Beet Armyworm (*Spodoptera exigua*), Western Yellowstriped Armyworm (*S. praefica*);
- Cutworms: Black Cutworm (*Agrotis ipsilon*), Variegated Cutworm (*Peridroma saucia*), and others;
- Corn Earworm (*Helicoverpa zea*);
- European corn borer (*Ostrinia nubilalis*);
- Loopers: Alfalfa Looper (*Autographa californica*), Cabbage Looper (*Trichoplusia ni*);
- Seed Corn Maggot (*Delia platura*);
- Root Lesion Nematode (numerous spp.);
- Wireworms (*Limonius* spp. and others);
- Garden Symphylans (*Scutigerella immaculata*);
- Slugs.

Snap Beans Quick Guide

Botanical Data	Environmental Conditions	Culture and Special Considerations
Beans (*Phaseolus vulgaris*) **Family:** Fabaceae **Life Cycle:** herbaceous, annual, wild forms perennial **Flowers:** hermaphroditic (perfect), flowers few to many, racemose or fascicled on axillary peduncles, white, yellow, red, purple. Five petals. In most conditions beans are self-pollinated, as the pollen is released a day before the flower opens; therefore, the flower is not dependent on insect pollination. Stamens 9 and 1; style bearded longitudinally. Pods with convex shape or compressed. Italian beans several- to many-seeded, dehiscent (opening by slits to release seeds). **Physiology:** cool-season vegetable, photosynthesis C_3 **Stems:** mostly twining, some forms erect **Leaves:** pinnately 3-foliolate, but sometimes consist of 1 leaflet, stipulate and stipellate (having a pair of leaflike structures, spines, glands, or scales at the leaf base or along a petiole), the stipules persistent, leaflets entire **Roots:** develop from the radicle at the lower end of the hypocotyl of the embryo, taprooted with lateral fine roots, lateral roots usually host nodulated outgrowths containing nitrogen-fixing bacteria (rhizobia) **Fruits:** legume, a dry fruit that is long and thin and has several seeds inside lined up in a row **Seeds:** germination 8–16 days at 60°F–85°F. Will not germinate at temperatures below 60°F. Bean seeds are sensitive to chilling during germination, and permanent damage may occur. 2–10 seeds/g. Viability 2–3 years when stored in cool, dry conditions. **Days to Maturity (DTM):** snap beans 50–65 days; pole beans 60–80 days; dry shelling beans 75–90 days to fresh shell stage; runner beans 75–80 days depending on cultivar.	**Growing Zones:** check state and county cooperative extension sites and guides for adaptability and recommended planting dates. **Optimal Temperature for Growth:** 70°F–80°F. Temperatures above 90°F, especially warm night temperatures, will result in poor pollen development, pollination, and flower drop. **Frost:** beans are very sensitive to frost (30°F–32°F). Tops are easily killed and turn dark green to black after 1 frost event. Lower parts of plant may survive, but tops, later-developing green pods, and flowers are easily damaged. **Sunlight:** full sun **Soil Conditions:** beans will grow on sandy loam to clayey soils, but medium-textured soils such as loams are best. Adequate drainage is essential. **Optimal pH:** 5.5 to 6.5 **Soil Moisture Content:** consistent moisture at surface since roots are shallow **Pollination:** bean flowers are perfect and normally self-pollinate; pollen is usually shed and fertilization occurs before the flower opens, but plants can cross-pollinate if bees manage to penetrate an unopened flower. If you wish to save seeds of a particular variety, do not grow different varieties side by side. **Nutrition Information:** Snap beans, green, raw. USDA Food and Nutrition Service. % Daily Value based on 2,000 calorie diet Serving size 1 cup Calories 34 Total fat 0% Cholesterol 0% Sodium 7 mg, 0% Total carbohydrate 8 g, 3% Dietary fiber 4 g, 15% Sugars 2 g Protein 2 g Vitamin A 15% Vitamin C 30% Calcium 4% Iron 6%	**Ease of Growing:** easy; stay within soil temperature guidelines **Site Preparation:** spade and loosen soil to 6–10 inches. Work in a 2-inch layer of compost, decomposed manure, and topsoil (optional) the previous fall. Do not work when soil is wet. **Fertilizer:** beans do not require high amounts of N, P, and K. Average recommendations are N = 40/lb./acre, P_2O_5 = 80 lb./acre low P, 60 lb./acre med. P, and 40 lb./acre high P per soil tests. K_2O = 60 lb./acre low K, 40 lb./acre med. K, and 20 lb./acre high K per soil tests. See appendix D for equivalent rates with selected fertilizers for circle plots. **Planting and Spacing:** direct seed, no advantage to transplants, snap beans 1–1½ inches deep, 2–4 inches apart. Traditional rows are spaced 18–36 inches apart. In circle plots space concentric circles at least 14 inches apart. Stagger plantings in separate plots every 14–21 days. **Thinning:** if seeding is heavier, thin to 2–4 inches apart **Inoculant:** dry and snap bean group (*Rhizobium leguminosarum* biovar *phaseoli*) **Weeding:** gentle cultivation since the roots are shallow **Cultivars:** many bush beans, pole beans, French/filet beans, edamame beans, dry shelling beans, and scarlet runner beans available—check seed catalogs **Harvesting:** for snap beans, harvest pods when slightly undersized and tender, about 2 weeks after flower bloom. Continually pick pods to extend harvest and increase yield. Dry shelling beans usually require 3–4 more weeks (weather dependent). Pods should be papery and dry. If rain threatens, dry the plants or pods in a covered dry area. **Storage:** beans should be completely dry; place in containers in freezer near 0°F for 2 weeks to kill weevils and other insect pests.

A

FIGURE 43. *A*, USDA ARS–bred carrots with different pigmentation. *B*, Carrot seed crop in Nyssa, Oregon. *C*, Harvested carrots ready for market. Courtesy of USDA Agricultural Research Service. *D*, Carrot illustration by Ernst Benary (1819–1893), a German entrepreneur who started a successful seed-breeding business (1 of 28 botanical plates produced in 1867). Courtesy of Wild Carrot Museum, http://www.carrotmuseum.co.uk/manuscripts.html.

Carrots

(*Daucus carota* subsp. *sativus*)

Samuel Ogden, in his classic book *Step-by-Step to Organic Vegetable Gardening*, said this about carrots: "Never underestimate carrots; what would a beef stew or a pot roast be without carrots?" Carrots are the orange vegetable with carotene, but the orange carrot has come into vogue in only relatively recent times. White and yellow varieties were preferred in Europe until a few centuries ago, purple carrots are more popular in Afghanistan, and pink carrots are de rigueur in India. Seed catalogs now offer a wide variety of colors, sizes, and lengths to suit many consumer preferences and soil growing conditions (fig. 43*A*). Your garden soil will dictate what type of carrot to grow. Carrots may be difficult to grow in very clayey soils, as they prefer lighter-textured loamy soils that are loose and fertile. They require a sunny location, although some vegetable guides mention that carrots can tolerate a little afternoon shade. In my experience, carrots will tolerate some shade, but their growth and development will not be as robust compared to those grown in full sun.

The carrot is a member of the parsley family (Apiaceae, formerly Umbelliferae) and has an edible, fleshy root with fine, feathery leaves. It is biennial and produces umbel-shaped flowers the second year; however, in the vegetable garden, carrots are treated as annuals (fig. 43*B*). Carrots are versatile, as they can be eaten raw in salads, juiced, cooked, or baked into carrot cakes, and they complement many meat and other vegetable dishes. In some countries, carrots are made into jams and sweetmeats. Carrots are an important part of good nutrition and a healthy diet. They provide many essential nutrients such

B

D

C

as beta-carotene, which is converted into vitamin A by the body. Carrots also contain vitamin C, vitamin B (riboflavin, niacin, thiamine, vitamin B_6, and folate), vitamin E (alpha-tocopherol), and vitamin K and are a rich source of dietary fiber and minerals such as manganese and potassium. Carrots also provide iron, copper, zinc, calcium, selenium, protein, carbohydrates, and biotin. One 7-inch-long root supplies about 35 calories, no fat, and 270% of the daily requirement for vitamin A and 10% for vitamin C.

Historical Background

The wild carrot, *Daucus carota*, is indigenous to Europe and areas in Asia. Fossil pollen belonging to the carrot family has been identified from the Eocene epoch (55 to 34 million years ago). The first cultivated carrots, branched purple or yellow roots, are believed to have originated over 5,000 years ago on the Iranian Plateau (Afghanistan, Pakistan, and Iran). Archaeologists believe that the wild carrot was not used for food, but the seeds were used medicinally to treat stomach ulcers, abscesses, and bladder, liver, and kidney problems, as well as in childbirth and as an aphrodisiac. Carrot cultivation spread to Spain in the 1100s from the Middle East and North Africa, to Italy in the thirteenth century, to Germany and the Netherlands in the fourteenth century, and to the British Isles in the fifteenth century. The Dutch developed the modern version of the carrot in the seventeenth century through selection and breeding. Up until then, carrots were purple, reddish, or yellow. The Dutch are usually credited with developing the orange color in carrots; however, early historical evidence shows that orange carrots existed much earlier, as illustrated in an alphabetical recension of the Materia Medica of Dioscorides, drawn in 512 in the Juliana Anicia Codex for presentation to Juliana Anicia, the daughter of Emperor Anicius Olybrius (fig. 44). The Dioscorides codex may have been copied from an earlier manuscript owned by Theodosius II (408–450 AD).

Culture

Carrots can be temperamental and they require more care than most vegetable crops. The seeds are small, although pelleted seeds now make the chore of seeding easier. Carrots require balanced and consistent moisture levels while growing. For this reason, I recommend that the beginning gardener work up to the task of growing carrots. If you are a beginning gardener and wish to experiment a bit, include some

A B

FIGURE 44. *A*, Cultivated and wild carrots from the Juliana Anicia Codex of 512 AD. *B*, Adam Lonitzer, a German botanist, noted for his 1577 revised version of Eucharius Rösslin's herbal, wrote *Kreuterbuch*, including this drawing labeled "Pastenachen Mören Pastinaca sativa, & sylvestris." Courtesy of Wild Carrot Museum, http://www.carrotmuseum.co.uk/manuscripts.html.

FIGURE 45. Carrot circle plot with mesh fencing for protection against rabbits. Photo by author.

carrots and radishes in your patch of lettuce and salad greens. If you have improved your garden soil with organic matter over several seasons, your success rate will be higher than if you just start with plots where lawn or miscellaneous grasses and weeds recently existed.

Carrots can be grown in spring, fall, and winter throughout the southern United States and in spring and summer in northern climates. Check your growing zone and spring and fall frost-free dates. Carrots require full sunlight and deep, well-drained, fertile soil that is free of stones and debris and has plenty of well-rotted organic matter, but not too much nitrogen. Commercial carrots are usually grown in finer-textured soils such as sandy loams to silt loams. If your garden soil has appreciable amounts of clay, try the short varieties (fig. 47). Carrots prefer somewhat acidic soils; the pH range should be 5.5 to 7.5 for best results.

Carrots are a cool-season crop and grow best during cooler spring and fall temperatures: night temperatures of 55°F and day temperatures of 75°F are ideal for carrots. At warmer soil temperatures of 82°F–95°F, carrot seed germination is reduced and erratic. Carrot roots obtain optimal color at temperatures of 60°F–70°F. Carrots grow slowly, especially in cool spring temperatures (below 50°F), and growth increases as temperatures rise. As temperatures warm up above 86°F, foliage growth slows, and strong flavors and bitterness can occur. It is important to plant carrots early in the spring because their germination time is longer than that of most vegetables (6–21 days) when soil temperatures are 55°F–80°F, so be patient and keep the seedbed moist. For fall crops, check your fall frost dates and consider days to maturity. Then back-calculate the planting time. In my Texas location, it is difficult to get a fall crop because of the high soil temperatures (> 82°F) at planting time in midsummer. Some overwintering carrot cultivars can be planted in late September or early October for spring carrots (May through June). Seed catalogs state that planting in PHZM zones 6 and above requires no mulch cover during the winter; however, in colder zones, 6–12 inches of mulch may be needed.

Soil preparation is critical for growing good carrots. Prepare the soil and circle by loosening soil down to about 12 inches. If your circle plots are new (1 to 3 years), enrich with well-decomposed compost (not woody material or wood chips), well-rotted manure, other organic or chemical fertilizer, and topsoil (optional; see chapter 4). Plant seeds when soil temperatures start reaching about 50°F. Keep the seedbed moist, and when optimal germination temperatures are reached, your carrot seeds will be ready to get a good head start. In the home garden, early spring planting is critical. Nature will determine, after a few weeks, when conditions are optimal for germination. Maintaining uniform moisture is essential for good color and root formation. Avoid drastic dry-wet cycles, as the roots are prone to splitting. Excessive moisture and/or watering can affect good coloration and may encourage disease. Overwatering, especially toward the end of the growing cycle, can also result in split carrots. There is some evidence that carrots will fork and not grow to potential if the soil is saturated during the first week after germination. 'Chantenay' and 'Danvers' are less prone to forking, but all carrot varieties will fork if the soil is dry, compacted, or rocky, or if the root hits an obstruction in the soil. Do not hesitate to pull up a carrot or two from time to time to check how they are progressing.

Crop rotation is an important practice in the garden, especially for carrots. The objectives for rotating carrot plots are to manage for pests, improve soil health, and help control weeds. Any prior knowledge about pests or disease can be helpful in planning and growing carrots. Cover crops and rotation can be used to assist in managing prior fungal diseases. Since other vegetable crops share the same hosts and problems (beans, potatoes, parsnips), grow a nonleguminous green manure cover crop (oats, barley, rye grain, ryegrass, wheat, corn, or other grain crop) in late summer, fall, or winter. When you incorporate the green matter into the soil, allow at least 2 weeks or more for the organic material to decompose so that there is no significant nitrogen deficit. Where nematodes are a problem (forking, galls on roots, small carrot stubs growing from roots), try a grain cover crop. Grain cover crops such as rye and oats are not host specific for root-knot nematodes. Legumes such as alfalfa, clover, beans, and soybeans are hosts to the root-knot nematode. A biofumigant cover crop may also be effective in managing nematodes and other pathogens. Crops such as Sudan grass, sorghum-Sudan grass hybrids, and brassica crops (mustards) release chemicals that can have a toxic effect on nematodes when tilled into the soil and degraded by soil microbes. Some varieties of mustards and arugula (e.g., 'Caliente 199 Mustard Blend' and 'Nemat') have been specifically bred as biofumigants.

Planting

Use your best soils for carrots, and the fewer obstructions such as rocks, the better. The objective with circle mounds is to improve the soil over time. If you are fortunate enough to be starting with fertile loamy soil, compost may be all that is needed to maintain organic matter content and soil condition. If you are starting with soil that needs improvement, keep working by adding manure and compost and allowing sufficient time for more complete decomposition. Some fertilizer (nitrogen, phosphorus, and potassium) may be needed from either organic or synthetic sources. Once the seedbed is friable (lighter and easily workable), you are ready for carrots. The carrot Quick Guide contains the details of spacing and so forth. The pelleted seeds (organic now available) are much easier to work with. Plant 2–3 seeds per inch at a depth of ¼ to ½ inch. After seeding, apply a thin layer of very fine compost to mulch the surface. This helps prevent soil crusting. For example, if you plant a circle 4 to 5 feet in diameter, start with the outside edge and move toward the center at either 4- to 6-inch intervals depending on the size of the carrot cultivar you are planting. Table 23 shows the number of plants in a 4½-foot-diameter circle with ring spacing at 5 inches and plants at either 3 or 4 inches apart. A 3-inch plant spacing equals 195 plants; 4-inch spacing, 146 plants.

Germination can take between 6 and 21 days depending on soil temperature. The germination percentage of carrot seeds and other factors should result in a stand that requires minimal thinning. If you overseed, thin plants out when you can distinguish one plant from the next. Frequent weeding results in less work in the end. Usually, a small tool or fingers work well.

Fertilization

The discussions of nutrient needs here are focused on home gardening; commercial growers depend on soil tests for both major nutrients and micronutrients. Nitrogen and phosphorus are essential for good carrot development; however, excess nitrogen causes excessive top growth, which can slow development of the root and cause branched, hairy, fibrous roots and root cracking, especially during harvesting. Fresh manure should also be avoided, as it promotes rough skins and root branching. Many commercial growing guides base fertilizer recommendations on soil tests. In the home garden, you can do a soil test, but you can estimate fertilizer needs from the performance of a previous crop and/or vigor of weeds. Fertility built up over several years from aged organic matter usually provides sufficient initial preplanting nitrogen, phosphorus, and potassium. Circle plots where previous crops of squash, beans, peppers, and so forth have been prolific and showed healthy green color are a good indication of adequate soil fertility for carrot success.

FIGURE 46. Carrot varieties. Photo by author.

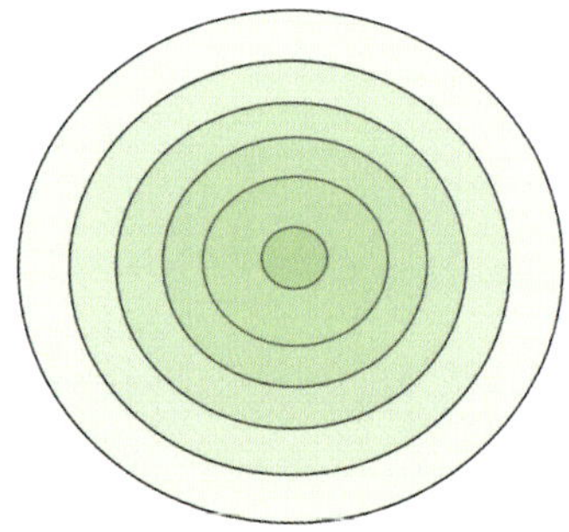

TABLE 23. Example of 4½-foot-diameter circle plot of carrots, with concentric rings 5 inches apart

Distance from center (radius), ring spacing @ 5 inches apart	Ring circumference (inches)	Number of plants	
		Plant spacing 3 inches	Plant spacing 4 inches
28	176	59	44
23	144	48	36
18	113	38	28
13	81	27	20
8	50	17	13
3	19	6	5
Total	583.8	195	146

Note: It is easier to start planting at the outer edge of the circle and progressively move toward the center. Start planting seeds in the outermost ring (28 inches from the center of the circle). Move inward 5 inches (23 inches from the center) and plant seeds. Continue planting at 18, 13, 8, and 3 inches from the center. Carrots are usually thinned to 3 or 4 inches depending on cultivar.

Synthetic fertilizer

Research shows that a carrot crop requires about 90 lb. N/acre, 120 lb. P/acre, and 160 lb. K/acre. Commercial growers usually use about 80–150 lb./N acre depending on conditions. Various studies have evaluated fertilizer rates with carrot yield and quality. Yields were greatest with 134–160 lb. N/acre in Florida sandy soils depending on season, 98 lb./acre in Oregon silt loams, and 98 lb./acre in Texas sandy loams. Nitrogen fertilizer rates that improve yield are also correlated with improved carotenoid and sugar content in carrots. High nitrogen rates in commercial carrot fields can result in nitrogen leaching into groundwater and being lost via runoff. In summary, research shows that nitrogen rates above 150 lb./acre seldom improve yield. The average recommended rate in soils with low organic matter (OM) is 120 lb. N/acre; with medium OM, 100 lb. N/acre; and with high OM, 80 lb. N/acre. These fertilizer rates are approximate so that the gardener can gain perspective on fertilization rates for carrots (see table 32 in appendix D for converting lb./acre to equivalent rates for selected fertilizers in circle plots). Use half of the total fertilizer requirement during seedbed preparation and apply the other half as a side dressing when plants are established.

Phosphorus and potassium fertilization should be based on a soil test. In a Florida study on sandy soils, research showed that 75 lb./acre was sufficient for optimal production, and carotenoid and soluble sugars in carrots were not affected by potassium fertilization. Aside from the scientific research, many gardeners credit solid sweet carrots to the addition of potassium (wood ashes contain soluble potassium). Remember, there are different phosphorus tests for different soils throughout the United States. Where phosphorus levels are greater than 51 ppm (Bray extraction used in slightly acidic to acidic soils, pH 6.0–7.2) or greater than 42 ppm (Olsen extraction used in alkaline soil pH > 7.2), no additional phosphorus is needed. When phosphorus levels are in the range of 11–20 ppm (Bray) and 8–15 (Olsen), about 100 lb. P_2O_5/acre is needed. Phosphorus applications can range from 0 to 150 lb. P_2O_5/acre depending on existing levels from a soil test. Potassium applications can range from 0 to 200 lb. K_2O/acre depending on the soil test. Once you have determined the needed phosphorus and potassium, use table 32 in appendix D to convert lb./acre to equivalent rates for selected fertilizers in circle plots.

Organic fertilizer

The common organic materials to use aside from cover crops and plant residues (mulches) are compost, decomposed animal manure, blood meal, bone meal, cottonseed meal, alfalfa pellets, greensand (phosphorus and potassium), phosphate rock, and wood ashes (potassium) (see chapter 9 for more information on organic matter and fertilization). Throughout the book, I discuss nutrient release

FIGURE 47. Size comparison of carrot varieties. Drawing by author.

FIGURE 48. "Baby-cut" carrots available in most grocery stores are actually not a short cultivar but are cut from regular-sized carrots that may have had slight imperfections. Photo by author.

from organic materials—nitrogen from organic sources is released slowly over several years.

Selecting Cultivars

Specific recommendations depend on climate, soils, and growing conditions. There are six basic categories of carrots, based on shape and length (fig. 47). Multiple cultivars are available in these groups:

- 'Imperator,' 8 to 10 inches long
- 'Danvers,' 6 to 7 inches long
- 'Nantes,' 5 to 7 inches long
- 'Chantenay,' 4 to 5 inches long
- 'Amsterdam,' 2 to 3 inches long
- 'Paris Market,' short and round

Diseases and Pests

In the home garden, with proper crop rotation and soil health, problems are usually minimal. However, if problems arise, the following key may assist in identifying the cause (note: only the most common problems are listed). Many good websites can aid diagnosis with color photos. The cooperative Cornell University extension publication 2013 Organic Carrots for Processing (NYS IPM No. 133) is an excellent reference for organic and chemical pesticides labeled for carrots.

Diseases

Leaves

- Leaves appear grayish white on upper surface. Fungal disease, **Powdery Mildew** (*Erysiphe heraclei*).
- Dark brown to black necrotic lesions exist along margins of leaves and petioles. Fungal disease, **Alternaria Leaf Blight** (*Alternaria dauci*). Alternaria is seed borne. Symptoms may appear on older leaves, then on younger leaves during warm, moist conditions—use disease-free seeds, crop rotation, and foliar fungicides. Leaves may shrivel entirely and die.

- Leaves curl and have small, circular, grayish spots; as disease progresses, entire leaf dies. Fungal disease, **Early** or **Cercospora Leaf Blight** (*Cercospora carotae*).
- Small yellow areas eventually become lighter brown and dry with water soaking and chlorosis around the lesions, yellow halo on leaf margins. Bacterial disease, **Bacterial Blight** (*Xanthomonas hortorum* pv. *carotae*). For leaf blights, use disease-resistant cultivars, crop rotation, high initial fertility (nitrogen). Late nitrogen applications may promote disease; destroy crop residues. Various biologicals, biofungicides, chemical fungicides, gibberellic acid, and hydrogen peroxide are available.
- Stunted plants have thin leaves and reddish tops. Viral diseases transmitted from aphids, **Carrot Motley Dwarf** and **Carrot Thin Leaf**.
- Leaves are yellowing, older leaves purple red with "witches broom" appearance. Mycoplasma-like organism, **Aster Yellows** (see root diagnostics). Transmitted by aster (formerly six-spotted) leafhopper.

Seedlings

Damping-off disease from soil-borne fungi (*Pythium* spp., *Rhizoctonia solani*). Wet conditions. Also **crown rot**; early symptoms are horizontal dark brown lesions. As carrots mature, the tops may die back and top part of the root is rotted (brown to black cankers). Avoid poorly drained soil, plant on elevated ridges or mounds, use crop rotation, handle carefully during harvest, maintain storage sanitation. Some biologicals and biofungicides available.

Roots

- Forking—can be due to obstructions in soil (rocks, woody twigs, and mulch); soil-borne fungi (*Pythium ultimum*, *P. irregulare*, *Rhizoctonia solani*, and *Macrophomina* spp.); fresh manure and excess nitrogen.
- Forking, galls on roots, small carrot stubs growing from roots. **Root-Knot Nematodes** (*Meloidogyne hapla*). Management includes crop rotation to non-root vegetables; fumigants are used in commercial fields (**WARNING:** not recommended for home gardens). Grain cover crops (rye, barley, oats, and wheat), corn, Sudan grass, tall fescue, and annual ryegrass are nonhosts or poor hosts to this nematode. Avoid alfalfa and other legumes as cover crops before

carrots. Try biofumigant cover crops (mustards and arugula—see discussion under carrot culture).

- Root splitting—overwatering, especially toward the end of the growing cycle.
- Stubby, short carrots. **Lateral Root Dieback**; fungus (*Pythium* spp.) causes stubby carrots. Avoid poorly drained soils prone to flooding.
- Very pale yellow roots. Hot weather and high soil temperatures can be responsible for poor color formation. Keep plants well watered and use fine mulch when temperatures go above 85°F.
- Soft rot of the root, wilting and dieback of leaves, pitting and carved-out appearance, discoloration of root, smelly decay. **Bacterial Soft Rot** (*Dickeya* spp. and *Pectobacterium* spp.). Losses in storage usually occur after other storage diseases have appeared. Handle carefully after harvest; plant on raised beds or ridges if in poorly drained soils.
- Small brown water-soaked lesions and depressions. **Cavity Spot,** caused by fungal pathogens (*Pythium violae* and *P. sulcatum*). Disease increases with successive carrot plantings. Alfalfa is also a host for *P. violae*. Some tolerant varieties are available. High nitrogen may contribute. More prevalent during wet conditions and in poorly drained soils. Improve drainage—plant in raised beds or ridges; may be a calcium deficiency. Some biologicals, biofungicides, fungicides, hydrogen peroxide, and preseed treatments may be effective.
- White mold or cottony rot, outbreaks on the stored roots. Fungal disease, **Cottony Rot**, **White Mold, Sclerotinia** (*Sclerotinia sclerotiorum* and *S. minor*). Use crop rotation, plant on raised beds, avoid shade. Management: clean storage areas and tools, frequent inspection, low temperatures, and aeration and washing in a diluted bleach solution may give adequate control. Some biologicals and biofungicides available.
- Scab lesions; lateral brown striations; sunken, dry corky lesions on carrot surface. **Common Scab** caused by *Streptomyces scabies* bacteria. Alkaline soils (avoid potato fields) or dry high-organic soils. Adjust soil pH if above 7.
- Hairy roots with massive proliferation of side roots, bronze foliage. Second-year seed heads (umbels) abnormal. Mycoplasma-like organism, **Aster Yellows**. This disease is spread by adult aster leafhoppers.

Insects and other pests

- Whiteflies: Greenhouse Whitefly (*Trialeurodes vaporariorum*), Iris Whitefly (*Aleyrodes spiraeoides*), Sweet Potato Whitefly (*Bemisia tabaci*), Silverleaf Whitefly (*Bemisia argentifolii* [= *B. tabaci*, Biotype B]);
- Saltmarsh Caterpillar (*Estigmene acrea*);
- Palestriped Flea Beetle (*Systena blanda*);
- Aphids: Willow Carrot Aphid (*Cavariella aegopodii*), Honeysuckle Aphid (*Hyadaphis foeniculi*), Green Peach Aphid (*Myzus persicae*), Cotton (Melon) Aphid (*Aphis gossypii*), Hawthorn/Parsley Aphids (*Dysaphis foeniculus* and *D. apiifolia*), Tulip Bulb Aphid (*D. tulipae*), Hawthorn Carrot Aphid (*Dysaphis crataegi*), Bean Aphid (*Aphis fabae*);
- Carrot Rust Fly (*Psila rosae*);
- Aster (formerly Six-Spotted) Leafhopper (*Macrosteles quadrilineatus*);
- Armyworm (*Pseudaletia unipuncta*);
- Parsleyworm or Black Swallowtail Butterfly (*Papilio polyxenes*)—note: I leave these caterpillars alone, as they turn into black swallowtail butterflies;
- Yellow Woollybear (*Diacrisia virginica*);
- Leafminers: Chrysanthemum Leafminer (*Liriomyza trifolii*), Serpentine Leafminer (*L. brassicae*), and Vegetable Leafminer (*L. sativae*);
- Tarnished Plant Bug (*Lygus lineolaris*);
- Vegetable Weevil and larva (*Listroderes costirostris obliquus*);
- Carrot Weevil (*Listronotus oregonensis*);
- Southern Potato Wireworm (*Conoderus falli*);
- Root-Knot Nematodes (*Meloidogyne hapla*)

Harvesting

Keep checking your crop by occasionally pulling up several random carrots to check for development and taste. Although seed catalogs may list 65–70 days to maturity, carrots can and often do take longer to develop—up to 100 days. This is usually due to climatic factors. One common mistake is to wait too long, thinking that your carrots will grow bigger. If you wait past the optimal harvest time, the roots can become woody and the flavor can deteriorate. If the soil is moist, carrots can be pulled out by the tops. If the tops break off while pulling, use a digging tool such as a pitchfork to unearth the roots, but take care to avoid damaging them. In cooler climates where carrots mature more toward the end of the growing season, roots can be left in the ground after light frosts—some people believe they become sweeter. In some climates, carrots may be left in the ground under heavy mulch during the winter. There is a limit to storing carrots in the ground; if your soil freezes hard during the winter, this may not be a good option. In my Texas garden, fire ants damage root crops left in the ground. In Kansas and Idaho, I stored carrots in insulated buried conical pits.

Carrots Quick Guide

Botanical Data	Environmental Conditions	Culture and Special Considerations
Carrot (*Daucus carota* subsp. *sativus*), *Daucus* from the ancient Greek for "carrot"; *carota*, variant of the Greek word *karoton*, meaning "red rooted"; *sativus*, cultivated **Family**: parsley family (Apiaceae or Umbelliferae) **Life Cycle**: classified as herbaceous biennials, but grown as annuals in vegetable gardens **Flowers**: terminal umbels, pale pink before opening, white in full flower, with 5 petals, sepals, and stamens. Carrots require cold weather (chilling) to form flowers. Early plantings can result in early flowering. **Physiology**: cool-season vegetable, photosynthesis C_3 **Stems**: located above the ground, solitary, usually freely branched, internodes not distinct. Upon flowering, stems elongate, narrow, become pointed, and terminate in a highly branched umbel inflorescence. **Leaves**: ovate-lanceolate, filiform, elongate, pinnately divided **Roots**: strong taproots typically conical in shape, depending on cultivar. Taproot consists of parenchymatous outer cortex (phloem) and inner core (xylem). Quality carrots have a large proportion of cortex compared to core. **Fruits**: schizocarp consisting of 2 mericarps; each mericarp is an achene or true seed. **Seeds:** viability 3 years under cool dry conditions, then rapid decrease. 650–750 seeds/g. Seed germination 6–21 days at 55°F–80°F. **Days to Maturity (DTM):** varies greatly depending on cultivar. Check seed catalogs. Ranges around 36 days for baby carrot cultivars; 56–75 days for early to late types. DTM may exceed seed catalog listing	**Growing Zones**: check state and county cooperative extension sites and guides for adaptability and recommended planting dates **Timing**: sow in early spring to mid-July depending on summer temperatures and growing zone. Plant overwintering cultivars in fall. **Optimal Temperature for Growth**: 60°F–70°F for optimal color development. At < 50°F, growth slow. Above 86°F, growth reduced; strong, bitter flavor can develop. **Frost**: can tolerate some frost **Sunlight**: full sun, will tolerate light shading during part of day **Soil Conditions:** prefers well-drained, fertile soil, light-textured soils such as sandy loams to silt loams. In clayey soils, use short adapted cultivars. **Optimal pH**: 5.5–7.0 **Moisture Content:** consistent moisture needed to develop good color and root shape. Erratic moisture can result in split roots. Excessive water affects color formation and encourages disease. Drip irrigation not effective for larger plots. **Nutrition Information:** Raw carrots, USDA Food and Nutrition Service, % Daily Value based on 2,000 calorie diet Serving size 1 cup Calories 52.5, 3% Total carbohydrate 12.3 g, 4% Total fat 0.3 g, 0% Protein 1.2 g, 2% Vitamin A 428% Vitamin C 13% Vitamin K 21% Calcium 42.2 mg, 4% Iron 0.4 mg, 2% Potassium 410 mg, 12% Phosphorus 44.8 mg, 4% Sodium 88.3 mg, 4% Magnesium 15.4 mg, 4%	**Site Preparation**: spade and loosen soil to 6–10 inches. Work in compost, decomposed manure, and topsoil (optional) the previous fall. Do not work when soil is wet. Avoid fresh manure and excess N; forking may result. When planting, cover seeds with sifted compost, vermiculite. After plants are established, mulch with fine materials (peat moss, compost). **Transplants**: no, direct seed **Spacing**: start with 2–3 seeds/inch, gradually thin growing carrots to 2–4 inches depending on desired size and cultivar. Optimal size—when tops have 7–10 leaves, thin to 4 inches for larger cultivars. Harvest and eat thinned-out carrots. Can interseed with some radish or turnip seeds to mark seed location. **Fertilizers**: N varies according to organic matter content in soil. Average rates for soils with low OM = 120 lb. N/acre, medium OM = 100 lb. N/acre, and high OM = 80 lb. N/acre. P applications can be based on soil test (0–150 lb. P/acre depending on existing fertility); K applications can range from 0 to 200 lb. K/acre depending on existing fertility. Soil tests can provide needed rates for P and K (see table 32 in appendix D for converting lb./acre to equivalent rates for selected fertilizers in circle plots). **Weeding**: gentle cultivation. Add compost after carrots start maturing and tops show at soil surface to avoid green shoulders. **Depth of Planting**: ¼–½ inch **Cultivars**: there are many good heirlooms and hybrid cultivars available; select according to climate and soil type, texture, and depth. Seed companies introduce new cultivars every year.

FIGURE 49. Vegetable harvest arrangement with broccoli and cauliflower. Photo by author.

Broccoli, Cabbage, Cauliflower, and Others *(Brassica oleracea)*

Historical Background

The family Cruciferae, or mustard family, contains many important food crops such as cabbage, broccoli, cauliflower, brussels sprouts, kale, kohlrabi, collard greens, turnips, rutabagas, and mustard, all of which can be found in most vegetable garden catalogs. In addition, many other crucifers are now available (Chinese cabbage, assorted mustard greens, and "microgreens") that are highly nutritious. The family name derives from the characteristics of the flower, which has 4 sepals and petals arranged in a cross. The word "cabbage" derives from *caboche*, a Middle French word from the fifteenth century that literally means "head" or "noggin." Cabbage, broccoli, cauliflower, kale, collard, Chinese cabbage, brussels sprouts, and kohlrabi have the same scientific name (*Brassica oleracea*) but are differentiated by their subspecies names (see botanical section of Quick Guide).

The mustard family has a long history as cultivated food crops. Some authorities believe that our modern varieties of *Brassica oleracea* originated from wild cabbage or sea kale, a plant native to the western and eastern coasts of Europe, the Mediterranean, and Asia Minor. Cabbage and kale were probably the first "cole crops" (those belonging to the mustard family) to be domesticated (around 2,000 years ago), although broccoli may have been known to the Greeks and Romans as far back as 2,500 years ago. The present-day forms of broccoli originated in Italy and have developed over the last 2,000 years. Cabbage was cultivated in Germany in the mid-twelfth century and was being grown in England by the fourteenth century. Cabbage may have been introduced to the American continent from seeds planted by Jacques Cartier, French mariner and explorer in Canada (around 1541). Thomas Jefferson grew an assortment of different cabbage varieties at his Monticello gardens.

Planting and Culture

Check the Quick Guide for specific information about the three main cole crops. As with all vegetable crops, good drainage is essential. The crucifers prefer acidic soils (pH 6.0–6.8) and will grow well in a variety of soil textures. In the circle gardening method, annual additions of compost, manure, and other soil amendments will maintain and improve soil physical properties, organic matter, and fertility. Cabbage is usually easiest to grow, followed by broccoli, then cauliflower.

Broccoli, cabbage, cauliflower, and other cruciferous vegetables are usually set out as transplants. If you live in an area where spring is fleeting, the South for example, you will need cultivars that bolt slowly and are tolerant of higher temperatures. Prolonged cool temperatures after planting can also affect the growth cycle and quality of the cole crops (see Quick Guide for specifics). If you buy your transplants, your selection is usually limited, but if you start your own plants from seeds, you can explore and test many more different cultivars (see chapters on starting the garden). Good-quality transplants are vital to a successful crop. Hardened-off cole crop transplants 5 to 6 weeks old are best. Older transplants that start producing small heads will not produce as well as younger plants that are still in the leaf stage.

It is not difficult to start cruciferous seedlings. The seeds are about the size of a poppy seed on a roll and are easy to distinguish and handle. I use gallon pots and plant 4 seeds per pot in February, more than 2 months prior to the last freeze. I fill the pots about three-quarters full with a purchased vegetable seedling soil mixture. I add the rest of the vegetable potting mix when the seedlings grow above the pot. This adds more support to the stem. I find that crucifer seedlings get a bit stemmy even when grown outside in cold frames. I then set the pots in a cold frame, in a plastic tentlike structure, or out in a sunny spot by my well. Crucifers are tough plants and can tolerate light freezes. When the conditions are right, the seeds will germinate; then I watch the seedlings on a daily basis. In the South, we often have periods of mild temperatures in late winter that are sufficient to germinate crucifers. However, in colder climates, use a cold frame. Keep the soil moist. If a freeze threatens and you do not have a cold frame, drape plastic over the plants and hold the edges down with rocks, or move plants to an enclosed area (shed or garage).

The best time to prepare your circle plots is in the fall. Dig in manure and compost at this time, and if your soil needs some extra improvement, add a bag of topsoil. If you miss the fall application, apply the manure, compost, and topsoil to each circle plot a few weeks before setting out broccoli and cabbage plants. Commercial growers broadcast about one-third of the total nitrogen requirement at planting, use another one-third as side dressing 2 weeks after planting, and apply the final one-third 5 weeks after planting. In the home garden, side dress 4 to 6 inches away from the base of the plant, along with good watering. Some commercial growers do not side dress nitrogen for cauliflower, as loose heads may form. Phosphorus and potassium are usually applied as a preplanting treatment when the seedbed is prepared.

Commercial fertilizer rates for cruciferous crops vary according to various authorities and extension publications. Soils with low soil organic matter (SOM < 2%) require 100–180 lb. N/acre; soils with medium SOM (2%–5%) need 80–160 lb./acre; and soils with high SOM (5%–10%) need 60–140 lb./acre. Phosphorus based on soil tests can range from 0 to 150 lb./acre, whereas potassium rates range from 0 to 250 lb./acre. See appendix D for equivalent fertilizer rates for circle plots.

FIGURE 50. Red cabbage, broccoli, and cauliflower transplants ready to set out in the garden. Photo by author.

Before setting out transplants, prepare a hole about 8 to 12 inches deep, place some organic fertilizer and well-rotted compost in the bottom, and cover with 2–3 inches of garden soil. Then place the transplant with the base of the stem at about the same depth in the pot. When transplants are grown in cold frames and/or outside and are hardened off in natural sunlight, the plants will be strong and will get off to a good start. Plant transplants 10 to 24 inches apart depending on cultivar size (fig. 51). The wider spacing will produce larger main broccoli heads, but closer spacing will encourage many side shoots, which may be harvested over a longer period. There should be 3 to 6 leaves on your transplants, and the leaves should have a thickened, leathery feel. After setting out the transplants, I place a small amount of mulch around the seedlings—fine compost (fig. 51) or peat moss works well—to lessen the amount of soil splash on the young leaves.

During the adaptation phase, be sure to provide consistent moisture, as well as weed and insect control to prevent "buttoning" (small, stunted heads, especially on broccoli and cauliflower). A cold snap (35 to 50°F) can also cause buttoning. To avoid buttoning, do not plant too early; plants will compensate if planted after cooler temperatures.

A

FIGURE 51. *A*, Red cabbage, *B*, broccoli, and *C*, kale transplants in circle arrangement (circle diameter 5 feet). Photos by author.

B

C

FIGURE 52. Compost and animal manure applied in fall. The time to side dress red cabbage plants with small amounts of fertilizer is 3–4 weeks after setting out; then 10–14 days later, followed by a third side dress 10–14 days after that. Commercial growers may use a fourth side dressing of fertilizer for cabbage, especially red cabbage, since it seems to require more nitrogen.

A

FIGURE 53. *A*, Red cabbage and *B*, broccoli in circle plots, with heads starting to form.

B

Diseases and Pests

Consult state and local extension bulletins for the latest treatments of diseases and pests. Remedies and controls are constantly being updated. The diseases below are not all-inclusive but represent the most common problems.

Diseases

Seedlings

- Reddish-brown coloration on seedlings or discoloration near base of plant. Stem appears bent or twisted, wirelike, without breaking. Seedling can eventually die. Soil-borne fungus, **Wire Stem** (*Rhizoctonia solani*). Disease favors cool, cloudy weather, high humidity, overcrowding, and poor soil drainage.
- Seedlings die soon after germination, or decay sets in and seedlings fall over and die. A lesion develops near the stem base in contact with soil. Fungal disease, **Damping Off** (*Pythium debaryanum*). Moist, wet conditions and high humidity favor damping off. Avoid overwatering, provide good soil drainage.
- See **Yellows** or **Fusarium Wilt** (*Fusarium oxysporum* f. sp. *conglutinans*).
- See **Clubroot** (*Plasmodiophora brassicae*).
- See **Black Leg** (*Phoma lingam*).

Leaves

- Infected plants can be at any stage of development, with yellow-green leaves, which eventually turn brown and die. Entire leaves may drop off as disease progresses. Warm, wet, high-humidity conditions favor the disease. Bacterial disease, **Black Rot** (*Xanthomonas campestris* pv. *campestris*). Use tolerant cultivars, seed treatments, crop rotation, and copper sprays.
- Lifeless leaves with yellow-green color, usually on one side of plant, curling of leaves. Leaf area near petiole or midrib dies. Disease starts on lower leaves and progresses upward. Usually appears 2 to 4 weeks after transplanting. Fungal disease, **Yellows** or **Fusarium Wilt** (*Fusarium oxysporum* f. sp. *conglutinans*). Disease overwinters in infected plant debris. Use disease-free seeds, seed treatments, crop rotation, and resistant cultivars. Destroy previous year's litter; fungicides available.
- Small dark yellow spots on leaves; spots enlarge and have a concentric ring appearance with a yellow halo. The entire plant may defoliate. Fungal disease, **Leaf Spot** and **Blight** (*Alternaria brassicae* and *A. brassicicola*). Wet, humid conditions. Use disease-free seeds, crop rotation. Fungicides available.
- Water-soaked circular areas on base of leaves or where foliage is in contact with the soil. The necrotic lesions quickly rot and become soft and watery. White, cottony mycelial fungal growth. Disease can colonize inside and outside stems, and heads have large black sclerotia. Fungal disease, **Sclerotinia Rot / White Mold** (*Sclerotinia sclerotiorum*). Soil borne; provide good air circulation, do not use other cole crops in rotations. No effective fungicides available.
- Small dark specks on top and bottom of leaves progressing to numerous water-soaked spots (⅛ inch in diameter). Spots may turn tan to brown and develop a purple border. Bacterial disease, **Bacterial Leafspot** (*Pseudomonas syringae* pv. *maculicola*). Disease occurs in greenhouses as well as fields (cauliflower is susceptible). Seed-borne bacterial disease, spread by rain or overhead irrigation, and soil splash onto leaves.

Leaves and heads

Small yellow-green lesions on upper leaf surfaces, progressing to underside of leaves. Grayish-white moldy growth on underside of leaves. Cabbage heads can develop sunken black spots, which are infected during the seedling stage, but symptoms do not appear until maturity. Fungal disease, **Downy Mildew** (*Peronospora parasitica*).

Develops in warm, wet, and high-humidity conditions. Fungicides available.

Seedlings, leaves, stems, and roots

Pale yellowish irregular spots on leaves, can become ashy gray with black spots. Stem lesions appear purple near ground level, causing black rot on lower stem and base of plant and roots. Plants are stunted, wilt, and often fall over because of root damage. Disease can spread to stored cabbage heads. Use crop rotations, remove previous year's crop litter. Fungal disease, **Black Leg** (*Phoma lingam*). Hot water treatments on commercial seeds, crop rotations every 4 years, avoid overhead irrigation and soil splash onto plants, avoid cultivation when soil is wet, control weeds, especially in the mustard family. Control insect pests. Fungicide labeled for broccoli.

Roots

Clubby, swollen, distorted appearance at base of plant and roots, larger club roots just below surface of soil. Disease usually appears about 3 weeks after infection and seedlings usually succumb to death. Plants may wilt in hot weather but recover during evening. Leaves appear stunted and yellow. Disease rarely kills more-mature plants, but roots are less able to absorb nutrients and water. Fungus, but more closely related to slime molds. **Clubroot** (*Plasmodiophora brassicae*). Disease prefers acidic soils; mix in lime, wood ashes to increase alkalinity (pH > 7). Alkaline soils not as susceptible, but not immune from outbreaks of clubroot. Use long rotations of 6 years, avoid poorly drained soil.

Insects

- Various caterpillars and loopers: Cabbage Looper (*Trichoplusia ni*), Alfalfa Looper (*Autographa californica*), Diamondback Moth (*Plutella xylostella*), Imported Cabbage Worm (*Pieris rapae*), Beet Army Worm (*Spodoptera exigua*), Cross-Striped Cabbageworm (*Evergestis rimosalis*), Garden Webworm (*Achyra rantalis*), Hawaiian Beet Webworm (*Spoladea recurvalis*), Southern Beet Webworm (*Herpetogramma bipunctalis*); Cutworms (*Agrotis* spp. and *Peridroma saucia*);
- Wireworms (Elateridae spp.);
- Aphids: Cabbage Aphid (*Brevicoryne brassicae*), Turnip Aphid (*Hyadaphis erysimi*), Green Peach Aphid (*Myzus persicae*);
- Flea Beetles (*Phyllotreta* spp., *Epitrix cucumeris*, and *Systena blanda*);

- Silverleaf Whitefly (*Bemisia argentifolii*);
- Cabbage and Seedcorn Maggots (*Delia* spp.);
- Harlequin Bug (*Murgantia histrionica*);
- Grasshoppers and Katydids.

The common White Cabbage Butterfly (*Pieris rapae*), with 1 to 4 black spots on the wings, is often seen fluttering around the garden. The larvae are the pests on cole crops.

Cruciferous Vegetables Quick Guide

Botanical Data		
Broccoli (*Brassica oleracea* var. *italica*) **Family:** mustard family (Cruciferae); derived from 4 flower petals resembling a cross. Latin *crux*, "cross," *fera*, "to bear." **Life Cycle:** classified as herbaceous biennials, but grown as annuals in vegetable gardens **Flowers:** perfect, 4 petals, stamens nearly always 6 in 2 whorls, genetically incompatible with self-pollination; pollination can occur from other crucifers (cauliflower, cabbage, kale, collard, kohlrabi, brussels sprouts, etc.) **Pollinators:** bees, flies, other insects **Physiology:** cool-season vegetable, photosynthesis C_3 **Stems:** tall, fibrous, freely branched, especially at top of plant **Leaves:** alternate, smooth, pinnatifid, margins entire, dentate, or broadly lobed, glaucous (with a whitish or bluish waxy covering) **Roots:** taproot with relatively shallow, extensive, fibrous root system **Fruits:** silique, 2-celled pod-like fruit; when mature, sides open, dehiscent, and separate **Seed Viability**: 3–5 years in uniform cool, dry conditions **Days to Maturity (DTM):** variable based on cultivar, 65–105 days for transplants, add 10–14 days if directly seeded	**Cabbage** (*Brassica oleracea* var. *capitata*) **Family:** mustard family (Cruciferae); derived from 4 flower petals resembling a cross **Life Cycle:** classified as herbaceous biennials, but grown as annuals in vegetable gardens **Flowers:** perfect, 4 petals, stamens nearly always 6 in 2 whorls, genetically incompatible with self-pollination; pollination can occur from other crucifers (cauliflower, kale, collard, kohlrabi, brussels sprouts, etc.) **Pollinators:** bees, flies, other insects **Physiology:** cool-season vegetable, photosynthesis C_3 **Stems:** short, fibrous at maturity **Leaves:** alternate, smooth or wrinkled depending on variety, glaucous (with a whitish or bluish waxy covering, may rub off), fleshy, repand (with a wavy surface or margin), toothed or lobed **Roots:** taproot with extensive, finely branched roots **Fruits:** silique, 2-celled pod-like fruit; when mature, sides open, dehiscent, and separate **Seed Viability**: 4 years in uniform cool, dry conditions **Days to Maturity (DTM):** variable based on cultivar, 49–71 days for transplants, add about 20 days if directly seeded	**Cauliflower** (*Brassica oleracea* var. *botrytis*) **Family:** mustard family (Cruciferae); derived from 4 flower petals resembling a cross **Life Cycle:** classified as herbaceous biennials, but grown as annuals in vegetable gardens **Flowers:** perfect, 4 petals, stamens nearly always 6 in 2 whorls, summer cauliflower usually self-compatible **Pollinators:** bees, flies, other insects **Physiology:** cool-season vegetable, photosynthesis C_3 **Stems:** short, fibrous at maturity **Leaves:** smooth, glaucous (with a whitish or bluish waxy covering, may rub off), fleshy, repand (with a wavy surface or margin), toothed or lobed **Roots:** taproot with well-branched laterals and profuse network of small fibrous roots, can be more extensive than in cabbage **Fruits:** silique, 2-celled pod-like fruit; when mature, sides open, dehiscent, and separate **Seed Viability**: 3–5 years in uniform cool, dry conditions **Days to Maturity (DTM):** variable based on cultivar, 50–80 days for transplants, add 10–14 days if directly seeded
Environmental Conditions		
Broccoli **Growing Zones:** check state and county cooperative extension sites and guides for adaptability and recommended planting dates **Timing:** set transplants out when there are 3–5 true leaves and after danger of hard frost **Optimal temperature for growth:** germination temperature is between 55°F and 75°F, optimal between 60°F and 70°F. Temps. below 40°F can cause chilling injury and/or early flower development.	**Cabbage** **Growing Zones:** check state and county cooperative extension sites and guides for adaptability and recommended planting dates **Timing:** set transplants out when there are 5–6 true leaves and after danger of hard frost **Optimal temperature for growth:** germination temperature is between 55°F and 75°F, optimal between 60°F and 75°F. Prolonged temps. of 50°F–60°F can produce premature seed stalks instead of heads.	**Cauliflower** **Growing Zones:** check state and county cooperative extension sites and guides for adaptability and recommended planting dates **Timing:** set transplants out when there are 6–8 true leaves and after danger of hard frost **Optimal temperature for growth:** germination temperature is between 55°F and 75°F, optimal between 68°F and 78°F. Most temperamental of cole crops regarding environmental factors and temps.

Cruciferous Vegetables Quick Guide *continued*

Environmental Conditions		
Broccoli	**Cabbage**	**Cauliflower**
Frost: can tolerate hard frost 28°F and colder (mid-20s) depending on conditions	**Frost:** can tolerate hard frost 28°F and colder (mid-20s) depending on conditions	**Frost:** can tolerate hard frost 28°F and colder (mid-20s) depending on conditions
Sunlight: full sun	**Sunlight:** full sun	**Sunlight:** full sun
Soil Conditions: prefers well-drained, highly fertile soils, tolerates wide range of soil texture (sandy loams to clay loams). Moderately sensitive to salts.	**Soil Conditions:** prefers well-drained, highly fertile soils, tolerates wide range of soil texture (sandy loams to clay loams). Moderately sensitive to salts.	**Soil Conditions:** prefers well-drained, highly fertile soils, tolerates wide range of soil texture (sandy loams to clay loams). Moderately sensitive to salts.
Optimal pH: 6.0–6.8	**Optimal pH:** 6.0–6.8	**Optimal pH:** 6.0–7.0
Soil Moisture Content: even moisture supply needed for establishing transplants; keep moisture consistent throughout growing season for constant, steady, and even growth	**Soil Moisture Content:** even moisture supply needed for establishing transplants; keep moisture consistent throughout growing season for constant, steady, and even growth	**Soil Moisture Content:** even moisture supply needed for establishing transplants; keep moisture consistent throughout growing season for constant, steady, and even growth

Culture and Special Considerations		
Broccoli	**Cabbage**	**Cauliflower**
Site Preparation: spade and loosen soil to 6–10 inches. Work in a 2-inch layer of compost, decomposed manure, and topsoil (optional) the previous fall. Do not work when soil is wet. After plants are established, mulch with fine materials (peat moss, compost).	**Site Preparation:** spade and loosen soil to 6–10 inches. Work in a 2-inch layer of compost, decomposed manure, and topsoil (optional) the previous fall. Do not work when soil is wet. After plants are established, mulch with fine materials (peat moss, compost).	**Site Preparation:** spade and loosen soil to 6–10 inches. Work in a 2-inch layer of compost, decomposed manure, and topsoil (optional) the previous fall. Do not work when soil is wet. After plants are established, mulch with fine materials (peat moss, compost).
Planting: in the home garden, use transplants to advance growth when temperatures are still cool in spring and fall	**Planting:** in the home garden, use transplants to advance growth when temperatures are still cool in spring and fall	**Planting:** in the home garden, use transplants to advance growth when temperatures are still cool in spring and fall
Direct seeding into the garden bed can be done where the growing season is sufficiently long and temperatures stay in optimal ranges. Care must be applied to reduce soil crusting, which is detrimental to tender seedlings.	Direct seeding into the garden bed can be done where the growing season is sufficiently long and temperatures stay in optimal ranges. Care must be applied to reduce soil crusting, which is detrimental to tender seedlings.	Direct seeding into the garden bed can be done where the growing season is sufficiently long and temperatures stay in optimal ranges. Care must be applied to reduce soil crusting, which is detrimental to tender seedlings.
Seeds: ¼ inch deep, usually planted in flats indoors or in cold frame	**Seeds:** ¼ inch deep, usually planted in flats indoors or in cold frame	**Seeds:** ¼ inch deep, usually planted in flats indoors or in cold frame
Spacing: depends on cultivar, transplants 12–24 inches apart. Traditional rows 18–36 inches apart.	**Spacing:** depends on cultivar, transplants 12–24 inches apart. Traditional rows 18–48 inches apart.	**Spacing:** depends on cultivar, transplants 12–24 inches apart. Traditional rows 18–36 inches apart.
Weeding: gentle cultivation, mulch after plants are actively growing	**Weeding:** gentle cultivation, mulch after plants are actively growing	**Weeding:** gentle cultivation, mulch after plants are actively growing
Cultivars: cultivars matter; choose adaptable cultivars recommended for your area	**Cultivars:** cultivars matter; choose adaptable cultivars recommended for your area	**Cultivars:** cultivars matter; choose adaptable cultivars recommended for your area

Culture and Special Considerations		
Broccoli **Specifics on Culture:** when heads appear, they mature quickly; harvest before yellow flowers open and heads yellow. Cut heads rather than breaking off; once the main head is cut, side shoots, which are never as large as the main head, may be harvested for an extended period, depending on temperatures. **Harvest:** harvest when heads and side shoots are compact and before flower buds open and yellow flowers appear. Average head diameter around 4–8 inches. Overmature heads and stems become woody. Cut side shoots below the florets, as it seems to stimulate new sprouts and side shoots. Cool broccoli quickly after harvest to maintain high quality. **Nutrition Information:** Broccoli, raw, USDA Food and Nutrition Service. % Daily Value based on 2,000 calorie diet Serving size 1 cup Calories 31 Total fat 0 g, 1% Total carbohydrate 6 g, 2% Protein 3 g, 5% Vitamin A 567 IU, 11% Vitamin C 81 mg, 135% Vitamin K, 92.5 mcg, 116% Folate 57 mcg, 14% Calcium 43 mg, 4% Iron 0.7 mg, 4% Phosphorus 60 mg, 6% Potassium 288 mg, 8% Manganese 0.2 mg, 10% Magnesium 19 mg, 5%	**Cabbage** **Specifics on Culture:** cabbage heads are mature when the outermost green leaves begin to curl slightly, exposing white leaves below. Cabbage can be harvested anytime the heads appear large enough. It is better to harvest sooner than later, as overmature heads can split open, leading to a greater chance for insect damage, especially cabbage worms. **Harvest:** harvest when heads are firm; soft spongy heads are not mature. Overmature heads will begin to split. Harvest in early morning. If the main head is removed carefully, several small heads may develop later. Cool cabbage heads after harvest to maintain high quality. **Nutrition Information:** Cabbage, raw, USDA Food and Nutrition Service. % Daily Value based on 2,000 calorie diet Serving size 1 cup Calories 22 Total fat 0 g, 0% Total carbohydrate 5 g, 2% Protein 1 g, 2% Vitamin A, 87 IU, 2% Vitamin C 32.6 mg, 54% Vitamin K 67.6 mcg, 85% Vitamin B_6 0.1 mg, 6% Folate 38 mcg, 10% Calcium 36 mg, 4% Potassium 151 mg, 4% Phosphorus 23 mg, 2% Manganese 0.1 mg, 7%	**Cauliflower** **Specifics on Culture:** as temperatures warm, the size of the head or curd will suffer. Avoid overmaturity; cut heads when they are snowy white and before yellowing. It is better to harvest early rather than wait, or quality can decrease. If the weather warms too quickly when cauliflower is maturing, the outer leaves can be tied over the head to prevent sunscald and slow blanching of the head. In high temperatures the heads can fail to form. **Harvest:** harvest when head (curd) diameter reaches 5–8 inches and before segments separate. Overmature curds will loosen and separate. When double, cut early rather than late. For pure white heads (white cultivars), pull 3–4 leaves and tie loosely over head. Color of cauliflower heads does not affect eating quality. Cool cauliflower heads after harvest to maintain high quality. **Nutrition Information:** Cauliflower, raw, USDA Food and Nutrition Service. % Daily Value based on 2,000 calorie diet Serving size 1 cup Calories 25 Total fat 0 g, 0% Total carbohydrate 5 g, 2% Protein 2 g, 4% Vitamin C 46 mg, 77% Vitamin K 16 mcg, 20% Vitamin B_6 0.2 mg, 11% Foliate 57 mcg, 14% Potassium 303 mg, 9% Manganese 0.2 mg, 8% Phosphorus 44 mg, 4% Calcium 22 mg, 2%

A

B

FIGURE 54. Cucumbers and assorted squash. Photos by author.

Squash and Cucumbers

(*Cucurbita* spp. and *Cucumis Sativus*)

There are about 125 genera and 825 species in the family Cucurbitaceae, including several prominent garden vegetables. Pumpkin and squash comprise mainly 6 species: field pumpkin (*Cucurbita pepo*), winter squash (*C. maxima*), crookneck squash (*C. moschata*), Asian or Malabar gourd (*C. ficifolia*), Missouri gourd (*C. foetidissima*), and cushaw, pipian, or calabaza squash (*C. mixta*). The word "pumpkin" is derived from the Greek *pepon* and Latin *pepo*. The Latin *pepo* describes large fruit and melons. The scientific name of cucumbers is *Cucumis sativus*.

Historical Background

The term "squash" is associated with Native Americans along the northeastern Atlantic coast (from *askutasquash*, their equivalent of vine apples). *Cucurbita pepo* is thought to be the earliest domesticated squash, with traces found in Florida (10,000 BCE), southern Mexico (8000 BCE and in cultivation by 7500 BCE), and in Illinois in the Mississippi Valley (5000 BCE, cultivated by 1500 to 1000 BCE). By the 1600s, the Wampanoag, a North American tribe in southeastern Massachusetts and Rhode Island, was growing many varieties of squash and pumpkin (*C. pepo*). Squashes and pumpkins were brought to the Old World, where they were being grown as early as 1542. In

C

D

E

F

TABLE 24. Scientific and common names of various species in the Cucurbitaceae family

Cucurbita pepo	*C. maxima*	*C. moschata*	*C. ficifolia*	*C. foetidissima*	*C. mixta*
Acorn squash	Hubbard	Butternut	Seven year melon	Buffalo gourd	Cushaw
Cocozelle	Banana	Cheese	Siam pumpkin	Missouri gourd	Seroria squash
Crookneck summer squash	Marrow		Malabar gourd or squash	Wild gourd	Giant pumpkin cultivars
Scallop squash	Turban		Asian pumpkin	Coyote gourd	Pie pumpkin
Zucchini	Buttercup		Pie melon	Wild pumpkin	
Vegetable marrow			Thai marrow		
Halloween pumpkin varieties			Fig leaf gourd		

England, pumpkins were grown during the mid-sixteenth century, and American colonists were already familiar with these plants.

Our garden cucurbits are frost-sensitive annuals, sometimes perennials, which have tuberous storage roots and grow mostly as vines. Cucurbits develop tendrils that help support the climbing and vining habit. Plant breeders have now produced bush-type squashes and cucumbers. Bees and moths pollinate the cucurbits and are attracted to the ultraviolet light reflected from the flower petals (fig. 54c). Refer to chapter 3, "Garden Ecology," for more details about cucumber reproduction.

Four important food crops originated in India: the cucumber, eggplant, Indian mustard, and cowpea. Cucumber, from the Latin word *cucumis*, was cultivated throughout western Asia for 3,000 years and in eastern Iran and China for 2,000 years. The cucumber originated north of the Bay of Bengal and in the Himalayas. Cucumbers spread from India to Greece and Italy, and later to China. The Romans took the vegetable to Europe during the ninth century, and cucumbers were cultivated in France and England in the fourteenth century. Cucumbers finally arrived in America in the mid-sixteenth century. Columbus brought the cucumber to Haiti and other islands in 1494. When French explorers arrived, they found Native Americans growing cucumbers in Canada (now Montreal) around 1535. Likewise, the Spanish explorer Hernando de Soto found cucumbers growing in Florida around 1540. The Mandan on the Great Plains along the Missouri River (now North Dakota) were advanced farmers who grew corn, beans, pumpkins, squashes, and gourds, and they obtained cucumbers and watermelons from the Spaniards.

Culture and Planting

Cucurbits grow best during warmer weather, when soil temperatures have risen past 60°F (optimal planting temperature is 70°F–95°F). Squash and cucumbers are very frost sensitive. I recommend planting the bush cultivars, as they are more compact (fig. 54). I do use vining winter squash and cucumber cultivars, but I plant them on the perimeter of the garden and let them trail outward. Squash and cucumbers are easy to plant since they have large seeds. Apply compost and decomposed manure as instructed in chapter 7, "Establishing the Garden." Soil texture can range from sandy loam to clay loam, and the pH should be acidic to neutral (5.8–7.0). If your soil is more toward the clayey side, you can modify it over time with additions of organic matter. Shape the soil in the circle into a conical shape, with the center mounded slightly, and create a border around the perimeter so that water does not run off the plot.

Fertilization rates vary; check local extension bulletins. Average commercial nitrogen rates are about 80 lb./acre. Broadcast about 30 to 60 lb. N fertilizer/acre (high-nitrogen organic and/or balanced synthetic fertilizer per your gardening preference) and mix into the upper 4 to 6 inches of soil several weeks before or at the time of planting. Preplanting rates for phosphorous and potassium range from 90 to 150 lb./acre depending on soil test results. After the plants are actively growing (about 2 to 3 weeks), side dress with an additional

30 to 50 lb. N/acre. See appendix D for equivalent fertilizer rates for circle plots.

Place 6 to 8 seeds in a circular arrangement about 12 inches from the perimeter of the circle. I do not recommend planting transplants, as they are very sensitive to transplant shock. Seeds work fine; they germinate in 5 to 7 days at optimal soil temperatures. Keep the soil moist to ensure rapid germination. After the seeds have germinated and the plants have developed a couple of leaves, select the best 3 or 4 plants (fig. 54). It is difficult to cull the other plants out, but if you don't, your plants will become too crowded and tangled and you will not be able to reach into the jungle and harvest your fruit. If you cannot bear to sacrifice the plants, try moving the culls to another plot. Scoop a good amount of soil around and under the plant and move it to a new location. With care, the plants usually survive the move.

Squash plants are monoecious; they produce separate male and female flowers on the same plant (see chapter 3, "Garden Botany"). The ratio of male to female flowers is usually 3:1 or higher. Female flowers are typically borne on short stems, whereas male flowers have longer stems. Honeybees are the primary pollinators and are extremely sensitive to insecticides. When squash fruit (a pepo) begins to develop, it grows fast, about 1 inch per day. Various squash cultivars will cross-pollinate—for example, zucchini will cross with crookneck, but not with cucumbers.

It is best to harvest summer squash when they are smaller, immature, and tender. At this stage you will be able to eat the skin and seeds. Zucchini have the habit of camouflaging themselves so that when you find them, they are baseball-bat size. In literally a few days, a 6- to 8-inch zucchini will become a foot long. Books have been written on what to do with so much zucchini. If you let your summer squash get too large, the skin will become tougher and the seeds hard and unpalatable. As a general rule, after you see a small squash emerging from a female flower, be ready to pick in three or four days. I have found the perfect solution for the "whale"-sized zucchinis—they go to the dairy goats, who love them raw.

Diseases and Pests

Diseases

Leaves

- Circular tan to brown spots, yellowing on perimeter. Spots can enlarge to 1½ inches in diameter. Spots may have a target or "bull's-eye" appearance. Conditions favorable for disease are

FIGURE 55. *A*, Squash bug. Photo by benjamint444. http://en.wikipedia.org/wiki/File:Male_Amorbus_rubiginosus.jpg. *B*, Adult squash vine borer. (*Melittia satyriniformis*) is a common clearwing-moth; symptoms of infestation are a runner or entire plant that wilts and sawdust-like frass near the base of the plant. C, The larvae (caterpillars) reach a length of 1 inch and have a brown head and a cream-colored body; larvae feed on the plant for approximately 4 weeks and tunnel along the stem of the plant. D, Most summer squash varieties and Hubbard squash with succulent stems are very susceptible to vine borers. Pumpkins, Green Striped Cushaw, and butternut squashes are more resistant. Drawings by author.

A

B, C, and D

bright sunshine, frequent heavy dew and rain, and temperatures of 60°F–90°F. Overwinters on plant residue and is spread by insects, water splash, tools, and implements. Fungus, **Alternaria Leaf Spot** (*Alternaria cucumerina*). Fungicides effective.

- Dark spots, circular to irregularly shaped (lighter in center, darker around perimeter). Leaf tissue around spots often yellow. Centers of spots become papery and dry and fall out, leaving holes in leaves. The entire leaf may eventually be affected. Overwinters on cucurbit residue and weeds; spores (conidia) are wind borne and spread by water splash and irrigation. Direct water on leaves is necessary for infection. Disease usually increases rapidly at 78°F to 90°F; infections are cyclic and can reoccur every 7 to 10 days. Fungus, **Cercospora Leaf Spot** (*Cercospora citrullina*). Disease is most common in watermelon, other melons, and cucumber. Clean up all previous year's litter, space plants for good airflow, avoid wetting leaves, and rotate crops every 2 to 3 years. Fungicides effective.

Vines, stems, and leaves

- Wilting followed by rapid decline and death. More severe on cucumber and cantaloupe, less severe on squash and pumpkin. Bacteria, **Bacterial Wilt** (*Erwinia tracheiphila*). Disease is spread by striped or spotted cucumber beetle; no control is available, other than control of cucumber beetles. *Erwinia tracheiphila* overwinters in the beetles that hibernate in plant debris, litter, and weeds near the garden. Usually, plants are infected before symptoms show; when the vines begin to wilt, the disease has progressed and death is imminent. Pull plants and discard.
- White powdery growth on leaf surfaces and stems. Fruits are not directly affected, but size and growth can be stunted. Fungus, **Powdery Mildew** (*Erysiphe cichoracearum*). Disease spreads during wet conditions, high humidity (50°F–90°F). Avoid wetting foliage during irrigation and water in early morning so that aboveground plant parts will dry. Mulch in and around plants to avoid soil splash. Do not crowd plants; good air circulation is essential. Seems to affect late-planted squash. Use resistant cultivars; fungicides effective.
- Small yellow spots on upper leaf surfaces; spots develop brown irregular margins and coalesce with each other. A gray mold may appear on lower leaf surfaces. Leaves may wither and die; fruit is not affected. Fungus, **Downy Mildew** (*Pseudoperonospora cubensis*). Wet, warm, humid weather favors the disease. Avoid wetting leaves during irrigation, mulch in and around plants, and use resistant cultivars; fungicides available.
- Plants wilt; symptoms improve during evening, but plant eventually succumbs to permanent wilting. Yellowing on older leaves, progresses to younger leaves. Initially, only one vine on plant may be affected while other vines remain unaffected. As disease progresses, the entire plant may wilt and die. Plants that survive are stunted, and production is greatly reduced. A white mold may

appear on dead vines. In watermelon and muskmelon, a brown necrotic streak can be observed externally on the lower stem and extending along the length of the vine. Fungus, **Fusarium Wilt** (*Fusarium oxysporum*). Soil-borne disease, lives for many years in soil. Plant resistant cultivars, buy disease-free seeds, avoid irrigation and soil splash on leaves. Watermelon should be rotated every 5 to 7 years with noncucurbit crops. No effective chemical controls.

- Yellow, V-shaped lesions form around margins of older leaves. As disease progresses, the lesions enlarge and dominate the leaf. Plants wilt and die. This disease is often confused with bacterial wilt and gummy stem blight. Fungus, **Verticillium Wilt** (*Verticillium dahliae* and *V. albo-atrum*). The fungi survive in soil for many years as dormant sclerotia. This disease affects many vegetable crops. Sclerotia germinate in soil and infect plant roots. Verticillium wilt is most severe during cool periods and subsides somewhat during the hot summer. Plants may wilt when stressed, especially after fruit set. *Verticillium dahliae* grows in plant xylem and interferes with water transport within the plant. No effective controls.

Leaves, stems, and fruit

- Brown, red, or tan spots, irregularly shaped and sized, spots usually larger than with downy mildew. Spots may cover entire leaf. Stems may split, and brown gummy slime may be evident on open wounds. Disease is usually observed as a wet rot on the lower portion of the vine and stem. Vines eventually wilt and die, and fruit can be affected and can also develop circular spots. Fungus, **Gummy Stem Blight** (*Didymella bryoniae*). No resistant cultivars, disease may be seed borne. Remove all cucurbit litter, rotate crops, and avoid wetting leaves during irrigation. Some fungicides available.
- Yellow water-soaked spots turn brown, then black. Spots dry out and fall out of leaf, creating holes. Fruits can be affected and can have circular black cankers. Fungus, **Anthracnose** (*Colletotrichum orbiculare*). Seed-borne disease, overwinters in litter; remove all cucurbit litter, use crop rotation, buy disease-free seeds. Several genetically resistant cucumber and watermelon cultivars available. Fungicide treatments available.
- White to gray spots on leaves, sometimes with yellow halo. Spots become papery and fall out, leaving holes in leaves. Cucumber,

summer squash, and pumpkin have sunken fruit spots (greenish to black velvety fungal growth). Infected winter squash fruits develop raised corky areas on rind. Fungus, **Scab** (*Cladosporium cucumerinum*). Buy disease-free seeds; disease-resistant cultivars available for cucumber. Rotate every 2 or more years, avoid overhead irrigation and soil splash on leaves, do not work or disturb plants when wet, and discard all cucurbit litter and residue at end of season. Fungicides available.

- Leaves mottled, with distorted, deformed, curled, or twisted appearance much like herbicide damage. Fruits are also affected; can appear as warts on fruit, green spots on yellow fruit, ring spots, uneven coloration, deformity and discoloration, and significantly reduced yield. A number of viral diseases, **Cucumber Mosaic Virus, Zucchini Yellows Mosaic Virus, Squash Mosaic Virus, Watermelon Mosaic Virus,** and **Tobacco Ringspot Virus**. Viral symptoms develop rapidly in warmer temperatures (79°F–89°F). Viral symptoms are similar among the different diseases, and identification is impossible from symptoms alone. Laboratory and greenhouse investigations are required to identify the virus. Viral diseases, depending on the disease, are transmitted by a number of insects: leafhoppers; over 60 species of aphids (especially the green peach aphid); spotted, western striped, and banded cucumber beetles as well as other beetles; and dagger nematodes (*Xiphinema americanum*). Numerous plants serve as reservoir hosts (common weeds, flowers, and vegetables). There are no effective controls other than managing and eradicating all weeds around the garden. This is usually difficult and impractical for the home vegetable gardener, as is using insecticides to control insects that transmit viral diseases. The best defense is to find resistant cultivars.

Fruit

Water-soaked, sunken spots, rot and mold on the blossom end of the fruit (opposite the stem). Rot is usually confined to the blossom end or tip of the fruit. **Blossom End Rot**. The condition can occur from calcium deficiency, fluctuations of moisture levels in the soil, or poor pollination (it is difficult to distinguish). Ensure that plants are growing in well-drained soil, check pH of soil, add calcium to soil (liquid fertilizers), limit the use of fresh manure and high-ammonia fertilizer, mulch in and around plants, water regularly, and maintain even moisture levels in soil, especially during dry periods.

Insect pests

- Seedcorn Maggot (*Delia platura*);
- Wireworms (*Agriotus* spp., *Melanotus* spp., and other Elateridae);
- Squash Bugs (*Anasa tristis*);
- Squash Vine Borer (*Melittia cucurbitae*);
- Cucumber Moth (*Diaphania indica*);
- Leafminers (*Liriomyza sativae*, *L. trifolii*);
- Cucumber Beetles, Spotted (*Diabrotica undecimpunctata howardi*) and Striped (*Acalymma vittatum*);
- Squash Beetle (*Epilachna borealis*);
- Pumpkin Beetle (*Aulacophora hilaris*);
- Beet Armyworm (*Spodoptera exigua*), Western Yellowstriped Armyworm (*S. praefica*), Yellowstriped Armyworm (*S. ornithogalli*);
- Cabbage Looper (*Trichoplusia ni*);
- Pickleworm (*Diaphania nitidalis*);
- Silver Leaf Whiteflies (*Bemisia tabaci*, Biotype B [= *B. argentifolii*]);
- Melon or Cotton Aphid (*Aphis gossypii*);
- Green Peach Aphid (*Myzus persicae*);
- Melon Thrips (*Thrips palmi*), Tobacco Thrips (*Frankliniella fusca*);
- Two-Spotted Spider Mites (*Tetranychus urticae*);
- Nematodes (*Steinernema carpocapsae*).

Squash bugs

The squash bug is the most common pest I have encountered in growing squash (fig. 55). Squash bugs seem to prefer the more delicate varieties of squash (yellow zucchini, yellow squash, and pattypan varieties). However, after they have decimated these varieties, they will move on to green zucchini. If you are not squeamish, hand pick squash bugs as they first appear. As I water the circle plots with a hose at the base of the plants, the squash bugs will start migrating up the stems and leaves of the plant to escape the water. If you ignore them, they will multiply into the thousands. If the population builds to this level, the battle is lost, and it is time to pull up the squash plants and discard them away from the garden. Wait a week and replant. Squash bugs are members of the insect order Hemiptera and have piercing-sucking mouthparts that remove sap from plants, causing them to wilt and collapse. Therefore, if your squash plants suddenly become wilted, look for squash bugs or the stem vine borer.

Adult insects overwinter in plant debris near the previous crop. As the days warm in late spring, they emerge and travel to squash plants. There they mate and feed around mid-June. The small masses or clusters of brownish-red eggs are easy to see. Destroy these egg clusters by mashing them. Some people use masking tape to remove the eggs, and others lay boards down around their squash—the bugs hide underneath the boards, where they can be caught and killed. Another remedy is diluted liquid dish soap (some people add sugar and a little oil), sprayed onto the clusters and adults. Squash bugs are very resilient, and they usually infest plants in great numbers.

Pale green nymphs hatch in a week, and as they molt over time, they increase in size. If you are diligent and inspect your squash on a regular basis, you will see the nymphs. During the final molt, the insects become adults and hide on the underside of leaves and near the base of the plant. A second generation can be produced in late summer and early fall. These are the adults that overwinter. Squash bugs feed on all parts of the squash plant, including the fruits. Squash bugs are the vector of another disease of cucurbits, yellow vine decline, caused by the bacteria *Serratia marcescens*. These bacteria live in overwintering squash bugs and are spread to cucurbits during the next spring when the bugs begin feeding. Watermelon growers in Texas grow early-maturing straight-neck summer squash in border rows as trap plants for squash bugs. There they are killed with insecticides.

Squash vine borer

The adult squash vine borer is a clear-winged moth in the Sesiidae family that attacks summer squash, winter squash, and pumpkins (fig. 55). Vine borers seem less interested in butternut squash, cucumbers, and watermelons. They are often misidentified as a bee or wasp because they have orange markings on their abdomen and hind legs, and clear wings. Adult vine borers resemble wasps in flight and fly during the day, while many moths fly at night. Female vine borers lay eggs at the base of leaf stalks, and larvae hatch in about a week. The white to cream-colored larvae have brown heads and feed inside the stalk, killing the leaf. They migrate to the main stem for 4 to 6 weeks, grow to almost an inch in length, and then exit the stems, travel to the soil, and pupate. They remain in the soil until the following summer, producing one generation per year. A second crop of squash planted in early July will usually be able to avoid the squash vine borer.

A telltale sign of the squash vine borer is wilting of the vine, and signs of sawdust-like frass or tissue protruding from holes in the stem. There is little a gardener can do at this point. There are a couple of treatments, including using a stiff narrow wire, needle, or toothpick to try to kill the borer. Other management methods include watching for the adults and then using floating row covers to protect the plants from the moths, wrapping the lower stem with aluminum foil, and covering some of the trailing stem nodes with soil to allow the plant to root in several places. However, the bush varieties of squash do not develop trailing vines. Other home remedies include filling a yellow bowl or trap pan with water in the hope of drowning some of the adults. Squash vine borers are attracted to the color yellow, and if you catch some adults, it is time to resort to covers or chemical means to control them. If you decide to use pesticides, consult a local extension for recommendations and use.

Squash and Cucumbers Quick Guide

Botanical Data		
Zucchini, Acorn, Crookneck, Pattypan, Field Pumpkins (*Cucurbita pepo*)	**Butternuts, Other Winter Squash** (*Cucurbita moschata*)	**Hubbards** (*Cucurbita maxima*)
Family: cucurbit family, Cucurbitaceae	**Family**: cucurbit family, Cucurbitaceae	**Family**: cucurbit family, Cucurbitaceae
Life Cycle: classified as herbaceous annual; prostrate, bushy, climbing, trailing vines with tendrils	**Life Cycle**: classified as herbaceous annual; prostrate, bushy, climbing, trailing vines with tendrils	**Life Cycle**: classified as herbaceous annual; prostrate, bushy, climbing, trailing vines with tendrils
Flowers: monoecious, solitary in axils of leaves; male staminate flowers on long, strongly ridged peduncles, 3 stamens; female pistillate flowers near base of plant on short peduncles, corolla 5-lobed; open 1 day in morning	**Flowers:** monoecious, solitary in axils of leaves; male staminate flowers on long, ridged peduncles, 3 stamens; female pistillate flowers near base of plant on short peduncles, corolla 5-lobed, open 1 day in morning	**Flowers:** monoecious, solitary in axils of leaves; male staminate flowers on long, not prominently ridged peduncles, 3 stamens; female pistillate flowers near base of plant on short peduncles, corolla 5-lobed, open 1 day in morning
Pollinators: honeybees; crossing does not occur between species; cucurbit pollen is not easily dispersed by wind	**Pollinators**: honeybees; crossing between *C. moschata* and *C. mixta* can occur; cucurbit pollen is not easily dispersed by wind	**Pollinators**: honeybees; crossing does not occur between species; cucurbit pollen is not easily dispersed by wind
Physiology: cool-season vegetable, photosynthesis C_3	**Physiology**: cool-season vegetable, photosynthesis C_3	**Physiology**: cool-season vegetable, photosynthesis C_3
Stems: hollow, with stiff hairs	**Stems**: hollow, hairy, not spiny, sometimes rooting at nodes	**Stems**: somewhat prickly, not spiny
Leaves: alternate, cordate at base, lobed	**Leaves**: alternate, dark green, lobed, can have whitish spots	**Leaves**: large, not lobed except on young shoots
Roots: intricate and extensive root system, 5–7 main roots, taproot branches extensively with laterals and fibrous roots, roots can grow up to 4 feet deep, majority at 12–18 inches	**Roots**: intricate and extensive root system, 5–7 main roots, taproot branches extensively with laterals and fibrous roots, roots can grow up to 4 feet deep, majority at 12–18 inches	**Roots**: intricate and extensive root system, 5–7 main roots, taproot system better developed at deeper depths, roots can grow up to 4 feet deep, majority at 12–18 inches
Fruits: pepo, often large	**Fruits:** pepo	**Fruits**: pepo, can have musky flavor
Seeds: viability 3–4 years, max. 6 years if stored in uniform cool, dry conditions. Zucchini 5–8 seeds/g; yellow summer 9–13 seeds/g, pattypan 7–10 seeds/g, acorn 9–16 seeds/g, field pumpkins 5–10 seeds/g; colored seeds have been treated with fungicide.	**Seeds**: viability 3–4 years, max. 6 years if stored in uniform cool, dry conditions. Butternut 4–6 seeds/g; colored seeds have been treated with fungicide.	**Seeds**: viability 3–4 years, max. 6 years if stored in uniform cool, dry conditions. Hubbard 4–6 seeds/g; colored seeds have been treated with fungicide.
Days to Maturity (DTM): variable based on cultivar, yellow summer 39–60 days, zucchini 38–60 days, pattypan 55–63 days, acorn 70–100 days, field pumpkins 80–120 days	**Days to Maturity (DTM)**: variable based on cultivar, 85–110 days	**Days to Maturity (DTM):** variable based on cultivar, 92–115 days

Environmental Conditions		
Zucchini, Acorn, Crookneck, Pattypan, Field Pumpkins	**Butternuts, Other Winter Squash**	**Hubbards**
Growing Zones: check state and county cooperative extension sites and guides for adaptability and recommended planting dates	**Growing Zones**: check state and county cooperative extension sites and guides for adaptability and recommended planting dates	**Growing Zones**: check state and county cooperative extension sites and guides for adaptability and recommended planting dates
Timing: plant seeds after all danger of frost has passed and soil temp. reaches 60°F	**Timing**: plant seeds after all danger of frost has passed and soil temp. reaches 60°F	**Timing**: plant seeds after all danger of frost has passed and soil temp. reaches 60°F

Squash and Cucumbers Quick Guide, *continued*

Zucchini, Acorn, Crookneck, Pattypan, Field Pumpkins	Butternuts, Other Winter Squash	Hubbards
Optimal Temperature for Growth: germination temperature is between 70°F and 95°F, optimal growing temp. between 65°F and 75°F **Frost**: easily damaged by frost **Sunlight**: full sun **Soil Conditions**: well-drained, highly fertile soils, tolerates wide range of soil texture (sandy loams to clay loams) **Optimal pH**: 5.8–7.0 **Soil Moisture Content**: keep moisture consistent, with regular deep watering throughout growing season for constant, steady, and even growth, especially during fruit development; water in morning at base of plants; avoid water from lawn sprinklers; pointed fruits are an indication of moisture stress	**Optimal Temperature for Growth**: germination temperature is between 70°F and 95°F, optimal growing temp. between 65°F and 75°F **Frost**: easily damaged by frost **Sunlight**: full sun **Soil Conditions**: well-drained, highly fertile soils, tolerates wide range of soil texture (sandy loams to clay loams) **Optimal pH**: 5.8–7.0 **Soil Moisture Content**: keep moisture consistent, with regular deep watering throughout growing season for constant, steady, and even growth, especially during fruit development; water in morning at base of plants; avoid water from lawn sprinklers	**Optimal Temperature for Growth**: germination temperature is between 70°F and 95°F, optimal growing temp. between 65°F and 75°F **Frost**: easily damaged by frost **Sunlight**: full sun **Soil Conditions**: well-drained, highly fertile soils, tolerates wide range of soil texture (sandy loams to clay loams) **Optimal pH**: 5.8–7.0 **Soil Moisture Content**: keep moisture consistent, with regular deep watering throughout growing season for constant, steady, and even growth, especially during fruit development; water in morning at base of plants; avoid water from lawn sprinklers

Culture and Special Considerations		
Zucchini, Acorn, Crookneck, Pattypan, Field Pumpkins	**Butternuts, Other Winter Squash**	**Hubbards**
Soil Preparation: apply decomposed manure and compost and work into soil (6–10 inches). Do not work when soil is wet. **Planting**: plant in full sun; avoid cool, shaded locations. Maintain uniform moisture and add N as recommended. Thin fruits that are misshapen and pointed on the end are a sign of uneven moisture. **Transplants**: not recommended; plants very susceptible to transplant shock **Seeds**: plant seeds ¾–1½ inches deep, depending on soil texture **Spacing**: in hills and circle plots, plant 6–10 seeds, select the best 3 plants evenly spaced in mound **Weeding**: gentle cultivation; use mulch to control weeds, conserve moisture, and limit diseases by protecting leaves from soil splash **Irrigation**: irrigation interval and amount increase as the plant develops and temperature increases. Water demands are greatest during fruit set and fruit sizing stages. Maintain soil moisture for high-quality fruit.	**Soil Preparation**: apply decomposed manure and compost and work into soil (6–10 inches). Do not work when soil is wet. **Planting**: plant in full sun; avoid cool, shaded locations. Maintain uniform moisture and add N as recommended. Thin fruits that are misshapen and pointed on the end are a sign of uneven moisture. **Transplants**: not recommended; plants very susceptible to transplant shock **Seeds**: plant seeds ¾–1½ inches deep, depending on soil texture **Spacing**: in hills and circle plots, plant 6–10 seeds, select the best 3 plants evenly spaced in mound **Weeding**: gentle cultivation; use mulch to control weeds, conserve moisture, and limit diseases by protecting leaves from soil splash **Irrigation**: irrigation interval and amount increase as the plant develops and temperature increases. Water demands are greatest during fruit set and fruit sizing stages. Maintain soil moisture for high-quality fruit.	**Soil Preparation**: apply decomposed manure and compost and work into soil (6–10 inches). Do not work when soil is wet. **Planting**: plant in full sun; avoid cool, shaded locations. Maintain uniform moisture and add N as recommended. Thin fruits that are misshapen and pointed on the end are a sign of uneven moisture. **Transplants**: not recommended; plants very susceptible to transplant shock **Seeds**: plant seeds ¾–1½ inches deep, depending on soil texture **Spacing**: in hills and circle plots, plant 6–10 seeds, select the best 3 plants evenly spaced in mound **Weeding**: gentle cultivation; use mulch to control weeds, conserve moisture, and limit diseases by protecting leaves from soil splash **Irrigation**: irrigation interval and amount increase as the plant develops and temperature increases. Water demands are greatest during fruit set and fruit sizing stages. Maintain soil moisture for high-quality fruit.

Culture and Special Considerations, *continued*		
Zucchini, Acorn, Crookneck, Pattypan, Field Pumpkins **Fertilizer**: avg. commercial rate 30–60 lb. N/acre (0.015–0.3 lb./20 $ft.^2$ (5-ft. diam. circle). Side dress N again 2–3 weeks later with 30–50 lb./acre. P and K range from 90 to 150 lb./acre (0.04–0.7 lb./20 $ft.^2$). See appendix D for equivalent rates for circle plots. **Harvest**: yellow squash and zucchini are picked in the immature, tender stage. Pumpkins take much longer to mature; wait until vines begin to die back and rinds on fruit are toughened. Test by pressing thumbnail against skin; nail should not leave a dent. Harvest pumpkins before hard frost. **Crop Rotation**: no cucurbits for 2–3 years **Cultivars**: many heirlooms and hybrids to choose from. Many cultivars have disease resistance. **Nutrition Information**: Zucchini, raw. USDA Food and Nutrition Service. % Daily Value based on 2,000 calorie diet Serving size 1 cup Calories 20 Total fat 0.2 g, 0% Total carbohydrate 4.2 g, 1% Protein 1.5 g, 3% Vitamin A 248 IU, 5% Vitamin C 21 mg, 35% Vitamin K 5.3 mcg, 7% Vitamin B_6 0.3 mg, 14% Riboflavin 0.2 mg, 10% Folate 36 mcg, 9% Thiamin 0.1 mg, 4% Pantothenic acid 0.2 mg, 2%	**Butternuts, Other Winter Squash** **Fertilizer**: avg. commercial rate 30–60 lb. N/acre (0.015–0.3 lb./20 $ft.^2$ (5-ft. diam. circle). Side dress N again 2–3 weeks later with 30–50 lb./acre. P and K range from 90 to 150 lb./acre (0.04–0.7 lb./20 $ft.^2$). See appendix D for equivalent rates for circle plots. **Harvest**: mature when rind is hard and cannot be punctured by thumbnail. Leave 1 inch of stem during storage. Store fruits at 50°F and 50%–75% relative humidity. Check days to maturity. Acorn squash have the shortest storage time, 5–8 weeks. **Crop Rotation**: no cucurbits for 2–3 years **Cultivars**: many heirlooms and hybrids to choose from. Many cultivars have disease resistance. **Nutrition Information**: Butternut, raw. USDA Food and Nutrition Service. % Daily Value based on 2,000 calorie diet Serving size 1 cup Calories 63 Total fat 0.1 g, 0% Total carbohydrate 16.4 g, 5% Protein 1.4 g, 3% Vitamin A 14,883 IU, 298% Vitamin C 29.4 mg, 49% Vitamin E 2 mg, 10% Thiamin 0.1 mg 5% Niacin 1.7 mg, 8% Folate 37.8 mcg, 9% Pantothenic acid 0.6 mg, 6%	**Hubbards** **Fertilizer**: avg. commercial rate 30–60 lb. N/acre (0.015–0.3 lb./20 $ft.^2$ (5-ft. diam. circle). Side dress N again 2–3 weeks later with 30–50 lb./acre. P and K range from 90 to 150 lb./acre (0.04–0.7 lb./20 $ft.^2$). See appendix D for equivalent rates for circle plots. **Harvest**: mature when rind is hard and cannot be punctured by thumbnail. Leave 1 inch of stem during storage. Hubbard types can be stored much longer than other winter squash (5–6 months) at 50°F–55°F and relative humidity of 70%–75%. Check days to maturity. **Crop Rotation**: no cucurbits for 2–3 years **Cultivars**: mostly heirloom types **Nutrition Information**: Hubbard, raw. USDA Food and Nutrition Service. % Daily Value based on 2,000 calorie diet Serving size 1 cup Calories 46.4 Total fat 0.6 g, 1% Total carbohydrate 10 g, 3% Protein 2.3 g, 5% Vitamin A 1,586 IU, 32% Vitamin C 12.8 mg, 21% Thiamin 0.1 mg, 5% Niacin 0.6 mg, 3% Folate 18.6 mcg, 5% Pantothenic acid 0.5 mg, 5%

Botanical Data	Environmental Conditions	Culture and Special Considerations
Cucumber (*Cucumis sativus*) **Family**: cucurbit family, Cucurbitaceae **Life Cycle**: classified as herbaceous annual; prostrate, bushy, climbing, trailing vines with tendrils **Flowers**: monoecious, dioecious, hermaphroditic, some modern cultivars almost all female flowers. Male flowers in 3–7-flowered fascicles, stamens 3. Female flowers solitary, with short, thick pedicel, ovary inferior, ellipsoid, prickly, hairy, warty, stigma 3-lobed.	**Growing Zones**: check state and county cooperative extension sites and guides for adaptability and recommended planting dates **Timing**: plant seeds after all danger of frost has passed and soil temp. reaches 70°F. Seeds will not germinate at temps. < 50°F. **Optimal Temperature for Growth**: cucumbers grow best at 75°F–85°F **Frost**: easily damaged by frost	**Soil Preparation**: apply decomposed manure and compost and work into soil (6–10 inches). Do not work when soil is wet. **Planting**: plant cucumbers in full sun; avoid cool, shaded locations. Maintain uniform moisture and add N as recommended. Thin fruits that are misshapen and pointed on the end are a sign of uneven moisture. **Transplants**: not recommended; plants very susceptible to transplant shock

Squash and Cucumbers Quick Guide, *continued*

Botanical Data	Environmental Conditions	Culture and Special Considerations
Pollinators: bees. All cucumbers will cross; isolate by at least ½ mile. Does not cross with muskmelons, watermelons, squash, pumpkins, or gourds. **Physiology**: cool-season vegetable, photosynthesis C_3 **Stems**: rough, hispid (bristlelike hairs), sparingly branched, 6–15 feet long. Tendrils up to 12 inches. **Leaves**: alternate, simple, stipules absent, subcordate to triangular ovate, palmately 3- to 7-angled or lobed, almost as wide as long, deeply cordate at base, acute at apex, toothed, bristly, and hairy **Roots**: extensive, horizontal laterals (3–4 feet), taproot (3½ feet) **Fruits**: pendulous, globose to cylindrical berry, slightly curved, with spinous tubercles and warts, skin usually green but some varieties white, yellow, and brown. Poor fruit set is common during rainy weather when bees are inactive. **Seeds**: usual seed life 3 years under cool, dry conditions **Days to Maturity (DTM)**: variable based on cultivar, 54–63 days	**Sunlight**: full sun; avoid shady areas **Soil Conditions**: well-drained, highly fertile soils, tolerates wide range of soil texture (sandy loams to clay loams) **Optimal pH**: 6.8–7.2 **Soil Moisture Content**: keep moisture consistent, with regular deep watering throughout growing season for constant, steady, and even growth, especially during fruit development; water in morning at base of plants; avoid water from lawn sprinklers **Bitterness in Fruit**: Bitterness is due to the formation of 2 cucurbitacins (terpenoid compounds). Terpene compounds in cucumbers played an evolutionary role in deterring herbivores. **Harvest**: For specific cultivars, pick by size, color, and firmness. Pick cucumbers early and often to stimulate more production. Overmature and large cucumbers can develop a bitter taste.	**Seeds:** plant seeds ½–1 inch deep, depending on soil texture **Spacing**: in hills and circle plots, plant 6–10 seeds, select the best 3 plants evenly spaced in mound **Weeding**: gentle cultivation; use mulch to control weeds, conserve moisture, and limit diseases by protecting leaves from soil splash **Irrigation**: irrigation interval and amount increase as the plant develops and temperature increases. Water demands are greatest during fruit set and fruit sizing stages. Maintain soil moisture for high-quality fruit. **Fertilizer**: avg. commercial rate 30–60 lb. N/acre. Side dress N again 2–3 weeks later with 30–50 lb./acre. P and K range from 90 to 150 lb./acre. See appendix D for equivalent rates for circle plots. **Crop Rotation**: no cucurbits for 2–3 years **Cultivars**: cultivars available as gynoecious—all female flowers; hermaphroditic—both male and female parts in same flower; and monoecious—separate male and female flowers on same plant; parthenocarpic, has ability to set fruit without pollination. Cultivars vary widely in their tendency to be bitter. **Nutrition Information:** Cucumber, raw. USDA Food and Nutrition Service. % Daily Value based on 2,000 calorie diet Serving size 1 cup Calories 8 Total fat 0.1 g, 0% Total carbohydrate 2 g, 1% Protein 0.3 g, 1% Vitamin A 54.6 IU, 1% Vitamin C 1.5 mg, 2% Vitamin K 8.5 mcg, 11% Folate 3.6 mcg, 1% Calcium 8.3 mg, 1% Iron 0.1 mg, 1% Magnesium 6.8 mg, 2% Phosphorus 12.5 mg, 1% Potassium 76.4 mg, 2%

FIGURE 56. Onions growing in circle plot arrangement and close-ups of onions maturing. Photos by author.

Onions

(*Allium cepa*)

Botanically, the onion family (Liliaceae) is diverse and prolific, providing us with a variety of culinary jewels and flowering plants. There are about 850 species of *Allium*, distributed throughout Europe, North America, North Africa, and Asia. Where would food preparation be without onions and their allies, garlic, leeks, shallots, and chives? The onion is an essential ingredient in many dishes and has been used by many cultures for thousands of years. The garden onion comes in many different varieties—red, yellow, white, and green—each with its own unique flavor, from very strong to mildly sweet. Onions can be eaten raw or cooked in a variety of ways.

Many different native species of wild onion can be found throughout our prairies and rangelands (fig. 57). How can you find onions and garlic in the wild? Your nose will tell you. Walking through a patch of wild onions near a creek will arouse the familiar onion scent. Some wild plant guides state that any plant that smells and looks like an onion or garlic is most likely edible. There are plants that have all the appearance of a wild onion without the onion smell. Beware, they may be death camas (*Zigadenus* spp.), a plant dreaded by ranchers, as it is highly poisonous to livestock (and people). All parts of death camas are poisonous (from alkaloids), and fatality occurs with consumption of 2 to 6% of an animal's body weight. As with any wild plants, it is best to receive field instruction from trained botanists, because many plants look alike. Even experts misidentify wild plants.

Onions can be grown in almost any soil, ranging from sandy loams to clayey-textured soils. Onions require well-drained, fertile conditions and full sunlight. The soil surface should be loose and friable and should have at least a moderate amount of organic matter. The basic plant nutrients, nitrogen, phosphorus, and potassium, must be available in large amounts to produce large bulbs.

Medical research shows that onions may help guard against many chronic diseases. Onions and their vegetable allies are rich in thiosulfinates, sulfides, sulfoxides, and other odoriferous sulfur compounds. The cysteine sulfoxides are primarily responsible for the onion flavor and produce the eye-irritating compounds that induce weeping. Onions have about one-quarter the sulfur compounds of garlic.

FIGURE 57. *A, Allium abramsii,* Abram's onion. Courtesy of Kier Morse, Cal Photos, University of California, Berkeley. *B, Allium anceps*, twinleaf onion. Courtesy of Mary Winger, Cal Photos, University of California, Berkeley. *C, Allium campanulatum*, dusky onion. Courtesy of Steven and Shellie Perry, Cal Photos, University of California, Berkeley.

Historical Background

Many botanists and archaeologists believe onions originated in central Asia. Research suggests that Iran and western Pakistan first grew onions, and Chinese gardens have included onions for 5,000 years. Onions may have been one of the earliest cultivated crops because they were easy to grow and could be stored, transported, and consumed when needed. Onions were used symbolically in Egypt and were considered an object of worship. Onions symbolized eternity to the Egyptians and were buried with the pharaohs. The Roman legions ate onions and carried them across Europe. During the Middle Ages, the three main vegetables were cabbage, beans, and onions. The Pilgrims brought onions with them on the *Mayflower* but

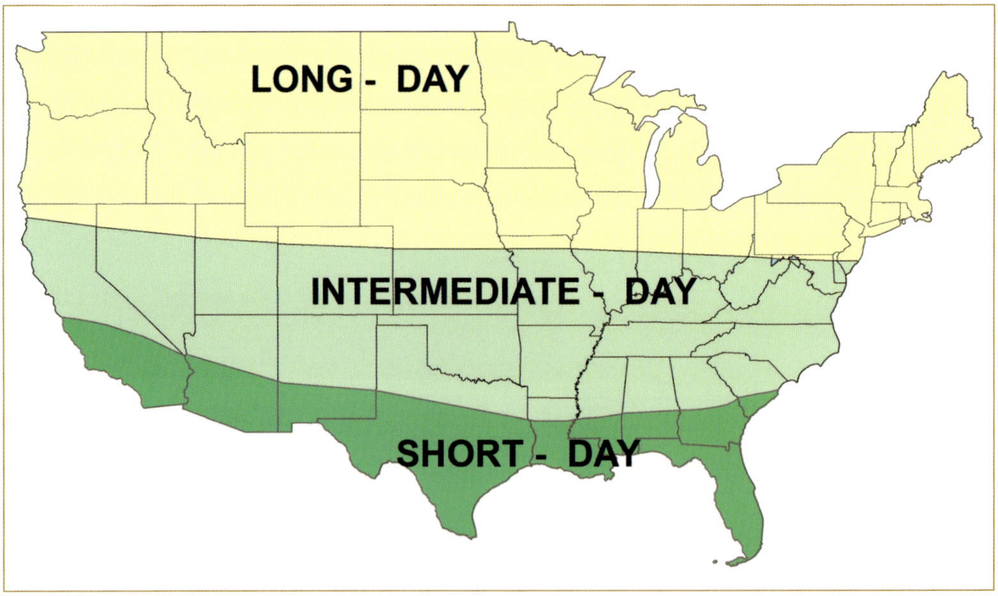

FIGURE 58. Day-length map for onion cultivars in the United States. Courtesy of Dixondale Farms, Carrizo Springs, Texas, http://www.dixondalefarms.com/.

later found that the Native Americans were already using onions in a variety of ways. Onions were included in the first Pilgrim gardens in 1648. The rest is history: What would Italian, French, Asian, Arabic, Mexican, South American, Indian, and other cuisines throughout the world be without the onion and its allies?

Culture and Planting

Short-day onions

- Start bulbing process when day length reaches 10–12 hours.
- Mature in 110 days when planted in the South during winter or early spring.
- Mature in 75 days when planted in northern states in late spring but will not get very large.
- The earlier you plant them, the larger they get.

Intermediate-day onions

- Start bulbing process when day length reaches 12–14 hours.
- Will produce nice-sized bulbs unless you live in far south Florida or South Texas.

- Mature in 110 days when planted at the proper time.
- Exceptionally sweet.

Long-day onions

- Start bulbing process when day length reaches 14–16 hours.
- Do extremely well in northern states.
- Sweet, storage, and specialty long-day varieties available.
- Excellent for long-term storage.

Use the onion Quick Guide at the end of the chapter for detailed information about soils and culture. Onions can be planted from sets, transplants, and seeds. Growing onions is relatively easy, but there are some particulars that the gardener needs to know. First, you must choose the right cultivar for your region and climate. Onion bulbs develop according to the hours of daylight. There are short-, intermediate-, and long-day cultivars. The short-day cultivars produce bulbs when day length reaches 10 to 12 hours of daylight, whereas long-day onions require 14 to 16 hours of daylight. Figure 58 shows the latitudinal ranges for the three day-length classes of onions.

Onion transplants and sets are easy to plant (fig. 59). There are many more cultivar choices if you buy onion transplants than if you buy sets. Onion sets are small onions grown from seeds and are about the size of a large marble. All the onion guides I have read mention that smaller sets (about ½ to ¾ inch in diameter) are best. In my experience, the slightly larger onion sets produce better onions, so the debate is on. I often find that there are not many cultivars to choose from when buying onion sets, and it may be hard to find the right day-length onion. You may find onion sets for sale at local nurseries, but ask the vendor about the variety and day length.

If a set and developing plant grows only one stalk, harvest it as a green onion, as the plant will put all its energy into forming a seed head. Onion sets are a great way to introduce gardening to children because they find it interesting to watch the small onion develop into a large bulb.

I have had mixed results with onion sets throughout the years, but I have had consistent success with onion transplants. Try both sets and transplants and decide for yourself. Onion transplants should be planted as soon as you receive them. Upon receipt in the mail, they may look dried out because they are dormant. In the dry state, the onion plant can sustain itself from the bulb for about 3 weeks. If you cannot plant them immediately, keep them in a cool,

A

B

FIGURE 59. *A*, Yellow and white onion sets. *B*, Onion transplants. Courtesy of Harris Seed and Peaceful Valley Farm and Garden Supply, Inc. GrowOrganic.com.

well-ventilated area until planting. Do not immerse them in water or wet soil, as they will rot.

The third option, and probably the least popular among home gardeners, is growing onions from seeds, which requires a longer time. In climates where spring is a fleeting event, temperatures may warm up too quickly—thus the advantage of planting a set or transplant. One advantage of planting seeds is the large number of cultivars available in seed catalogs.

Onions can be grown in many types of soils and textures, from sandy loams to clay loams. The key to successful onions is soil fertility and good drainage. As you follow the circle gardening method and add organic matter to your plots, the soil will become looser and more friable. The added organic matter will also provide more moisture-holding capacity. Sandy loams may dry out quickly, and nutrients may leach out more quickly. On the other end of the soil texture spectrum, clays and alluvial soils may be sticky, clumpy, and hard, but they typically have more natural fertility.

Fertilizer recommendations are difficult to make without a reference, either from a soil test or performance of previous crops (see section on fertilizer rates and individual plants). Commercial onion growers may use some preplant nitrogen and phosphorus and continue fertilizer applications with irrigation water or apply fertilizer every 2 to 3 weeks. Stop fertilizing about 4 weeks prior to harvest. Onions require a high amount of nitrogen. The total nitrogen fertilizer need is spaced out in intervals and may range from 130 lb. N/acre on soils with low organic matter, to 110 lb. N/acre on medium organic soils, to 90 lb. N/acre on high organic soils. Start with 30–50 lb. preplant N/acre, then side dress with 30–50 lb. N/acre (3–4 times) at 2- to 3-week intervals. Use table 32 in appendix D to convert lb./acre rates to equivalent rates for circle plots. Low nitrogen levels in the soil can induce early maturity and reduce bulb size, whereas excess nitrogen will promote bulbs with large necks, which do not store well.

Some onion plant suppliers recommend a fertilizer with higher phosphorus in the mixture, for example, 10-20-10. Phosphorus and potassium are applied prior to planting onions, and rates can range from 0 to 150 lb./acre depending on soil tests. Use plant diagnostics and onion development to evaluate fertilizer needs. Onion plants and sets usually start off slowly, but growth speeds up with the subsequent development of leaves as temperatures warm up. The perfect onion should have 13 leaves, which correspond to 13 rings of scales in the bulb.

Onion sets should be planted 1 to 2 inches deep and about 3 to 4 inches apart. If you are planting onion transplants, bury the roots about 1 inch lower than the white portion of the plant. Use the same spacing as for sets, about 4 inches apart. Figure 60 shows a 4-foot-diameter circle plot with spaced rings (radii of 3, 6, 12, 18, and 24 inches) and plant spacing of 3 and 4 inches respectively between sets or transplants. After planting the set or transplant, pat the soil down, as this will prevent the plant from unearthing itself after you water it. Onion sets and transplants can be planted in early spring, about 4 to 6 weeks before the last estimated spring freeze. Check with your local county extension office. Mail-order vendors that specialize in onions often have planting dates that match your zip code and Plant Hardiness Zone. If the temperature drops below 20°F, the plants can be damaged, so on cold nights cover the onion patch with a tarp and weigh down the edges so the covering does not blow off and expose the onions.

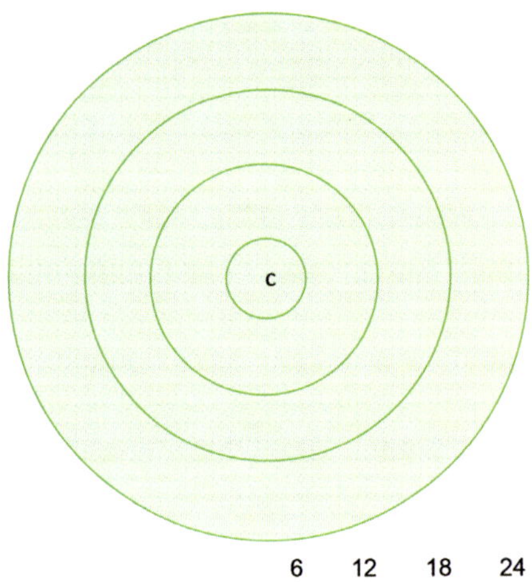

FIGURE 60. Planting onions in a circle plot. This example uses a circle 4 feet (48 inches) in diameter. Plant in concentric rings, starting with the outer edge, and work toward the center. Table 25 shows the number of plants at 3- and 4-inch spacings.

TABLE 25. Number of plants at 3- and 4-inch spacings in circle plot rings of different size

Radius (inches)	Diameter (inches)	Circumference (inches)	Plants @ 4-inch spacing	Plants @ 3-inch spacing
24	48	151	38	50
18	36	113	28	38
12	24	75.4	19	25
6	12	37.7	9	13
3	6	18.9	5	6
Total plants			99	132

In the circle plot, keep up with weeding. Mulches such as peat moss or decomposed compost can be applied to help maintain even moisture, smother weeds, and prevent new weeds from establishing. Consistent moisture is essential for good onion bulb formation. If onion bulbs do not receive adequate moisture, they will be small and certain diseases can appear. Onions have shallow roots; therefore, do not let the soil become noticeably dry and cracked at the surface. You also do not want saturated conditions; good drainage is essential. Overwatered or saturated conditions can cause leaves to turn yellowish. Irrigate (water) onions regularly to maintain moisture at the stem-bulb level. Frequency of watering depends on the weather. It is impossible to recommend how many inches of water per week because of soil texture and climate differences. When the bulbs start maturing and the tops begin to fall over naturally, the bulbs will be near maturity. At this point, discontinue watering and let the soil begin to dry out. If a wet weather cycle occurs during this time, it is worth covering the circle with a tarp, as too much water at the end of maturity can cause split bulbs and rotting problems, and it will interfere with curing and storage.

In my Texas garden, a few onion flower stalks appear every year. Many gardeners wonder why the plant is flowering and what they should do about it. Will removal of the flower stop the plant from producing an inferior onion? The truth is that once the onion stalk flowers, there is nothing you can do about it. These are the onions you should harvest green and use in the kitchen. They are usually lighter, about half the weight and size of a nonflowering onion bulb. An onion that produces a single stalk with a flower will not store well. What causes the onion to produce a flower stalk? An onion is actually a biennial plant, meaning it takes 2 growing seasons to complete its life cycle, flower, and produce seeds. When an onion plant flowers during the first growing season, it has received some environmental signal that stimulates flowering. Several factors can cause premature flowering, the most common of which is temperature fluctuation (alternating cold and warm temperatures). In my Texas climate, there are always extreme temperature fluctuations. Flowering can occur if you have the wrong day-length cultivar, so make sure you buy adapted cultivars. I find that seeded onions and transplants are less likely to flower than onions grown from sets.

Harvest and Storage

Onions are ready to harvest after about 80% of the tops have fallen over. Avoid watering and irrigation at this time. Do not water for 5–8 days in sandy soils, longer in loams and clays (2 weeks). This is a critical time, so do not wait too long and let the tops deteriorate to nothing, or expose the bulbs to very hot sun, as they can be damaged and start rotting. If rain is forecast, it is better to harvest the onions and set them in a dry shed. Do not let your curing onions get rained on. Lift the bulbs carefully out of the soil, perhaps using a small hand spade to pry them loose. If any onions are accidentally damaged, use them immediately. Brush off loose dirt; cleaning is easier once the outer layer becomes papery and falls off. I usually leave the onions to cure in the sun for a few days and then move them to a dry location in the barn. A cured onion skin will appear papery and the roots will be dry. For onion tops that are completely dry, cut the leaf stem 2–3 inches above the bulb. For onion tops that are still slightly green, cut at 12 inches and braid the onions into ropes. Ideally, onions should be stored in a cold (32°F–40°F; onions freeze at 31°F; at temperatures > 50°F onions are subject to sprouting), dry location. I do not have a place to store my onions at that temperature, but surprisingly, they store very well in the food pantry in my air-conditioned house (76°F) in mesh netting. Keep an eye on your stored onions: one rotten onion will ruin others that touch it. If any onions develop a black mold, use them first.

Notable Onion Allies

Onion lovers may want to consider growing garlic (*Allium sativum* var. *sativum*), elephant garlic (*Allium ampeloprasum* var. *holmense*), leeks (*Allium ampeloprasum* var. *porrum*), chives (*Allium schoenoprasum*), and shallots (*Allium cepa* var. *aggregatum*). Garlic, leeks, and shallots are grown much like onions as far as soil requirements, light, fertilizer, and water, and they do well in circle plots.

Chives

Chives are nice to have around, as they are inconspicuous, perennial, and easy to grow. They also need little care, and they are wonderful as a garnish (fig. 61A). I plant chives in a small patch in the herb garden, where they multiply and produce attractive white and lavender flowers. Chives are native to Asia and are the mildest and smallest member of the onion family. They have been used as a seasoning for nearly 5,000 years. I mix chives into our homemade chèvre (goat

FIGURE 61. *A*, Chives in the herb bed. *B*, Fall garlic. Photos by author.

A

B

cheese) with a little salt. Chives are grown for the flavor of the leaves and edible flowers. Chives produce rhizomes, are semibulbous, and will grow in a bunch. They can be started from seeds, rhizomes, or a nursery transplant in a pot.

Garlic

Garlic appears in seed catalogs in two types, hardneck and softneck. The hardneck cultivars are more cold tolerant and hardy, have a milder flavor, and are the gourmet varieties. Softneck cultivars have a stronger flavor and store better than hardneck cultivars. Garlic rarely produces fertile flowers; therefore, plants are propagated vegetatively by planting the individual cloves. The larger the clove, the larger the bulb.

Garlic is very frost hardy; about 6 to 8 weeks before the ground freezes in the fall is the best time to plant it. In some climates where temperatures do not warm up quickly, garlic can be planted in very early spring. Separate the individual cloves at planting time. Some garlic references state that the bulbs should not be refrigerated prior to planting, as it causes them to become nubby and rough. Also, bulbs should not be kept in an unduly warm room, as premature sprouting may occur.

During the fall while the weather is cool, the planted cloves sprout roots. Garlic is usually not planted in the spring because warming temperatures and increasing day length will stimulate premature bulbs.

Garlic culture is much like that of onions. Plant the garlic cloves 2–3 inches deep and 4–6 inches apart, with the clove pointed up. When freezing temperatures arrive, apply 4–6 inches of mulch to prevent soil frost heaving. In the spring when it starts to warm up, remove some of the mulch to the outside of the circle plot, depending on how much decomposition has occurred since the fall. As the garlic grows, decomposed compost can be used to mulch it and add organic matter to the soil surface. Garlic requires moderate amounts of nitrogen applied in 2 to 3 small applications (⅓ at planting, ⅓ as tops emerge in spring, and ⅓ one month later). Avoid fertilizing with nitrogen 60 days before harvest.

All onion cultivars have insect-repellent properties (except against those insects that attack onions), but garlic is especially pungent. As with all onion cultivars, use only shallow cultivation, or smother young weeds with mulch and compost. Garlic is mature when the tops die back. Like onions, garlic bulbs can be harvested prior to maturity for use in the kitchen; however, the flavor will be milder.

Elephant garlic

Elephant garlic is not really garlic—it is related to the leek. Elephant garlic resembles garlic, but it is taller and has wider leaves as well as larger flower heads and bulbs. Elephant garlic tends to bloom every other year, and the bulb does not separate into cloves until the plant flowers. It is slightly less hardy than garlic and the flavor is milder than that of common garlic—somewhere between the taste of leeks and garlic. Plant elephant garlic much as you would garlic, but place cloves 2–3 inches deep and 6–8 inches apart. As the plant grows, mound the soil up 2–3 inches. Elephant garlic is a heavy nitrogen user—it needs about three times more than garlic.

Leeks

Leeks are winter-hardy biennials that are harvested as an annual (fig. 62). Leeks do not form bulbs like onions, garlic, or shallots. The long, thick, white stem is used; it imparts a creamy texture when cooked and has a mild, sweet taste. Try potato-leek soup (à la *Mastering the Art of French Cooking* by Julia Child, Simone Beck, and Louisette Bertholle), and you will become a leek fan.

Leeks perform best in slightly acidic soil (pH 6.0–6.8) but will grow well in slightly alkaline soil. Leek transplants are planted the same as onion transplants, but set plants 4–6 inches apart, with 12–18

FIGURE 62. Leeks planted in circle arrangement. Photo by author.

inches between rows or concentric circles, and 5–6 inches deep with 1–2 inches of leaf extending above the soil surface. Burying the leek transplant more deeply produces the desirable blanched white stem. As the plant grows, systematically mound up soil on the stem to produce more of the white stem, but not to the point where the bottom leaves attach to the stem. Leeks grow and mature more slowly than onions (often 120–150 days). A light application of organic or synthetic fertilizer (equivalent of 10–10–10) at the time of planting will ensure that the plants start off well. Then side dress several more times throughout the season. The top leaves, called the flag, should be dark blue green. Be careful during cultivation, as leek roots are fibrous and shallow—mulch to smother weeds. Keep leek plots moist, but not wet, throughout the growing season.

Unlike onions and garlic, leeks are harvested while they are still green and actively growing. Leeks are mature when the white stem portion is more than 1 inch wide and the shaft is more than 3 inches long. Start harvesting a few plants for the kitchen when they are about 1 inch wide. Leek stems can grow to 3 inches thick, but be careful, as they may become more fibrous and less desirable. When harvesting leeks, wash them well, cut off some of the green top, and refrigerate. Leeks can be frozen and used later in soups and sauces.

Shallots

Shallots are a culinary delight: gourmet cooks and chefs know that shallots transform ordinary dishes into something extraordinary. Shallots have a firm texture and are sweet yet aromatic. They are more delicately flavored than regular onions, and their young outer leaves can be used like chives. The true French gray shallot, *eschalot*, is considered the true shallot, and it grows wild from central to southwest Asia. Shallots are usually the size of a chestnut, more or less pear shaped and firm, and the outer skin can vary from grayish to golden brown, rosy, or purple tinged. The flesh is an off-white tinged with green or magenta.

Shallots are easier to grow than onions and are the most prolific multiplier. Shallot culture (soil, fertilizer, watering, and weeding) and care are much the same as they are for onions. The outer leaves can be used like chives, and immature green shallots can be used as scallions when their tops are 6–8 inches tall and the stem is ⅜ inch in diameter. Single bulbs are spaced 6–8 inches apart with the tops even with the soil surface. Shallots will form a cluster of 5–12, and up to 20 bulbs will spread out from the original bulb; thus they require more space between plants. Young shallot sprouts are delicate, so avoid thick mulches until the plants are well established. Shallot bulbs often develop exposed on top of the ground; do not cover them with soil. Make sure your soil has ample phosphorus. Gophers love shallots, as they do garlic, so protect your beds with gopher wire or traps.

Shallots are harvested the same as onions, after the tops of the plants die back in mid to late summer. Cure shallots in a warm, dry location for a week and then store them in mesh bags in a cool, dry place. Small bulbs can be replanted since they will not store well. Many shallot cultivars are good keepers and will last all winter.

Diseases and Pests

Below is a key to help identify onion diseases and pests. This list is not all-inclusive, but common problems are included. Various USDA, university, and extension publications have diagnostic photos. I refrain from including remedies for the problems, as the treatments are too numerous to list and, depending on the problem, include management-oriented solutions, organic treatments, and pesticide-related measures. Onions in the home garden are usually free of major problems. Well-drained soil, plenty of organic matter, adequate nutrient levels (nitrogen, phosphorus, potassium) and moisture, rotation (every 5 years), and cleanup of all onion litter and undesirable bulbs will arm the home gardener with an arsenal of preventive measures.

Diseases

Leaves and bulbs

- General wilting, yellowish dieback of leaf tips, soft stems and necks, double bulbing, and cracked bulbs occur mid to late season until harvest. Can occur from contaminated transplants or sets. Fungus enters roots and base of plant through wounds caused by cultivation and other stress. Roots may rot, and the bulb may show a gray to brown discoloration. A white to pink fungal growth may show up between and on scales. Sometimes, onion maggots are a secondary infection, as they are attracted to the diseased tissue. If the infection occurs late in the season, decay of the bulb may occur during storage. Fungal, **Fusarium Basal Rot** (*Fusarium oxysporum* f. sp. *cepae*).
- Brown to purplish velvety appearance on healthy green leaves; as disease progresses, lesions may girdle the leaf and develop a pale yellow coloration followed by brown necrosis and collapse of

the leaf. Develops from fungal spores during rainy periods, high humidity, and wet weather, from splashing of soil up onto leaves (mulch onion plots). Bulbs may rot in storage. Fungal, **Downy Mildew** (*Peronospora destructor*).

- Oval water-soaked leaf lesions, tip burn and varying lengths of yellow to grayish leaf streaking, which darken to black. As the disease progresses, the entire leaf collapses and dries up. Dark spots appear on the outer scales of the bulb and reddish-brown discoloration occurs on inner scales. Occurs in cool, wet periods. Bacterial, **Bacterial Leaf Streak** and **Bulb Rot** (*Pseudomonas viridiflava*).
- Numerous white flecks on leaves, develops rapidly during wet weather and in temperatures above 69°F. If fungus infects the bulb, a brown stain appears on the neck and outer scales. Fungal, **Botrytis Brown Stain** or **Botrytis Blast** (*Botrytis cinerea*).
- Bleached white appearance on leaf tips. Wilting of tissue and drying, thus the bleached white appearance. Onion bulbs rot in storage. Wet conditions, high humidity, and low temperatures (below 59°F). Spores survive for long periods in the soil. Water-splashed soil onto leaves can contain the infectious sporangia. Fungal, **White Tip** (*Phytophthora porri*).
- Small yellow spots, swelling, and open lesions on leaves. Leaf tips can also develop gray to black necrosis. Stems and necks are soft, onions double, bulbs crack, and secondary infections can rot the bulbs before and after harvest and storage. **Stem and Bulb Nematode** (*Ditylenchus dipsaci*).

Bulbs

Black powdery or peppery mold at the neck of the bulb. Common problem, fungal spores common in soil and air. Can develop from injured roots or improper harvest and damp or wet curing environment. Black spores form along veins and outer papery scales of bulbs. Soft rot can follow infections. Fungal, **Black Mold** (*Aspergillus niger*). Keep onions dry during curing. If onions are wet for 6 hours or longer and temperatures are higher than 86°F, black mold can start. Separate out any onions with mold, wipe mold off, and use quickly.

Insects

- Tiny yellow or dark brown–specked flying insects (1 mm long). Tiny dark green specks caused by piercing and rasping mouthparts, spots on leaves turn grayish white or silvery. Under severe infestation, leaves can collapse. **Onion Thrips** (*Thrips tabaci*), **Western Flower Thrips** (*Frankliniella occidentalis*), and other species. Thrips have been referred to as "enemy number one" to onions, more than other insects and diseases combined. Thrips overwinter as larvae or pupae in leaf litter, mulch, and soil, and on other host plants. Life cycle is rapid (eggs to adult in 2 weeks). Thrips can hide where the leaf and bulb meet. Damage is usually during hot, dry weather conditions. Cool and rainy periods decrease thrip populations and damage. Do not confuse with onion flies, whose larvae are the onion maggot. Onion flies are about the size of a housefly. Thrips overwinter in onion residue, discarded onions, and stored bulbs. They also overwinter on other host plants, making control difficult. Rainstorms can wash thrips from the plants and decrease populations; ladybugs can be useful.

- White worm feeds on seedlings, roots, or bulbs. **Onion Maggot** (*Hylemya* spp.). Adult is onion fly, light greenish to gray, long legged, with large wings, and about the size of a housefly; can have 3 generations per year. Female flies lay eggs (30–40) in leaf axils or in crevices near the soil. Eggs hatch in 2–8 days and larvae crawl down into the soil where they feed (maggots), then enter the pupal stage. In 2–3 weeks, the flies emerge to repeat the cycle. The complete life cycle lasts from 45 to 65 days. Some gardeners plant onions randomly throughout the garden so plants are not highly concentrated in one spot. Organic gardeners apply ground cayenne pepper, ginger, chili powder, wood ashes, and diatomaceous earth at the base of the plants. Onion maggots thrive in poorly drained soils.
- Plant is sheared off at the base. **Cutworm** (*Agrotis segetum*, *A. ipsilon*). Cutworms, gray to brown caterpillars, are the larval forms of night-flying moths. Adult moths can lay up to 1,500 eggs, and there can be 4 generations in one year. The larval stage can last for several months and can overwinter in the garden.
- Deformed seedlings and plants, stunted growth, pale, limp foliage, leaves that turn brown and die. Bulbs are short, with very few fine roots, unhealthy color, swelling or galls. Plants do not respond to adequate fertilizer and watering. **Nematodes** (numerous species: lesion nematode, *Pratylenchus penetrans*; Root-Knot Nematode, *Meloidogyne* spp.; Stem and Bulb Nematode, *Ditylenchus dipsaci*; Stubby Root Nematode, *Paratrichodorus allius*, *P. minor*). Nematodes seem to be more prevalent in sandy soils and in some heavy clay and muck soils.

Onion Quick Guide

Botanical Data	Environmental Conditions	Culture and Special Considerations
Onion (*Allium cepa*) **Family:** Liliaceae **Life Cycle:** classified as herbaceous biennial monocot, but grown as annual in vegetable gardens **Inflorescence:** a spherical terminal false umbel **Flowers:** perfect flower, can be protandrous (pollen is released before stigmas mature). White, pink, or purple, stamens 6, stigma single or shortly trifid (divided into 3 lobes), ovary superior. **Pollinators:** bees, flies, and other insects **Physiology:** cool-season vegetable, photosynthesis C_3 **Stems:** scapose (bearing a naked flowering stem rising from the ground without proper leaves); truncated bulbs range from spherical to nearly cylindrical and cone-like. Membranaceous skin coloring may be white, yellow, brown, red, or purple. **Leaves:** basal or confined to lower ½ of stem, green to blue-green, hollow, narrowly linear, closed at the tip. Older leaves on outside of bulb, young leaves emerge up through the center of the sheath of the preceding leaf. **Roots:** adventitious, fibrous, and shallow (fibrous tuft) **Fruits:** short, globose-ovoid capsule **Seeds:** black, about 200 seeds/g. Germination standard a minimum of 75%. Seeds with 50% germination for 2 years if stored in cool, dry, dark conditions. Pelleted seeds available. **Days to Maturity (DTM):** variable based on climate. Avg. transplants about 95–115 days, sets 85 days, seeds 90–125 days.	**Growing Zones:** check state and county cooperative extension sites and guides for adaptability and recommended planting dates **Day Length:** Important! Match day length (short, intermediate, long) with your region of the United States and Canada. More cultivar choices available for seeds and transplants. **Timing:** sets 4–6 weeks before last spring freeze; transplants are hardy to 20°F; plant early according to Plant Hardiness Zone Map **Optimal Temperature for Growth:** germination temperature is between 59°F and 77°F, optimal between 68°F and 77°F. Higher temperatures favor bulbing and curing. **Frost:** can tolerate some frost, damage at < 20°F **Sunlight:** full sun **Soil conditions:** prefers well-drained, fertile soils that do not crust easily. Light-textured soils such as sandy loams, loams, and silt loams. **Optimal pH:** 6.0–6.8, can tolerate some alkalinity. Sensitive to acidic soils—associated with trace element deficiencies, or occasionally aluminum or manganese toxicity. **Soil Moisture Content:** consistent and constant moisture levels needed throughout growing season. Interruption of moisture (dry conditions) causes outer scales to mature. When moisture resumed, inner scales reinitiate growth and the final onion may split or form a double. Lighter, sandier soils need more water. At bulbing stage, substantial amounts of water are needed, but avoid excessively wet conditions throughout the growing season.	**Site Preparation:** spade and loosen soil to 6–12 inches. Work in a 2-inch layer of compost, decomposed manure, and topsoil (optional) the previous fall. Do not work when soil is wet. After plants are established, mulch with fine materials (peat moss, compost). **Planting:** direct seeding is used where growing season is sufficiently long and temperatures stay in optimal ranges. Transplants should have 3–5 well-formed leaves at transplant time. Plant 1 inch deep. Make sure the top of the transplant's neck is not buried too deep. Sets should be 1 inch deep, 3–4 inches apart. If hard freeze is imminent, cover plot with mulch. **Seeds:** should be ½ inch deep, usually planted in flats indoors or in a cold frame **Spacing:** 3–4 inches apart and 6 inches between rings in circle plot **Weeding:** gentle cultivation **Crop Rotation:** every 5 years **Fertilizer:** preplant N 30–50 lb./acre, side dress 3–4 times with 30–50 lb./acre every 2–3 weeks. No N 4 weeks prior to harvest. P and K preplant 0–150 lb./acre based on soil test. See appendix D for equivalent rates for circle plots. **Nutrition Information:** Onions, raw. USDA Food and Nutrition Service. % Daily Value based on 2,000 calorie diet Serving size 1 cup Calories 64 Total fat 0 g, 0% Total carbohydrate 15 g, 5% Protein 2 g, 4% Vitamin A 0% Vitamin C 20% Vitamin B_6 10% Calcium 37 mg, 4% Phosphorus 46 mg, 5% Potassium 234 mg, 7% Manganese 0.2 mg, 10%

FIGURE 63. Peppers, eggplants, and other vegetables harvested from circle plots. Photo by author.

Peppers

(*Capsicum annuum*)

Peppers are a popular and widely used vegetable throughout the world. About a quarter of the world's population consumes chilies every day. Bell peppers are classified as *Capsicum annuum*, but hot peppers can belong to several other species. Peppers range from sweet to extremely hot. One of the hottest chili peppers, the Trinidad Moruga Scorpion (*Capsicum chinense*), native to the district of Moruga in Trinidad and Tobago (fig. 64C), has the world record as the hottest chili pepper, at 2,009,231 Scoville heat units (SHU). Habaneros reach 350,000 SHU, and jalapeños 2,500–10,000 SHU. The heat from peppers is caused by capsaicinoids, which are alkaloids found in sacs or glands along the juncture of the placenta and inner wall of the fruit. Contrary to common belief, chili seeds do not produce capsaicin, but they can absorb the compound. Capsaicin in pure form is a volatile, colorless, crystalline to waxy compound with 16 million SHU; however, there are far hotter compounds in nature. Resin spurge (*Euphorbia resinifera*), a cactus-like succulent indigenous to the slopes of the Atlas Mountains in Morocco, contains resiniferatoxin, a naturally occurring chemical with 16 *billion* SHU, 1,000 times higher than the SHU of pure capsaicin (fig. 64*B*).

Peppers have many nutritional benefits—they contain high amounts of vitamin C and are rich in beta-carotene, potassium, and fiber. The pepper is a member of the nightshade family, Solanaceae (tomatoes, eggplants, potatoes, and tobacco), but it is not related to the black pepper spice (which is in an entirely different family, Piperaceae). One circle plot of peppers does not take up much space, but the productivity of one circle will astound you. I sincerely hope that you are a pepper lover; if not, try to acquire a taste for peppers, as they are fun to grow. Grow an assortment of cultivars in your circle and watch the fruits develop. You can easily grow large bells and an assortment of horn, cylindrical, and cherry types. If you are a seed saver, be aware that the hot gene in peppers is dominant and insects can cross-pollinate plants.

A

FIGURE 64. *A*, Botanical illustration of wild chile piquin (*Capsicum annuum*). *Köhler's Medizinal-Pflanzen*, 1887. *B*, This plant, resin spurge (*Euphorbia resinifera*), is not a pepper but a cactus-like succulent indigenous to the slopes of the Atlas Mountains in Morocco. Contains resiniferatoxin (16 billion SHU). Courtesy of HortipediaCommons. Photo by Dr. K. D. Zinnert. *C*, Trinidad Moruga Scorpion (*Capsicum chinense*), world's hottest chili pepper (2 million SHU). Photo by Stefano Fabrizio, courtesy of Wikimedia Commons.

B

C

One small anecdote about peppers: you would expect common names of plants to be different around the world, but there are also different common spellings. "Chilli" is common in England and Europe, and "chile" in the southwestern United States. More names for peppers that you may encounter are ají, pimiento, peperone, paprika, and mango or mango pepper (for the association with tropical pickled mangoes).

Historical Background

People have a long history with peppers, especially chilies. Native Americans started domesticating peppers as far back as 10,000–12,000 years ago, most likely from the wild chile piquin (*Capsicum annuum* var. *aviculare*; 100,000–140,000 SHU) (fig. 64a). There are at least 20 other wild pepper species. Archaeologists have found pepper plant remnants in caves that date to 7000 BC. The origin of peppers probably centers in south-central Bolivia and extends into the Andes and Amazonia. Another region of pepper domestication and diversity includes Central America and southern Mexico. Native Americans undoubtedly spent considerable time and effort domesticating and rearing chili peppers. Peppers were revered by the Inca, Aztec, and Maya, who used them for food, spices, and treatment of various ailments. Columbus encountered peppers in the New World (1493) but thought they were related to the black pepper spice. He introduced *Capsicum* to Europe, and it later spread to Africa and Asia.

There are 5 domesticated species of chili: *Capsicum annum*, most of the cultivated peppers including the bells, cherry, yellow wax, ancho, cayenne, jalapeño, and serrano; *C. chinense*, the habaneros and Scotch bonnet; *C. frutescens*, Tabasco; *C. battacum*, yellow Peruvian pepper; and *C. pubescens*, *manzano* and *peron*. Peppers exhibit tremendous diversity in size, color, taste, and spiciness. Some seed companies cater to pepper lovers.

Culture and Planting

Peppers are planted as transplants. Direct seeding is not advisable for several reasons: the time it takes for germination, the slowness of initial seedling growth, and the expense of seeds, especially for hybrids. It is much more economical to start your own pepper seedlings and raise plants to transplant size (4 to 8 inches in height and ⅜ to ¼ inch in stem diameter) (fig. 65). The techniques for starting pepper seedlings and raising transplants are very similar to those for tomatoes and eggplants. Refer to the pepper Quick Guide for specifics. Here, I wish to concentrate on a few issues that are specific to peppers. Peppers are subject to diseases that are similar to those of tomatoes; however, I find that peppers are much less problematic if you follow some basic rules. Hybrid specialty colored bells are gorgeous, and although they can be more difficult to grow and usually have less disease resistance, the effort is worth it. Plant the specialty bells in the inner part of the circle arrangement for more protection against wind and possible fruit sunscald.

In setting out transplants, dig a hole 1 foot deep and 8–12 inches wide. Sprinkle some blood meal in the bottom of the hole and fill with 2 inches of soil, add 6 inches of compost, and then mix in 4 inches of soil. Use your hand or a small trowel to create a depression deep enough to accommodate the transplant and root ball. Place the plant in the hole about 1 to 2 inches below the soil line. Leave a slight depression so water does not run off during irrigation. After planting, place a small amount of mulch around and under the new plants to prevent soil splash onto the tender leaves. More mulch can be added later when the soil heats up and the plants grow taller (fig. 66). Peppers seem to be more prone to transplant shock, so try to pick an overcast day and be careful not to disturb the roots when removing the plant from the pot. If you purchase transplants in smaller pots, plant them in larger half-gallon or 1-gallon pots and let the plants grow to the size in figure 29*B* and *C* in chapter 9. If you move them to bigger pots, they will be stronger for the eventual move to the garden.

The following is a summary of pepper culture:

1. Many pepper diseases are seed borne; that is, the seeds can be contaminated with bacterial spot, pepper mild mottle virus (PMMV), Cercospora leaf spot, and anthracnose.

2. Start seedlings in a cold frame, or cover pots with plastic. Use a potting mix with slow-release fertilizers and organic amendments. Be patient, as germination is slow, depending on current diurnal temperatures. I put an extra seed or two in my pots and thin to the best plant later. Pepper seedlings grow slowly; don't forget to keep the soil moist, and check every morning and at midday.

3. Plant transplants in well-drained areas; elevated circle mounds or other raised beds work well. Remove flower blooms on transplants. Plants that flower early usually indicate stress.

4. Peppers tolerate a wide range of soils. Improve with organic matter and be judicious with fertilizer, especially nitrogen. Optimal pH is between 6 and 6.8.

5. Do not plant peppers where peppers, tomatoes, potatoes, or eggplants were grown during the last 4 years.

6. Plant peppers about a week to 10 days after the optimal time to transplant tomatoes. Peppers like a warmed soil (above 60°F).

7. Pepper seeds tend to germinate slowly (7–10 days), but some species

and cultivars require even longer germination times. Some specialty peppers (*C. frutescens*) have been known to take up to 100 days to germinate.

8. During cold snaps, cover plants at night to avoid damage to leaves.

9. In the home garden, larger container-grown transplants are preferable to small pots (< 2 inches). Avoid disturbing roots as much as possible.

10. As with tomatoes, flower set in peppers depends on ambient temperatures. Many pepper cultivars will drop their blooms when temperatures rise above 90°F and when night temperatures drop below 75°F. Flower drop is also common in peppers when springtime temperatures are cool. Hot pepper cultivars such as jalapeños can tolerate hot weather and still produce fruit. Some hot pepper cultivars set fruit better in warmer weather than specialty colored bells. Maximum flower set on sweet bells occurs at between 60 and 70°F.

11. The optimal temperature range for both sweet bells and hot peppers is between 70 and 85°F.

12. My pepper plants stop producing fruit during the hot Texas summer days; however, some of the hot cultivars keep producing. Throughout the summer, take care of your peppers with frequent watering, mulching, and some fertilizer if needed. When temperatures start dropping in the fall, your pepper plants will start producing again—with a vengeance.

13. The quality of red and yellow pigments in peppers is temperature dependent (65°F–77°F). At temperatures above 75°F, red coloration tends toward a washed-out yellow. Color development ceases at temperatures below 55°F.

14. Cover large exposed fruits to avoid fruit scalding during hot sunny weather. I use handfuls of hay or straw, or cloths.

15. Water pepper plants at soil level and try to avoid frequent water spray on leaves.

16. Mulch plants in a circle arrangement to maintain soil moisture. Uneven or dry soil can cause poor fruit set, fruit drop, and uneven fruit development. Even though mulch helps maintain more constant moisture levels, temperatures above 90°F in Texas signal that I still need to water circles every 2–3 days.

17. As plants grow taller, I pile in more mulch (hay, straw) around the plants to support them. The loose material can be up to 8 to 10 inches in depth and tucked around the plants. The mulch decomposes rap-

idly during hot weather and from consistent watering, so keep adding mulch throughout the growing season. I rarely use stakes except near the end of the season, when fruit set is heavy.

18. I use 2-foot-high wire mesh borders to protect plants from digging animals such as rabbits, skunks, and armadillos (fig. 66). The mesh fencing also provides support to the plants on the outer perimeter of the circle.

19. You can mix pepper cultivars in the same circle. However, you may get interesting results if you save seeds. Seed growers must isolate cultivars at least 500 feet apart to maintain seed purity.

20. Many garden guides recommend using various concoctions of pepper sprays made from cayenne pepper and hot peppers. These preparations are used as a repellent, not as a pesticide. **I recommend against using pepper sprays, as one small accident, such as wind blowing in the wrong direction or an inadvertent touch to your eyes, will create a burning experience that you will never forget.** Find other solutions for repelling pests.

FIGURE 65. Pepper transplants in circle arrangement. These circle plots can produce 2 or more bushels of peppers. Photo by author.

21. Peppers can be harvested at any stage of development. Use a knife or scissors to cut the stem. Pepper stems are brittle and often break off if you twist or pull fruits from the plant.

22. Some pepper cultivars require staking as they grow, especially when fruit is heavy.

FIGURE 66. A 4½-foot circle bed, with an assortment (10 plants, 18 inches apart) of Italian sweet, bell, and mild hot southwestern chili cultivars (same plot as in fig. 65). The mesh fencing inhibits small digging animals and provides support to the outside plants. Some staking may be needed as plants become heavy with fruit. These circle plots have received manure and compost applications for 8 years; no other fertilizers have been used. Photos by author.

Diseases and Pests

Below is a key to common pepper diseases and pests. It is not possible to cover all aspects of this subject in this book, or to include photos of problems. Search out USDA, university, and extension publications with photos. If you have a particular problem that stumps you, contact your county extension office.

Diseases

Leaves and stems

Severe defoliation of plant, round to oblong lesions with light gray centers, premature leaf drop. Disease prevalent in wet, humid weather. Fungal disease, **Cercospora Leaf Spot** (*Cercospora capsici*). Fungi from contaminated seeds, also carried over from previous pepper crop litter. Fungal spores dispersed by wind can be controlled by fungal sprays.

Leaves, stems, and fruit

- Round lesions on ripe fruits, start out as small pinkish lesions; as they progress the lesions contain concentric pink-to-salmon rings. Disease associated with warm, wet, humid conditions. Fungal disease, **Anthracnose,** caused by *Colletotrichum acutatum* and *C. gloeosporioides*. Fungi from contaminated seeds, also carried over from previous pepper crop litter. Use disease-free seeds, crop rotations, and preventive fungicide applications.
- Water-soaked lesions on leaves and stems, necrosis develops with brown coloration in center. Premature leaf drop; disease spreads rapidly in warm, wet conditions. On fruits, lesions are small, round, and dark brown to black. Bacterial disease, **Bacterial Spot** (*Xanthomonas campestris* pv. *vesicatoria*). Bacteria are seed borne; buy uncontaminated seeds. Some seed companies advertise that they test their seeds.
- Stunted plants; ring spots, mottling, and necrosis on leaves. Fruits misshapen, raised ring spots, and black specks. Viral disease, **Tomato Spotted Wilt Virus (TSWV).** Virus transmitted by tobacco thrips (*Frankliniella fusca*) and western flower thrips (*F. occidentalis*). Plant resistant cultivars and use reflective colored mulches.
- Stunted plants, leaf symptoms variable, slight to severe leaf curling, mottling, lighter coloring (light to dark green) showing a mosaic pattern, and necrosis on leaves. Fruits distorted and

malformed. Viral disease, **Cucumber Mosaic Virus (CMV).** Virus transmitted by many species of aphids. Plant resistant cultivars and use reflective colored mulches.

- Chlorotic mosaic pattern on leaves. Fruits have sunken, distorted, discolored areas. Viral disease, **Pepper Mild Mottle Virus (PMMV).** Virus is seed borne and is spread by contact with other plants. Use noninfected seeds.
- Plants stunted, unthrifty, with premature wilting, slow recovery from dry soil, and leaf chlorosis—pale yellow to light green. Symptoms characteristic of nutrient deficiencies. Roots contain galls. **Root-Knot Nematodes** (root-knot nematode, *Meloidogyne* spp., and sting nematode, *Belonolaimus longicaudatus*). Soil and root tissue analysis needed for positive identification. Life cycle consists of 4 larval stages (4–8 weeks), then development into adult male or female. First-stage larvae hatch from egg and molt; larvae in second stage infect plant roots. Three more molts occur, and larvae then mature to adults. Optimal life cycle occurs when soil temperatures are 70 to 80°F. Integrated control measures depend on soils and climate and include crop rotation, resistant cultivars, fallowing, biological controls, soil amendments (animal manure, poultry litter, cover crop residues), soil solarization with transparent plastic tarps, and chemical controls (nonfumigant and fumigant nematicides).

Insect pests

Many common insect pests are associated with peppers.

f = fruit, l = leaves, s = stems, r = roots

- Western Yellowstriped Armyworm (*Spodoptera praefica*), Yellowstriped Armyworm (*S. ornithogalli*) (s, 1, f)
- Tomato Fruitworm (*Helicoverpa zea*) (f)
- Beet Armyworm (*Spodoptera exigua*) (1, f)
- Cabbage Loopers (*Trichoplusia ni*) (1, s)
- Aphids: Green Peach Aphid (*Myzus persicae*), Melon Aphids (*Aphis gossypii*), Potato Aphids (*Macrosiphum euphorbiae*) (1, s)
- Tomato Psyllid (*Bactericera cockerelli*) (1)
- Whiteflies: Silverleaf Whitefly (*Bemisia argentifolii*), Greenhouse Whitefly (*Trialeurodes vaporariorum*), Bandedwinged Whitefly (*T. abutilonia*) (1)
- Twospotted Spider Mites (*Tetranychus urticae*) (s, 1)
- Flea Beetles (*Epitrix hirtipennis* and others) (1)

- Leafminers (*Liriomyza sativae*, *L. trifolii*, and *L. huidobrensis*) (1)
- Omnivorous Leafroller (*Platynota stultana*) (1, f)
- Pepper Weevil (*Anthonomus eugenii*) (f)
- Thrips: Western Flower Thrips (*Frankliniella occidentalis*), Onion Thrips (*Thrips tabaci*), and other species (s, 1, f)
- Colorado Potato Beetle (*Leptinotarsa decemlineata*) (s, 1)
- European Corn Borer (*Ostrinia nubilalis*) (1)
- Stink Bugs: Brown (*Euschistus servus*) and Green (*Acrosternum hilare*) (f)
- Pepper Maggot (*Zonosemata electa*) (f)

What is Pepper Corking?

Do your jalapeños have white lines that look like "stretch marks" or striations on the skin? They may appear at the green and red stage. This condition is called "corking," and it is a genetic trait associated with specific pepper varieties (Mexican and cayenne). Contrary to popular myth, corking has no effect on taste or heat level. Some sweet bell peppers can also carry this genetic trait. Most gardeners strive for blemish-free fruit and view "corkiness" as an undesirable pepper trait; however, in Mexico it is desirable.

FIGURE 67. "Corking" is a genetic trait associated with specific pepper varieties. Photo by author.

Peppers Quick Guide

Botanical Data	Environmental Conditions	Culture and Special Considerations
Pepper (*Capsicum annuum*) **Family:** Solanaceae **Life Cycle:** classified as herbaceous annual **Flowers:** solitary or rarely 2 or 3 at first node; protogynous white flowers (has perfect flowers, but female organs develop and mature before male organs produce pollen). Stamens 6 or 7 attached to base of corolla. Anthers release pollen 2–3 days after flowers open. Stalks thicken in fruit. **Physiology:** warm-season vegetable, photosynthesis C_3 **Stems:** many stemmed, with woody caudex (base) **Leaves:** alternate, glabrous or pubescent, ovate to lanceolate, entire, apex acute to acuminate, base wedge shaped **Roots:** moderately deep rooted, strong taproot with numerous branched fibrous laterals **Fruits:** true berry, erect or hanging; varied shapes (spherical, ovoid, conical), sweet to pungent **Seeds:** kidney shaped, white; about 140 seeds/g. Usual seed life about 2 years under good storage conditions. Germination time is 8–25 days. **Days to Maturity (DTM):** variable based on climate. DTM is from date of transplant to fruiting. DTM varies greatly among cultivars, average is 50–85 days. **Cultivars:** choose adaptable cultivars. Huge selections of sweet and hot peppers available. Disease-resistant cultivars available.	**Growing Zones:** check state and county cooperative extension sites and guides for adaptability and recommended planting dates **Optimal Temperature for Growth:** germination at 70°F–90°F; pepper seeds germinate slowly at cooler temperatures; optimal growing temperature for sweet peppers is between 70°F and 75°F; for hot peppers 70°F–85°F **Frost:** easily damaged or killed by light frost (28°F–32°F) **Sunlight:** full sun. Fruits can scald on hot, sunny days; use a floating cover, cloth, or wads of hay for prevention. **Soil Conditions:** prefers well-drained, loamy soils, will also grow in sandy soils. Constant moisture balance is important. **Optimal pH:** 6.0–6.8 **Soil Moisture Content:** consistent and constant moisture levels needed throughout growing season. Mulch around plants. **Nutrition Information:** Peppers, bell, green, raw. USDA Food and Nutrition Service. % Daily Value based on 2,000 calorie diet Serving size 1 cup Calories 30 Total fat 0.3 g, 0% Total carbohydrate 7 g, 2% Protein 1.3 g, 3% Vitamin A 551 IU, 11% Vitamin C 120 mg, 200% Vitamin K 11 mcg, 14% Vitamin E 0.6 mg, 3% Niacin 0.7 mg, 4% Vitamin B_6 0.3 mg, 17% Folate 15 mg, 4% Calcium 15 mg, 1% Iron 0.5 mg, 3% Magnesium 15 mg, 4% Phosphorus 30 mg, 3% Potassium 261 mg, 7% Copper 0.1 mg, 5% Manganese 0.2 mg, 9%	**Site Preparation:** spade and loosen soil to 6–10 inches. Work in a 2-inch layer of compost, decomposed manure, and topsoil (optional) the previous fall. Do not work when soil is wet. After plants are established, mulch with fine materials (peat moss, compost, hay, straw). **Planting:** tobacco users should disinfect hands when planting and working with peppers (tobacco mosaic virus) **Transplants:** harden transplants at temperatures around 65°F and expose them gradually to increased light and higher temperatures. Taproot is easily damaged during transplanting—use care. Remove any flower blooms on transplants. Plant on a cloudy or overcast day. **Seeds:** 6–8 weeks prior to transplanting, sow seeds in pots or shallow flats 1/4 inch deep in a cold frame **Spacing:** 12–18 inches apart **Weeding:** gentle cultivation; use mulch to control weeds and maintain even moisture. Tuck loose mulch around bases of plants for additional support. **Fertilizer:** abundant P, 0–150 lb./acre per soil test; 0–200 lb./acre K per soil test. Calcium is important; do not use N in excess as it promotes extensive leaf growth at expense of flowering and fruiting. N requirement is 140 lb./acre in low SOM, 120 lb./acre in medium SOM, and 100 lb./acre in high SOM soils. Broadcast ½ fertilizer requirement at planting, ½ when fruits develop. See appendix D for circle plot fertilizer equivalents. **Crop rotation:** every 4 years

A

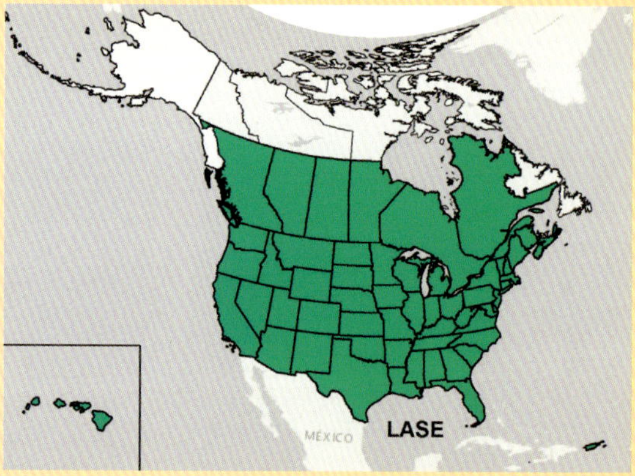

C

FIGURE 68. *A*, Botanical illustration of wild prickly lettuce, *Lactuca serriola*. Prof. Dr. Otto Wilhelm Thomé, *Flora von Deutschland, Österreich und der Schweiz*, 1885, Gera, Germany, http://www.biolib.de. *B*, Swiss chard, spinach, beets, and lettuce circle plots in foreground. Photo by author. *C*, Extent of wild prickly lettuce in North America. Courtesy of USDA NRCS Plants Database, http://plants.usda.gov/java/.

B

Salad Greens

Lettuce (*Lactuca sativa*)
Spinach (*Spinacia oleracea*)
Swiss Chard (*Beta vulgaris* var. *cicla*)
Beets (*Beta vulgaris* ssp. *vulgaris*)

Lettuce (*Lactuca sativa*)

Historical background

Wild lettuce (*Lactuca serriola*), or prickly lettuce, is a common weed around our homes and gardens. Wild lettuce has a milky white latex, which is noticeable when the stems or leaves are damaged or removed. The garden lettuce we grow today is related to prickly or China lettuce, which was introduced into the United States from Eurasia (Europe, Asia, and North Africa) (fig. 68*A*). Prickly lettuce is now established in every state in the United States (except Alaska) and in Canada. Our modern cultivars are not found in the wild. Plant breeders have concentrated on increasing the time before bolting occurs, increasing disease resistance, and developing a wide variety of colors, leaf shapes, and flavors. Average lettuce consumption in the United States exceeds 25 pounds per year.

The literature mentions that wild lettuce may have first originated in Turkey, Iran, Siberia, and North Africa. Carvings in Egyptian tombs dating back to 4500 BC show lettuce with pointed leaves. The Egyptians cultivated lettuce for edible oil extracted from the seeds, and archaeologists state that lettuce was at the table of Persian kings in the fifth century BC. The following are some notable events in history regarding lettuce:

- Theophrastus identified 3 varieties in his *History of Plants*, 350 BC.
- In the year 1 AD the Romans referred to 12 lettuce varieties; in ancient Rome, lettuce was a luxury and was used during feast days.
- Charlemagne may have brought lettuce to France in 780 AD.
- Columbus brought lettuce seeds to the New World, and records show its cultivation in Hispaniola (now the Dominican Republic), a colony (1,500 settlers) established in 1494 during his second voyage.
- In colonial times, lettuce was planted in gardens of the gentry—George Washington planted 16 of his 61 garden beds to lettuce.

Throughout the ages, lettuce has been grown for its medicinal properties. Lettuce can cause allergic contact dermatitis in sensitive individuals (food handlers, chefs, and gardeners). In some people, contact with lettuce can result in immediate hypersensitivity, which includes urticaria (hives) and life-threatening anaphylaxis.

There are 4 common distinct lettuce types: iceberg or crisphead (*Lactuca sativa* var. *capitata*); butterhead, Bibb, or Boston (*L. sativa* var. *capitata*); leaf (*L. sativa* var. *crispa*), and cos or romaine (*L. sativa* var. *longifolia*). Iceberg or crisphead lettuce is commonly found in grocery stores and restaurant salads and has compact folded heads

FIGURE 69. Fall-planted mixed lettuce varieties in circle arrangement. Photo by author.

that are brittle and can be peeled off or broken up for use in food preparation. This lettuce is usually a lighter green and has a lower concentration of chlorophyll in its cells. The butterhead cultivars have more open, loose heads with soft, delicate leaves. Leaf lettuce cultivars produce individual leaves, are popular in the home garden, and are very adaptable. The cos or romaine types do not form a head but grow upright and have elongated leaves. The leaves of butterhead, leaf lettuce, and romaine can be harvested individually instead of picking the entire plant.

Culture and planting

Lettuce is easy to grow, but there are some particular requirements that must be considered (see lettuce Quick Guide). Lettuce is an annual cool-season crop and grows best at temperatures between 55°F and 70°F, but it can germinate at temperatures as low as 35°F–40°F. When temperatures rise to 85°F and above, thermal dormancy begins and seed germination is inhibited. Seed companies state that pelleted seeds broaden the range of seed germination in lettuce. Since lettuce is an annual plant, its natural inclination is to produce seeds during the life cycle year. Warmer temperatures initiate bolting, emergence of a seed stalk and flowers. Another unpleasant characteristic that plagues lettuce is the development of bitterness as temperatures increase and bolting begins. The compounds that cause bitterness in lettuce are called bitter sesquiterpene lactones (BSLs) (lactucin, 8-deoxylactucin, and lactucopicrin).

Many of the leafy salad greens such as lettuce, spinach, and Swiss chard can withstand light to medium frosts, and they can be the first vegetables seeded into the garden. Fall-planted lettuce can be perpetuated in cold frames or by floating row covers when frost threatens. I have noticed that during heavy frosts (around 25°F), lettuce is damaged quite severely, but often the plant bases are still alive. In the South, a sequence of frosts will arrive and knock back the cool-season salad greens, followed by rising temperatures that remain in the 40s and 50s for several weeks, and then the trend is repeated. In these climates, remove the dead and wilting leaves and you may be surprised by new growth from the plant crowns—if you protect the plants from future hard frosts.

Lettuce can tolerate a wide range of soil textures, but the main concern is that the soil be well drained. Heavier-textured soils with higher clay content store more water that is available for plant growth. Lettuce prefers a soil pH of between 6.0 and 6.6, or neutral, and high fertility. Fertility levels in your soil can be diagnosed by evaluating past plant performance in the garden and/or by a soil test. If your lettuce germinates but does not show sufficient growth after 2 weeks, your soil is probably nutrient deficient. Commercial growers use 80–120 lb. N/acre, half broadcasted and half used as a side dressing 3–5 weeks after establishment. Phosphorus rates range from 0 to 150 lb./acre, and potassium from 0 to 200 lb./acre depending on soil test analyses. See appendix D for equivalent fertilizer rates for circle plots.

In established home vegetable gardens where adequate amounts of sustained compost, manure, and other organic amendments containing nitrogen, phosphorus, and potassium have been added to the soil over a period of 3 or more years, there should be adequate nutrients. In a newly established garden, your fertility levels may not be adequate. How well does your lawn grow around your property? Does it need regular applications of fertilizer? If the answer is yes, you will need to boost your nitrogen, phosphorus, and potassium levels with organic and/or synthetic fertilizer formulations. If you use a synthetic fertilizer, use a balanced formulation of nitrogen, phosphorus, and potassium. I mention this theme continually throughout the book, as many beginning gardens fail, and gardeners become discouraged by the performance of their garden because they assume that manure and compost will initially provide for the nutrient needs of the plants. Organic gardening is a process in which soil health improves over time with the addition of organic matter. In newly established vegetable gardens, the addition of manure and compost may not provide enough nitrogen to meet plant needs.

Plant lettuce seeds as soon as the soil can be worked early in the spring—this means about a month before the last spring frost. Lettuce seeds are small, and unless you have deft fingers, placing individual seeds is almost impossible. Seed companies have gadgets to help plant small seeds, but the best solution is pelleted seeds. This makes the chore of seeding lettuce in the home garden much easier—the cost is worth it! Planting lettuce using the circle method is easy: start with the outside diameter and plant seeds shallowly (⅛ to ¼ inch deep), ½ inch apart or closer. Move inward 8 to 18 inches and start the next concentric row (table 26). Continue the process inward. I like to plant more seeds than some guides recommend because I want a good stand; I can thin to larger spacings later. I would rather have a denser stand than a spotty stand that has to be replanted. I like to plant mixtures that seed companies prepare, as this provides variety to the salad (fig. 69). As a side note, those of us who are not as exacting and particular will tend to use more seeds and have denser stands. No problem—that is what thinning was invented for! As soon as the conditions are right for germination in the spring, seedlings will appear. Let nature determine when the plants germinate and start to grow; your concern is to get these salad greens planted early. These leafy salad greens can be planted in fall gardens as well. If you are new to gardening, determine your plant growing zone and talk with other local gardeners and your extension service for information about fall planting.

In the South, fall planting of these salad greens can be somewhat tricky, as the soil temperatures can still be above 90°F during the daytime throughout September and October. These salad greens require cool soil temperatures to germinate (see individual Quick Guides for specific data).

TABLE 26. Example of 4½-foot-diameter circle plot of lettuce with concentric rings 12 inches apart

Radius of circle or distance from center (inches), with rings spaced 12 inches apart	Ring circumference (inches)	Plant spacing		
		3 inches	6 inches	12 inches
27	170	57	28	14
15	94	31	16	8
3	19	6	3	2
Total Plants		94	47	24

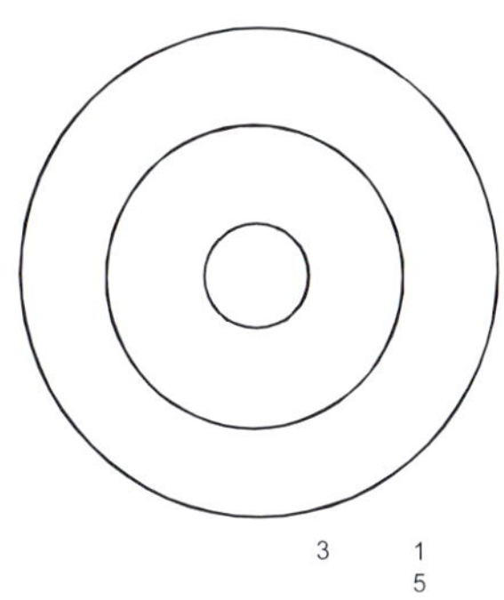

Note: Start planting at the outer edge of the circle and progressively move toward the center (27, 15, 3 inches).

SCIENCE NOTE • Safety Concerns and Salad Greens

There are risks associated with eating raw foods, although they are slight. First, let's be clear on one point: millions of bags of salad greens are sold in the United States without incident. However, outbreaks of food-borne illness do occur from time to time. When contamination does occur, two bacteria are usually the culprits (*Salmonella enterica* and *Escherichia coli*). These pathogens can be killed by cooking. If they reside in the soil, they can occur inside and outside the plant. For example, during commercial harvesting of lettuce, workers cut and core the lettuce with a knife, which can then pick up pathogens from infected soil. Lettuce produces a milky latex or sap (spinach and Swiss chard do not), which can trap these pathogens in the plant tissue. Washing and cleansing during processing does not affect pathogens that are living in the internal tissues of the plant. Where do these pathogens come from? Usually they come from raw contaminated animal manure. *E. coli* and *Salmonella* are gram-negative bacteria that live comfortably inside the animal gut, but when they are excreted in feces, they face a new, inhospitable environment (with varying temperatures, low nutrients, different pH levels, and predation from other microbes). *E. coli* has a low rate of survival outside the animal host. *E. coli* populations in the environment must be replenished by new additions of contaminated manure or by other sources. *E. coli* has an average survival of 3 days in the soil environment. However, in tropical climates, *E. coli* is able to survive longer in freshwater and soil.

Salmonella is more insidious, as it can live in the environment for long periods. *Salmonella* is associated with a large number of animal species. Birds and flies (including the common housefly) are vectors that spread it in the environment. Most infections in humans come from eating undercooked meats, seafood, and eggs. *Salmonella* outbreaks are also linked to fruits and vegetables from contaminated raw manure fertilizers. How does *Salmonella* infect fruits and vegetables? The bacteria can be external or internal in plant tissues. For example, in tomatoes, if *Salmonella* comes in contact with flowers, stems, or fruits, it can infiltrate and colonize inside plant tissues, where washing cannot remove it. Tomato plants have also been known to take up *Salmonella* via hydroponic solutions. Some characteristics of *Salmonella* include the following:

- Can survive for 10–15 days in septic systems.
- Can survive in aquatic environments.
- Can survive in soil and sediments for at least a year.

Common lettuce disease promotes colonization of human pathogens: Carefully controlled laboratory experiments have shown that wet conditions, high relative humidity, and the presence of downy mildew (*Bremia lactucae*) in lettuce was associated with proliferation of *E. coli* and *Salmonella enterica*. The occurrence of downy mildew in lettuce may increase the risk of these two pathogens contaminating a crop.

In conclusion, the odds are that you will not get ill from eating packaged lettuce greens. Millions of packages of salad greens are sold in the United States each year. Many states and individual farms train employees and maintain safety protocols to manage potential contamination from food-borne pathogens. The data from the USDA seems to show that contamination is not specific to either large or small farms—the potential risks are about the same.

Lettuce diseases and pests

Diseases

The disease list below will help identify common problems. Seek additional information from your state cooperative extension office for pesticide recommendations. Crop rotation, uninfected seeds, removal of the prior year's plant residues, minimal leaf wetness, no overhead irrigation or watering, and, for some diseases, resistant varieties are all good management tools to manage lettuce diseases. Biological and chemical controls are available for some of the diseases below.

- Wilting of lower leaves, rotting at base of plant, entire plant can wilt and turn slimy. Fungus, **Sclerotinia Rot** (*Sclerotinia sclerotiorum* and *S. minor*). Soil borne, also carried by wind and infected equipment, irrigation water, and seeds. Overwinters in soil. Do not plant after beans, peas, carrots, cabbage, tomatoes, or potatoes, as they are hosts to *Sclerotinia*. Plant after corn, broccoli, or grain cover crops.
- Yellow spots and cottony growth under leaves. Cool, humid conditions. Fungus, **Downy Mildew** (*Bremia lactucae*). Soil borne; spreads by soil splash and wind. Control methods are those listed above under diseases; use resistant varieties.

- Powdery growth on both sides of leaves, starting with small yellow dots that turn gray; thick mold may develop on older leaves, leaves become slimy. Cool, damp conditions. Fungus, **Gray Mold** (*Botrytis cinerea*). Control methods are those listed above under diseases.
- Sunken, water-soaked spots on lower leaves, eventually turn brown and become slimy. Can cause damping off of seedlings. Fungus, **Bottom Rot** (*Rhizoctonia solani*). Spreads from infected soil, soil-water splash, boots, and machinery. Control methods are those listed above under diseases.
- Mosaic and necrotic yellowing, pale veins, and stunted plants. Virus, **Lettuce Mosaic Virus** (LMV). Seed-borne disease, infected seeds. Transmitted by aphids from wild lettuce (*Lactuca serriola*). Place bag over infected plants to prevent escape of aphids, discard plants. Treat aphids.
- Tips of internal leaves turn brown or gray. **Tipburn**. Physiological disorder caused by calcium deficiency, excess nitrogen, and hot temperatures.

Insect pests

- Western Flower Thrips (*Frankliniella occidentalis*);
- Silverleaf Whitefly (*Bemisia argentifolii*);
- Leafminers: Pea Leafminer (*Liriomyza huidobrensis*); Serpentine Leafminer (*L. trifolii*), Vegetable Leafminer (*L. sativae*);
- Darkling Beetles (*Blapstinus* spp., *Caelus* spp., and others);
- Aphids: Green Peach Aphid (*Myzus persicae*), Potato Aphid (*Macrosiphum euphorbiae*), Lettuce Aphid (*Nasonovia ribisnigri*), Lettuce Root Aphid (*Pemphigus bursarius*), Foxglove Aphid (*Aulacorthum solani*);
- Bulb Mites (*Rhizoglyphus* spp., *Tyrophagus* spp.);
- Beet Armyworm (*Spodoptera exigua*);
- Armyworm (*Pseudaletia unipuncta*);
- Cutworms: Black Cutworm (*Agrotis ipsilon*), Variegated Cutworm (*Peridroma saucia*), Granulate Cutworm (*Feltia subterranea*);
- Garden Symphylans (*Scutigerella immaculata*);
- Loopers: Cabbage Looper (*Trichoplusia ni*), Alfalfa Looper (*Autographa californica*);
- Corn Earworm (*Heliothis zea*);
- Tobacco Budworm (*Heliothis virescens*);
- Saltmarsh Caterpillar (*Estigmene acrea*);
- Slugs

SCIENCE NOTE • Intercropping or Companion Cropping of Lettuce and Alyssum (*Lobularia maritima*) to Control Aphids

Lettuce is an economically important crop in California (worth about $2.3 billion/year). Alyssum is a perennial ornamental flowering plant from the Mediterranean area that blooms over an extended period. Organic growers in California use interplanted strips of alyssum to attract hoverflies (Syrphidae) to control aphids. Hoverfly larvae are natural enemies of aphids: 1 larva can kill up to 160 aphids per day. Lettuce-alyssum intercropping is an effective biological control system that is commonly used by organic lettuce growers.

FIGURE 70. Intercropping of alyssum with organic romaine lettuce for aphid control at USDA ARS fields in Salinas, California. Courtesy of USDA ARS, http://www.ars.usda.gov/is/AR/archive/jan14/lettuce0114.htm.

Lettuce Quick Guide

Botanical Data	Environmental Conditions	Culture and Special Considerations
Lettuce (*Lactuca sativa*); *lactis* means "milk," *sativa*, "grown from seeds" **Family**: Asteraceae **Life Cycle**: herbaceous, self-pollinating annual **Inflorescence**: a diffuse conical panicle, flower heads few to many, each made up of 15–25 or more flowers **Flowers**: perfect flowers, with ligulate corollas only (yellow, bluish, rarely white), ovary inferior. Mostly self-pollinated; some insects can cross-pollinate; some authorities state that 5% of crossing may occur between different cultivars, partially cleistogamous (pollen is released and fertilization occurs before flower opens); will cross with prickly lettuce (*L. serriola*). **Physiology**: cool-season vegetable, photosynthesis C_3 **Stems**: erect, arising singly or clustered **Leaves**: vary by cultivar. Can be linear-ovate, obovate, or lanceolate. **Roots**: taprooted, with fine fibrous roots **Fruits**: achene, white to black **Seeds**: germination 2–15 days at 40°F–75°F. Temperatures above 80°F cause poor to nonexistent germination. 800–850 seeds/g. Viability up to 3 years when stored in cool, dry conditions. Pelleted seeds available. **Days to Maturity (DTM)**: calculated from germination date. Most cultivars 28–58 days. Cool weather can delay maturity 1–3 weeks.	**Growing Zones**: check state and county cooperative extension sites and guides for adaptability and recommended planting dates. Lettuce is hardy and can be planted as soon as soil can be worked in spring. **Timing**: seed in early spring; seeds can germinate in soil at 35°F–40°F. Can be grown continuously at temperatures of 40°F–75°F. Spring and fall crops are common throughout the United States. **Optimal Temperature for Growth**: 55°F–65°F; temperatures above 75°F cause the plants to bolt. With the development of the seed stalk, lettuce leaves become bitter and tough. **Frost**: can withstand light frost (28°F–32°F). Extend fall season with clear plastic or other protective floating row gardening covers. **Sunlight**: full sun, partial shade **Soil Conditions**: prefers well-drained, loose, N-rich soils. Soil texture can range from mucks to sandy loams to clays or clay loams. Clay loams and silty clay loams retain moisture for growing lettuce. **Optimal pH**: 6.0–6.8 **Soil Moisture Content**: consistent moisture at surface since roots are shallow **Nutrition Information**: Lettuce, green leaf, raw. USDA Food and Nutrition Service. % Daily Value based on 2,000 calorie diet Serving size 1 cup Calories 5.4 Total fat 0.1 g, 0% Total carbohydrate 1 g, 0% Protein 0.5 g, 1% Vitamin A 2665 IU, 53% Vitamin C 6.5 mg, 11% Vitamin K 62.5 mcg, 78% Potassium 70 mg, 2% Calcium 13 mg, 1% Iron 0.3 mg, 2% Manganese 0.1 mg, 5%	**Ease of Growing**: easy, stay within soil temperature guidelines **Site Preparation**: spade and loosen soil to 6–10 inches. Work in a 2-inch layer of compost, decomposed manure, and topsoil (optional) the previous fall. Do not work when soil is wet. **Fertilizer**: 40–50 lb. N/acre preplant, side dress with 40–50 lb. when leaves are 2–4 inches high, optional side dress of 40–50 lb./acre 10–14 days later. Preplant P and K at 120–150 lb./acre depending on soil test. Refer to appendix D for equivalent fertilizer rates for circle plots. **Planting**: ⅛–¼ inch deep, usually seeded directly into garden. Can be sown into small pots or flats and transplanted. Plant every 2 weeks for successive harvests. **Spacing**: direct seeding at ½–1 inch apart depending on cultivar. Leaf types can be grown close together, thinned, and harvested progressively. Romaine types 8–12 inches apart, large iceberg types 12–18 inches apart. In row plantings spacing is 18–30 inches between rows. In circle arrangements spacing between rows can vary depending on goals. Successively harvested leaf and romaine types can be spaced 8–12 inches apart because of individual leaf harvest. For full-sized plants spacing can be increased to 12–18 inches. **Thinning**: when 2–3 leaves appear, thin plants **Weeding**: gentle cultivation since the roots are shallow **Cultivars**: common types are iceberg or crisphead; butterhead, Bibb, or Boston; cos or romaine; leaf; and Latin. Cultivar selection is important, as each responds differently to warming and hot temperatures—check seed catalog data. **Harvest**: anytime from baby greens to mature leaves; do not harvest when leaves are wet; periodically taste leaves before maturity and before hot weather ensues, as bitterness occurs

Where western flower thrips are a problem (spread viral diseases), remove surrounding flowering weeds to manage pests. Consult university extension bulletins for control and management of specific insect pests.

Spinach (*Spinacia oleracea*)

Historical background

Spinach is another cool-season plant and has many of the same growing requirements as lettuce. Spinach has increased in popularity with the advent of the salad bar, fancy salad offerings in restaurants, and prewashed spinach in containers at the grocery store. We have come a long way since the canned spinach days, which probably turned you away from this vegetable, regardless of the powers it provided "Popeye the Sailor Man." Spinach is rich in many nutrients, not just the iron that gave Popeye strength; these include vitamins A, C, E, K, B_2, B_6, B_9 (folic acid), and niacin; the minerals calcium, potassium, magnesium, manganese, phosphorus, copper, zinc, and selenium; the carotenoids lutein and zeaxanthin; and betaine, omega-3 fatty acids, and protein.

FIGURE 71. Spinach growing throughout the winter, planted in fall. Photo by author.

Botanically, the Latin word *spinacia* refers to the seeds, which have a prickly appearance, like those of many plants in the family Chenopodiaceae (goosefoot family). The species name *oleracea* refers to an edible plant. Like most of our cultivated crop plants, spinach originated from wild plants, *Spinacia tetrandra* and *S. turkestanica* (fig. 72*A*). Our present garden varieties do not exist in the wild; they were developed from wild plants native to northern Iran, Afghanistan, and Turkmenistan. Wild spinach, *S. tetrandra*, is still gathered as a wild edible green in Asia Minor. Wild spinach migrated from ancient Persia, most likely with traders, and found its way to India and then China (around 647 AD). Spinach was introduced to Sicily in the Mediterranean around 827 AD and was documented in early medical and agricultural writings in the tenth century. In the twelfth century, the Arab agronomist Ibn al-'Awwam called it the "captain of leafy greens." By the thirteenth century, spinach was known in Germany, and the smooth-leaved variety was botanically described in 1552; during the fourteenth century, spinach was being grown in England and France.

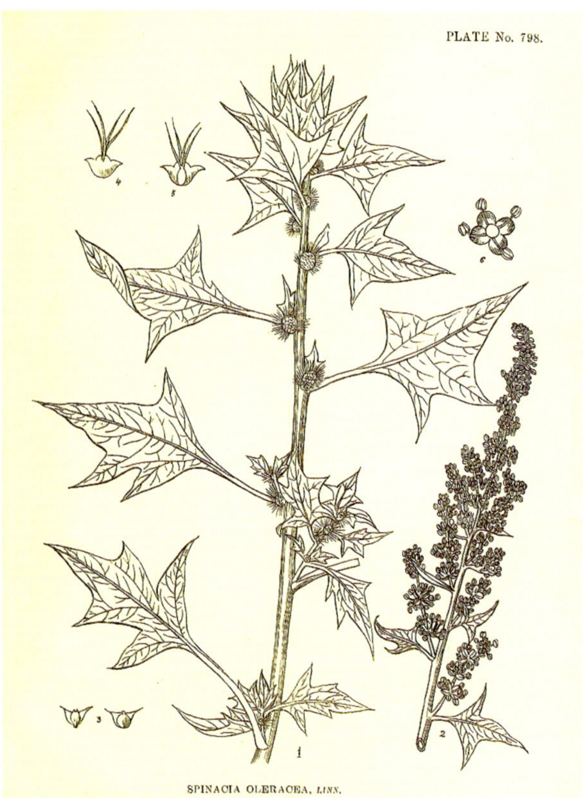

A

FIGURE 72. *A*, Garden spinach, *Spinacia oleracea* L. Kirtikar, K. R., Basu, B. D., Indian medicinal plants, *Plates*, vol. 4: t. 798 (1918). *B*, Garden spinach, *Spinacia oleracea*. Prof. Dr. Otto Wilhelm Thomé, *Flora von Deutschland, Österreich und der Schweiz*, 1885, Gera, Germany, http://www.biolib.de.

B

In seed catalogs, you will find spinach cultivars with smooth leaves or crinkled savoy leaves. Some new cultivars have green oval leaves with red stems. I recommend growing both types, although some cooks find the smooth-leaved cultivars easier to clean.

Culture and planting

The culture and planting of spinach resemble the procedures described for lettuce. Although spinach and lettuce belong to completely different plant families, they both share the habit of bolting with the advent of warming, hot temperatures, and long days. I find that unlike lettuce, which develops an unpalatable bitter taste when it bolts, spinach does not develop that attribute, at least to the extent that lettuce does. I harvest the bolting head on spinach when it appears and coax the plant along by harvesting leaves for as long as possible. Finally, hot weather signals the end of spinach—seed again in fall. During single-event hard freezes, I find spinach to be the most resilient plant in the garden: it outsurvives lettuce and

FIGURE 73. Malabar spinach is a vining plant that needs support (post or trellis) and thrives in hot, humid climates. Photo by author.

Swiss chard. When hot weather arrives and your spinach has completed its productive life cycle, try Malabar spinach (*Basella alba*, Basellaceae family) and New Zealand spinach (*Tetragonia tetragonioides*, Aizoaceae family), which are not related to the goosefoot family (Chenopodiaceae) (fig. 73). Malabar spinach is native to the tropical monsoon regions of southern Asia (coast of India and Sri Lanka). It is a perennial vine grown as an annual or biennial potherb. It prefers hot, humid climates and moist, fertile, well-drained soil. The leaves are glossy, ovate, deep green, thick, mucilaginous, and rich in phytonutrients.

Spinach is a cool-season vegetable and prefers temperatures of 55 to 60°F with medium day length. The seeds can germinate between 45 and 75°F (70°F is optimal), and young plants can withstand temperatures as low as 18°F without damage. At 15°F, damage can be severe, and lower temperatures usually kill the plants. When temperatures start reaching the mid-80s, pollination and seed development begin to suffer and seeds many be smaller and have lower yields and germination rates. If your spinach is growing well and temperatures start exceeding 75°F, you can alleviate the impact of warming temperatures by daily irrigation to cool the soil and microenvironment around the plants. Floating row covers, Reemay garden blankets, and similar products can significantly reduce soil surface temperatures during warmer days.

Spinach plants have separate sexes and appear morphologically distinct when they reach maturity. Female spinach plants produce flowers, while male plants produce an elongated spike up to 3 inches long. The dustlike pollen grains are easily blown about by the wind. In seed production, when female spinach plants are isolated from male plants during flowering, they can reverse sex, producing male flowers with female flowers for pollination.

Many hybrid spinach cultivars are available in seed catalogs. During the last decade, the baby leaf spinach market has grown tremendously. In California, where a lot of spinach is grown, breeders strive for resistance to downy mildew, especially since plants harvested as baby spinach are planted more densely and are closer to the ground. Spinach breeders select for seedling vigor; leaf shape (arrow shaped, lobed); leaf texture (smooth versus crinkled [savoy]; smooth leaves are easier to wash and clean for market); leaf color (darker colors are preferred and give the impression of higher nutritional content); and plant stature (sturdy upright stems keep leaves off the soil, where fungal diseases reside, and reduce soil splash).

Spinach can tolerate a wide range of soil textures (sandy loams to loams are ideal), but it will also grow well in clayey soils. Improving soil humus with additions of organic matter in circle plots (compost, decomposed manure, and a nitrogen fertilizer added prior to preparing the seedbed for each crop) will improve soil quality and support soil microbes and nutrients for plant growth. The pH range for spinach is 6.5 to 7.5, but plants are more tolerant of alkaline soils than most vegetables. On average, spinach requires from 60 (in soils with high organic matter) to 100 lb. N/acre (in soils with low organic matter), with half broadcasted during planting, and half as a side dressing 3 to 4 weeks later. Preplanting applications of phosphorus and potassium range from 90 to 150 lb./acre depending on soil tests. See appendix D for equivalent fertilizer rates for circle plots.

Spinach seeds are about the size of a peppercorn and are not difficult to space evenly (about 1 inch apart, followed by thinning to 3 inches) in the circle rows. If you drop a few extra ones, plants can be thinned out later as you harvest tender young leaves. When the plants are about 3 inches high, go over the plot and remove plants that are clustered together or those that are crowding larger, more robust plants. Spinach leaves can be harvested when they are about 3 inches above the ground. Be careful to snap the stem near the base with your fingers, or use fine scissors. If you pull on the leaf, you may uproot the entire plant.

Spinach diseases and pests

Diseases

LEAVES

- Yellowish, random chlorotic lesions that enlarge. Undersides of leaves develop gray to bluish fungal growth. Leaves may eventually become curled, distorted, and die. May be seed borne, spread by wind and water splash from soil to leaves. Disease overwinters in live spinach plants and seeds. Turn under all previous year's litter and residue. Not an overwintering soil-borne disease, does not survive after microbial decomposition in soil. Cool, wet conditions favor fungal disease (48°F for germination and 54°F–60°F for development). **Downy Mildew** or **Blue Mold** (*Peronospora farinosa* f. sp. *spinaciae*; *P. effusa*). Use resistant cultivars.
- Overall general wilted appearance, pale to yellowish green, roots become blackened. Disease can occur at any stage of plant growth. Warm conditions favor disease, suppressed in alkaline soils. Soil-borne fungi survive in soil. Crop rotations necessary, at least every 5 years. Some cultivars are more sensitive. Brassica cover

crops show promise as natural biofumigants. Use pathogen-free seeds. Fungal disease, **Fusarium Wilt** (*Fusarium oxysporum* f. sp. *spinaciae*).

- Interveins show chlorosis and necrosis on older leaves. Wilting as disease progresses, may appear during bolting of plant. Seed- and soil-borne disease, persists in soil for years, crop rotations necessary. Use nonhost cover crops (grains, flowers, *Brassica* spp.). Fungal disease, **Verticillium Wilt** (*Verticillium dahliae*).
- Disease starts out with small, concentric, water-soaked spots on young and old leaves. Progresses to larger spots, black fruiting bodies (acervuli), and lesions. Thrives in wet, cool conditions. Spreads by water splash from soil onto leaves and from infected seeds. Disease overwinters on spinach residues left in garden or field; eliminate all last year's litter. Fungal disease, **Anthracnose** (*Colletotrichum dematium* f. sp. *spinaciae*).
- White, blistered pustules form on lower side of leaves and advance to upper leaf surfaces. Plants appear weak and wilt. Disease can appear after heavy rains and soil splash onto leaves. Fungus survives in soil during summer as oospores and spreads by wind. Fungal disease, **White Rust** (*Albugo occidentalis*). Partially resistant varieties are available; use long crop rotations and control with fungicides.
- Seedlings and young plants develop lesions, have water-soaked appearance, wilt, and eventually die. Cool, wet conditions favor disease. Avoid excess irrigation; disease-resistant cultivars available. Some pathogens are seed borne (*Fusarium*), others soil borne (*Pythium, Rhizoctonia*, and *Fusarium*). Fungal diseases, **Damping Off** and **Root Rots** (*Pythium aphanidermatum* and other spp., *Rhizoctonia solani* and other spp., and *Fusarium cochlioides* and other spp.
- Viral diseases have many of the same symptoms and are difficult to sort out in the field. More than 100 viruses can infect spinach, and while some are asymptomatic, others produce severe symptoms that affect the plants. Leaves develop yellow blotches, chlorosis, and brittleness; they curl, wrinkle, roll inward, have a stunted appearance and poor growth, and eventually die. Symptoms can be confused with those of severe nutrient deficiencies. Aphids and leafhoppers can transmit viral diseases. **Cucumber Mosaic Virus, Tomato Spotted Wilt Virus, Beet Curly Top Virus, Beet Western Yellows Virus**. Resistant cultivars are available for cucumber mosaic virus, but no control measures are known for many other viral diseases.

- Climatic Stress can be indicated by leaf yellowing; spinach vigor and quality can deteriorate in high temperatures or wet, soggy, humid conditions, especially if there is poor soil drainage.

Insect pests

- Spinach Leafminer (*Liriomyza huidobrensis*, *L. sativae*, and *L. trifolii*);
- Aphids: Green Peach Aphid (*Myzus persicae*), Potato Aphid (*Macrosiphum euphorbiae*), Black Bean Aphid (*Aphis fabae*);
- Wireworms (*Limonius* spp. and others);
- Spinach Crown Mite (*Rhizoglyphus* spp.);
- Garden Symphylans (*Scutigerella immaculata*);
- Caterpillars (Lepidoptera): Western Yellowstriped Armyworm (*Spodoptera praefica*), Beet Armyworm (*S. exigua*), Cabbage Looper (*Trichoplusia ni*), Corn Earworm (*Helicoverpa zea*), Black Cutworm (*Agrotis ipsilon*), Variegated Cutworm (*Peridroma saucia*), Granulate Cutworm (*Agrotis subterranea*);
- Nematodes

Swiss Chard (*Beta vulgaris* var. *cicla*)

Historical background

Swiss chard is highly prized by Mediterranean cooks and is used in soups and rice dishes; it is also a popular salad green. Swiss chard is a good dietary source of vitamins K, A, C, E, B_1, B_2, and B_6; minerals magnesium, manganese, phosphorus, potassium, iron, copper, calcium, and zinc; and dietary fiber, protein, and antioxidants (syringic acid and flavonoids [kaempferol]) in leaves.

Swiss chard is not native to Switzerland, as the name implies. Garden beets (*Beta vulgaris* ssp. *vulgaris*) and Swiss chard (*Beta vulgaris* var. *cicla*) are members of the goosefoot family (Chenopodiaceae) and are thought to have originated from the sea beet (*Beta maritima*), which is native to southern Europe (Sicily, etc.). The sea beet grows in slightly saline soils along the Mediterranean coast. The common weed lamb's-quarters (*Chenopodium album*) and spinach are also in the Chenopodiaceae family. Swiss chard was cultivated by the Greeks, who called it *teutlon* or *teutlion* (the foliage resembled squid tentacles), and by the Romans, who named it *beta*. Swiss chard has many names throughout the world: chard, white beet, seakale, strawberry spinach beet, Sicilian beet, Roman kale, silverbeet, cardoon, and carde. The word "chard" is from the Latin *cardus*, meaning

Spinach Quick Guide

Botanical Data	Environmental Conditions	Culture and Special Considerations
Spinach (*Spinacia oleracea*); *Spinacia* (Latin) refers to "spines" and the prickly appearance of the seed; *oleracea* refers to an edible plant **Family**: Chenopodiaceae (goosefoot family) **Life Cycle**: herbaceous, annual, rarely biennial or perennial **Inflorescence**: typically clustered into small, compact, dense spikes **Flowers**: dioecious; plants produce either male (staminate) or female (pistillate) flowers. Pollinated by wind. Female inflorescence an axillary cluster, in male plants elongated and spikelike, up to 4 inches long. **Physiology**: cool-season vegetable, photosynthesis C_3 **Stems**: erect to spreading, solitary to branched at base of plant **Leaves**: alternate, simple, linear, deltoid, ovate to triangular; larger leaves at the base of the plant and smaller leaves higher on the flowering stem. Leaves form a basal rosette and are then arranged spirally on stems. Pale to dark green. **Roots**: characterized by a strong, vertical, deeply penetrating taproot with fine fibrous roots **Fruits**: utricle, pericarp separable or attached **Seeds**: roughened seeds with honeycombed surface, germination 6–21 days at 35°F–65°F. Temperatures above 85°F cause erratic and low germination. 80 seeds/g, optimal longevity about 1 year, 50% germination of seeds properly stored for 5 years. **Days to Maturity (DTM):** 21–40 days	**Growing Zones**: check state and county cooperative extension sites and guides for adaptability and recommended planting dates. Plant 4–6 weeks before last frost. **Timing**: seed in early spring; seeds can germinate in soil at 32°F–60°F. Spring and fall crops are common throughout the United States. Overwintering possible in many climates with and without protective floating coverings. **Optimal Temperature for Growth**: optimal quality 55°F–60°F, general temp. range 55°F–65°F. Longer day length (12.5–15 hours), and alternating cold and hot temperatures at less than 12.5 hours cause bolting, and warmer temps. cause bolting (seed stalk emergence). **Frost**: can withstand frost (air temperatures down to 18°F). Extend fall season with clear plastic or other protective floating row gardening covers. **Sunlight**: full sun, partial shade **Soil Conditions**: well-drained, loose, N-rich soils. Spinach grows best in sandy loams and loams but can be grown successfully in sandy to clayey soils. Spinach is sensitive to acidic soils. **Optimal pH**: 6.5–7.5, sensitive to acidic soils **Soil Moisture Content**: needs regular supply of moisture at surface since roots are shallow **Nutrient Needs**: nitrate levels in leaves can reach toxic levels with too much N fertilizer; oxalates in leaves can interfere with calcium absorption in humans **Nutrition Information:** Spinach, raw. USDA Food and Nutrition Service. % Daily Value based on 2,000 calorie diet Serving size 1 cup Calories 7 Total fat 0.1 g, 0% Total carbohydrate 1 g, 0% Protein 0.9 g, 2% Vitamin A 2813 IU, 56% Vitamin C 8.4 mg, 14% Vitamin E 0.6 mg, 3% Vitamin K 145 mcg, 181% Folate 58 mcg, 15% Calcium 30 mg, 3% Iron 0.8 mg, 5% Magnesium 24 mg, 6% Potassium 167 mg, 5% Manganese 0.3 mg, 13%	**Ease of Growing:** easy, stay within soil temperature guidelines **Site Preparation:** spade and loosen soil to 6–12 inches. Work in a 2-inch layer of compost, decomposed manure, and topsoil (optional) the previous fall. Do not work when soil is wet. **Planting:** ¼–½ inch deep seeded directly into garden. Plant every 2 weeks for successive harvests. **Spacing and Thinning:** direct seeding at 1 inch apart. Can seed more closely, then thin plants to 3 inches apart. Crowded plants have a tendency to bolt more quickly. **Fertilizer**: preplant 30–50 lb. N/acre, side dress 30–50 lb. N/acre 3–4 weeks later, P and K 90–150 lb./acre depending on soil test. See appendix D for equivalent fertilizer rates for circle plots. **Weeding:** gentle, shallow cultivation **Cultivars:** leaf types—savoy (wrinkled), semisavoy, and smooth. Smooth cultivars are used for baby spinach. Some cultivars are more bolt resistant as weather warms. **Harvest:** harvest anytime from small tender leaves to mature leaves; do not harvest when leaves are wet; avoid rough handling, as leaves bruise; snap lower stem off with fingers or use scissors; remove stems later in kitchen; leave plant intact for continued harvest; wash leaves, as they tend to collect soil and sand particles; can store in plastic bags in refrigerator

FIGURE 74. Swiss chard is available in many different cultivars and colors. Photos by author.

"thistle." The "Swiss" designation originated in order to distinguish the plant from French spinach varieties. Swiss chard came to America via seeds; a letter from Gideon Smith (Baltimore, October 30, 1829) acknowledges receipt of seeds from Europe. Swiss chard became a popular garden vegetable in the United States after the Civil War.

Culture and planting

There are many interesting cultivars now available with white, yellow, red, peppermint, and rainbow colors (fig. 74). I have grown many of them and find that the original white-stemmed 'Fordhook

FIGURE 75. *A*, Swiss chard seedlings sowed in higher density in circle plot arrangement. Greens will be thinned out as plants grow and used as "baby greens"; final spacing is 9–12 inches apart. B, Swiss chard mature, plants thinned out. Photos by author.

A

B

Giant' is the most robust in relation to climatic stressors. The rainbow cultivars of Swiss chard are a beautiful addition to the garden but are more fragile. Swiss chard is a tough plant and will withstand temperatures into the teens (around 18°F), but I find that it is not as frost hardy as spinach. Spinach is at the top of the list for frost tolerance in the garden.

The culture and planting of Swiss chard are very similar to the methods for beets and spinach, with some minor differences. After spinach has bolted and waned, Swiss chard is a good replacement. The young leaves are tender and can be used as a spinach replacement in salads and other dishes. I find that substituting Swiss chard for spinach in recipes is for the most part unnoticeable. Another nice aspect of Swiss chard is that as you harvest the leaves from the outside of the plant, new leaves emerge—it is perpetual.

Swiss chard will survive hot summers if irrigated often. If you keep your chard alive during the hot summer, it will reward you with a flourish of new growth in the fall. Unlike some leafy greens, Swiss chard will not turn bitter to the taste. If you let the leaves grow very large, they can be tough, but they cook down well. Over time, the stems of Swiss chard can become quite robust (thick and woody, similar in appearance to those of brussels sprouts, but note that chard is not in the Cruciferae family). The stalks are also edible; I find them similar in texture to celery. If you keep Swiss chard in the refrigerator in an open plastic zip-type bag with a little moisture, it will remain fresh and sweet for some time.

In climates with mild winters, Swiss chard will grow as a biennial or short-lived perennial, depending on the care it receives. Figure 69 shows Swiss chard planted in circle plots. The following are some important guidelines for growing Swiss chard:

- Plant several weeks before last frost (2–3 weeks).
- Plant in full sun or partial shade.
- Work compost, decomposed manure, and some additional nitrogen fertilizer into the soil. Follow instructions in chapter 7, "Establishing the Garden."
- Well-drained soil is essential.
- Chard can tolerate most garden soil textures, even clays, since there is no beet root. Chard does develop a robust taproot with extensive fibrous roots.
- Maintain pH at 6.0 to 7.0.
- For medium fertility, side dress with fertilizer as needed. Com-

mercial fertilizer rates range from 50 to 120 lb. N/acre, half broadcast, half as side dressing 3–5 weeks after planting. Phosphorus and potassium rates range from 0 to 150 lb./acre depending on soil test. See equivalent fertilizer rates in table 32 in appendix D.

- Directly sow seeds ½ inch deep.
- Like beets, Swiss chard requires thinning because the seeds are actually dried berries that contain at least two seeds (2–5).
- Plant 8–10 seeds per foot, thin plants for "baby greens"; final spacing 9–12 inches.
- Maintain even moisture levels, frequent and uniform; water needs are high.
- Use shallow cultivation.
- As plants get larger, mulch around plants with compost or fine hay/straw.
- Leaves about 6–8 inches long are tender.
- Gently snap off leaves at base of plant; do not haphazardly pull off leaves. Keep the plants pruned nicely.
- Use as a great supplement for homestead livestock (goats, chickens, and ducks).

Garden Beets (*Beta vulgaris* ssp. *vulgaris*)

The beet is propagated in the same manner as Swiss chard. There are now many cultivars, heirlooms, and hybrids available in seed catalogs. In my opinion, golden beets seem less hardy than their red counterparts, but they are worth growing. Seeds are planted (in clusters holding from 3 to 5 seeds) ½ inch deep every 2 to 5 inches, with about 8 inches between circular rows. Overall plant density should be about 8 plants per foot. This may seem a bit dense; however, the home gardener should harvest the roots at 2¼ to 3 inches. You can also harvest beets when they are smaller and more tender—use them raw in salads. I plant a little on the heavy side to get a good stand because the federal germination standard is around 75%. I thin plants after they are about an inch tall, and again after they are well established (fig. 76). Some gardeners presoak seeds for 12 hours to promote rapid germination, but I find that the seeds are more difficult to handle when wet, as they tend to stick together. Watering the beet bed after planting and keeping it moist is sufficient. Make sure you keep the newly planted beet bed moist, as excessive drying of the new planting seems to damage germination, and a poor stand

A

B

FIGURE 76. *A*, Beet greens can be used in salads. *B*, Garden beets, ready for second thinning. Photos by author.

can result. Beets typically germinate in 5–10 days with soil temperatures from 55°F to 80°F. Beets are a spring and early-summer crop, as they prefer moderate temperatures between 60°F and 78°F. As temperatures increase into the mid to high 80s, development of the roots suffers and the plants wilt if there is not sufficient moisture. Garden beets can tolerate higher temperatures (at or above 86°F) if sufficient vegetative growth has occurred during cooler spring temperatures.

If you wish to save beet seeds, be aware that the plant is a biennial and seeds are produced the second year. Garden beets and chard can also cross, as beets are wind pollinated. Beets do not flower until the roots have matured, and a vernalization period occurs after the first season (roots exposed to temperatures at or below 50°F, but not extensive hard freezes below 28°F, for at least 8 weeks).

Garden beets do best in lighter-textured soils (sandy loams to loams) that are deep and well drained. I grow beets in a clay loam, but I have improved the soil with additions of compost over the years. Beets prefer acidic soils (pH between 5.8 and 6.2) and are somewhat salt tolerant, more so than many other vegetable crops. The genetic history of the related sea beet may be responsible for this trait, as it grows along the Mediterranean coast. Boron deficiencies can occur in alkaline soils. Avoid excess nitrogen, as it promotes vegetative growth instead of root development. Overall, strive for a soil rich in humus with active microbes and nutrients.

Diseases and pests

Diseases

LEAVES

- Small, circular, light yellow-gray necrotic spots with dark purple outline, also occurs on beets, affects appearance and quality of leaves, can result in death of leaves. Moist, humid conditions in midsummer to early fall favor this disease, optimal temperature for development is between 77°F and 86°F. Dispose of all previous year's debris and litter, use crop rotation every 2 years or more. Fungal disease, **Cercospora Leaf Spot** (*Cercospora beticola*; less frequently *Phoma betae*). Fungicide treatments available.
- Yellowish, random chlorotic lesions that enlarge. Undersides of leaves develop gray to bluish fungal growth. Leaves may eventually become curled, distorted, and die. May be seed borne, spread by wind and water splash from soil to leaves. Disease overwinters in live spinach plants and seeds. Turn under all previous year's litter and residue. Not an overwintering soil-borne disease, does

not survive after microbial decomposition in soil. Cool, wet conditions favor fungal disease (48°F for germination and 54°F–60°F for development). Fungal disease, **Downy Mildew** or **Blue Mold** (*Peronospora farinosa* f. sp. *spinaciae*; *P. effusa*). Fungicide treatments available.

- Small, white, powdery spots on leaves, especially older leaves. Usually occurs 8–12 weeks after seedling emergence. Fungal mycelium grows over leaf surface from epidermal cells (upper leaf tissue). Fungal disease, **Powdery Mildew** (*Erysiphe polygoni* [*E. betae*]). Sulfur and fungicides available.
- Yellowing of leaves between veins and subsequent browning of leaf edges. Eventually, disease progresses to complete yellowing of the plant, wilting, and premature death. Slice open infected beet roots; darkening of the rings may be visible. Infection typically occurs during hot weather when plants are stressed. Fungal disease, **Fusarium Wilt** (*Fusarium oxysporum*). The disease is seed borne. Use crop rotations, avoid poor drainage, avoid hoeing soil up onto plant crowns, and buy disease-free seeds and varieties with some resistance.
- Seedlings and young plants develop lesions, have water-soaked appearance, wilt, and eventually die. Cool, wet conditions favor disease. Avoid excess irrigation; disease-resistant cultivars available, some pathogens are seed borne (*Fusarium*), others soil borne (*Pythium*, *Rhizoctonia*, and *Fusarium*). Fungal diseases, **Damping Off** and **Root Rots** (*Pythium aphanidermatum* and other spp., *Rhizoctonia solani* and other spp., and *Fusarium cochlioides* and other spp.).
- Yellow-, red-, or purple-mottled leaves; plants appear stunted, puckered; leaves curl; death of seedlings and older plants. Assorted **Viral Diseases** (Beet Mosaic Virus [BtMV], Beet Western Yellows Virus [BWYV], Rhizomania, Beet Necrotic Yellow Vein Virus [BNYVV]). Keep garden areas and edges of garden weed-free and eliminate volunteer beet plants, control aphids and leafhoppers, plant early, and avoid warm to hot temperatures and high humidity.

Insects

- Aphids: Green Peach Aphid (*Myzus persicae*), Potato Aphid (*Macrosiphum euphorbiae*);
- Whiteflies: Sweet Potato Whitefly (*Bemisia tabaci*), Silverleaf Whitefly (*B. argentifolii*);

- Thrips: Western Flower Thrips (*Frankliniella occidentalis*), Onion Thrips (*Thrips tabaci*);
- Striped Flea Beetle (*Phyllotreta striolata*);
- Potato Flea Beetle (*Epitrix cucumeris*);
- Western Black Flea Beetle (*Phyllotreta pusilla*), Western Striped Flea Beetle (*P. ramosa*);
- Darkling Beetle (*Blapstinus* spp.);
- Rove Beetle (Staphylinids);
- Cricket (*Gryllus* spp.);
- Spur-Throated Grasshopper (*Schistocerca* spp.); Desert Grasshopper (*Melanoplus sanguinipes*);
- Leafminers (*Liriomyza* spp.);
- Cutworms: Black Cutworm (*Agrotis ipsilon*), Variegated Cutworm (*Peridroma saucia*), Granulate Cutworm (*Agrotis subterranea*);
- Saltmarsh Caterpillar (*Estigmene acrea*);
- Diamondback Moth (*Plutella xylostella*);
- Loopers: Cabbage Looper (*Trichoplusia ni*), Alfalfa Looper (*Autographa californica*);
- Beet Armyworm (*Spodoptera exigua*);
- Corn Earworm (Bollworm) (*Helicoverpa zea*);
- Tobacco Budworm (*Heliothis virescens*);
- False Chinch Bug (*Nysius raphanus*);
- Lygus Bug (*Lygus hesperus*);
- Three-Cornered Alfalfa Hopper (*Sissistilus festinus*);
- Potato Leafhopper (*Empoasca fabae*);
- Slugs.

Swiss Chard Quick Guide

Botanical Data

Swiss Chard (*Beta vulgaris* var. *cicla*)

Family: Chenopodiaceae (goosefoot family), related to beets and spinach

Life Cycle: herbaceous plant, usually biennial, can persist as perennial in some climates, usually grown as an annual

Inflorescence: dense, cymes (flower clusters) 2–8-flowered

Flowers: hermaphroditic (perfect flowers, male and female); beets and chard will cross-pollinate, wind pollinated

Physiology: cool-season vegetable, photosynthesis C_3

Stems: erect to spreading, solitary to branched at base of plant

Leaves: glabrous, ovate to cordate, dark green or reddish, frequently forming a rosette from an underground stem; leaves have thickened midribs

Roots: characterized by a strong, vertical, deeply penetrating taproot with fine fibrous roots

Fruits: multiple fruit; multiple separate flowers in an inflorescence coalesce to form a single "fruit" at maturity

Seeds: seed clusters, germination 5–17 days at 50°F–86°F, max. temp. 95°F. 50 seeds/g. Usual seed longevity about 2 years. Pelleted seeds available.

Days to Maturity (DTM): 53–60 days

Environmental Conditions

Growing Zones: check state and county cooperative extension sites and guides for adaptability and recommended planting dates. Plant 4–6 weeks before last frost.

Timing: seed in early spring; seeds can germinate in soil at 32°F–60°F. Spring and fall crops are common throughout the United States. Overwintering possible in many climates with and without protective floating coverings.

Optimal Temperature for Growth: optimal quality 50°F–64°F, general temp. range 55°F–65°F.

Frost: Swiss chard can remain fresh in the garden through the first snowfall or until temperatures fall into the teens (around 18°F). Extend fall season with clear plastic or other protective floating row gardening covers.

Sunlight: full sun, partial shade

Soil Conditions: well-drained, loose, N-rich soils. Swiss chard does well in any soil where lettuce and spinach grow.

Optimal pH: 6.0–7.0

Soil Moisture Content: regular supply of moisture throughout upper 6 inches

Culture and Special Considerations

Ease of Growing: easy

Site Preparation: spade and loosen soil to 6–10 inches. Work in a 2-inch layer of compost, decomposed manure, and topsoil (optional) the previous fall. Do not work when soil is wet.

Planting: ¼–½ inch deep, seeded directly into garden. Can be started in pots for transplanting.

Spacing and Thinning: commercial fields plant 9–12 inches apart with rows 40 inches apart. For circle plots, direct seed at 1 inch apart for baby greens, 2–3 inches apart for larger growth. Thin to 6–12 inches after the plants reach a height of 3 inches. Space concentric rows 10–14 inches apart.

Fertilizer: preplant 25–60 lb. N/acre, side dress with 25–60 lb. N /acre 3–5 weeks later. Preplant P at 0–150 lb./acre and K at 0–200 lb./acre depending on soil test. See appendix D for equivalent fertilizer rates for circle plots.

Weeding: gentle, shallow cultivation

Cultivars: leaf types—white stemmed to multicolored (red, pink, orange, yellow, green)

Nutrition Information: Swiss chard, raw. USDA Food and Nutrition Service. % Daily Value based on 2,000 calorie diet
Serving size 1 cup
Calories 7
Total fat 0 g, 0%
Total carbohydrate 1 g, 0%
Protein 1 g, 1%
Vitamin A 2,202 IU, 44%
Vitamin C 11 mg, 18%
Vitamin K 299 mcg, 374%
Vitamin E 0.7 mg, 3%
Calcium 18 mg, 2%
Iron 0.6 mg, 4%
Magnesium 29 mg, 7%
Phosphorus 17 mg, 2%
Potassium 136mg, 4%
Manganese 0.1 mg, 7%

FIGURE 77. Tomatoes planted about 3 to 3½ feet apart. A depression or moat is built up around each plant to prevent runoff during watering. Mulch is essential to help prevent soil splash and fungal diseases, and to conserve moisture during hot weather. At this stage, I place mesh fencing around each plant with a stake to hold the fencing upright. Stakes, trellises, or tomato cages can also be used to provide support and help keep leaf/soil contact to a minimum (see fig. 79 for an assortment of ideas). Notice the green coloration of these plants—an indication of adequate nutrients. No additional fertilizer has been used, and compost and manure have been added annually to this soil for 10 years. About 6 different heirloom and hybrid cultivars are planted in this group. A drip system can be set up to make watering easier if you have many plants. Photo by author.

Tomatoes

(*Solanum lycopersicum* var. *lycopersicum*)

The tomato is likely the most popular homegrown vegetable. Tomatoes can be grown in the garden, along fences, in greenhouses, and in containers on patios and decks. Each tomato plant, grown properly, can yield 10 to 15 pounds or more of fruit. Homegrown sun-ripened tomatoes are superior in taste to those from the store, so it is worth the time and effort to grow your own.

Tomatoes are an integral part of cuisine throughout the world, especially in the United States—they truly are a beloved food. Surprisingly, the tomato is not "number one" in terms of vegetables consumed in the United States: it ranks fourth, after potatoes, head lettuce, and onions. The average American consumes about 18 pounds of fresh tomatoes and 69 pounds of processed tomato products a year. The USDA Economic Research Service estimates that the largest use of processed tomatoes is in sauces (35%), followed by paste (18%), canned whole tomato products (17%), and ketchup and juice (about 15%). Personally, I am still trying to duplicate my Aunt Susan's tomato sauce (gravy), and I am forever searching for an equivalent to her spaghetti and meatballs.

As of 2012, the United States and China were the world's leading producers of tomatoes—$2 billion in US annual farm cash receipts. Fresh-market and homegrown tomatoes are produced in every state in the nation. California is the leader in processed tomato products and shares the market with Florida for fresh-market tomatoes (about 30,000–40,000 acres). Other important tomato-producing states are

Virginia, Georgia, Ohio, Tennessee, North Carolina, New Jersey, and Michigan.

Tomatoes have significant nutritional value. One ripe tomato (6 ounces) can provide up to 32% of the recommended Daily Value of vitamin C and 25% of vitamin A, as well as B vitamins and many minerals. Tomatoes have been linked to cardiovascular and bone health, along with alleviating gastrointestinal problems, improving night vision, and reducing the risk of some cancers.

Historical Background

The tomato is thought to have originated along the coastal strip of western South America. Wild tomatoes grow between Ecuador and Chile and on the Galápagos Islands. The Mayan people most likely domesticated the tomato from a wild variety (*Solanum lycopersicum* var. *cerasiforme*), which they called *xitomati*. Seeds were transported to Europe after Cortés conquered Mexico City in 1519. In Europe, the tomato was grown as an herbal but was not commonly eaten except in Italy and Spain, as it was considered poisonous like its other nightshade counterparts. Not until the eighteenth century were tomatoes used as an edible food. George Washington Carver grew tomatoes, and Thomas Jefferson grew them as ornamentals at Monticello in 1781.

Selecting Cultivars

In choosing the best tomato cultivars for your garden, first consider your growing zone, length of growing season, amount of garden space, known disease problems in your area, and, finally, your preference. There are early-, mid-, and late-season tomato cultivars; determinate and indeterminate forms; large to medium-sized globe-shaped, plum-shaped, or cherry types; table, sauce, and paste tomatoes; and a wide variety of hybrids and heirlooms (fig. 77). Various cultivars come and go, while some have stood the test of time. In choosing the best cultivars for your area, it is best to consult your local cooperative extension, local Master Gardener websites, and fellow gardeners.

Culture

Tomato plants can be planted in rows, hills, and raised beds. For home gardens, the circle technique works well since the soil around the plant has been enhanced and raised to overcome any poor drain-

SCIENCE NOTE • Tomato Flavor

Which is the best-tasting tomato? Are heirlooms and modern hybrids equal in taste? There are many staunch heirloom aficionados, but taste tests have shown that hybrids can now stand up with their counterparts. Check the Internet and seed catalogs for hybrids that are getting good reviews. If you live in a humid climate, tomato diseases can be more of a problem; therefore, it is wise to try some of the disease-resistant cultivars. Try heirlooms as well—this is where the fun comes in.

Tomato flavor is related to sugars (fructose and glucose) and acids (citric and malic) in the fruit. Research has shown that tomatoes with high sugar and acid content are the best tasting. Flavor also depends on volatile compounds in the fruit that enhance the inherent sweet tomato flavor; these are detected by the olfactory nerve in the nose, not the tongue. Studies show that tomatoes with a high apocarotenoid content taste sweeter.

What causes the difference in flavor between homegrown and artificially ripened tomatoes? The factors are complex, but they are related to the cultivars used and the growing conditions. Commercial growers may select cultivars that rank higher for disease resistance and fruit resilience to harvesting and shipping conditions. Commercial tomatoes shipped to distant markets are typically picked at the "mature green" stage because they ship better than ripe tomatoes. In about 24 hours, this fruit will begin to show some pink coloring. These mature green tomatoes are often exposed to ethylene, a gaseous plant hormone that induces ripeness at produce-distributing facilities. During the natural ripening process, ethylene is produced in many fruits and vegetables (apples, apricots, cantaloupes, avocados, unripe bananas, peaches, pears, plums, and tomatoes). Tomatoes picked at the "breaker" stage do not need ethylene to ripen, since they have started to ripen naturally in the sun. Breaker tomatoes are sold in stores as "vine ripened."

Have you noticed that heirloom tomatoes naturally ripen unevenly, with green patches on the shoulders and variations in redness? Uniform ripening from a light green to red was discovered in natural tomato mutations in the 1920s, and this trait has been very important to tomato growers and markets. The drawback of the uniform ripening gene is that fruit quality (sugar content) is compromised. Researchers at the University of California and Cornell University located the gene responsible for uniform ripening. With this knowledge, they could decipher the gene coding for the protein that controls photosynthesis levels in tomatoes. Typically, leaves are the primary source of photosynthesis in the tomato plant; however, a developing tomato fruit can contribute up to 20% of its own photosynthates. This research could provide a strategy to enhance quality characteristics that have been inadvertently bred out of modern cultivated tomatoes.

age. Plant tomatoes in 2–3-foot circles (smaller for determinate, larger for indeterminate; see chapter 3, "Garden Ecology"). If you are planning to plant a garden in the spring, the fall is the best time to prepare. You can also start in early spring and build up your soil with decomposed manure, compost, and other soil amendments; however, be aware that the nutrients in manure and compost are slow-release fertilizers. In new garden plots, you need to use a fast-acting preparation as well. In areas with long growing seasons, the circle bed can be reenriched with decomposed manure and compost for a fall crop after determinate tomatoes have produced their crop and declined. Fast-growing crops such as lettuce, spinach, Swiss chard, short-season zucchini cultivars, radishes, and beets can be used as a second crop. The following are the basic steps of tomato culture and setting out transplants:

1. Select tomato plot location.

2. Loosen and dig soil in main circle 8–12 inches deep.

3. Start with the in situ compost method (see information in chapter 9 on organic matter and compost). If initial fertility is low, add fertilizer and soil amendments.

4. When compost is decomposed, soil resembles a homogeneous mixture, and litter components are barely recognizable, incorporate it into soil by turning over soil at shovel depth over the entire circle.

5. Excavate a hole about 12 inches in diameter and 12 inches deep in the circle plot.

6. Place a small amount of organic fertilizer in the bottom of the hole (e.g., blood meal, fish meal, 10–10–10 or other balanced fertilizer).

7. Place about 2 inches of soil-compost mixture over the fertilizer and set plant in hole.

8. Bury tomato plant roots and raise soil level slightly above the crown of the plant. If the plant is spindly, set plant deeper and cover more stem (more detail included later in this chapter). Leave a depression of about 2 inches in the excavated area to act as a well to prevent water runoff during irrigation. This depression can be mulched.

9. Mulch around the tomato circle with hay, leaves, grass clippings, or a combination of materials to control weeds and lawn grass invasion. Use periodic applications of fertilizers (see discussions on fertilizer and soil amendments). Be careful with fertilizer applications; the plant should be a healthy green, with no yellowish-green

tints. Too much nitrogen favors plant growth at the expense of fruit production.

10. Pruning is an optional step based on gardener preference.

In the North, both the roots and most of the stem should go into the hole. A healthy, robust top leaf cluster should protrude above the ground. Since tomato roots will also grow from the stem, the plant will develop a larger root structure, which has two advantages: it gives the plant a more stable base, and it allows the plant access to more nutrients. In the South, where there is high humidity, there is a risk of rot and fungus infections; therefore, some extension publications recommend planting at soil level in the pot. I have had no problems with deep planting of tomatoes in Kansas, Texas, Wyoming, Idaho, and Virginia.

Seeding

Starting plants from seeds requires some diligence, but the process can be fun and rewarding. A packet containing 20–30 seeds is close to the price of one nursery transplant in a 4-inch pot. If you buy transplants, buy seedlings in the bigger 4-inch pots. Often you see packs of very small 1-inch containers. These plants are more economical, but they are usually too small and fragile. Avoid these unless you wish to replant into bigger pots and grow them to transplant size (6–8 inches in height). Also, avoid buying pale, spindly, or wilted transplants. About 6 to 8 weeks before the last spring frost, sow seeds by any of the methods listed below that you prefer (I prefer the cold frame, or minigreenhouse):

- The sunny windowsill method—after germination move to cold frames or minigreenhouse to avoid spindly, weak plants.
- Hot and/or cold frames.
- Greenhouse or minigreenhouse.
- Grow lights.

I fill 1-gallon pots with a 1:1 mixture of vegetable potting medium and topsoil/compost mix from the garden. I find that most potting mixes with a high percentage of peat do not have adequate consistency, are somewhat water repellent, and dry out quickly, especially the surface zone where your seeds are. I use some of the slow-release pelleted fertilizers and mix them according to directions with the soil medium. In my experience, seed starter mixes that advertise that fertilizer is included do not really demonstrate much in the way of reserve fertilizer during the growth phase of seedlings. I do not criticize the commercial seed-starter soil mixes because there is a very fine level beyond which fertilizers can burn and injure tender seedlings. Many gardeners are concerned about damping-off disease (see disease guide below); it is generally not a problem if you have good ventilation and do not overwater. My philosophy is not to pamper the seedlings; they have to adjust to outside garden conditions eventually.

I plant 2–3 tomato seeds per gallon pot (2 if you are using a 4–5-inch peat or plastic pot) and place in a cold frame or plastic greenhouse tent outside. Tomato seeds germinate at between 70 and 80°F. At the optimal germination temperature of 85°F, seedlings should emerge in about 5–6 days. At the lower temperature range, germination will take longer—up to 2 weeks. Once the seedlings emerge, make sure the planting medium stays moist, but not oversaturated and wet. With larger pots, watering every day is not necessary; just make sure the soil is moist to the touch. If 2–4-inch pots are used, warm, sunny days can dry out the soil quickly and your seedlings will wilt and possibly not recover if they became too desiccated—use 1-gallon pots. Fortunately, you can revive slightly wilted seedlings. As the seedlings grow, I choose the two best plants in gallon pots because I cannot bear to eliminate them all. I will carefully dig out the extra seedling later and transplant it to another gallon pot.

On warm, sunny days, open the cold frame for ventilation, but close it in the evening. If a very cold night or freezing temperatures are expected, you could move the plants into a garage or shed. For cold above freezing, an extra layer of plastic will help maintain higher temperatures in the frame. *Four-Season Harvest: Organic Vegetables from Your Home Garden All Year Long* is an excellent book by Eliot Coleman on growing vegetables in plastic greenhouses and cold frames. Coleman states that adding an extra layer of plastic is like moving your garden 500 miles south. The temperature inside the cold frame can be increased by 5°F with an extra layer of plastic.

The main thing to remember is not to let too much moisture or heat build up in the cold frame or greenhouse. The plants could succumb to wilt diseases or rot, and/or the warmer temperatures could cause the plants to grow more rapidly than normal, causing them to become spindly. Young tomato seedlings are more durable than you think—they need to adapt to the outside world, so do not baby them too much.

The most important point in raising or buying tomato seedlings is to avoid spindly, light green, or weak-stemmed plants. Also, you want to plant large transplants so that you maximize your chances of obtaining ripe fruit. If you live in a short, cool growing zone, choose varieties that mature quickly (55–60 days). In locations where hot and/or humid weather advances quickly, you especially want to plant the largest transplants you can find because hot temperatures inhibit fertilization of the flowers—meaning no fruit development.

Transplants and the Hardening-Off Process

On average, tomatoes require about 5 to 7 weeks to grow into a viable transplant that is ready to set out into the garden. If tomato plants are growing in larger pots, that is, about 1 gallon, the hardening-off process will involve mostly gradually exposing the plants to full sunlight. If your tomato seedlings were purchased and are growing in smaller 2- to 4-inch pots, I recommend transplanting them to a 1-gallon pot as part of the hardening-off process. Use a fertile medium (1:1 mixture of vegetable potting medium and topsoil/compost) in the pot with some slow-release fertilizer pellets, or use a liquid organic fertilizer 2–3 days after transplanting. If your plants are already in larger pots, start using a liquid organic fertilizer as per directions; some are specially formulated for tomatoes. These starter fertilizers are usually low in nitrogen, phosphorus, and potassium and contain micronutrients (e.g., 3-0-4, 6-4-4, 4-2-6, 4-5-3, etc.). This is the first step in hardening off tomatoes in the home garden because the plants will be more robust when the time comes to move them to the garden. When transferring a plant from a smaller pot to a larger one, trim off any damaged or weak lower branches and bury the plant deep, with about 4 to 6 inches of exposed stem and leaves (fig. 78). Keep newly transferred plants in a shady spot out of the wind. If you are using the cold frame in hardening off your tomatoes, provide some shade over the glass or plastic until the plant roots have adapted and the plant shows no signs of wilt. If you did not disturb the roots when taking the plant out of the smaller pot, there should not be much trauma or transplant shock to the plant. The root mass should be well distributed throughout the potting medium. Research shows that lightly brushing your tomato seedlings helps strengthen the plants (see Science Notes later in this chapter).

When the time comes to move the transplant to the garden, the next step in the hardening-off process is to acclimate the plant to full sunlight. This is done in stages. When I take my plants out of the cold frame, I locate them on the north side of the house or in another shady spot for 2–3 days. Then I move them to a location with more light (usually full sun) for 2–3 days. I then wait for cloudy skies; this is a good time to move them out to the open garden. When sunny skies arrive, the plants will be able to withstand full sun. You will know if you moved the plants too suddenly into full light: they will show signs of wilt, and worse, the leaves will show sunscald and have a white, bleached appearance. If this happens, move plants back to a slightly shadier location and they will usually recover. The whole process of hardening off is a slow, step-by-step procedure. Gradual changes are the rule for hardening off transplants. The ideal tomato transplant for the home garden is 6–10 inches tall and has a stem diameter of 1/4–3/8 inch, a deep green color, and no flowers or small fruits (fig. 78). Several days before setting out the hardened plant, decrease watering but do not let the plant completely dry out.

When setting plants, place them 3 to 3½ feet apart, and upright so that about half of the plant is buried and the other half exposed (fig. 79). Roots should be at least 3–4 inches deep; cover the root ball with a mixture of half soil and half compost. Place a small amount of organic fertilizer in the bottom of the hole (e.g., blood meal, fish meal, 10–10–10 or other balanced fertilizer), place about 2 inches of soil-compost mixture over the fertilizer, and set the plant in the hole. Raise the soil level slightly above the crown of the plant. If the plant is spindly, set the plant deeper and cover more stem. Create a small well or depression around the plant to prevent water runoff during irrigation. Place some fine mulch material around the plant and in the well. Many tomato references state that mulch should be placed around tomatoes after the soil has warmed; they warn that mulching prematurely slows down the growth of the plant. I do not find any significant effects of mulching after I set out my transplants. In my opinion, it is better to mulch and prevent soil splashing onto the leaves and possibly incurring foliar fungal diseases (fig. 79). A starter solution of liquid organic fertilizer is also advisable several days after the plants show no stress.

The first 2 weeks: Keep soil moist around plants during the first 2 weeks. If conditions are rainy and wet, consider mulching around the base of the plants with hay or straw to protect lower leaves from soil splash and from having direct contact with the soil. This mulch can be pulled away when conditions are drier and the sun comes out. Use permanent mulch when temperatures start warming up (above 70°F).

Two weeks to maturity: As the plants mature and warm to hot temperatures occur, mulch around the base of the plants if you have not done so already. I have found that mulching around the plants and letting them crawl over the mulch works well if you (1) have the space, at least a 5-foot diameter around the plant, and (2) your climate is dry and arid. In more humid climates, I have found that tomato cages help support the plant as it grows and also facilitate air flow around the plant, reducing the incidence of disease. Research shows that cages or trellis arrangements can significantly improve tomato yield and quality.

In the home garden, apply water as needed. The 3 main factors that drive the need for irrigation are (1) the amount and timing of rainfall, (2) evapotranspiration (water release via plant stomata and evaporation from the soil), and (3) soil texture and water-holding capacity. As these variables change, so do the timing and amount of irrigation.

I use about 4 inches or more of mulch around the plants when they reach about a foot in height and try to keep the soil moist, but not constantly wet. Keep track of air temperature; as temperatures increase toward the 90s with no overcast sky, I have to water every other day. When temperatures reach the upper 90s and toward 100°F, I find that

FIGURE 78. Tomato seedlings in gallon pots ready for transplanting to the open garden. Photo by author.

A B

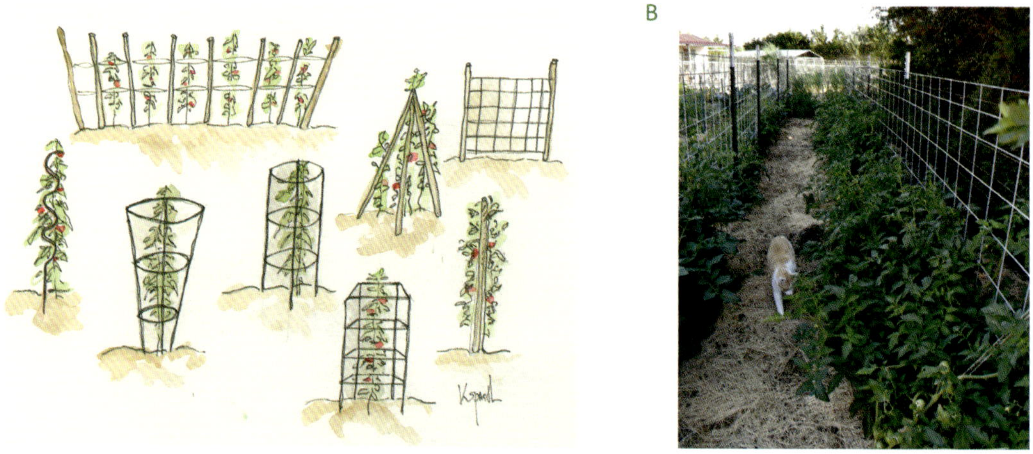

FIGURE 79. A, Tomatoes planted about 3 to 3½ feet apart. A depression or moat is built up around each plant to prevent runoff during watering. Mulch is essential to help prevent soil splash and fungal diseases, as well as to conserve moisture during hot weather. At this stage, I place mesh fencing around each plant with a stake to hold the fencing upright. Stakes, trellises, or tomato cages can also be used to provide support and help keep leaf/soil contact to a minimum. Notice the green coloration of these plants—an indication of adequate nutrients. No additional fertilizer has been used, and compost and manure have been added annually to this soil for 10 years. About 6 different heirloom and hybrid cultivars are planted in this group. A drip system can be set up to make watering easier if you have many plants. Drawing by author. B, Tomato trellis is 4-foot hog wire. Tomatoes are tied to hog wire for support; many plants intertwine in the wire without tying them. Huntley is inspecting the crop. Photo by author.

SCIENCE NOTE • Mechanical Conditioning of Tomato Seedlings

Brushing and stimulating 2-week-old tomato seedlings reduced the rate of stem growth, which resulted in stockier, tougher, darker green plants. Chilling tolerance is another benefit to daily brushing of tomato leaves. During chilling treatments, soluble sugars in leaves increased 15-fold compared to a 5-fold increase in sugars in nonbrushed plants. Science shows that daily brushing of young tomato seedlings results in stronger, more chill-resistant transplants.

daily watering is needed, and even then, it is difficult to keep up. At temperatures of 100 to 105°F, my tomato plants decline. I try to keep my indeterminate cultivars alive until fall, when they will revive and produce flowers and fruit. Daytime temperatures above 85°F–90°F (depending on humidity) and nighttime temperatures lower than 75°F inhibit flower fertilization (pollen becomes unviable).

SCIENCE NOTE • Pruning Tomatoes

What are the benefits of pruning tomatoes? Some gardeners swear by pruning, while others see no benefit. If you think there is an advantage, by all means continue pruning. Most experts report that pruning major stems of homegrown tomatoes is not beneficial, as fruit production can be decreased and the incidence of sunscald increased. Recent scientific research shows that there is little benefit to pruning to 1, 2, or 3 stems in field-grown tomatoes. Early pruning of tomatoes was found to temporarily affect plant architecture, but this characteristic disappeared later in the growing season. By not pruning, market growers can save an estimated $40 per acre. In contrast, greenhouse cluster varieties have shown a marketable yield and weight increase when fruit clusters are pruned to 3 fruits each.

Pruning determinate tomatoes is counterproductive—the plants are bred to be compact. Removal of suckers may cause fruit production to drop. In Florida trials, light pruning of suckers did not increase productivity. Heavy pruning reduced yields but resulted in larger fruit.

Figure 80*B* shows the ultimate pruned tomato, a "tomato tree" in The Land pavilion at Disney's Epcot Center, recognized by Guinness World Records as both the largest and most productive tomato plant in the world.

Fertilizers

Use of organic and/or synthetic fertilizers is entirely up to the gardener. Commercial rates are useful in understanding nutrient needs of tomatoes; rates and timing vary slightly among states and localities. Fertilizer rates for smaller plots and examples of how to calculate rates for areas of any size are given in chapter 7 and appendix D. The commercial rates given here are averages from many different sources. I advise home growers to check university and cooperative extension information for their state and local growing area. Soil type, inherent organic matter, and fertility are of course different from location to location. Nitrogen fertilizer rates are given to provide maximum quality and production. Nitrogen is a fleeting nutrient in soils and varies at any given time because of climatic factors, soil moisture, organic matter, existing growing plants, and degree of decomposition of organic materials in the soil. Phosphorus and potassium rates are best determined through a soil test. If soil tests

PERSONAL NOTE • Pruning Tomatoes

I personally do not prune tomatoes except for removing some suckers when I think about it. I usually have too many other chores; however, my lack of time to prune does not seem to affect the health and productivity of my crop. I usually plant upward of 2 dozen or more tomato plants, so pruning is not a practical option for me. If you are interested in pruning your tomatoes, here are some guidelines. The objective of pruning is to encourage a strong main stem and promote fruit size. Pruning should be limited mostly to indeterminate tomatoes, as improper removal of leaf and stem material from determinate tomatoes will reduce your crop. Limit pruning to suckers below the first flower cluster. During the first month of growth, tomatoes can double in size every 12 to 15 days. Tomato plants produce side shoots or "suckers" at the junction or axil of the stem and leaf. Usually suckers grow at 45° angles to the main stem, and if left unpruned they can grow large and produce flowers and fruit. The idea of pruning is to remove suckers and strengthen the main stem and fruit production. Simple pruning of tomatoes involves pinching off these suckers in the leaf axils. Tomato suckers below the first flower/fruit cluster can compromise the integrity of the main stem. Suckers in the upper parts of the plant receive less translocated sugar and are considered weaker. For a multi-stemmed tomato plant, the goal is to develop main stems with about the same diameter; however, the main stem should be the strongest stem. Let the second stem grow from the first node above the first fruit cluster, the third stem from the second node above the cluster, and so on—usually to 4 stems. Removing lower branches that come in contact with the ground and soil is a good idea, as rain or soil splash onto the leaves invites disease. I always mulch around my tomato plants so that no leaf material or stems come in contact with the soil. Mulch conserves water, reduces evaporation, helps minimize disease from soil splash, and adds organic matter to the soil surface as it decomposes. Do not overprune plants in hot climates with intense sunlight, as your fruits may be exposed to sunscald.

Small suckers pinch off easily, but larger ones may require rocking the sucker back and forth until it snaps off, or, with practice, the larger sucker can be snapped off with a quick movement. Avoid removing suckers in the upper 10 inches of the plant, as you do not want to remove the apical meristem at the growing tip of the plant. For larger neglected suckers, you can employ a method called "Missouri pruning" in which only a portion of the sucker is pinched off, leaving 1 or 2 remaining leaf stems. Removing large suckers can become problematic, as you may do more harm than good. Avoid using tools (scissors or pruning tools) to prune large suckers because you may open a wound that could be subject to the transmission of an infectious tomato disease. My recommendation is to experiment: if you have enough plants, remove varying degrees of leaf material and compare the results.

FIGURE 80. *A*, Pruning tomato suckers. Figure by author. *B*, "Tomato tree" in The Land pavilion at Disney's Epcot Center, recognized by Guinness World Records as both the largest and most productive tomato plant in the world (the plant has yielded more than 32,000 tomatoes weighing a total of 1,151.84 pounds). Courtesy of Wikipedia, photo of Epcot tomato tree by Deror Avi, grown hydroponically in greenhouse with strategic pruning.

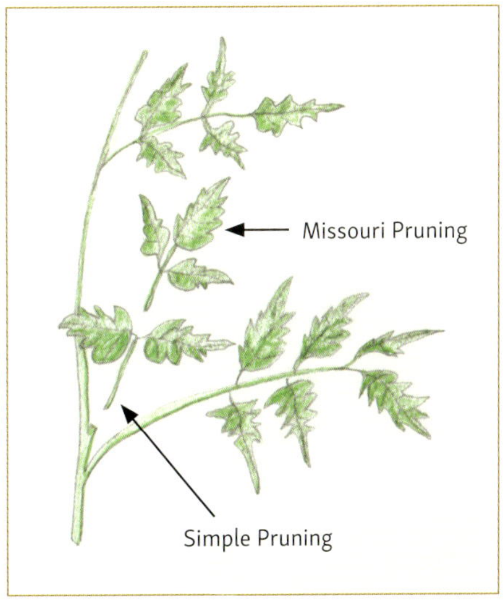

A

B

are not available, use moderate amounts of these nutrients as a start. Seek information from local cooperative extension personnel and fellow gardeners.

Soils with low, medium, and high organic matter generally require 130, 110, and 90 lb. N/acre, respectively. See appendix D for equivalent fertilizer rates for circle plots. Many extension bulletins recommend half as a preplant and half as a side dressing when fruit appears. After applying some initial nitrogen during planting, some growers side dress with 30–50 lb./acre at first fruit set, and 30–50 lb./acre when the third and fourth flower clusters appear. Phosphorus applications range from 0 to 150 lb./acre depending on soil test. Potassium levels can range from 0 to 250 lb./acre depending on soil test. Some growers split potassium applications after an initial application and side dress with 60 to 100 lb./acre at first fruit set to aid in additional fruit firmness.

Spacing varies depending on cultivar. Staked plant rows are typically 30–48 feet apart, with 24–30 inches between plants in a row. Determinate plants rows are usually spaced 24–30 inches apart. I plant tomatoes 3 feet apart. A 3-foot-diameter circle is about 7 square feet. Professional growers apply half of the fertilizer as a preplant and half as a side dressing when fruit appears. When setting out a transplant, I also place a small amount of organic fertilizer in the bottom of the hole (e.g., blood meal, fish meal, etc.), place about 2 inches of soil-compost mixture over the fertilizer, and then place the plant and cover with soil. Save eggshells to place around tomato roots when planting, and also use an organic fertilizer with calcium if you experience blossom end rot (see tomato diseases).

Diseases and Pests

Diseases

In commercial farming, speedy and accurate diagnosis of plant diseases is essential. Tomatoes can be plagued by a wide variety of diseases that affect leaflets and leaves, roots, stems, collars, fruits, and the entire plant. It is not practical to address tomato diseases in detail in this book; however, some of the more common diseases are categorized in the key below. For commercial growers and those who wish to know about tomato diseases in detail, there are many good extension, USDA, university, and agricultural publications with extensive information and photographs. In general, some preventive measures can be taken to limit tomato diseases in the home garden.

Where diseases are a problem, choose cultivars with disease resistance. Seed catalogs list disease resistance with symbols: VF indicates resistance to verticillium and fusarium wilts; VFN means the plants are resistant to verticillium, fusarium, and nematodes; and VFNT includes resistance to tobacco mosaic virus.

1. Eliminate and discard previous year's nightshade plants (do not add dead plants to compost).

2. Use clean, disease-free seeds.

3. Use healthy, robust transplants.

4. Plant cultivars adapted to your area and climate.

5. Where specific diseases are a problem, search out hybrids with specific disease resistance.

6. Do not work with tomato plants when wet, or when using tobacco.

7. Do not crowd plants; plant where there is good air movement.

8. Mulch plants after soils warm up, and stake or use tomato cages to keep leaves and fruits out of contact with soil.

9. Water plants at ground level—avoid wetting leaves and top sprinkling.

10. Provide adequate nutrient levels throughout the growing season.

11. Rotate plants at least every 3 to 4 years.

Leaf and leaflet deformities

Concentric (target-like) irregular spots on leaflets. Leaf spots, occurring anytime, generally more severe after flowering and fruit set.

- Water-saturated appearance on lower leaves, moving upward. Lesions turn gray and margins are darker to black in color. Leaves may have a scorched or wilted appearance. Common fungal disease, **Septoria Leaf Spot** (*Septoria lycopersici*).
- Leaf spots irregular, concentric (target-like), brown, and up to ½ inch in diameter. Lesions may merge, causing leaves to turn yellow and dry up. Lesions can appear on stems and fruit (tan to brown and leathery). Common fungal disease, **Early Blight** (*Alternaria solani*).
- Beige to brown flame-shaped concentric rings on edge of leaflets, wrinkled appearance on top of leaflet, small translucent white rings on fruit, or gray mold covering flowers. Fungal disease, **Gray Rot** (*Botrytis cinerea*).

For fungal diseases that overwinter and survive on plant litter, seeds, or other weeds in the nightshade family, use mulches under and around the plants to prevent soil water splash, which can cause spores to come in contact with leaves. Diseases are more prevalent during warm and rainy periods of high humidity.

Spots on leaves and leaflets

- Brown to black spots with yellow halo on leaves, center of leaf may rot out. Bacterial disease, **Bacterial Spot** (*Xanthomonas campestris* pv. *vesicatoria*). Associated with high temperatures and humidity. Carryover on plant litter, seeds, and soil.
- Brown to black spots with yellow halo on leaves, spots fused into groups in some areas. Bacterial disease, **Bacterial Speck** (*Pseudomonas syringae* pv. *tomato*). Enters through stomata or wounds.
- Other causes of leaf spots include transmission by aphids of **Alfalfa Mosaic Virus (AMV)** and **Potato Virus (PV).**

Wilting diseases

Leaflets and leaves wilt and/or dry out; can affect entire plant, growth stage where plants heavy with fruit.

- Wilting and yellowing of lower leaves and branches, moves up the plant, leaves may yellow and drop prematurely, plant may wilt entirely and die. Also affects vascular system of plant, inside of stem shows brown discoloration. Common fungal disease, **Fusarium Wilt** (*Fusarium oxysporum*). Can occur at any time in the season and at any growth stage, associated with warm air and soil temperatures (78°F–90°F) and poorly drained soils. Survives for long periods in soil, has resistant spores, found throughout soil profile to deep layers. Fungus enters feeder roots.
- **Verticillium Wilt** (*Verticillium albo-atrum*). Field symptoms similar to those of fusarium wilt. To distinguish between fusarium and verticillium wilt, lab analysis is necessary. Attacks many plants including eggplant, okra, pepper, potato, strawberry, and 300 or more other herbaceous and woody plants. One diagnostic feature of verticillium wilt is that it prefers cooler air and soil temperatures (60°F–75°F) and moist soil. Attacks in spring or fall.
- Wilting and leaf yellowing, stem at soil level soft, rotted, sunken, and brown to black. White fungal growth may be seen at stem/soil junction. Fungal disease, **Southern Blight, White Mold,** and **Stem Rot** (*Sclerotium rolfsii*). Soil-borne disease, spreads in infected organic matter and from plant to plant. Carryover on plant litter and dying plants.

Stunted, dwarfed, and curled leaflets, appearance similar to herbicide damage, black streaks on stem. Can affect entire plant.

- Any of the following: leaves slightly rolled, wrinkled, blistered, mottled, stunted, distorted (like herbicide damage). Viral disease,

Cucumber Mosaic Virus (CMV). Transmission by aphids from a host of different weeds, infested tomato litter, seeds, tobacco products, contact (from pruning, harvesting fruits, fingers, tools, clothing). Disease can occur without observed aphids on plants; disease overwinters and survives on host plants. Many vegetables affected (pepper, cucumber, melons, squash, spinach, celery, and beets).

- Plant with stunted, completely pathetic bushy appearance; wrinkled, gnarled, curled leaflets. Viral disease, **Tomato Yellow Leaf Curl Virus (TYLCV).** Transmitted by tobacco white fly (*Bemisia tabaci*). Several weeds are host to this virus.
- Any of the following symptoms: stunting, ring spots, bronzing of leaves, misshapen fruits. Affects plant at any stage of development. Viral disease, **Tomato Spotted Wilt Virus (TSWV).** Transmitted by western flower thrips (*Frankliniella occidentalis*) and tobacco thrips (*F. fusca* and *F. bispinosa*) from many different weed hosts. Find resistant cultivars.

Yellow leaflets with chlorotic appearance

- Chlorosis, yellowing starting with young leaves near apex or tip of plant (deficiency in any of the following micronutrients: boron, calcium, copper, iron, manganese, zinc). Deficiency symptoms vary by micronutrient—for example, dull green or pale yellow foliage and browning of terminal bud are signs of calcium deficiency; yellow to white leaf veins indicate iron deficiency.
- Chlorosis, yellowing starting with old leaves at base of plant (deficiency in any of the following nutrients: nitrogen, magnesium, molybdenum, phosphorus, potassium, sulfur). For example, pale green, yellowish leaflets on weak plants indicate nitrogen deficiency; dull green leaflets tinged bluish on the underside, plant stunted, entire plant affected—phosphorus; patchy yellowing of leaflets, dry edges, soft fruits—potassium.

Fruits: Small spots

- Grayish-brown corky centers with irregular oily halo, can coalesce or merge together. Spots first appear on green fruit as black, raised, pimple-like dots surrounded by halo. **Bacterial Spot,** caused by *Xanthomonas campestris* pv. *vesicatoria*. Bacteria overwinter on seeds and infected garden litter and can be spread from transplants.
- Birds-eye lesions on fruit, brown spots with surrounding yellow to white halo $1/16$–$1/8$ inch in diameter. Can affect young transplants

with sudden complete wilt; older plants can develop brown edges that die back to the midrib. **Bacterial Canker,** caused by *Clavibacter michiganensis* subsp. *michiganensis.*

Fruits: Larger rotting spots

Sunken, concave, black rotting spots on ripe and overripe fruit, can have concentric rings surrounding sunken area. During wet, moist weather, these lesions can exude spores. Fungal disease, **Anthracnose** (*Colletotrichum coccodes*). Fungi overwinter on diseased vines and litter, and in soil. Can be spread by soil water splash and warm, humid conditions. Disease can develop after infection by other fungal diseases and insect damage.

Fruits: Physiological disorders

- Fruits develop a hardened, papery, irregular, white to gray patch where exposed to sun. Sunscald spots may eventually turn into more hardened gray patches. **Sunburn.** In areas of intense sun, especially from western exposures during the late afternoon, use row covers, wads of hay straw, or cloth to protect exposed fruits.
- Small to large necrotic spots on bottom of fruit, concave rotting spot that can penetrate into fruit, black end on fruit. Physiological nonparasitic disease, **Blossom End Rot**. Contributing factors are irregular rainfall, lack of calcium in soil or lack of calcium transfer to fruit because of extreme fluctuations in moisture, infrequent then sudden heavy rainfall or irrigation, excess salinity, and excess nitrogen. Secondary infection from fungus (*Alternaria* spp.) can occur. Some cultivars are more susceptible. Staking and pruning may be associated. Mulch plants, make small, frequent applications of liquid fertilizers with calcium, apply frequent light watering to maintain static moisture levels. There are several remedial measures to reduce blossom end rot of tomatoes: (1) raise soil pH and calcium levels; (2) maintain adequate and even moisture, irrigate during dry weather; (3) avoid overfertilization of nitrogen; (4) do not create saturated soil conditions, and alleviate poor drainage; and (5) apply weekly foliar sprays of CaCl or $CaNO_3$. A homemade calcium solution can be prepared from 20 discarded eggshells. Place them in 1 gallon of water and bring to a rolling boil. Remove from heat, cool for 24 hours, and strain contents. Use as a spray on tomato plants.
- Corky, dry, irregular scars on ends of fruits. Physiological, **Corky Stylar Scar** (catface). Caused by unfavorable climatic conditions, low temperatures during flowering and fruit development.

- White tissue inside fruit. **White Tissue.** Not understood; potassium supplements seem to help.
- Small transverse cracks on skin of fruits. Cracks usually heal. May be related to irregular wet-dry cycles. **Rain Check.**
- Night temperatures above 70°F can cause **Blossom Drop.** Beat the heat by planting large transplants of early-maturing cultivars as early in the spring as possible.

Fruits: Concentric, target-like circles or rings

Sunken, rotten, brown to black spots, can be corky, with numerous surrounding concentric rings or circles. Fungal disease, ***Rhizoctonia solani.*** Survives on litter from many vegetable species (tomatoes, lettuce, cucumbers, leeks, beans, and weeds).

Fruits: Discoloration

- Yellow mottling on ripe fruit. Viral disease, ***Rhabdovirus*** and other viruses.
- Blotchy ripening of fruit. Physiological, some cultivars are prone to this condition; contributing factors are potassium and boron deficiencies, shaded locations, and lack of sun.

Fruits: Massive damage

Numerous pronounced, severe, grayish to light brown spots, mottling of fruit, shriveled and deformed fruits and plants. For plant shriveling, see diagnostics for viral diseases. **CMV, TMV, Alfalfa Mosaic Virus (AMV).** Also fungal diseases, **Mildew** and **Late Blight** (*Phytophthora infestans*).

Insect pests

f = fruit, l = leaves, s = stems, r = roots

Common insect pests on tomatoes include

- Tomato Fruitworm (*Helicoverpa zea*) (f)
- Tomato Hornworm (*Manduca quinquemaculata*) (s, l)
- Tobacco Hornworm (*Manduca sexta*) (s, l)
- Yellowstriped Armyworm (*Spodoptera ornithogalli*) (s, l, f)
- Beet Armyworm (*Spodoptera exigua*) (s, l, f)
- Loopers: Alfalfa Looper (*Autographa californica*), Cabbage Looper (*Trichoplusia ni*) (s, l)
- Colorado Potato Beetle (*Leptinotarsa decemlineata*) (l)
- Variegated Cutworm (*Peridroma saucia*) (s)

- Black Cutworm (*Agrotis ipsilon*) (s)
- Flea Beetles (*Epitrix hirtipennis* and others) (l)
- Green Peach Aphid (*Myzus persicae*) (l, s)
- Potato Aphid (*Macrosiphum euphorbiae*) (l, s)
- Tomato Psyllid (*Bactericera cockerelli*) (l)
- Western Flower Thrips (*Frankliniella occidentalis*), vector of spotted wilt virus (l, flowers)
- Leafminers: (*Liriomyza sativae, L. trifolii,* and *L. huidobrensis*) (l)
- Whiteflies: Silverleaf Whitefly (*Bemisia argentifolii*), Greenhouse Whitefly (*Trialeurodes vaporariorum*), Bandedwinged Whitefly (*T. abutilonia*) (l)
- Tomato Bug (*Cyrtopeltis modesta*) (s)
- Stink Bugs: Consperse Stink Bug (*Euschistus conspersus*), Redshouldered Stink Bug (*Thyanta pallidovirens* [= *T. acerra*]), Say's Stink Bug complex (*Chlorochroa sayi* and *C. uhleri*), Southern Green Stink Bug (*Nezara viridula*) (s, l, f)
- Twospotted Spider Mites (*Tetranychus urticae*) (s, l)
- Potato Leafhopper (*Empoasca fabae*) (s)
- Root-Knot Nematode (*Meloidogyne* spp.) (r)

PERSONAL NOTE • Harvesting Tomatoes

Your tomatoes are progressing well and there are some big luscious "berries" (see chapter 5). Do you decide to harvest when tomatoes are fully ripened or when partially green with red or pink tints? Your decision should vary with existing conditions in the garden.

Supermarket tomatoes are most likely harvested before they are table ripe because a ripe tomato does not ship well. Tomatoes harvested in the "breaker stage" (when the color changes from green to yellow to pink or red on not more that 10% of the tomato surface) are often advertised as vine ripened, but this is a misnomer. What is the chemistry of tomato flavor as ripening progresses? There is a diverse set of chemical compounds, including sugars (glucose and fructose), acids (citrate, malate, and glutamate), and over 400 volatiles (16 primary volatiles), that are associated with tomato flavor. Research finds: 1) total solids and sugars increase progressively as tomatoes mature and ripen from green to red; 2) tomato acidity increases from green to the green-yellow state and then remains relatively constant; 3) taste tests confirm that vine ripened tomatoes are more flavorful (higher sugar content) than room ripened tomatoes; and 4) tomatoes picked at earlier stages of maturity have an "off flavor" (volatile organic compounds, Peak 43, a-terpineol) that varies among different varieties.

In my Texas garden, if I wait until the tomato is fully ripened, there is a high probability that the best and largest tomatoes will have sustained damage from either sunscald, birds, insects, or other animals. As tomatoes mature and enlarge, some varieties are prone to cracking, especially large heirloom varieties, which is often followed by mold and rot. I almost always harvest when the tomato is about 50% green and pink-red. I am willing to sacrifice a little flavor and have a viable tomato that is not spoiled. Personally, I do not really detect "off flavors." If you are determined to pick when fully ripe, you must be on constant alert or else you may be disappointed and find a damaged tomato.

Tomato Quick Guide

Botanical Data	Environmental Conditions	Culture and Special Considerations
Tomato (*Solanum lycopersicum* var. *lycopersicum*); *Solanum* derived from Latin *sol*, meaning "sun"; *lycopersicon* derived from Greek, translated as "wolf peach" **Plant Family:** Solanaceae (nightshade) **Life Cycle:** classified as herbaceous perennials, but grown as annuals in vegetable gardens **Growth Form:** determinate are short and bushy (2–3 feet), most do not need staking, cages helpful and provide support; indeterminate grow as long vines (up to 6 feet). Plant spread is 2–6 feet. **Physiology:** photosynthesis C_3 **Flowers:** perfect or complete, yellow. Bloom in midsummer, late summer, early fall. See chapter 3, "Garden Ecology," with diagram. **Stems:** stems and leaves are densely glandular-hairy **Leaves:** compound, reticulate veined, odd pinnate with 5–9 leaflets on petioles, leaflets with serrated margins **Roots:** fibrous root system if plant grown from cuttings, taproot with fibrous network if grown from seeds. Tomatoes are considered to be deep rooted—the majority of roots are 12–24 inches deep. **Fruit:** classified botanically as a berry. All or most of the pericarp is soft and fleshy. **Seeds:** viability 3–5 years under cool, dry conditions; 250–380 seeds/g; germination 5–15 days at 70°F–80°F; seed planting depth ¼–½ inch **Plant Toxicity:** for a poisoning emergency in the United States call 1-800-222-1222 (American Association of Poison Control Centers) Leaves and stems are not edible. Leaves, stems, and green unripe fruit of the tomato plant contain small amounts of the toxic alkaloids tomatine and solanine, which are also found in potato leaves and other plants in the	**Growing Zones:** check state and county cooperative extension sites and guides for adaptability and recommended planting dates Be conservative and wait 2 weeks past your average safe date before planting (the safe date is the date the last frost occurs 90% of the time according to meteorological records). **Optimal Temperature for Growth:** 70°F–80°F during the day and 55°F–70°F during the night. When daytime fall temperatures are consistently below 60°F, the fruit will no longer ripen on the vine, so it is time to pick the larger mature green fruits and bring them indoors. Leave the smaller fruits to maximize size before frost. **Sunlight:** full sun, at least 8 hours of direct sun daily **Soil Conditions:** prefers well-drained, fertile soil, high in organic matter. Clays, loams, and sandy loams are suitable. Lighter-textured soils that drain and warm quickly can produce earlier harvests. Tomatoes cannot tolerate poorly drained or waterlogged soils. Parasitic nematodes (sting and stubby root) prefer sandy soils. **Optimal pH:** 6.0–7.0, can tolerate slightly acidic soils, as low as pH 5.5 **Moisture Content:** consistent moisture needed to prevent wilting and blossom end rot **Days to Maturity (DTM):** seed catalogs usually provide information about DTM. Add 30–35 days if direct seeding. DTM is the projected time from setting out healthy, well-formed, vigorous transplants and is only a guide; it is highly dependent on climate and environmental conditions. The following is a realistic assessment: early, 55–65 days; midseason, 65–80 days; and late, over 80 days.	For a family of four, 10–20 plants suffice. **Spacing:** in the home garden, spacing depends on the variety and the training system. Commercial growers also need to space plants for spray equipment. Staked plant rows are 30–48 feet apart, and distance between plants in rows is 24–30 inches depending on cultivar. Determinate plant rows are usually spaced 24–30 inches apart. In home gardens, a uniform spacing of 36 inches is usually adequate. Nonstaked, crawling vines need row spacing of 6 feet with plant spacing at 4 feet. For support, use wire cages or wooden stakes (40–72 inches tall). **Crop Rotation:** every 3 to 4 years **Depth of Planting:** seeds ¼–½ inch deep. Use 1:1 mixture of vegetable potting medium and topsoil/compost mix from the garden. **Starting Transplants:** various methods can be used: inside with grow lights, outside in cold frames, and greenhouses. Do not allow seedlings and transplants to develop flowers or fruit. For plants in more northern climates, roots and most of stem should be covered in hole; leave only top canopy leaves. In the South, fungi can be a problem, so don't bury as much stem. **Planting:** usually transplants in the home garden, but can be directly seeded with good soil preparation. Add 30–35 days if direct seeding. Transplants are usually 5–6 weeks old at time of planting. Hardened-off container plants are best. Set transplants out after danger of frost has passed. A cloudy, windless day is best. If frost threatens, cover with a tarp, towel, old sheet, or plastic shields (see nursery supply and seed catalogs). Dig hole 12 inches deep, add small amount of fertilizer, cover fertilizer with 2 inches of soil, place transplant in hole with soil/compost mixture. **Fertilizer:** soils with low, medium, and high organic matter generally require 130, 110, and 90 lb. N/acre, respectively. Many extension bulletins recommend ½ as a preplant and ½ as a side dress when fruit appears. After applying some initial N

Tomato Quick Guide *continued*

Botanical Data	Environmental Conditions	Culture and Special Considerations
nightshade family. Levels of tomatine in foliage and green fruit are generally not dangerous unless large amounts are consumed. Tomato plants can be toxic to dogs and other pets if they eat large amounts of the fruit, or chew plant material. **Cultivars:** There are many good heirlooms and hybrid cultivars. It may be difficult to choose (seed companies estimate that there are 25,000–40,000 cultivars worldwide). The choice of cultivar is important: Consider your climate and growing zone * Days to maturity before harvest (early and late cultivars), growth form (determinate vs. indeterminate) * Fruit type and use (table, canning, juice, sauces, cooking styles) * Appearance: fruit color any shade of red, yellow, pink, purple. All shapes and sizes, large, round fruits (7–16 oz.); plum/roma types, cluster, and cherry and grape types * Jointless or jointed—when picked, jointless fruits leave the stem on the plant, resulting in a smooth fruit surface. In jointed fruits, the stem and a few leaves remain with the fruit, which has appeal in stores. * Disease resistance or tolerance. Hybrids are bred for various disease resistance (check seed catalog descriptions). * Fruit resilience—firmness of fruit for shipping or home use	**Nutrition Information:** Tomatoes, red, raw. USDA Food and Nutrition Service. % Daily Value based on 2,000 calorie diet Serving size 1 cup Calories 26.8 Total carbohydrates 5.8 g, 2% Total Fats 0.3 g, 0% Protein 1.3 g, 3% Vitamin A 25% Vitamin C 32% Vitamin K 15% Potassium 10% Phosphorus 4% Manganese 8% Magnesium 4%	during planting, some growers side dress with 30–50 lb./acre at first fruit set, and 30–50 lb./acre when the third and fourth flower clusters appear. P applications range from 0 to 150 lb./acre depending on soil test. K levels can range from 0 to 250 lb./acre depending on soil test. Some growers split K applications between an initial application and a side dressing with 60–100 lb./acre at first fruit set to aid in additional fruit firmness. See appendix D for equivalent fertilizer rates for circle plots. **Pruning:** controversial, sometimes recommended; however, scientific research shows that there is little benefit for increasing yield (see Science Notes) **Weeding:** cultivate about 1 inch around plant. Mulch when soil warms up. **Health:** tomatoes are an excellent source of potassium and several vitamins: A, C, E, and folic acid. The main tomato carotenoids (antioxidants) are * beta-carotene, an orange pigment also found in carrots and sweet potatoes * lycopene, a red pigment having anticancer effects * phytoene and phytofluene, newly discovered anticancer compounds in tomatoes The health benefits of tomatoes are enhanced by cooking. Carotenoid and flavonoid absorption in the body is greater from cooked tomatoes than from fresh tomatoes, since cooking breaks down the tomato cell matrix. Also, the addition of olive oil to diced tomatoes during cooking greatly increases the absorption of lycopene. Oil is essential for absorbing carotenoids from tomatoes in salads or salsa. There is almost no absorption of these vital nutrients from salad eaten with a nonfat dressing.

ADDITIONAL TOOLS and INFORMATION

Site Notes:

Assessment Completed By: ____________________ Date: ____________________

Name of Site: ____

Location: ____

Weather Conditions: ____

Current Use of Site: ____

Future Plans: ____

____

Site Drawing and Notes:

Appendix A

Garden Site Indicator Scorecard and Soil Health/Quality Indicator Scorecard

General instructions:

- Go to the garden site that you wish to evaluate.
- Evaluate each indicator (Poor, Tolerable, Best).
- After a suitable garden site has been located, proceed to the Soil Health/Quality Indicator Scorecard.

The Garden Site Indicator Scorecard is a subjective evaluation, but it can provide relative baseline conditions based on the number of indicators in each column.

Notes: Some indicators, highlighted in red, are critical. If an indicator score occurs in a red box, find another garden location. Other indicators that are not in red but have a poor rating may be improved or corrected depending on the extent of the situation.

- If there is a particular area of interest on the site, concentrate the assessment there.
- Complete the field notes section below for future reference.
- Rate each indicator by marking an X in the appropriate box.
- Tally the scorecard.

TABLE 27

GARDEN SITE INDICATOR SCORECARD		Date:________ Site Name: ________ Assessment Completed By: ________	
	(circle appropriate category)		
Indicators	**Poor**	**Tolerable**	**Best**
1. Distance from house and kitchen	Not convenient	Somewhat convenient	Conveniently close
2. Visibility from house	Not visible	Partially visible	Totally visible
3. Privacy	Not private, open view	Partially private	Private
4. Potential aesthetic value with home	Low	Medium	High
5. Fencing	No fencing	Partially fenced	Completely fenced
6. Distance to trees, shrubs, windbreaks	1–5 feet (shade over garden most of the day)	5–20 feet	More than 20 feet (no shadows)
7. Distance to walls and barriers	1–5 feet	5–20 feet	More than 20 feet
8. Potential disturbance and trampling from humans	High	Medium	Low or none
9. Potential disturbance and trampling from pets	High	Medium	Low
10. Potential disturbance from marauding wildlife	High	Medium	Low
11. Water access—city water, well, pond, creek, etc.	No water available on site, and no access to water	Water available, but expensive	Cheap, abundant water available
12. Irrigation water quality (municipal, water well, or from irrigation district)	Poor (salts, sewage, potential pathogens)	N/A	Good
13. Sun exposure during the day	Low	Moderate	Maximum
14. Drainage	Very poor	Somewhat poor	Adequate
15. Ponding of water after rainfall	Longer than 1 hour	15 minutes to 1 hour	Rapid, less than 15 minutes
16. Potential flooding	High	Occasional	Low to none
17. Debris, trash (glass, construction materials, nails, bricks, concrete, etc.)	Considerable amount	Some	None
18. Stoniness of site	Considerable	Some	None
19. Erosion risk	Considerable	Some	None
20. Potential damage from high winds	High	Medium	Low
21. Slope	Steep	Moderate	Flat
22. Direction of facing slope or pitch of garden	North	East, west	South

23. Trees and brush currently growing on the site	Lots of trees and brush	Some unwanted trees and brush	No interfering trees or brush
24. Grasses and weeds currently growing on the site	Low amount of vegetation (very patchy), weedy, little plant vigor	Moderate vegetation cover, ½ herbaceous plants, ½ grasses	Vigorous vegetation cover, mostly grasses
25. Droughtiness of site (potential water-holding capacity)	Soil dries out quickly, droughty. Plants wilt the day after watering in hot weather.	Some plant wilting or curling on very hot days, but recover quickly	Plants maintain turgidity several days after watering or in hot weather
26. History of site	Unknown	Some information	Known
27. Potential past hazards (chemical)	High	Moderate to low	None
28. Potential current hazards (chemical)	High	Moderate to low	None
Preponderance of evidence, total number of red indicators (if any score is in red box, find another garden location).			
Preponderance of evidence, other indicators (total number of indicators in each column).			

Soil Health/Quality Indicator Scorecard

Equipment required:

- Shovel
- Tape measure or ruler
- 1 gallon of water for each soil scorecard
- Pen or pencil

General instructions:

- Go to the site you wish to evaluate.
- Select a typical spot to sample; if the area is variable, you may need to complete more than one scorecard.
- Dig a hole approximately 1–2 feet deep. This hole will be used for the soil quality assessment.
- Complete the field notes section on the next page.
- Circle each indicator rating.

- Complete additional soil scorecards for other potential locations.
- Tally the scorecard.

Notes: The Soil Health/Quality Indicator Scorecard is a subjective evaluation, but it can provide a relative baseline based on the number of indicators in each column. Note that not all the indicators represent an unhealthy situation; the rating for a particular indicator may be normal for the soil type. For example, the color, infiltration capacity, and structure may be normal or expected for that soil. Infiltration capacity can be improved with organic matter and soil improvement measures.

Site Notes:

Date: ____________________

Name of Site: ____________________

Location: ____________________

Weather Conditions: ____________________

Current Use of Site: ____________________

Future Plans: ____________________

____

Length of garden area (   ) x *width of garden area* (   ) = *square feet* (   )

Drawing and Notes:

TABLE 28

<table>
<tr><td colspan="2">SOIL HEALTH/QUALITY INDICATOR SCORECARD</td><td colspan="2">Date:____________________
Site Name: ____________________
Assessment Completed By: ____________</td></tr>
<tr><td></td><td colspan="3">(circle appropriate category)</td></tr>
<tr><td>Indicators</td><td>Undesirable and/or Unhealthy</td><td>Moderately Healthy</td><td>Desirable and/or Healthy</td></tr>
<tr><td>1. Is there a sufficient topsoil layer?</td><td>Subsoil is exposed or very near the surface.</td><td>Topsoil is thin, about 4–6 inches. Some topsoil may be needed.</td><td>More than 6 inches deep</td></tr>
<tr><td>2. Depth of surface and immediate subsoil layer</td><td>Less than 1 foot</td><td>1–2 feet</td><td>More than 2 feet</td></tr>
<tr><td>3. During hot and dry climatic conditions, are there soil cracks?</td><td>Obvious and many</td><td>Occasional</td><td>None</td></tr>
<tr><td>4. Color of topsoil layer (moist)</td><td>Yellow, gray, light gray, mottled</td><td>Light brown</td><td>Black, dark brown, dark red, color uniform</td></tr>
<tr><td>5. Ease of digging hole 1 foot deep</td><td>Not possible or very difficult</td><td>Moderately difficult</td><td>Relatively easy</td></tr>
<tr><td>6. Soil compaction</td><td>Dense, tight, and compacted. Hard layer inhibits plant roots, roots grow laterally.</td><td>Moderately compacted, few roots grow laterally</td><td>Not compacted, many vertical roots with adequate side branching</td></tr>
<tr><td>7. Soil structure</td><td>Hard, dense, or dusty powdery when dry. Surface crust forms after hard rain. Difficult to prepare smooth seedbed.</td><td>Lumpy, crumbles with pressure. Moderate crusting after hard rain.</td><td>Very crumbly, no crusting after hard rain. Soil is mellow and seedbed is easy to prepare.</td></tr>
<tr><td>8. Odor of soil</td><td>Oily, chemical, gasoline, rotten eggs, other foul odors</td><td>No chemical smell, but slightly disagreeable</td><td>Fresh, earthy smell</td></tr>
<tr><td colspan="4">Warning: Certain contaminants such as lead and other pollutants may not have an odor. If you suspect chemical pollutants, or if the soil has a noticeable disagreeable odor, do not do the smell test. Send a soil sample to an appropriate lab.</td></tr>
<tr><td>9. Existing plant cover under normal undisturbed conditions (if not mowed or clipped)</td><td>Low</td><td>Medium</td><td>High</td></tr>
<tr><td>10. Vigor of existing vegetation (plant coloration and growth)</td><td>Many dead or stressed plants, yellow coloration, and bare patches</td><td>Some dead or stressed plants, growth sporadic, a few bare patches</td><td>High plant vigor, good green coloration, growth rapid, no bare patches</td></tr>
<tr><td>11. Plants reproducing</td><td>None</td><td>Some</td><td>Many</td></tr>
<tr><td>12. Plant roots in upper 4–12 inches</td><td>None</td><td>Few</td><td>Many</td></tr>
</table>

TABLE 28 ***continued***

Indicators	Undesirable and/or Unhealthy	Moderately Healthy	Desirable and/or Healthy
13. Current plant health	Yellow, discolored, blighted, streaky, spotty, or many dead, dry leaves and stems. Plants spindly, thin, and weak.	Yellow to green coloration. Plant color falls off or discolors as season progresses, and with hot weather.	Green to dark green coloration. Plants upright with healthy stems.
14. Bare ground	Patchy and connected areas of bare ground	Some bare ground and patchiness	No bare ground, plant cover exists throughout entire area
15. Biological activity, earthworms, insects	None	Some	High
16. Decomposition, biological activity, microbes (decomposition speed of litter and organic material when soil conditions are moist)	Old plant litter, very slow or almost no decomposition of organic materials	Moderate decomposition of plant litter and organic materials (months)	Rapid decomposition of plant litter and organic materials (several weeks to a month)
17. Water-holding capacity	Soil dries out quickly, droughty. Plants wilt quickly after watering in hot weather.	Some plant wilting or curling in hot weather, but recover quickly	Soil retains moisture. Plants maintain turgor and structure in hot weather.
18. Infiltration (estimate based on observations during rainfall)	Rapid to immediate or very slow (over 1 hour)	Most water infiltrates in about 20 minutes to 1 hour	Most water infiltrates in 10–20 minutes
Data from Web Soil Survey or soil test (if no data, then omit)			
19. Organic matter (obtain from Web Soil Survey and/or soil test)	Less than 2%	2%–4%	4%–6%
20. pH (obtain from Web Soil Survey and/or soil test)	Less than 6.4 or greater than 7.2	—	—
21. N, P, K	Low	Medium	Adequate or high
22. Micronutrients	Low	Medium	Adequate or high
Preponderance of evidence (total the number of indicators in each column).			

Appendix B

Organic Materials, Carbon/Nitrogen Ratios, Composting Information

Weighted Average Technique for Calculating the C/N Ratio of Compost Based on Its Organic Components

For example, common materials in my barnyard are discarded Bermuda grass hay, some snippets of leftover alfalfa stems, goat and llama manure, and soil. First, estimate how much of each available material is in your mix (for example, 10 parts hay in 16 total parts), and multiply by the C/N ratio. Sum up the total parts in the mix and the total of the C/N ratios multiplied by the parts. Divide as shown in table 31. If you are knowledgeable with spreadsheets, set up the calculations and evaluate different scenarios. Keeping the compost pile moist, not wet, and periodically mixing it are essential.

Pearson Square Method for Compost Mixture Determinations Using Two Materials

These calculations are provided to give you an approximate idea of how to determine the mixture needed for certain common organic materials. The carbon-to-nitrogen (C/N) ratio in a compost pile needs to range from 25:1 (25 parts of carbon for every part of nitrogen) to 40:1 (40 parts of carbon for every part of nitrogen). The ideal ratio is 25:1 to 30:1. When the ratio is below the target C/N ratio, excess

TABLE 29. Average N, P, and K, timing of release, effect on pH, and notes for commonly used organic fertilizers

Material	Total N (%)	Total P (%)	Total K (%)	Nutrient release	Effect on pH	Notes
Cattle manure, dry	0.5–2	0.5–0.7	0.5–2.0	slow	slightly acidic	may contain soluble salts*
Cattle manure, fresh	0.6–2.5	0.3	0.5	slow	slightly acidic	may contain soluble salts*
Poultry manure, dry	1.5–4.4	2.1	2.6	medium to rapid		can burn plants,* strong odor, decomposed has less burn risk
Sheep manure, dry	3.5	0.6	1	slow	slightly acidic	*
Hog manure, dry	2.1	0.8	1.2	slow	slightly acidic	*
Horse manure, fresh	0.7	0.3	0.6	slow	slightly acidic	weed seeds
Swine manure, dry	2.25	2	1	slow	slightly acidic	*
Swine manure, fresh	0.6	0.5	0.4	slow	slightly acidic	*
Rabbit manure, dry	2.25	1	1	slow	slightly acidic	
Blood meal	12	0–1	0–1	medium to rapid	acidic	$, can burn plants
Cottonseed meal	6–7	0.4–2	1–1.5	slow to medium	acidic	pesticide residues and GMO
Soybean meal	7	2	1	slow, 1–4 months		$, can be GMO
Fish meal	10	3–6	2–3	slow, 1–4 months	acidic	$, odor
Feather meal	10–14	0	0	slow, 6–9 months		$, odor
Fish emulsion	4–5	1–2	1–2	slow		micronutrients, odor
Bone meal, steamed	1–6	15–30	0	slow to medium	alkaline	$, can burn
Hoof and horn meal	13	0	0	slow to medium	alkaline	$
Bat guano, high N	10	3	1	slow, 4+ months		$, stimulates microbes
Bat guano, high P	3	10	1	slow, 4+ months		$, stimulates microbes
Green manure (grain crop)	2.5	0.2	2.1	medium		nutrient content decreases with age of plant

Alfalfa meal, pellets	2–3.6	2	1	slow, 1–4 months		micronutrients
Seaweed	1.7	0.75	5	slow		micronutrients
Kelp	1–1.5	0.5–1	5–10	medium		$, zinc, iron
Wood ashes	0	1–2	5–10	medium	alkaline	use sparingly and with care
Compost	0.5–3.5	0.5–2	0.5–2	slow to very slow	acidic to alkaline	pH depends on materials, gradual increase in P and K
Rock phosphate	0	30	0	slow to medium for sedimentary RP; apply 4 to 5 weeks before planting	acidic	a mined resource; igneous RP deposits are less soluble than sedimentary RP and are not very effective when applied directly to the soil
Greensand	0	1	6	slow release, does not burn plants, beneficial to soil microbes, good soil conditioner to loosen heavy and tight soils	slightly acidic to slightly alkaline, usually has little effect on soil pH	mined from ocean deposits, "glauconitc," a sedimentary rock

Sources: Zibilske (1998); USDA NRCS (2010); NRAES (1992, 1999).

*Growing scientific evidence shows that pathogens, antimicrobials, and hormones may exist in commercially produced livestock and poultry manure across the United States.

$ = cost consideration.

nitrogen is converted to ammonia and escapes into the atmosphere, which affects your air quality. If the target C/N ratio is too high, the decomposition process slows and does not progress. In this example, leaves and cow manure are available. The gardener wants to make compost with a C/N ratio of 30:1. What percentage of the compost pile should be leaves, and what percentage fresh manure? Be sure to mix in soil with the leaves and compost.

From table 30, find the C/N ratios for leaves and fresh cow manure. Leaf C/N = 34:1; fresh cow manure C/N = 20:1.

TABLE 30. Average carbon and nitrogen content and C/N ratio for commonly available organic materials

Organic material	Carbon (%)	Nitrogen (%)	C/N ratio
Blood meal	43	13	3.3:1
Chicken manure (fresh)	15	1.8	8:1
Topsoil (high organic matter)	56	4.9	11:1
Broiler litter	38	2.7	14:1
Alfalfa pellets	40	2.7	15:1
Kitchen vegetable wastes	40	2.7	15:1
Finished garden compost	30	0.5–2.0	15:1
Alfalfa hay	40	2.5	16:1
Bluegrass from fertilized lawn	42	2.2	20:1
Cow manure (fresh)	16	0.6–4.2	20:1
Decomposed barnyard manure	41	1–2.0	20:1
Leaf litter	48	1.4	34:1
Horse manure (fresh)	27	0.7	38:1
Sphagnum peat moss	43	0.9	48:1
Bermuda grass hay	44	1.1	49:1
Corn stalks	40	0.7	57:1
Timothy grass hay	52	0.9	58:1
Wheat straw	38	0.5	80:1
Paper	39	0.3	120:1
Sawdust (hardwood)	46	0.1	400:1
Sawdust (spruce)	50	0.05	600:1

Sources: USDA NRCS (2010); NRAES (1992, 1999).

Step 1. Leaf C/N – manure C/N = 34 – 20 = 14

Step 2. Leaf C/N – target C/N = 34 – 30 = 4. Divide 4 by answer in step 1: 4 ÷ 14 x 100 = 28.6%.

Step 3. Target C/N – manure C/N = 30 – 20 = 10. Divide 10 by answer in step 1: 10 ÷ 14 x 100 = 71%

To achieve a target C/N ratio of 30, about 71% of the compost pile should be leaves and 28% cow manure. The range of moisture in the compost pile should be between 40 and 65%.

TABLE 31. Sample calculations of C/N ratio for compost based on its organic components

Scenario 1

	C/N ratio	Parts in mix	C/N ratio x parts
Hay	40	10	400
Alfalfa stems	18	1	18
Manure	20	2	40
Soil	12	3	36
Sum		16	494
C/N ratio 494 ÷ 16 = 30.9			

Scenario 2

	C/N ratio	Parts in mix	C/N ratio x parts
Leaves	34	10	340
Lawn clippings	20	5	100
Manure	20	2	40
Soil	12	2	24
Sum		19	504
C/N ratio 504 ÷ 19 = 26.5			

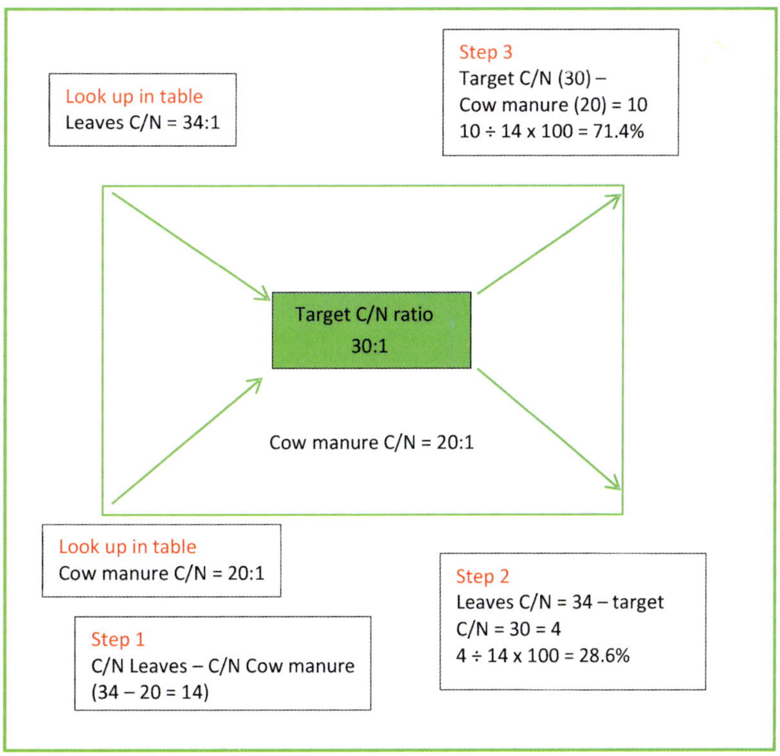

FIGURE 81. Calculating a target C/N ratio of 30:1.

Organic Matter Fact Sheet

- Soil organic matter (SOM) is an integration of biological and mineral components.
- One gram of soil can contain up to 10^{10} to 10^{11} bacteria, 6,000–50,000 bacteria species, and up to 656 feet of fungal hyphae.
- Microorganisms in the soil mineralize nitrogen, phosphorous, and sulfur as they decompose organic matter. Nutrients are released slowly, over years.
- Additions of organic matter to the soil may not supply the nutrient needs of vegetable plants in newly established gardens. SOM and nutrients accumulate over time. Additional nutrients from soil amendments may be needed to supply macronutrients for plants in new garden soils.
- SOM and soil microorganisms function together to improve soil physical properties that are related to greater soil resilience and resistance to erosion. As organic matter is added to the soil, biological activity increases, soil porosity is greater, and more-stable soil aggregates are formed, which is related to greater infiltration capacity.
- In an average soil, about 50% of the mass is carbon.
- SOM contains 5% nitrogen, on average.
- Soil scientists estimate that for each 1% change in SOM via tillage and erosion, about 1,000 lb. organic N/acre and an inch of potential water storage capacity are lost.
- Organic compounds have a tenuous hold on soil nitrogen (90%–95%), which is unavailable to plants.
- Plants can take up soluble organic compounds (mostly soluble proteins and amino acids), which make up about 0.3%–1.5% of the total organic nitrogen in soils.
- SOM is the primary source of nitrogen, phosphorus, and sulfur.
- For each 1% organic matter, on average there are 1,000 lb. of nitrogen and 100 lb. of phosphorus and potassium in the upper 6 inches of soil.
- In plant ecosystems, the primary source of SOM is plant tissues; animal waste products are secondary.
- SOM sustains and regulates nutrient cycling in soils.
- Potential SOM content and the endpoint in the soil depend on the soil parent materials, soil environment, climate, and native vegetation.

- SOM accumulates over long periods (centuries) and eventually reaches equilibrium (levels off).
- Once optimal soil organic carbon levels are reached (equilibrium), the annual increase in SOM fluctuates between positive and negative values, but the long-term average is approximately a zero gain.
- Organic matter development is greater (1.5 to 3 times) in the soil surface layer of grassland communities compared to forests.
- During soil development, nutrients in the soil are derived from specific minerals in the parent material. As soils develop and become older, nutrients are supplied by the organic fraction of the soil.
- On average, after 1 year, most of the carbon from SOM added to the soil returns to the atmosphere as carbon dioxide (CO_2). About 25 to 33% remains in the soil (~ 5% in organism biomass, ~ 20% in humic substances, and ~ 5% in nonhumic fractions).
- SOM buildup in the soil is a slow process.
- The principal elements of SOM are carbon, hydrogen, oxygen, nitrogen, phosphorus, potassium, and sulfur.
- SOM enhances soil physical properties such as structure, aggregate stability, infiltration capacity, porosity, water-holding capacity, granulation, and friability (ease of working the surface).
- SOM is directly linked to soil health and productivity.
- SOM generally decreases with soil depth.
- SOM varies in content in different soils: soils in desert and arid regions contain on average less than 1.5% organic matter; soils developed with prairie grasses generally contain more organic matter (3% to 5%) than forested soils.
- The average carbon-to-nitrogen (C/N) ratio of undisturbed soils is relatively stable at 12:1.
- When native soils are first cultivated, about 20%–40% of the SOM is lost over a 5- to 20-year period.
- SOM affects chemical processes in the soil: it increases the cation exchange capacity (CEC) and acts as a buffer to maintain soil pH.
- SOM enhances microbial biodiversity in soils.
- Organic residues on the soil surface decompose more slowly than if incorporated into the soil, because aboveground material is beyond the reach of soil microorganisms.
- Organic matter content depends on plant productivity. Grassland soils develop higher organic matter content than forest soils. As SOM increases, plant productivity increases.

- Plant nutrients are retained by SOM; thus nutrients do not leach readily into subsurface soil layers (horizons).
- Soil pathogens are suppressed to a large extent in natural ecosystems and undisturbed soils. Nonpathogenic and pathogenic microorganisms coexist.
- The incorporation of organic materials (compost, decomposed manure, cover crops) can stimulate nonpathogenic antagonist microorganisms and suppress pathogenic microorganisms.
- Hydrophilic and hydrophobic aspects of SOM and inherent minerals adsorb pesticides and other toxic compounds in the soil.

Compost

- Compost is an integral part of organic farming and gardening.
- During the composting process, microbial decomposition aerobically transforms organic substrates into a humus-like material.
- About 4%–20% of carbon in compost degrades relatively rapidly.
- During organic matter microbial decomposition, about 80% of the total is emitted as carbon dioxide gas. Eventually the remaining organic matter stabilizes and resists further microbial decomposition.
- On average, compost contains 40%–60% organic matter.
- The advantages of using compost are increased water-holding capacity, improved soil structure and friability, enhanced biological properties, and addition of slow-release nutrients over time.
- Before planting, work 2–3 inches of compost into the top 6 inches of soil. If you use circle plots, you will require much less compost compared to covering the entire garden area.
- Compost can be used as a mulch around your plants during the growing season.
- Composts made with organic litter materials and manure from cows, horses, and hogs have a nitrogen content of 0.5%–0.7% (less than 1%). On average, compost made with poultry manure can contain up to 1.5%, and phosphorus and potassium range from 0.5 to 2%.
- The pH of compost can range from 6.0 to 8.5; manure-based composts usually have a pH of 7.0 to 8.0.
- Decomposition of SOM depends on adequate supplies of oxygen and moisture, the proper composition of organic material, microorganisms, and temperatures above 50°F.

- Nitrogen from organic fertilizers and compost is often not immediately available to plants because it needs to be mineralized by microorganisms and environmental factors such as temperature, soil moisture, and the characteristics of the organic materials.
- Release of nitrogen from organic sources involves a biological process—microbial decomposition.
- Microbial respiration and SOM decomposition virtually cease below 41°F.
- There are four stages of compost decomposition: mesophilic, thermophilic, cooling, and maturing.
- In order to kill or pasteurize harmful organisms in compost, temperatures of 105°F or higher are needed for 5 days, and a temperature above 131°F is needed for 4 hours during the thermophilic stage. Even then, research has shown that not all potentially harmful pathogens are eliminated or killed.

Appendix C

Climate Tools

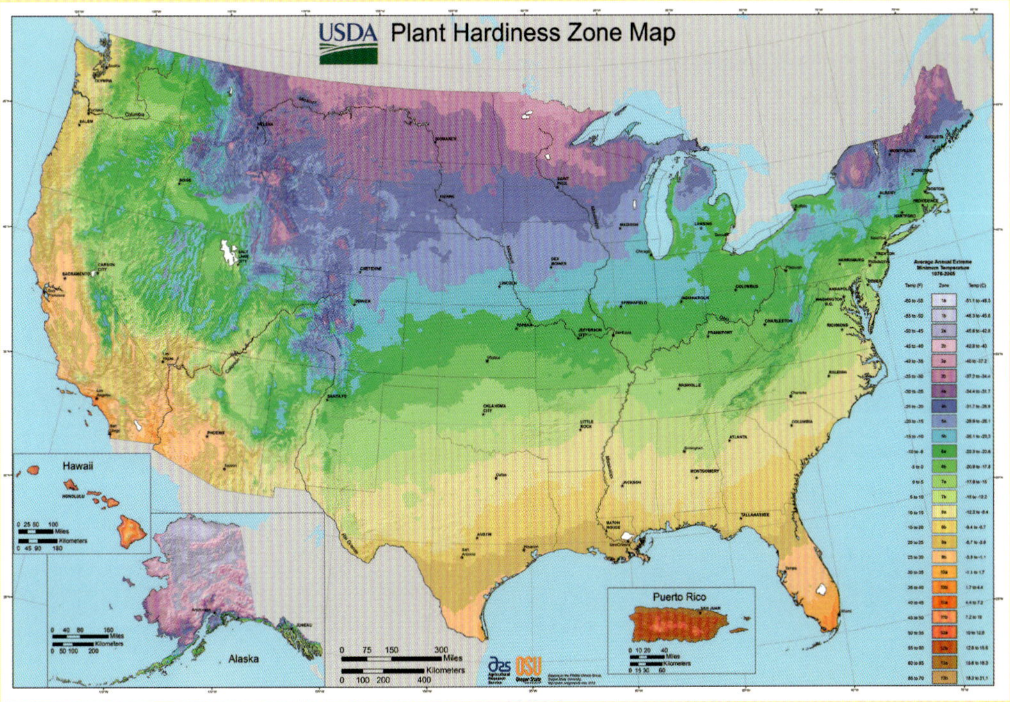

FIGURE 82. USDA Plant Hardiness Zones. Courtesy of USDA ARS, http://planthardiness.ars.usda.gov/PHZMWeb/Downloads.aspx.

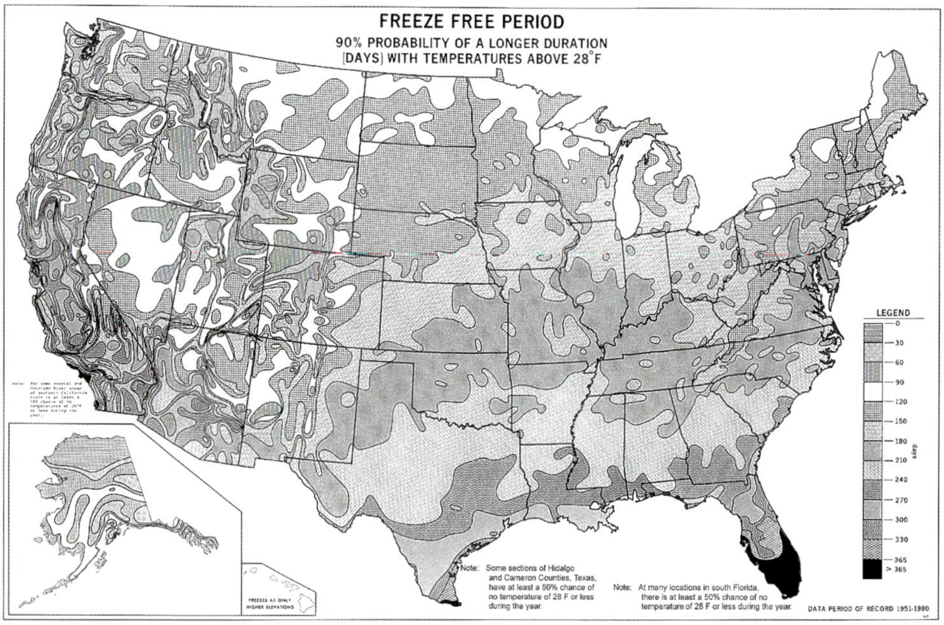

FIGURE 83. Freeze-free periods in the United States (90% probability of days with temperatures above 28°F). http://www.noaa.gov/.

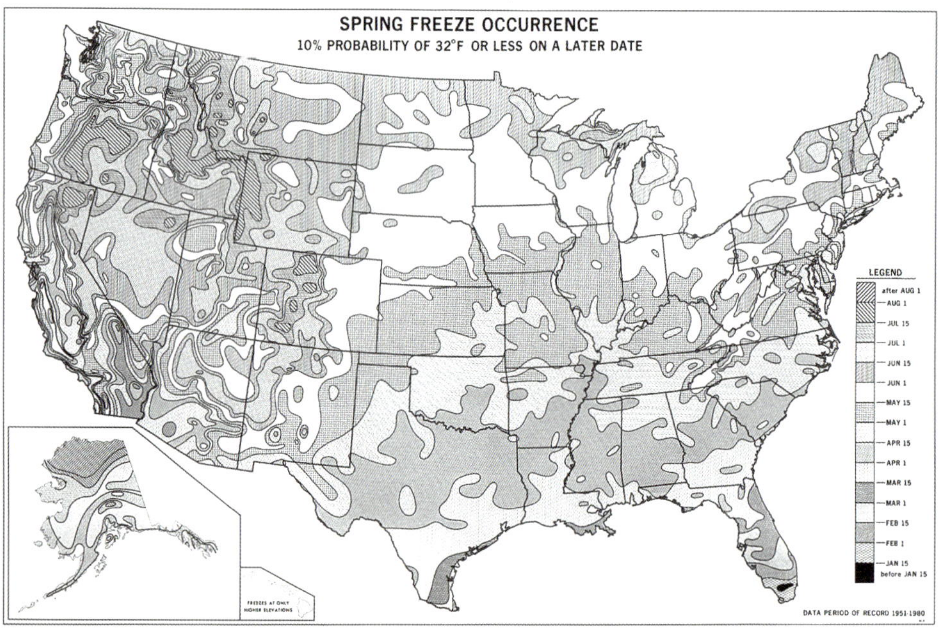

FIGURE 84. Spring freeze occurrence in the United States (10% probability of 32°F or less on a later date). http://www.noaa.gov/.

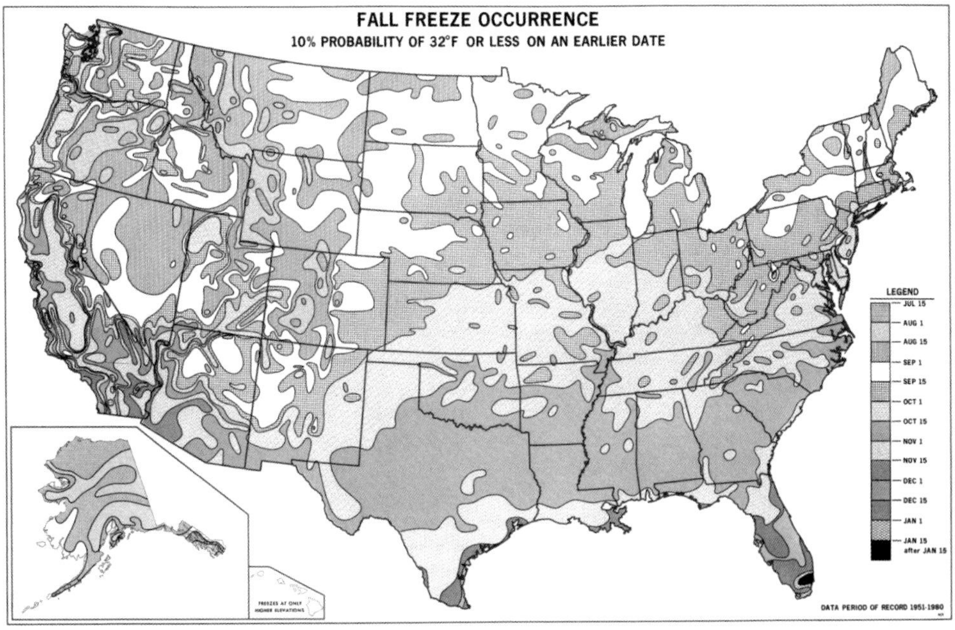

FIGURE 85. Fall freeze occurrence in the United States (10% probability of 32°F or less on an earlier date). http://www.noaa.gov/.

Appendix D

Equivalent Fertilizer Application Rates

Example 1

You want to apply 100 lb./acre of nitrogen, phosphorus, or potassium. What is the equivalent amount needed in an area of 16 ft.^{2} (4½-foot-diameter circle plot) using decomposed cow manure (0.5–0.5–0.5)? Using table 32, find the equivalent N rate (100 lb./acre) for a 16 ft.^{2} plot (7.3 lb.). Note: research shows that about 18% of the nitrogen in decomposed cow manure is available to the crop the first year. Under the column for decomposed cow manure with 18% available, adjusted for 100%, the amount would be 40.5 lb. The following steps show the calculations:

Step 1.

$$\frac{0.5 \textit{ lb. N, P, or K in manure}}{100 \textit{ lb. product}} = \frac{100 \textit{ lb. rate needed for 16 ft.}^2}{x = \textit{lb. product needed}}$$

Cross multiply 100 x 100 ÷ 0.5 = x
x = 20,000 lb.

Step 2.

$$\frac{20{,}000}{1 \textit{ acre} = 43{,}560 \textit{ ft.}^2} = \frac{x \textit{ lb. rate needed for 16 ft}^2}{16 \textit{ ft.}^2 \textit{ circle plot}}$$

TABLE 32. Equivalent nitrogen rates for circle plots 4½ feet and 5 feet in diameter using various soil amendments and fertilizers

	Decomposed cow manure	Decomposed cow manure	Compost	Compost	Blood meal	Bone meal	Fish meal	Synthetic	Synthetic	Synthetic
	0.5–0.5–0.5	18% avail.	1–1–1	11.5% avail.	12–0–0	5–12–0	10–6–5	10–10–10	20–20–20	33–0–0
	N (%)	Adjusted for	N (%)	Adjusted for	N (%)	N (%)	N (%)	N (%)	N (%)	N (%)
	0.5	100%	1	100%	12	5	10	10	20	33
Target amt. (lb. N/acre)	Circle plot 4½ feet in diameter, 16 square feet N equivalent: pounds of fertilizer product needed to achieve equivalent nitrogen fertilizer rate from column 1 (target lb. N/acre)									
200	14.60	81.10	7.30	63.47	0.61	1.46	0.73	0.73	0.36	0.22
150	10.95	60.82	5.47	47.60	0.46	1.09	0.55	0.55	0.27	0.17
125	9.12	50.68	4.56	39.67	0.38	0.91	0.46	0.46	0.23	0.14
120	8.76	48.66	4.38	38.08	0.36	0.88	0.44	0.44	0.22	0.13
100	7.30	40.55	3.65	31.73	0.30	0.73	0.36	0.36	0.18	0.11
90	6.57	36.49	3.28	28.56	0.27	0.66	0.33	0.33	0.16	0.10
80	5.84	32.44	2.92	25.39	0.24	0.58	0.29	0.29	0.15	0.09
70	5.11	28.38	2.55	22.21	0.21	0.51	0.26	0.26	0.13	0.08
60	4.38	24.33	2.19	19.04	0.18	0.44	0.22	0.22	0.11	0.07
50	3.65	20.27	1.82	15.87	0.15	0.36	0.18	0.18	0.09	0.06
25	1.82	10.14	0.91	7.93	0.08	0.18	0.09	0.09	0.05	0.03
Circle plot 5 feet in diameter, 20 square feet										
200	18.02	100.12	9.01	78.35	0.75	1.80	0.90	0.90	0.45	0.27
150	13.52	75.09	6.76	58.76	0.56	1.35	0.68	0.68	0.34	0.20
125	11.26	62.57	5.63	48.97	0.47	1.13	0.56	0.56	0.28	0.17
120	10.81	60.07	5.41	47.01	0.45	1.08	0.54	0.54	0.27	0.16
100	9.01	50.06	4.51	39.18	0.38	0.90	0.45	0.45	0.23	0.14
90	8.11	45.05	4.05	35.26	0.34	0.81	0.41	0.41	0.20	0.12
80	7.21	40.05	3.60	31.34	0.30	0.72	0.36	0.36	0.18	0.11
70	6.31	35.04	3.15	27.42	0.26	0.63	0.32	0.32	0.16	0.10
60	5.41	30.04	2.70	23.51	0.23	0.54	0.27	0.27	0.14	0.08
50	4.51	25.03	2.25	19.59	0.19	0.45	0.23	0.23	0.11	0.07
25	2.25	12.51	1.13	9.79	0.09	0.23	0.11	0.11	0.06	0.03

Note 1: Equivalent rates are the same for P and K using decomposed cow manure (0.5–0.5–0.5), compost (1–1–1), and synthetic fertilizers on chart.

Note 2: For balanced fertilizers or soil amendments (equal amounts of N-P-K), equivalent rates from table 32 will be the same or equal.

Cross multiply 20,000 x 16 ÷ 43,560 = x
x = 7.3 lb.

To adjust for 18% availability during year 1,

$$\frac{7.3 \text{ lb.}}{18\%} = \frac{x \text{ lb. rate needed for 16 ft.}^2}{100\%}$$

x = 40.5 lb

Example 2

You want to apply 100 lb./acre of nitrogen, phosphorus, or potassium. What is the equivalent amount needed in an area of 16 ft.^{2} (4½-foot-diameter circle plot) using a balanced 10–10–10 fertilizer? Using table 32, find the equivalent N rate (100 lb./acre) for a 16 ft.^{2} plot (0.36, or round to 0.4 lb.).

$$\frac{10 \text{ lb. N, P, or K in fertilizer}}{100 \text{ lb. product}} = \frac{100 \text{ lb. rate needed for 16 ft.}^2}{x = \text{lb. product needed}}$$

Cross multiply 100 x 100 ÷ 10 = x
x = 1,000 lb.

$$\frac{1{,}000}{1 \text{ acre} = 43{,}560 \text{ ft.}^2} = \frac{x \text{ lb. needed for 16 ft.}^2}{16 \text{ ft.}^2 \text{ circle plot}}$$

Cross multiply 1,000 x 16 ÷ 43,560 = x
x = 0.36, or round to 0.4 lb.

To convert pounds to ounces (16 ounces in 1 pound), multiply 0.4 pound x 16 = 6 ounces.

Example 3

You want to apply 100 lb. phosphorus (P_2O_5)/acre to tomatoes. What is the equivalent amount needed in an area of 16 ft.^{2} (4½-foot-diameter circle plot) using bone meal (5–12–0)? Note that the amount of P and K in fertilizer is always expressed as P_2O_5 and K_2O. There are 12 lb. of P_2O_5 in 100 lb. of product.

$$\frac{12 \text{ lb. } P_20_5 \text{ in fertilizer}}{100 \text{ lb. product}} = \frac{100 \text{ lb. rate needed for 16 ft.}^2}{x = \text{lb. product needed}}$$

Cross multiply $100 \times 100 \div 12 = x$
$x = 833.3$ lb.

$$\frac{833.3}{1\ acre = 43{,}560\ ft.^2} = \frac{x\ lb.\ needed\ for\ 16\ ft.^2}{16\ ft.^2\ circle\ plot}$$

Cross multiply $833.3 \times 16 \div 43{,}560 = x$
$x = 0.31$, or round to 0.3 lb.

To convert pounds to ounces (16 ounces in 1 pound), multiply
0.3 pound x 16 = 4.8 ounces.

Example 4

You want to apply 100 lb. potassium (K_2O)/acre to tomatoes. What is the equivalent amount needed in an area of 16 ft.^{2} (4½-foot-diameter circle plot) using the fertilizer blend (10–6–5)? Note that the amount of P and K in fertilizer is always expressed as P_2O_5 and K_2O. There are 5 lb. of K_2O in 100 lb. of product.

$$\frac{5\ lb.\ K_2 0\ in\ fertilizer}{100\ lb.\ product} = \frac{100\ lb.\ rate\ needed\ for\ 16\ ft.^2}{x = lb.\ product\ needed}$$

Cross multiply $100 \times 100 \div 5 = x$
$x = 2{,}000$ lb.

$$\frac{2{,}000}{1\ acre = 43{,}560\ ft.^2} = \frac{x\ lb.\ needed\ for\ 16\ ft.^2}{16\ ft.^2\ circle\ plot}$$

Cross multiply $2{,}000 \times 16 \div 43{,}560 = x$
$x = 0.73$, or round to 0.7 lb.

To convert pounds to ounces (16 ounces in 1 pound), multiply
0.7 pound x 16 = 11.7 ounces.

In addition, by applying this rate of potassium (100 lb./acre) or 0.7 lb. of fertilizer blend (10-6-5), you would also be applying the equivalent of 200 lb. of nitrogen and 120 lb. of potassium. Note that the nitrogen application is high (200 lb. N), so it you would want to reduce the target goal of 100 lb. potassium using (10-6-5).

$$\frac{10\ lb\ of\ N\ in\ fertilizer}{100\ lbs.\ of\ product} = \frac{x\ lb.\ \ N\ applied}{2{,}000\ lbs\ (10\text{-}6\text{-}5\ applied)} = 200\ lb.N$$

$$\frac{6\ lb\ of\ P\ in\ fertilizer}{100\ lbs\ of\ product} = \frac{x\ lb.\ \ P\ applied}{2{,}000\ lbs\ (10\text{-}6\text{-}5\ applied)} = 120\ lb.P$$

References

Alcorn, J. B. 1984. Development policy, forests and peasant farms: Reflections on Huastec-managed forests' contributions to commercial production and resource conservation. *Economic Botany* 38:389–406.

Ashworth, S. 1991. *Seed to Seed*. Decorah, IA: Seed Saver Publications.

Barrett, J. 2010. *What Makes Heirloom Plants So Great?* College Station: Texas A&M University Press.

Björklund, P. A. 2012. *Organic Matter: Ecology, Environmental Impact and Management*. Environmental Science, Engineering and Technology. New York: Nova Science Publishers.

Blancard, D. 1994. *A Color Atlas of Tomato Disorders: Observation, Identification, and Control*. London: Manson.

Borror, D. J., and R. E. White. 1970. *A Field Guide to the Insects of America North of Mexico*. Boston: Houghton Mifflin.

Brady, N. C., and R. R. Weil. 1996. *The Nature and Properties of Soils*. 11th ed. Upper Saddle River, NJ: Prentice Hall.

Brennan, E. B. 2013. Agronomic aspects of strip intercropping lettuce with alyssum for biological control of aphids. *Biological Control* 65:302–11.

Brush, S. B. 1982. The natural and human environment of the central Andes. *Mountain Resource Development* 2:14–38.

Butterly, C. R., J. A. Baldock, and C. Tang. 2013. The contribution of crop residues to changes in soil pH under field conditions. *Plant and Soil* 366:185–198.

California Institute of Technology. 2010. *The Feynman Lectures on Physics*. New York: Basic Books.

Champlain, Samuel de, and W. L. Grant. 1907. *Voyages of Samuel de Champlain, 1604–1618*. New York: C. Scribner's Sons.

Christanty, L., O. S. Abdoellah, G. G. Marten, and J. Iskandar. 1986. Traditional agroforestry in West Java: The *pekarangan* (homegarden) and *kebun-talun* (annual-perennial rotation) cropping systems. In *Traditional Agriculture in Southeast Asia: A Human Ecology Perspective*, edited by G. G. Marten, 132–58. Boulder, CO: Westview Press.

Coleman, E. 1999. *Four-Season Harvest: Organic Vegetables from Your Home Garden All Year Long*. White River Junction, VT: Chelsea Green.

Condé Nast. 2014. SELF Nutrition Data. 2014. http://nutritiondata.self.com/facts/vegetables-and-vegetable-products/2383/2.

Davidson, E. A., and I. L. Ackerman. 1993. Changes in soil carbon inventories following cultivation of previously tilled soils. *Biogeochemistry* 20:161–93.

Day, S. D., and P. E. Wiseman. 2009. At the root of it. *Arborist News*. International Society for Arboriculture. http://www.isa-arbor.com/education/resources/educ_Portal_RootGrowth_AN.pdf.

DeJong-Hughes, J. 2011. Does organic matter *really* matter? University of Minnesota Extension. http://www.pca.state.mn.us/index.php/view-document.html?gid=20970.

Deppe, C. 2000. *Breed Your Own Vegetable Varieties: The Gardener's and Farmer's Guide to Plant Breeding and Seed Saving*. White River Junction, VT: Chelsea Green.

Droffner, M. L., and W. F. Brinton. 1995. Survival of *E. coli* and *Salmonella* populations in aerobic thermophilic composts as measured with DNA gene probes. *Zentralblatt für Hygiene und Umweltmedizin* 197:387–97.

Drost, D., and W. Bitner. 2004. *Carrots in the Garden*. Utah State University Cooperative Extension. http://extension.usu.edu/files/publications/publication/HG_2004-12.pdf.

Eaton, E. R., and K. Kaufman. 2007. *Kaufman Field Guide to Insects of North America*. Boston: Houghton Mifflin.

Edmeades, D. C. 2003. The long-term effects of manures and fertilisers on soil productivity and quality: A review. *Nutrient Cycling in Agroecosystems* 66:165–80.

FAO (Food and Agriculture Organization of the United Nations). 2012. *The State of Food and Agriculture*. http://www.fao.org/docrep/017/i3028e/i3028e.pdf.

———. 2015. Fertilizer use to surpass 200 million tonnes in 2018. http://www.fao.org/news/story/en/item/277488/icode/.

FAO, WFP, and IFAD (Food and Agriculture Organization of the United Nations, World Food Programme, and International Fund for Agricultural Development). 2012. *The State of Food Insecurity in the World 2012: Economic Growth Is Necessary but Not Sufficient to Accelerate Reduction of Hunger and Malnutrition*. Rome, FAO.

Fengli, Z. 2009. Allelopathy of aerial part extracts from grafted eggplants. *Plant Physiology and Biochemistry* 10:76–78, 83.

Fernandez-Cornejo, J., R. Nehring, C. Osteen, S. Wechsler, A. Martin, and A. Vialou. 2014. *Pesticide Use in U.S. Agriculture: 21 Selected Crops, 1960–2008*. Economic Information Bulletin No. 124 (May). USDA Economic Research Service.

Ferrandino, F. 1999. *Pruning Tomatoes*. New Haven, CT: Taunton Press.

Fertilizer Institute. 2016. Fertilizer production: The logistics of making it and moving it. https://www.tfi.org/our-industry/intro-to-fertilizer/fertilizer-production.

Foley, J. 2014. A five step plan to feed the world. *National Geographic* (May).

Foster, B. L. 1999. Establishment, competition and the distribution of native grasses among Michigan old-fields. *Journal of Ecology* 87:476–89.

Francis, C. A., and M. E. Smith. 1985. Variety development for multiple cropping systems. *Critical Reviews in Plant Sciences* 3:133–68.

Franck, P., G. Kanny, B. Dousset, P. Nabet, and D. A. Moneret-Vautrin. 2000. Lettuce allergy. *Allergy* 55:201–12.

Gale, E. S., D. M. Sullivan, C. G. Cogger, A. I. Bary, D. D. Hemphill, and E. A. Myhre. 2006. Estimating plant-available nitrogen release from manures, composts, and specialty products. *Journal of Environmental Quality* 35:2321–32.

Gall, A. 2013. Why lettuce keeps making us sick. *Modern Farmer* (July 16).

Gatewood, J., and C. Lightfoot. 2013. Baby cut carrots: Healthy or harmful? Iowa State University Extension and Outreach. http://www.extension.iastate.edu/article/baby-cut-carrots-healthy-or-harmful.

Goldberg, D. E., T. Rajaniemi, J. Gurevitch, and A. Stewart-Oaten. 1999. Empirical approaches to quantifying interaction intensity: Competition and facilitation along productivity gradients. *Ecology* 80:1118–31.

Goldberg, D. E., R. Turkington, L. Olsvig-Whittaker, and A. R. Dyer. 2001. Density dependence in an annual plant community: Variation among life history stages. *Ecological Monographs* 71:423–46.

Gong, C. M., I. Koichi, I. Shunji, and S. Takashi. 2005. Survival of pathogenic bacteria in compost with special reference to *Escherichia coli*. *Journal of Environmental Science* 17:770–74.

Grime, J. P. 1977. Evidence for existence of three primary strategies in plants and its relevance to ecological and evolutionary theory. *American Naturalist* 111:1169–94.

Hanna, Y. 2009. Influence of cultivar, growing media, and cluster pruning on greenhouse tomato yield and fruit quality. *HortTechnology* 19:395–99.

Haynes, R. J., and R. Naidu. 1998. Influence of lime, fertilizer and manure applications on soil organic matter content and soil physical conditions: a review. *Nutrient Cycling in Agroecosystems* 51:123–137.

Hemphill, D. D., Jr., and T. L. Jackson. 1982. Effect of soil acidity and nitrogen on yield and elemental concentration of bush bean, carrot, and lettuce. *Journal of the American Society for Horticultural Science* 107:740–44.

Hipp, B. W. 1978. Response by carrots to nitrogen and assessment of nitrogen status by plant analysis. *HortScience* 13:43–44.

Hobbie, J. E., and E. A. Hobbie. 2006. N-15 in symbiotic fungi and plants estimates nitrogen and carbon flux rates in Arctic tundra. *Ecology* 87:816–22.

Hochmuth, G. J., J. K. Brecht, and M. J. Bassett. 1999. Nitrogen fertilization to maximize carrot yield and quality on a sandy soil. *HortScience* 34:641–45.

Horrocks, R. D., and J. F. Vallentine. 1999. *Harvested Forages*. San Diego: Academic Press.

Ianson, D. 2014. *Mycorrhizae in the Alaska Landscape*. HGA 00026. University of Alaska-Fairbanks Cooperative Extension Service.

Janzen, D. H. 1977. Promising directions of study in tropical animal-plant interactions. *Annals of the Missouri Botanical Garden* 64:706–36.

Johnson, N. C., J. H. Graham, and F. A. Smith. 1997. Functioning of mycorrhizal associations along the mutualism-parasitism continuum. *New Phytologist* 135:575–85.

Keller, E., and K. L. Steffen. 1995. Increased chilling tolerance and altered carbon metabolism in tomato leaves following application of mechanical stress. *Physiologia Plantarum* 93:519–25.

Koide, R. 1985. The nature of growth depressions in sunflower caused by vesicular-arbuscular mycorrhizal infection. *New Phytologist* 99: 449–62.

Kramer, P. J., and J. S. Boyer. 1995. *Water Relations of Plants and Soils*. San Diego: Academic Press.

Larcher, W. 2003. *Physiological Plant Ecology: Ecophysiology and Stress Physiology of Functional Groups*. New York: Springer.

Latimer, J. G., and P. A. Thomas. 1991. Application of brushing for growth control of tomato transplants in a commercial setting. *HortTechnology* 1:109–10.

Leake, J. R. 1994. The biology of myco-heterotrophic ('saprophytic') plants. *New Phytologist* 127:171–216.

Lehman, R. M., W. Taheri, S. L. Osborne, J. Buyer, and D. D. Douds. 2012. Fall cover cropping can increase arbuscular mycorrhizae in soils supporting intensive agricultural production. *Applied Soil Ecology* 61:300–304.

Lerner, R. B. 2001. *Growing Beans in the Home Vegetable Garden*. Vegetables HO-175-W. West Lafayette, IN: Purdue University Cooperative Extension Service. http://www.hort.purdue.edu/ext/ho-175.pdf.

Locey, K. J., and J. T. Lennon. 2016. Scaling laws predict global microbial diversity. *Proceedings of the National Academy of Sciences* 113. http://www.pnas.org/content/early/2016/04/26/1521291113.full.pdf.

Magkos, F., F. Arvaniti, and A. Zampelas. 2006. Organic food: Buying more safety or just peace of mind? A critical review of the literature. *Critical Reviews in Food Science and Nutrition* 46:23–56.

McCauley, A., C. Jones, and K. Olson-Rutz. 2017. *Soil pH and Organic Matter*. Montana State University Extension, Bozeman, MT.

McWilliams, J. 2009. Are organic veggies better for you? Maybe, or maybe not. Either way, it's a useless debate. News and commentary about environmental issues, August 5. The Slate Group. http://www.slate.com.

Motuzova, G. V., I. P. Motuzova, and H. M. Dergham, eds. 2011. *Soil Organic Matter and Its Interactions with Metals: Processes, Factors, Ecological Significance*. Environmental Science, Engineering and Technology. New York: Nova Science Publishers.

NRAES (Northeast Region Agricultural Engineering Service). 1992. *On-Farm Composting Handbook*. Edited by R. Rynk. Ithaca, NY: Cooperative Extension.

———. 1999. *Field Guide to On-Farm Composting*. Edited by M. Dougherty. Ithaca, NY: Cooperative Extension.

Olson, S. M. 1989. Pruning method effects on yield, fruit size, and percentage of marketable fruit of 'Sunny' and 'Solar Set' tomatoes. *Proceedings of the Florida State Horticultural Society* 102:324–26.

Organic Seed Alliance. 2007. *Principles and Practices of Organic Bean Seed Production in the Pacific Northwest*. Port Townsend, WA: Organic Seed Alliance. http://www.seedalance.org/uploads/pdf/BeanSeedManual.pdf.

Owen, J. 1991. *The Ecology of a Garden: The First Fifteen Years*. Cambridge: Cambridge University Press.

Paul, K. I., A. S. Black, and M. K. Conyers. 2003. Development of acidic subsurface layers of soil under various management systems. *Advances in Agronomy* 78:187–214.

Pocknee, S., and M. E. Sumner. 1997. Cation and nitrogen contents of organic matter determine its soil liming potential. *Soil Science Society of America Journal* 61:86–92.

Powell, A. L. T., C. V. Nguyen, T. Hill, K. L. Cheng, R. Figueroa-Balderas, H. Aktas, H. Ashrafi, et al. 2012. Uniform ripening encodes a Golden 2-like transcription factor regulating tomato fruit chloroplast development. *Science* 336:1711.

Rice, L. W., and R. P. Rice. 2006. *Practical Horticulture*. Upper Saddle River, NJ: Pearson Education.

Richie, G. S. O., and P. J. Dolling. 1985. The role of organic matter in soil acidification. *Aust. J. Soil Res* 23:569–76.

Riotte, L. 1998. *Carrots Love Tomatoes: Secrets of Companion Planting for Successful Gardening*. North Adams, MA: Storey.

Rodale, R., ed. 1971. *The Basic Book of Organic Gardening*. Compiled by G. Johns. New York: Ballantine Books.

San Miguel-Moncin, M., M. Krail, S. Scheurer, E. Enrique, R. Alonso, A. Conti, A. Cistero-Bahima, and S. Vieths. 2003. Lettuce anaphylaxis: Identification of a lipid transfer protein as the major allergen. *Allergy* 58:511–17.

Santos, B. M. 2008. Early pruning effects on 'Florida-47' and 'Sungard' tomato. *HortTechnology* 18:467–70.

Scheepers, J. 2014. Kitchen garden seeds. Bantam, CT. www.kitchengardenseeds.com.

Schnitzer, M., and S. U. Khan, eds. 1989. *Soil Organic Matter*. Vol. 8 of *Developments in Soil Science*. Amsterdam: Elsevier Scientific Publishing.

Schutz, H. G., and O. A. Lorenz. 1976. Consumer preferences for vegetables grown under 'commercial' and 'organic' conditions. *Journal of Food Science* 41:70–73.

Seaman, Abby, ed. 2015. *Production Guide for Organic Beans for Processing*. Geneva, NY: New York State Agricultural Experiment Station.

———. 2016. *Production Guide for Organic Carrots for Processing*. Geneva, NY: New York State Agricultural Experiment Station.

Seo, M. W., D. S. Yang, S. J. Kays, G. P. Lee, and K. W. Park. 2009. Sesquiterpene lactones and bitterness in Korean leaf lettuce cultivars. *HortScience* 44:246–49.

Shultz, J. N. 2007. Home-grown tomatoes. University of Illinois Extension.http://web.extension.illinois.edu/state/newsdetail.cfm?NewsID=6816.

Simard, S. W., D. A. Perry, M. D. Jones, D. D. Myrold, D. M. Durall, and R. Molina. 1997. Net transfer of carbon between ectomycorrhizal tree species in the field. *Nature* 388:579–82.

Simko, I., Y. Zhou, and M. T. Brandl. 2015. Downy mildew disease promotes the colonization of romaine lettuce by *Escherichia coli* 0157:H7 and *Salmonella enterica*. *BMC Microbiology* 15:19.

Smith, J. L., and H. P. Collins. 2007. Management of organisms and their processes in soils. In *Soil Microbiology, Ecology, and Biochemistry*, edited by E. A. Paul, 471–502. 3rd ed. Burlington, MA: Elsevier.

Smith, J. L., H. P. Collins, A. R. Crump, and V. L. Bailey. 2015. Management of soil biota and their processes. In *Soil Microbiology, Ecology and Biochemistry*, edited by E. A. Paul, 539–62. 4th ed. Burlington, MA: Elsevier.

Smith, S. E., I. Jakobsen, M. Grønlund, and F. A. Smith. 2011. Roles of arbuscular mycorrhizas in plant phosphorus nutrition: Interactions between pathways of phosphorus uptake in arbuscular mycorrhizal roots have important implications for understanding and manipulating plant phosphorus acquisition. *Plant Physiology* 156:1050–57.

Smith-Spangler, C., M. L. Brandeau, G. E. Hunter, J. C. Bavinger, M. Pearson, P. J. Eshbach, V. Sundaram, et al. 2012. Are organic foods safer or healthier than conventional alternatives? A systematic review. *Annals of Internal Medicine* 157:348–66.

Son, C. L., and S. E. Smith. 1988. Mycorrhizal growth responses: Interactions between photon irradiance and phosphorus nutrition. *New Phytologist* 108:305–14.

Spaeth, K. E. 2001. *Atmospheric Gas Exchange and Carbon Budgets in Grazingland Plant Communities*. Fort Worth, TX: USDA-NRCS Grazingland Institute.

Spaeth, K. E., M. A. Weltz, F. B. Pierson, and H. D. Fox. 1994. Spatial pattern analysis of sagebrush vegetation and potential influences on hydrology and erosion. In *Variability in Rangeland Water Erosion Processes*, 35–50. Soil Science Society of America Special Publication 38.

Stout, R., and R. Clemence. 1973. *The Ruth Stout No-Work Garden Book: Secrets of the Year-Round Mulch Method*. Emmaus, PA: Rodale Press.

Suding, K. N., and D. E. Goldberg. 1999. Variation in the effects of vegetation and litter on recruitment across productivity gradients. *Journal of Ecology* 87:436–49.

Tilman, D. 1988. *Plant Strategies and the Dynamics and Structure of Plant Communities*. Princeton, NJ: Princeton University Press.

USDA AMS (Agricultural Marketing Service). 2012. FAQ: Becoming a certified operation. http://1.usa.gov/organic-certification.

———. 2016. The National List of Allowed and Prohibited Substances. https://www.ams.usda.gov/rules-regulations/organic/national-list.

USDA ERS (Economic Research Service). 2012. Tomatoes. http://www.ers.usda.gov/topics/crops/vegetables-pulses/tomatoes.aspx.

———. 2014. Recent trends in GE adoption. http://www.ers.usda.gov/data-products/adoption-of-genetically-engineered-crops-in-the-us/recent-trends-in-ge-adoption.aspx.

USDA National Agricultural Statistics Service. 2003. Statistics of vegetables and melons. Chap. 4 in *Agricultural Statistics*. Washington, DC: US Government Printing Office.

USDA NRCS (Natural Resources Conservation Service) 2010. Composting. Part 637, Environmental engineering. *National Engineering Handbook*. Washington, DC.

US EPA (US Environmental Protection Agency). 2003. *Environmental Regulation and Technology: Control of Pathogens and Vector Attraction in Sewage Sludge*. EPA/625/R-92/013. Cincinnati, OH.

Van der Heijden, M. G. A., F. M. Martin, M. Selosse, and I. R. Sanders. 2014. Mycorrhizal ecology and evolution: The past, the present, and the future. *New Phytologist* 205:1406–23.

Weaver, J. E., and W. E. Bruner. 1927. *Root Development of Vegetable Crops*. New York: McGraw-Hill.

Whiting, D., A. Card, C. Wilson, C. Moravec, and J. Reader. 2011. *Managing Soil Tilth, Texture, Structure, and Pore Space*. CMG Garden Notes No. 213. Fort Collins: Colorado State University.

Winfield, M. D., and E. A. Groisman. 2003. Role of nonhost environments in the lifestyles of *Salmonella* and *Escherichia coli*. *Applied and Environmental Microbiology* 69:3687–94.

Winter, C. K., and S. F. Davis. 2006. Organic foods. *Journal of Food Science* 71:1–8.

Wolf, B., and G. Snyder. 2003. *Sustainable Soils: The Place of Organic Matter in Sustaining Soils and Their Productivity*. Boca Raton, FL: CRC Press.

Wszelaki, A. L., J. F. Delwiche, S. D. Walker, R. E. Liggett, J. C. Scheerens, and M. D. Kleinhenz. 2005. Sensory quality and mineral and glycoalkaloid concentrations in organically and conventionally grown redskin potatoes (*Solanum tuberosum*). *Journal of the Science of Food and Agriculture* 85:720–26.

Young-Hee, P., T.-C. Lee, L. Logendra, and R. T. Rosen. 2004. Antioxidant activity and phenolic compounds of Swiss chard (*Beta vulgaris* subspecies *cycla*) extracts. *Food Chemistry* 85:19–26.

Zeng, R. S., A. U. Mallik, and S. M. Luo, eds. 2008. *Allelopathy in Sustainable Agriculture and Forestry*. New York: Springer.

Zhao, X., E. Chambers, Z. Matta, T. M. Loughin, and E. E. Carey. 2007. Consumer sensory analysis of organically and conventionally grown vegetables. *Journal of Food Science* 72:S87–S91.

Zibilske, L. M. 1998. Composition of organic wastes. In *Principles and Applications of Soil Microbiology*, edited by D. M. Sylvia, J. J. Fuhrmann, P. G. Hartel, and D. A. Zuberer, 482–97. Upper Saddle River, NJ: Prentice Hall.

Websites

Chlordane for termites. Termites.com. http://www.termites.com/control/pesticides-chemicals/chlordane-for-termites.

Common insect pests of tomatoes. Texas A&M Agrilife Extension. http://aggie-horticulture.tamu.edu/vegetable/problem-solvers/tomato-problem-solver/insect-pests/.

Tomato insect pests. Colorado State University Cooperative Extension. http://www.colostate.edu/Depts/CoopExt/4DMG/Pests/tompests.htm.

Insect pests of tomato. University of Maryland Extension. https://extension.umd.edu/learn/insect-pests-tomato.

National Gardening Market Research Company. Garden Research.com. http://gardenresearch.com/national-gardening-survey-2016edition/.

Pests of tomato. Center for Integrated Pest Management, North Carolina State University. http://ipm.ncsu.edu/ag295/html/tomato_key.htm.

Tomato insect pests. Clemson Cooperative Extension. http://www.clemson.edu/extension/hgic/pests/plant_pests/veg_fruit/hgic2218.html.

Index

Note: Page numbers followed by *f* denote figures.